JN233400

KYOTO AREA STUDIES ON ASIA

CENTER FOR SOUTHEAST ASIAN STUDIES, KYOTO UNIVERSITY

VOLUME 2

One Malay Village

KYOTO AREA STUDIES ON ASIA
CENTER FOR SOUTHEAST ASIAN STUDIES, KYOTO UNIVERSITY

The Nation and Economic Growth: Korea and Thailand
YOSHIHARA Kunio

One Malay Village: A Thirty-Year Community Study
TSUBOUCHI Yoshihiro

Commodifying Marxism: The Formation of Modern Thai Radical Culture,
1927–1958
Kasian TEJAPIRA

KYOTO AREA STUDIES ON ASIA

CENTER FOR SOUTHEAST ASIAN STUDIES, KYOTO UNIVERSITY

VOLUME 2

One Malay Village:

A Thirty-Year Community Study

TSUBOUCHI *Yoshihiro*

TRANSLATED BY
Peter Hawkes

Kyoto University Press

TRANS PACIFIC PRESS

First published in Japanese in 1996 by Kyoto University Press as *Maree nōson no 20-nen*.
This English edition first published in 2001 jointly by:

Kyoto University Press,
Kyodai Kaikan,
15-9 Yoshida Kawara-cho,
Sakyo-ku, Kyoto 606-8305, Japan
Telephone: +81-75-761-6182
Fax: +81-75-761-6190
Email: sales@kyoto-up.gr.jp
Web: http://www.kyoto-up.gr.jp

Trans Pacific Press,
PO Box 120, Rosanna, Melbourne,
Victoria 3084, Australia
Telephone: +61 3 9459 3021
Fax: +61 3 9457 5923
E-mail: enquiries@transpacificpress.com
Website: http://www.transpacificpress.com

Copyright ©Kyoto University Press and Trans Pacific Press 2001

Set by digital environs Melbourne: enquiries@digitalenvirons.com

Printed in Melbourne by Brown Prior Anderson

Distributors

Australia
Bushbooks
PO Box 1958, Gosford, NSW 2250
Telephone: (02) 4323-3274
Fax: (02) 9212-2468
Email: bushbook@ozemail.com.au

USA and Canada
International Specialized Book
Services (ISBS)
5824 N. E. Hassalo Street
Portland, Oregon 97213-3644
USA
Telephone: (800) 944-6190
Fax: (503) 280-8832
Email: orders@isbs.com
Web: http://www.isbs.com

All rights reserved. No production of any part of this book may take place without the written permission of Kyoto University Press or Trans Pacific Press.

ISSN 1445–9663 (Kyoto Area Studies on Asia)
ISBN 4–876–984–50–6 (hardcover)
ISBN 1–876–843–99–3 (softcover)

National Library of Australia Cataloging in Publication Data

Tsubouchi, Yoshihiro, 1938–.
One Malay village: a thirty-year community study.

Bibliography.
Includes index.
ISBN 4 87698450 6 (Kyoto).
ISBN 1 876843 99 3 (pbk. : Trans Pacific).

1. Villages – Malaysia – Kelantan – Case studies.
2. Kelantan – Politics and government. 3. Kelantan – Social life and customs. 4. Kelantan - Social conditions.
5. Malaysia – Rural conditions. I. Title. (Series : Kyoto area studies on Asia ; v. 2).

307.72095951

Contents

Figures	viii
Tables	x
Plates	xiii
Biographical Note	xv
Preface	xvi

1. A Village in Kelantan	1
1.1 A History of Sparse Population	1
1.2 The Kelantan seen by Graham	4
1.3 The Establishment of Pioneer Villages	6
1.4 Relations with the Outside World	9
2. The Role of Rain-fed Paddy Farming	12
2.1 Land Clearance and Subsistence Farming	12
2.2 Unstable Yields	13
2.3 Simple Farm Implements	16
2.4 Family-based Paddy Farming	18
2.5 Changes in Paddy Farming	27
3. Rubber Tapping and Tobacco Cultivation	32
3.1 Small-scale Rubber Tapping	32
3.2 The Rapid Development of Tobacco Cultivation	38
3.3 Changes in the Composition of Tobacco Cultivators	43
3.4 Seasonal Contract Work	45
3.5 Tobacco Surpluses and their Effect on Income	46
3.6 The Impact of Tobacco Cultivation	49
3.7 The End of the Tobacco Boom	53
4. Other Income Sources and Changes	55
4.1 Increased Regular Employment	55
4.2 From Agricultural to Urban Migrant Work	56
4.3 Other Occupations	59
4.4 Other Sources of Income	65
5. Income and Lifestyle	69
5.1 Problems in Assessing Income	69
5.2 Villagers' Incomes by Source	70
5.3 Household Income	71
5.4 Income from Payment in Kind	75
5.5 Conditions in 1977	77
5.6 Conditions in 1992	80

6. Land and Residence   84
   6.1 Inheritance and Individual Ownership   84
   6.2 Changes in the Number of Landowners from 1957 to 1992   87
   6.3 Land Ownership and Postmarital Residence   88
   6.4 Residential Kin Groups   90
   6.5 Independent Residence   93
   6.6 The Mode of Life Among Kin and Neighbors   95
   6.7 The Village as a Series of Neighborhood Circles   98
   6.8 Summary   100

7. Marriage and Divorce   102
   7.1 Marriage   102
   7.2 Early Marriage and the Universality of Marriage   105
   7.3 The Range of Intermarriage   108
   7.4 Divorce   109
   7.5 Remarriage   115
   7.6 Polygyny   116
   7.7 Household Composition   119
   7.8 Divorce Trends in Kelantan   122

8. Islam and Divorce in Three Malay Villages   127
   8.1 Kinship Structure, Islamic Law, and Values   127
   8.2 Divorce Features   131
   8.3 Comparison and Observations   137

9. Changes in Population and Households   143
   9.1 The Follow-up Survey of 1991   143
   9.2 Changes in Population Composition   143
   9.3 Changes in Household Composition   154
   9.4 Various Aspects of Change in Household Structure   158
   9.5 A Summary of Changes in Population and Households   164

10. Multihousehold Compounds: Changes over Twenty Years
    and Their Significance   166
    10.1 Changes in the Population of Multihousehold Compounds   166
    10.2 Changes in the Composition of Multihousehold Compounds   173
    10.3 Summary and Observations   179

11. Life in a Minor *Pondok* and Changes, 1970–1992   182
    11.1 *Pondok* of Kelantan   182
    11.2 Establishment of a Minor *Pondok* and Transitions   183
    11.3 Location of Houses and Living Conditions   185
    11.4 The Guru's Family and Kin   190
    11.5 Residents of the *Pondok*   192
    11.6 The Changing Function of the *Pondok*   203

12. A Comparison of Two Villages	207
12.1 Occupation and Income	207
12.2 Some Aspects of Family Life	215
12.3 Education and Religion	219
12.4 The Concepts of "Town" and "Village" among Malays	223
13. The Study of Malay Villages and Related Subjects	227
13.1 Individuality and Universality	227
13.2 Galok and the Image of the Southeast Asian Village	229
13.3 Villages in the Malay Peninsula	229
13.4 Villages in Continental Southeast Asia	231
13.5 Villages in South Sumatra	233
13.6 Pioneer Settlements	234
13.7 Relationship to Southeast Asian Society	236
14. Galok Thirty Years On: The End of Ecological Adaptation	238
14.1 Changes in Occupations and Lifestyles	238
14.2 Changes in Population	244
14.3 Changes in Household Composition	249
14.4 Changes in Multihousehold Compounds	254
14.5 In Conclusion	256
Appendices	258
1 One Year in Kelantan	259
2 From Pasir Mas (Field Report 1)	265
3 From Alor Janggus (Field Report 2)	272
Bibliography	278
Glossary	285
Index	289

Figures

1-1. The Malay Peninsula	3
1-2. Kelantan State	5
1-3. Galok and Surroundings	7
1-4. Location of Houses in Galok	8
2-1. Rainfall and Cropping Seasons	13
2-2. Total Paddy Area and Planted Area (1970/71)	16
3-1. Composition of Galok Population by Age and Sex	52
6-1. Types of Neighborhood Kin Groups	91
7-1. Development of Household Composition	121
7-2. Changes in the Number of Marriages and Divorces in Kelantan	123
7-3. Divorce Rates for Each District in Kelantan	125
9-1. Population Pyramids for 1971 and 1991 (Actual Population)	144
9-2. Population Pyramids for 1971 and 1991 (Percentage in each Age Group)	145
9-3. Number of 1971 Residents Still Living in Galok in 1991	146
9-4. Number of 1971 Residents Still in Galok or Deceased in 1991	147
9-5. Number of 1991 Galok Residents who had been Resident Since 1971	148
9-6. In-migration and Out-migration	149
9-7. Stages of the Family Career	156
10-1. Changes in Multihousehold Compounds: Case 1	174
10-2. Changes in Multihousehold Compounds: Case 2	175
10-3. Changes in Multihousehold Compounds: Case 3	176
10-4. Changes in Multihousehold Compounds: Case 4	177
10-5. Changes in Multihousehold Compounds: Case 5	178
10-6. Changes in Multihousehold Compounds: Case 6	179
11-1. Location of Buildings in the *Pondok* (1971)	186
11-2. Location of Buildings in the *Pondok* (1992)	188
11-3. The Guru's Kin Living in the *Pondok*	190
11-4. Population Pyramids for *Pondok* Residents in 1971 and 1992	205
12-1. Proportion of Households Engaged in each Occupation	208

12-2. Proportion of Total Income from each Income Source	209
12-3. Distribution of Household Income	212
12-4. Distribution of Household Goods and Appliances	213
12-5. Size of House	214
12-6. Cost of House Construction	214
12-7. Cumulative Percentages of Ever-Married People by Age	216
12-8. Percentages of Ever-Married Persons by Number of Marriages and Number of Divorces	217
12-9. Percentages of Ever-Divorced Persons among Ever-Married	218
12-10. Duration of Marriage before Divorce (Aggregated Percentages)	220
12-11. Educational Experience by Age	221
12-12. Literacy by Age	222
12-13. Education among 15–19-year-olds	223
14-1. Population Pyramids for 1971, 1991 and 2000	246

Tables

2-1. Paddy Varieties and Number of Plots Planted (1970-1971)	14
2-2. Ownership of Main Farming Implements	17
2-3. Places Where Hoes and Sickles are Purchased	17
2-4. Household Work Force	19
2-5. Use of Draft Animals and Tractors for Paddy Land Preparation	20
2-6. Division of Labor for Bundling	22
2-7. Division of Labor for Transplanting	24
2-8. Division of Labor for Harvesting	25
2-9. Number of Plots Planted, by Variety, in 1970/1971 and 1976/1977	30
3-1. Number of Households Owning Paddy and/or Rubber Land by Size of Holding	34
3-2. Number of Households Engaged in Paddy Growing and Rubber Tapping by Scale of Operation	35
3-3. Changes in the Number of Households Cultivating Tobacco	42
3-4. Number of Households by Year Cultivation Started, and Sex and Age of Household Head	42
3-5. Number of Households by Year Cultivation Started, Sex and Age of Household Head, and Land Ownership	43
3-6. Male Household Heads Aged 20–39 who Began Tobacco Cultivation after the First Year	44
3-7. Age And Sex of Contract Workers at M.T.C. Station and the Percentage of the Population of the Same Age Group	46
3-8. Changes in Average Income Per 1000 Tobacco Plants	48
3-9. Households with Income from Tobacco Cultivation	48
3-10. Number of Bicycles, Radios and Sewing Machines Purchased by Year	53
5-1. Total Village Income, by Source (November 1970–October 1971)	70
5-2. Number of Households by Income and Size	73
5-3. Number of Households by Income and Number of Working Members	73
5-4. Number of Households by Income and Sex and Age of Householder	74

5-5. Number of Households by Residence and Income	75
5-6. Number of Households by Source and Amount Obtained in Paddy	76
5-7. Changes in Average Income by Income Source 1970/1971–1976/1977	78
5-8. Ownership of Specific Durable Consumer Items in 1970/1971 and 1977	79
6-1. Inheritance of Parents' Land	87
6-2. Relationship of Sellers to Buyers of Land	87
6-3. Changes in the Number of Landowners Listed in One Land District of Central Galok, 1957-1992	89
6-4. Postmarital Residence According to Relative Scale of Land Held by Husband and Wife	89
6-5. Ownership of Residence in Independent Households	92
6-6. Relationship of Tenants to Landlords (For Landlords Resident in Galok)	96
6-7. Relationship of Landlords to Tenants (For Tenants Resident in Galok)	96
7-1. Marriage Payments for First Marriages	105
7-2. Age at First Marriage	107
7-3. Kinship between Spouses	109
7-4. Person Seeking Divorce	111
7-5. Number of Ever-divorced People and their Percentage Relative to Ever-married People	111
7-6. Ever-married People by Number of Times Divorced	111
7-7. Number of Divorces by Duration of Marriage and Number of Children (not including *pasah*)	113
7-8. Custody of Children after Divorce	113
7-9. The Relation of Kinship to Marriage and Divorce	114
7-10. Number of Divorces for All Marriages Compared to Those for Inter-Galok Marriages	114
7-11. Ever-married Persons by Number of Marriages	117
7-12. Number of Marriages by Age at Remarriage	117
7-13. Interval between Divorce or Death of Spouse and Remarriage	118
7-14. Couples by Number of Marriages	118
7-15. Marriage and Divorce in Kelantan (1948–1990)	124
7-16. Number of Marriages and Divorces in Each District of Kelantan	126
8-1. Yearly Changes in Marriage and Divorce in Kelantan, Kedah and Melaka	133

8-2. Number and Percentage of People Divorced in Galok and
Padang Lalang — 134
8-3. Number of Ever-married People in Galok and Padang
Lalang by Number of Times Divorced — 135
8-4. Number of Divorces by Duration of Marriage in Galok and
Padang Lalang — 135
8-5. Number of Divorces by Number of Children in Galok and
Padang Lalang — 136
8-6. Marriage and Divorce among Muslims in Singapore,
1921–1991 — 138
8-7. Marriage and Divorce among Muslims in Indonesia — 141
8-8. Marriage and Divorce among Muslims in Java — 142
9-1. Destinations for Out-migration from the 1971 Population — 150
9-2. Age-specific Fertility and Total Fertility Rates (1972–1991) — 151
9-3. Average Life Expectancy Estimated from the Model Life
Tables — 153
9-4. Family Composition of Households in 1971 — 155
9-5. Family Composition of Households in 1991 — 155
9-6. Present Situation of Married Couples Resident in 1971 — 159
9-7. Households in 1991 by Reason for Living in Galok — 163
10-1. Number of Households in 1991 in Multihousehold
Compounds of 1971 — 170
11-1. *Pondok* Experience by Age (For Men in Galok) — 184
11-2. Literacy of *Pondok* Pupils in 1971 by Period of Stay (For male
residents of Galok who had received only *pondok* education) — 184
11-3. Number of Households in the *Pondok* by Category and Period
of Stay, 1971 and 1992 — 189
11-4. Situation of Elderly Residents According to Income — 195
11-5. *Pondok* Residents by Sex and Age, 1971 and 1992 — 204
12-1. Family Composition of Households in Kubang Bemban — 215
14-1. Age-specific Fertility and Total Fertility Rates — 247
14-2. Destinations for Out-migration from 1970/71 to 1991 — 248
14-3. Destinations for Out-migration from 1991 to 2000 — 250
14-4. Family Composition of Households in 1971 — 251
14-5. Family Composition of Households in 1991 — 251
14-6. Family Composition of Households in 2000 — 252
14-7. Number of Households in 1991 in Multihousehold Compounds
of 1971 — 255
14-8. Changes in Number of Households from 1991 to 2000 in
Multihousehold Compounds of 1971 — 255

Plates

2-1. Plowing with a water buffalo. A rubber grove can be seen in the background. 23
2-2. The use of a knife *(tame)* to harvest rice has become very rare in Galok. 26
2-3. Harvesting and threshing work. 29
3-1. A rubber grove. Trees are not necessarily planted in straight rows. 32
3-2. Rubber tapping. 37
3-3. Adding acid to the collected latex to make it coagulate. 38
3-4. Tobacco plants starting to grow after transplanting. 39
3-5. Seasonal workers at a tobacco station (1971). 40
3-6. Weighing tobacco leaves brought to the station. 40
4-1. Using a roller to press rubber into sheets. 57
4-2. A rubber dealer who travels from house to house by bicycle. 60
4-3. Weaving roof thatch *(atap)* from palm fronds. 61
4-4. A fruit and vegetable stall. 63
4-5. A meat stall. 64
4-6. A fruit and vegetable stall. 66
5-1. A house on stilts with wooden siding and tiled roof (1971). 81
5-2. A house on stilts with thatched roof and woven bamboo walls (1971). 81
5-3. The house of a teacher who moved to the village and bought land (1991). 82
5-4. A new bungalow-style house made of concrete blocks and brick (1991). 82
6-1. A village residence (1971). 94
6-2. A compound in 1991. Bricks are used for a part of the traditional wooden house. 99
7-1. Wedding presents from the groom's family for the bride. Money constituting the marriage payment has been folded and assembled into a decorative arrangement. 103
7-2. The bride and groom seated upon a decorated bed. 106
9-1. A village family (1971). 161
10-1. A village family (1971). 172

11-1. View of the pondok in 1971; no. 1.	187
11-2. View of the pondok in 1971; no. 2.	187
11-3. View of the pondok in 1971; no. 3.	193
11-4. The pondok in 1991.	203
12-1. Ujung Galok mosque in 1971.	225
12-2. The same mosque in 1991.	225
14-1. A furniture factory adjacent to Galok.	242
14-2. A peddler preparing for her rounds.	242
14-3. Vegetable cultivation.	243
14-4. A family with children.	253

Biographical Note

Tsubouchi Yoshihiro, currently Professor at Konan Women's University, spent most of his academic life at Kyoto University where he was Dean of the Graduate School of Asian and African Area Studies from 1998 to 2000 and Director of the Center for Southeast Asian Studies from 1993 to 1998. He has published extensively on the historical demography of sparsely populated areas and on the ethno-demography of Southeast Asia.

Preface

Located on the east coast of the Malay Peninsula, the state of Kelantan has a predominantly Malay population. This preponderance of Malays in a society known for being multiracial, the strongly ethnic flavor of traditional events that can be seen there, such as shadow plays and kite flying, and the distinctive brand of Islam adopted there, sometimes seen as nativized, sometimes branded as fanatical, has led people to seek a concentration of Malayness in Kelantan, despite its peripheral location in the Malay world.

More than thirty years have passed since I began a community study here in 1970. From July 1970 to August 1971, I spent thirteen months in Kelantan, made up of one year of settled study and one month for preparation and clearing up. Since then I have visited Kelantan on more than ten occasions, on four of which I carried out substantial surveys. In 1977, during a three-week stay, I conducted a small sample survey of residents of the same village. In 1984, I spent about one month surveying changes in household composition. Then from September to November of 1991 and in July and August of 1992, I again visited all residents, mainly to investigate changes in family and kin. The changes I observed between 1971 and 1991 are the subject of my book *Marē Nōson no 20 nen* (Twenty years of a Malay Village), published by Kyoto University Press in 1996, which is reproduced here in translation. In July and August 2000, I again surveyed changes in the villages, and the results are presented here in Chapter 14.

The purpose of the first survey was to examine the nature of a Malay rice-growing village. Behind this may have been the tacit premise that rice-growing is at the basis of Malay society. It formed one part of a comparative study of rice-growing villages in the Malay Peninsula. In terms of rice-growing technology, irrigated wet-rice cultivation is central. But for the Malays, wet-rice cultivation by means of irrigation is not necessarily a traditional technique: it can also be claimed that their traditional rice-growing was rain-fed cultivation of wet rice and upland rice. In this sense, from the viewpoint of rice-growing, a different type of society had come into being, and this study was an attempt to clarify the structure of such a society.

The 1977 survey aimed to discover the changes in rural areas against the background of the "green revolution" brought about by the introduction of high-yielding varieties. Of course, because the survey village lacked irrigation facilities, this influence was no more than indirect. At this time, for most of the peasants of Kelantan, industrialization was also a phenomenon of the remote urban areas. Shortly thereafter, Singapore's construction boom and the development of Kuala Lumpur would attract many migrant workers away from Kelantan. On the other hand, the education of their children to become school teachers, which many villagers cited as their ideal in 1977, became reality for many families thanks to the government's policy of giving priority to Malays.

Such changes are difficult to foresee, but after the event become no more than commonplace facts. The view that the traditional occupation of the Malays is typified by rice-growing can itself be seen to be mistaken in some respects when viewed in a wider spatial field or on a longer temporal axis. However, this thirty-year period can be considered a long term within the framework of sociological or anthropological field survey, and it is one that encompasses important changes in rural areas. The rapid changes experienced by the Malay community expose the limitations of such frameworks as urban-rural continuity, modernization, and urbanization, and are of such magnitude as to raise Malaysia from the ranks of the developing nations.

So-called community studies became popular in the 1960s and 1970s. At this time, it was significant simply to comprehend the lifestyles of people in Southeast Asia through long-term observation and describe them as a single structure. Subsequently, Malaysian and foreign researchers conducted surveys that, for example, had the explicit aim of promoting development or focused on a cultural structure. In this situation, continuous community study was either neglected or dealt with changes in the shorter term. In fact, sociologists rarely maintain a single interest over a long term; rather the problems they perceive change over time.

The changes I shall describe in this book, in this sense, are not a continuous, systematic record made with change itself in mind but merely a description of cross-sections through the time axis. Nevertheless, I have ventured to publish this incomplete record because it captures, through the eyes of one researcher, consciously and over a continuous period, the details of a process of change which today even the Malays are on the verge of forgetting. I do not know how it will be used in the future, but it is my hope that this record will one day be useful to the Malays themselves in looking back at their own past.

Among the various changes recorded, I have followed relatively intensively those related to family and kin. If changes in the family are sought in the age at first marriage or the decline in divorce, then they are drastic. Despite such changes in certain elements, however, structures remain that have persisted unchanged. Nevertheless, closer inspection reveals subtle changes in the composition of household members. And to apply a formula such as the nuclearization of the family to such changes is an oversimplification. The direction of change may in fact represent a detour around a more drastic process.

The various chapters of this book are for the most part updated versions of earlier published articles. Over the course of three decades, my interpretation of certain phenomena has changed, and in this sense, each chapter is the result of a comprehensive review rather than a simple reproduction. The main articles related to each chapter are as follows.

Chapter 2: "Marēshia higashi kaigan no tensuiden chiiki ni okeru inasaku" (Rice cultivation in the region of rain-fed rice fields on the east coast of Malaysia), *Tōnan Ajia Kenkyū (Southeast Asian Studies)* 10, no. 2 (1972).

Chapter 3: "Kurantan no ichi nōson ni okeru tabako kōsaku no dōnyū to shakaikeizaiteki henka" (The introduction of tobacco cultivation and socioeconomic change in a farming village in Kelantan), *Tōnan Ajia Kenkyū (Southeast Asian Studies)* 9, no. 4 (1972).

Chapters 4 and 5: "Marēshia higashi kaigan no sonraku jūmin no shūnyū to shūnyūgen—Kanpon Garo ni okeru kēsu sutadi" (Income and income sources of residents in a village on the east coast of Malaysia: A case study of Kampong Galok), *Tōnan Ajia Kenkyū (Southeast Asian Studies)* 10, no. 4 (1973).

Chapter 6: "Higashi kaigan Marē nōmin ni okeru tochi to kyojū" (Land and residence among Malay peasants on the east coast), *Tōnan Ajia Kenkyū (Southeast Asian Studies)* 10, no. 1 (1972).

Chapter 7: "Higashi kaigan Marē nōmin ni okeru kekkon to rikon" (Marriage and divorce among Malay peasants on the east coast), *Tōnan Ajia Kenkyū (Southeast Asian Studies)* 10, no. 3 (1972).

Chapter 8: "Marē nōson no 20 nen—jinkō to kazoku no henka wo chūshin ni" (Twenty years in a Malay village: Focusing on changes in population and the family), *Tōnan Ajia Kenkyū (Southeast Asian Studies)* 30, no. 2 (1992).

Chapter 9: "Marē nōson ni okeru yashikichi kyōjūshūdan—20 nenkan ni okeru henka to sono imi" (Multihousehold compounds in a Malay village: Changes in twenty years and their significance), *Tōnan Ajia Kenkyū (Southeast Asian Studies)* 31, no. 1 (1993).

Chapter 10: "Kurantan no nōson ni okeru pondo (kishuku shūkyōjuku)—sono henyō to genjō" (A *pondok* [religious boarding school] in a village in Kelantan: Its transformation and present situation), *Tōnan Ajia Kenkyū (Southeast Asian Studies)* 11, no. 2 (1973).

Chapter 11: "Kurantan no futatsu no nōson—machi ni chikai mura to tōi mura no hikaku" (Two villages in Kelantan: A comparsion of a village

near a town and one far from town), *Tōnan Ajia Kenkyū (Southeast Asian Studies)* 11, no. 4 (1974).
Chapter 12: "Marē nōson ni okeru Isurāmu to rikon" (Islam and divorce in a Malay village), *Tōnan Ajia Kenkyū (Southeast Asian Studies)* 13, no. 1 (1975).
Chapter 14: "Marē nōson no 30 nen—seitaitekiō no shūen wo haikei toshite" (Thirty years of a Malay village: With the end of ecological adaptation as a background), *Ajia-Afurika Chiiki Kenkyū (Asian and African Area Studies)* 1, no. 1 (2001).

I am indebted to many people for their assistance during my surveys in Malaysia. These include the late Dr. Joji Tanase, the team leader when the Malaysia project began in 1964 (then associate professor, Faculty of Letters, Kyoto University); the late Dr. Shinobu Iwamura, then director of the Center for Southeast Asian Studies, Kyoto University; and the team members, Masuo Kuchiba (professor emeritus, Ryukoku University; then a lecturer in the Faculty of Letters, Ryukoku University), and Narifumi Maeda (now Tachimoto) (now director and professor, Center for Southeast Asian Studies, Kyoto University; then a research student in the Faculty of Letters, Kyoto University Graduate School). Following the sudden death of Dr. Tanase, my work in Malaysia was supported by the late Dr. Takeshi Motooka (then professor at the Center for Southeast Asian Studies, Kyoto University); Dr. Masamichi Inoki (then professor, Faculty of Law, Kyoto University); Dr. Keizaburo Kawaguchi, leader of the project to compare rice-growing villages in the Malay Peninsula (then professor, Faculty of Agriculture, Kyoto University); and Dr. Shinichi Ichimura (then director of the Center for Southeast Asian Studies, Kyoto University), who raised funds for my survey when a donation from the Ford Foundation had been returned. In Kuala Lumpur, Professor Ungku Aziz, then Vice-Chancellor of the University of Malaya, and Mokhzani bin Abdul Rahim and Leo Frederiks, then lecturers in the Faculty of Economics and Administration of the same university supported my efforts. My fieldwork in Kelantan was facilitated by the cooperation of the late Tengku Rahim, then District Officer of Pasir Mas, and by his successors and their deputies and other officials; my stay in Pasir Mas owes much to the kindness of Haji Ramly Yaacob, my landlord Abdul Rahman and his wife Esah; and the surveys would not have been possible without my assistants Wan Junoh, Nik Azman, Khalid, and the many informants in the village who provided a variety of information, most notably the late Ismail bin Setapa, the late Dir bin Ismail, the late Haji Yusof, guru of the *pondok,* and the late Daud, the *penghulu* who lived in the neighboring village.

In the publication of this book, I offer my heartfelt thanks to my colleagues at the Center for Southeast Asian Studies for their support and to Mr. Tetsuya Suzuki of Kyoto University Press for his careful attention. I am grateful to the two anonymous referees for their valuable comments and Ms Motoko Kawano for preparing the index, and also to Matsushita International Foundation for funds that allowed the extension of my analyses, the results of which are in part incorporated herein.

In the past thirty years, almost half of the people acknowledged above have passed away. Among them is Ismail, who in 1970 told me, "The land is important. As long as we have land we can eat." Since then the significance of land in Galok has changed. Ismail's daughter lived by looking after the children of a couple who both worked as teachers, and who had moved into Galok after buying land there. Always cheerful despite the unremitting poverty of her livelihood, she too was no longer in Galok in 2000.

Awareness of privacy is beginning to emerge in the villages of Malaysia. Surveys into income have acquired difficult aspects, and questions about the niceties of family relations with regard to divorce may become difficult to ask. Nevertheless, I would like, if it is possible, to conduct one more survey in the village on occasion of the fortieth anniversary of my first survey.

Lastly I would like to mention with thanks that a grant-in-aid for publication of scientific research result by Japan Society for the Promotion of Science was awarded for the publication of this book.

1
A Village in Kelantan

1.1. A History of Sparse Population

This book primarily presents an account of a village in Kelantan in the thirty years from 1970 to 2000. While this period of observation is longer than the conventional community study, this account nevertheless covers only a limited time and space. In addition to being a small historical record, in the wider perspective it also has features of a comparative study; and in this sense, it has speculative aspects that are undesirable from the standpoint of objectivity. Questions arise that have long been debated in the social sciences, concerning the role of the so-called historical view or the objectivity of description. It is not my intention here to restrict myself to pseudo-objectivity or the simple presentation of data. Nevertheless, if questions should be raised in future, I am confident that these will concern the interpretation rather than the objectivity of my data.

Concerning the data collected in the community study that occupy the greater part of this book, I am willing to assert their objectivity on the grounds of my direct involvement. However, my discussions of Kelantan state rest on certain assumptions and inferences that go beyond my own observation. These bear upon my characterization of Kelantan as a sparsely populated state with relatively weak ruling structures, and my discussion of the process of population growth and land clearance, particularly since the mid-nineteenth century. These phenomena were not peculiar to Kelantan but common to Sumatra, the Malay Peninsula, Borneo and other parts of insular Southeast Asia. Within the Malay Peninsula, Kelantan's population was comparatively substantial. Although there were scattered communities of Thais and of overseas Chinese, Kelantan was characterized by a strong monoethnic character in that the majority of residents were Malays. And in that Kelantan lagged behind somewhat in the processes of colonization and development in the Malay Peninsula from the mid-nineteenth century, changes in the character of its population were also delayed. In the following, I shall outline Kelantan's history to the extent that I believe it necessary in order to understand the character of the survey area.

In Chinese historical materials, an old account of Kelantan (Chi-Lan-Tan) appears in Wang Ta-yūan's *Tao-i Chih-lioh*, which describes the situation in the fourteenth century. This account reveals that this part of the Malay Peninsula was already populated to some extent; but there is no way of knowing how large the population was or how it subsequently changed. What is important here is that Kelantan was not isolated from the outside world; it had relations at least with China. A little later, in the fifteenth century, Kelantan underwent Islamization. The influence of Islam from the west reached Kelantan slightly later than other Malay states, no doubt due to its more distant location on the east coast. Nevertheless, it cannot be said that Islamization was remarkably late in comparison with other areas of insular Southeast Asia, such as Sulawesi, and it is probably appropriate to evaluate it as following the mainstream of change. In the late fifteenth century, Kelantan is said to have become a tributary state of the Melaka kingdom. However, whereas the present sultans of various Malay states claim descent from the Melaka kingdom as legitimation of their rule and the source of their authority, the rulers of Kelantan are outside this area, and in the genealogy of the rajahs of Kelantan, this goes no further than marriage with a princess of Melaka.

From the late 1830s, the population of Kelantan is mentioned in several accounts by British visitors. At this time, Kelantan had become a tributary state of Siam. Writing in 1837, Moor estimated the non-Chinese population of Kelantan at 50,000, resident in 50 Islamic parishes *(mukim)* (Moor 1837: 245). Two years later, Newbold also estimated the population of Kelantan at 50,000, although in this case it is unclear whether Chinese are excluded (Newbold 1839: 418-419). A decade later, in 1849, Low put the figure at 40,000 (Low 1849: 606-607). The territory of Kelantan at the time is thought to be slightly larger than at present; but if we provisionally adopt the area of 5,746 square miles (14,882 square kilometers) recorded in the 1947 census, which is thought to equal the present area, then the population density in the mid-nineteenth century can be at 2.7 or 3.4 persons per square kilometer. These populations are thought to have been concentrated along the sea coast and the lower reach of the Kelantan River rather than being evenly distributed across the entire territory of the state.

Early in the twentieth century, Graham, who was resident in Kelantan as an advisor dispatched from Siam, estimated the population of Kelantan at the time to be 300,000. This was based on an adult male population of 60,000 listed for purposes of capitation tax. To this was added an equal number of adult females, each with three children, to give the total of 300,000. In addition, Graham states that the native population of the mountain areas might well exceed 10,000 (Graham 1908: 17). He further notes that Kelantan was divided into 250

Figure 1-1. The Malay Peninsula

mukim. This represents a fivefold increase in the period of approximately 70 years since Moor's report of 50 mukim in 1837. And since Moor had estimated the non-Chinese population at 50,000, the population had increased by almost sixfold in the same period. Although the reliability of the figures requires examination, it is certain that the population of Kelantan grew rapidly from the mid-nineteenth century.

The earliest comparatively reliable figures on the populations of states in the Malay Peninsula are provided by the census of 1911. Combining these with Newbold's 1839 figures for each of the Malayan states gives an average annual population growth rate over the period of 1.8 percent for the Malay population of Malaya (peninsular Malaysia). By state, Negeri Sembilan had the lowest rate of 0.9 percent, and Kelantan had the highest rate of 2.6 percent. Dodge claims that the high growth rate on the east coast of the peninsula, including Kelantan, derives from an underestimation of the population at the starting point. He starts with the official census figures and applies growth rates of 1.0 percent and 0.3 percent to estimate retrogressively the population of 1835 (Dodge 1980: 450-453). From this standpoint, the early population of Kelantan would have to be revised upward. However, the growth rates that Dodge applied in his retrogressive estimation are merely *a posteriori* values, and while they may be of service to some extent in estimations for wider areas such as the whole of Malaya, it would be dangerous to consider that they can be applied directly to Kelantan.

In the 1911 census, the population of Kelantan was 286,751 people, and the population density was still fairly low, at 19.3 per square kilometer. Thereafter the population continued to grow, reaching 309,574 in 1921, 362,517 in 1931, 448,572 in 1947, 505,522 in 1957, 684,738 in 1970, 859,270 in 1980, and 1,181,680 in 1991, in which year the population density reached 79.4 per square kilometer. This last figure is less than one quarter of the corresponding figure for Japan (332 in 1990), though higher than Hokkaido's 67.7. During this process of growth, the availability of land for reclamation approached the limit; but the fact that land was being reclaimed somewhere in Kelantan as a whole is suggestive of the basic character of Kelantan as pioneering society.

1.2. The Kelantan seen by Graham

Graham lists the principal settlements of Kelantan at the start of the twentieth century. These were Kota Bharu (population 10,000), Tumpat (4,000), Tabar (3,000), Bacho (2,000), Semarak (500), Kampong Laut (population not recorded), Pasir Puteh (1,000) and Wachap Nau (1,000) (Graham 1908: 29; place names follow the original). Of these, the first six are located on the lower reach of the Kelantan River or on the coast. Kota Bharu was a town, while the remainder were all villages with an administrative office, a police post, and a market. Besides the above, one place is named on the upper reach of the Kelantan River, the old Chinese gold collectors' settlement of Pulai (population 500), lying about 160 kilometers from the estuary.

In the early 1900s, Kota Bharu was the only town in Kelantan. Recent immigration of Chinese and Indian Muslims from the British-ruled Straits Settlements and of Malays from other parts of the Peninsula had swelled the population to around 10,000. In addition to the rajah's palace, the town's principal buildings included a court house, a revenue office, a post and telegraph office, a customs house, and a market, and outside the town was a jail. Separated from the west of the town by a narrow creek was the Chinese quarter, known as

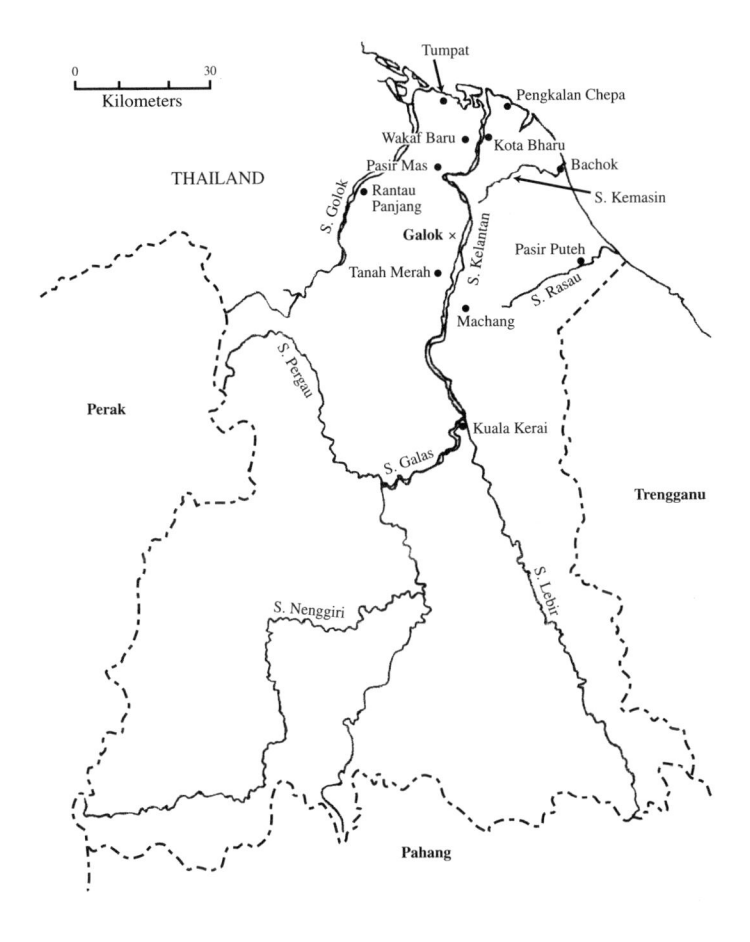

Figure 1-2. Kelantan State

Kampong China, where 1,000 people lived under a "Captain China." By this time many Chinese watch-menders, tailors, carpenters, and general dealers had begun to leave Kampong China to set up store in the main town.

That the greater part of Kelantan's population was concentrated in the coastal region can also be inferred from the distribution of major settlements cited above. In Graham's time, some 30,000 people, ten percent of the state's population, lived by sea-fishing (Graham 1908: 66). The catch, while providing food for the table, was in part salted and dried and sent to settlements inland. Salted fish was also one of the main export items to such places as Singapore. At this time salt was not produced in Kelantan, and the salt used for preserving fish was brought in from Patani in South Thailand. This salt was also used with small fish to produce a sauce called *budu*. Salted fish and *budu* were traditional fare of the Kelantanese people, and residents of the plains where rice was produced would flavor their daily meals with small amounts of these.

In the early twentieth century, about 70,000 tons of unhulled rice was produced in Kelantan, enough to feed the state's entire population and provide a surplus of 4,000 to 5,000 tons for export (Graham 1908: 71). In 1906/1907 (A.H. 1824), exports of unhulled and polished rice were valued at 109,161 Straits dollars, exceeding the value of salted fish exports of 62,104 dollars. However, as a proportion of total production, the volume of rice exported was minimal, suggesting that rice was grown essentially for home consumption. More important agricultural export items were copra (298,458 dollars) and betel nuts (153,691 dollars). In the same period Kelantan's exports included products of the upper reach, gold valued at 212,984 dollars and gutta-percha valued at 25,288 dollars. Gold was thus the state's most valuable export after copra. Rubber cultivation had begun in the early years of the twentieth century, but Graham remained skeptical about the new crop, of which the import of seeds and seedlings had become conspicuous. The villages of Kelantan, which housed the majority of the state's population, had a minor economic role in relation to the size of their population, and although not isolated, they were relatively independent, self-supporting entities.

Pasir Mas, the administrative seat of the district (*jajahan*) in which the survey village of Galok is located, lies on a bend on the lower middle reach of the Kelantan River just 16 kilometers upstream of Kota Bharu. The name of Pasir Mas appears on the fold-out map in Graham's volume. However, it is not listed among the principal settlements cited earlier. The same is true of Tanah Merah, the center of the present-day Jajahan Tanah Merah. And Kuala Kerai, which would later become the center of Jajahan Ulu Kelantan, is not even marked on the map. These settlements along the Kelantan River had not yet developed sufficiently. According to Graham, in addition to the principal settlements that he named, there were settlements of from 6 to 50 households scattered through the plain and along the Kelantan River (Graham 1908: 30). Pasir Mas was one of the more prominent of these.

1.3. The Establishment of Pioneer Villages

The growth of Kelantan's population involved the establishment and expansion of pioneer settlements. Such settlements were located in the Kelantan Plain, the earlier settlements apparently being opened in places with better communications and better availability of water in suitable quantity. Traditional rice cultivation depended to a large extent on rain-fed lowland

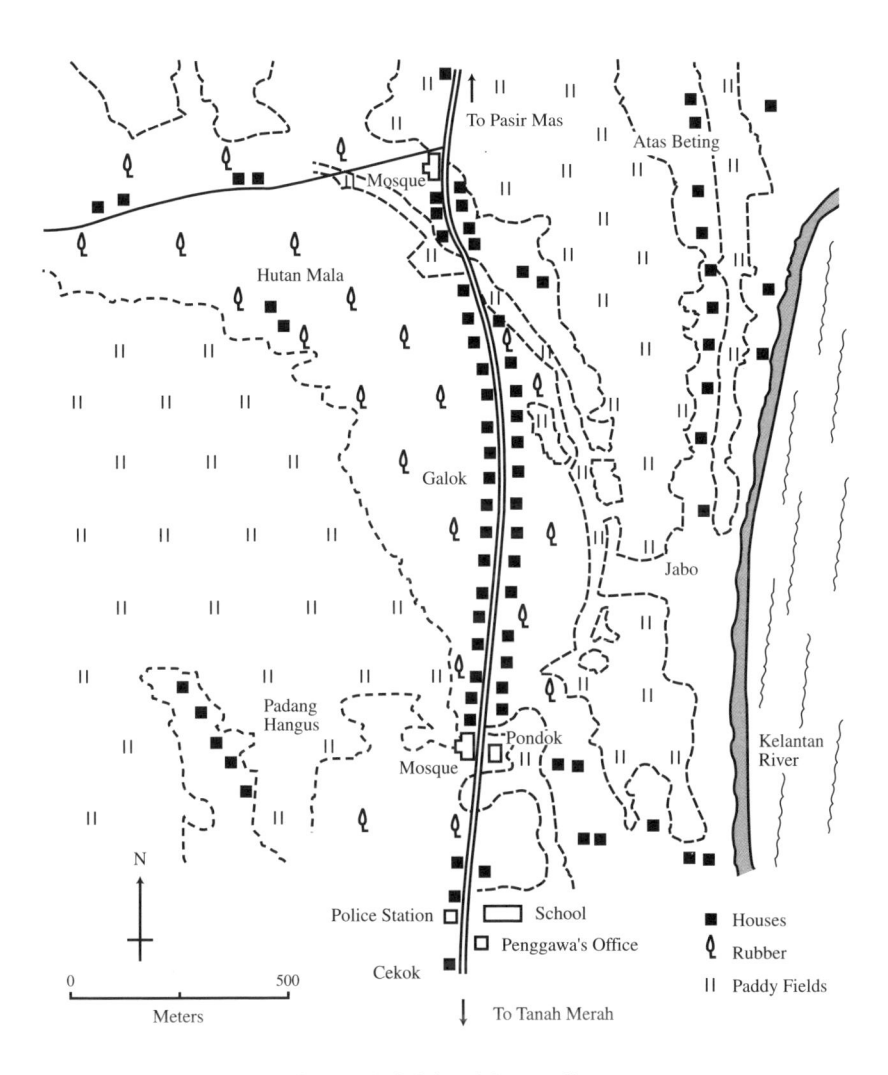

Figure 1-3. Galok and Surroundings

fields and upland cultivation. Rainfall in Kelantan in the rainy season is heavy, exceeding 500 millimeters in November and December. Irrigation plans involving raising water from the Kelantan River did not proceed on a large scale and permit double cropping of rice until much later. Undoubtedly, the speed of land clearance was also remarkable in cases that did not involve the construction of irrigation facilities. The formation of the countless small settlements described above can also be thought to be the result of such expansion. And rubber cultivation would further accelerate land clearance.

The survey village of Galok is a Malay settlement dotted along a roadside some 15 kilometers upstream of Pasir Mas. The middle reach of the Kelantan River begins from around the large bend in the river at Pasir Mas. Galok lies between 400 and 800 meters from the river. It was opened in around 1890. The name of Galok derives from a local word meaning a deep and narrow stream, which is said to have run behind the present-day mosque, where there is said

Figure 1-4. Location of Houses in Galok

to have been a marsh known as Kubang Galok. Traces of this remain in a patch of unused marshland, but the name may have referred to the entire length the old river bed (*alor*) that follows the line of the settlement and is today rice fields. The neighboring village of Atas Beting, which lies along the Kelantan River, was reportedly opened in around 1870, while Padang Hangus, which lies further from the river, dates back to around 1915. These are all pioneer villages opened for rain-fed rice cultivation. While there is some doubt about the dates of their founding, Atas Beting and Galok probably predate rubber cultivation. Villages further from the river appear to be of later opening, with higher proportions of rubber land and plots of larger area recorded in the land register. Kelantan's major produce before the introduction of rubber were, as mentioned, rice and copra, and the introduction of rubber in the early years of the twentieth century spurred the development of the middle and upper reaches of the Kelantan River. If the conversion of the jungle of the upper reaches to rubber and oil palm plantations were the late phase of development of Kelantan State, the development of the area around Galok can be said to represent the end of the early phase or the beginning of the middle phase.

In the 1960s, areas emerged where double cropping of rice was possible by use of irrigation water pumped up from the Kelantan River. By 1970, some 42 percent of rice land in Kelantan, namely, 79,500 acres (32,100 ha) out of a total of 188,000 acres (76,000 ha), was included in the Lemal, Pasir Mas, Alor Pasir, Salor, Kemubu, and other irrigation schemes. The Malaysian government's agricultural policy of raising self-sufficiency in rice had by this time increased the degree of specialization in rice cultivation in the Malay settlements and strenthened their image as rice-growing villages. The survey village of Galok lies upstream of the areas covered by the irrigation schemes. Thus, while agricultural development in Kelantan proceeded in the jungle area on the upper reach of the Kelantan River and the lowland on the lower reach, an area emerged that was left behind. Here the introduction of new crops such as tobacco would eventually be tried.

1.4. Relations with the Outside World

From the time that Kelantan appeared in the historical record, it had some remarkable dealings with the outside world. It is probably more apt to say that it was because it had dealings with the outside world that it appeared in the records of history. It dealt with the kingdoms of Melaka and Siam as a tributary state with a high degree of autonomy and little evidence of direct rule. In 1903, Siam for the first time despatched Graham to Kelantan as British Adviser with the intention of strengthening its control over the state; but in the end, with the

Bangkok Treaty of 1909, Kelantan came under British protection together with Trengganu, Kedah, and Perlis. Subsequently, Kelantan became one of the Unfederated Malay States; and in 1957, with the founding of the Federation of Malaya, it became a member, and the Federation of Malaya eventually joined with Sabah, Sarawak, and Singapore to form Malaysia.

In Graham's time in the early twentieth century, shipping was the most important means of communication linking Kelantan with the outside world. In 1931, a railway line was opened between Tumpat in Kelantan and Gemas in Negeri Sembilan. After World War II, a highway of about 400 miles (640 kilometers) was opened that reached Kuala Lumpur, passing through Kuala Trengganu and Kuantan. When I began my survey in 1970, Kuala Lumpur and Kota Bharu were linked by two flights daily and three mail trains weekly. By 1992, there were six daily flights and two weekly mail trains, and jet planes had replaced the propeller-powered machines. Rail users continued to decline, and with the completion of a new road across the center of the peninsula, night buses to Kuala Lumpur and Singapore began operating not only from Kota Bharu but also from major towns in the state.

The development of transportation in Kelantan is a twentieth-century phenomenon. In the early 1900s, there were virtually no cars in the state, not even ox carts (Graham, 1908: 57). By 1970, the network of trunk roads in the state was fairly well developed, and most major roads were surfaced. The trunk road between Pasir Mas and Tanah Merah was completed in 1935 and surfaced in 1940. Galok is located on this road exactly midway between these towns. Formerly, the most important means of transportation between the village and Pasir Mas was by small boat. Pasir Mas District is separated from the state capital of Kota Bharu by the Kelantan River, which was formerly crossed by ferry, but when the state government built a bridge in 1964, transportation was markedly improved. A toll was levied on traffic over the bridge, but this was subsequently removed. By 1992, a second bridge had been built, and the trunk road had been widened. The red clay road formerly known, among other names, as Jalan Penggawa was also widened and surfaced sufficiently to allow easy passage even in the rainy season. Cars and motorcycles increased rapidly. In 1970, telephone lines had reached Pasir Mas but not Galok. Electricity was also enjoyed only by residents of the town and its immediate vicinity. Mail was delivered in bulk to Galok, but not distributed to individual houses. By 1992, telephone lines and electricity had reached the rural villages. Electricity arrived in Galok in around 1988, and the telephone in around 1991. The volume of mail had also increased, but the method of delivery was unchanged.

In 1970, the town of Pasir Mas had a population of 11,228. Near the bank of the Kelantan River, the former traffic route, were the district office and the post office. A little further from the river was the road entering the town from Kota Bharu, and further inland yet was the railway station. Between the road and the station stood a market where small retailers of rice, fish, meat, vegetables, cloth, and other goods carried on their business. Across the roads around the market were the shops of Chinese, Indian, and Malay merchants that made up the commercial center of the town, and in the vicinity were primary and secondary schools, a hospital, clinic, police station, and two cinemas. Subsequently, the town of Pasir Mas stagnated rather than developed. Its population was 13,402 in 1980 and 13,275 in 1991. The wooden district office was replaced by a concrete structure, but the market building was abandoned following a fire, and the cinemas closed. In the midst of the overall stagnation, however, flower beds have been laid out at the entrance to the town maintaining a neat appearance. The only slightly lively place is the area around the bus station, the new hub of transportation. While the relationship between the survey village of Galok and Pasir Mas has remained unchanged from the standpoint of administration, for bigger purchases, many villagers go beyond Pasir Mas to the supermarkets and other shops of Kota Bharu, and for work, villagers have stronger links with Tanah Merah, where there has been rapid growth of lumber mills and other factories.

2
The Role of Rain-fed Paddy Farming

2.1. Land Clearance and Subsistence Farming

As mentioned in the previous chapter, the population of Kelantan grew rapidly from the mid-19th century and many new lands were cleared to accommodate this increase. When all available land had been cleared in one settlement, the pioneering spirit of the people carried them to neighboring areas with uncleared land. Like many parts of the Malay peninsula, Kelantan was characterized by land clearance. Even though in later times land was cleared for the monoculture of cash crops like rubber and oil palm, this pioneering character remained unchanged.

This chapter will outline the features of paddy cultivation in this type of area using data from fieldwork conducted in 1970/1971, and discuss the role of paddy growing in Malay farm villages. For the most part, food production in Galok and other settlements that were opened around the same time fulfilled local needs. Although a considerable amount of time has passed since the area was first settled, irrigation and other more recent cultivation methods have not been introduced, and many aspects of paddy farming remain unchanged.

Landholdings in Galok in 1970 were generally small, with an average size of 1.2 acres (0.48 ha). Of the 146 households in the village, 107 or 73.3 percent owned paddy land. However, only 4 of these owned large holdings of more than 3 acres (1.21 ha), while 63 (58.9 percent) owned less than 1 acre (0.40 ha) and 39 (26.7 percent) owned none at all. Rubber is another important land category in Galok, and 88 households (60.3 percent) owned rubber holdings, the average area of which was 1.7 acres (0.69 ha). Thirteen households owned more than 3 acres, 48 households (54.4 percent) owned less than one acre (0.40 ha) and 58 households (39.7 percent) owned none. Twenty-seven households (18.5 percent) owned neither paddy nor rubber holdings.

These figures show that a broader section of the population owns paddy, indicating that paddy farming is the primary occupation. The small size of holdings may be due to Islamic and traditional laws encouraging equalized inheritance, a point that will be covered later in the book. The resultant subdivision of land with each successive generation could also explain the occurrence of households with no landholdings. With sufficient rainfall and no fertilizer, the average holding of 1.2 acres will yield 360 *gantang* (1 *gantang* equals 1 imperial gallon or 4.546 liters) of paddy but, as will be discussed in more detail below, this is not enough to feed an average household when the standard annual consumption per capita is estimated at 100 *gantang*. Thus, although earlier settlements were basically self-sufficient, this is no longer the case in Galok.

2.2. Unstable Yields

The banks of the Kelantan River are too high to divert water by traditional methods and there are no tributaries near Galok. For this reason, paddy growing has been entirely dependent on rainwater. Fortunately, monthly rainfall from June to January exceeds 200 mm (Figure 2-1), and the clayey soil retains water very well. By surrounding each field with high, sturdy bunds it is possible to

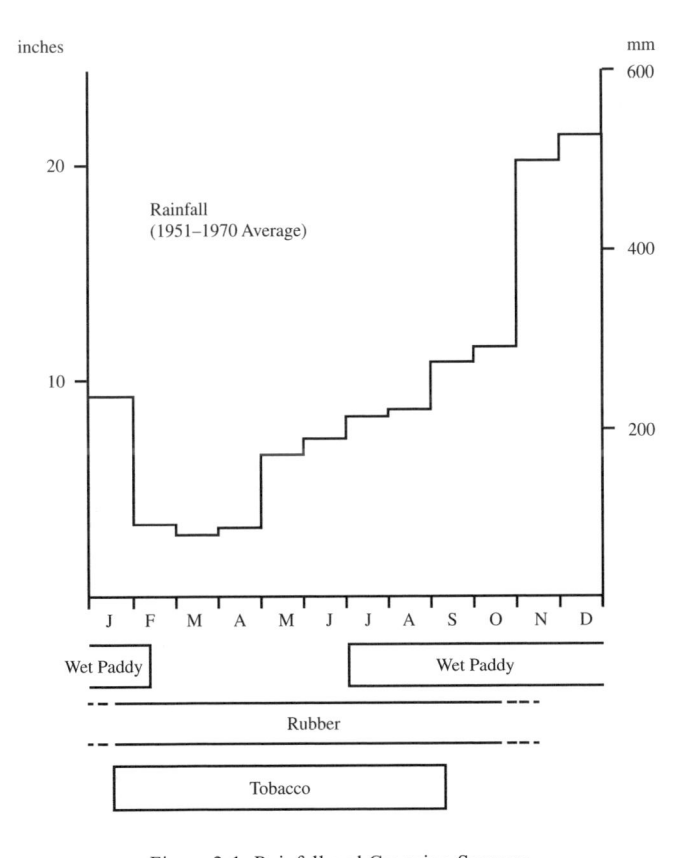

Figure 2-1. Rainfall and Cropping Seasons

reserve rainwater for paddy cultivation. Due to the gently undulating terrain around Galok, which is located part way up the river, water collects more easily in some spots than in others. *Tanah alor*, land situated on old river channels and natural depressions where water tends to pool after rain, is considered optimum for paddy growing. The villagers categorize paddy plots into *tanah dalam*, "deep-water land," where water readily ponds, including *tanah alor*, and *tanah darat*, "dry land," where water pools less readily. In addition, the steeper areas where water does not pool at all are planted with *padi tugalan* ("rice sown with a dibble"), a variety of upland rice suitable for dry field cultivation. The paddy holdings in Galok mentioned in the previous section fall into one of these three categories.

Paddy varieties grown in Galok during the study period are listed in Table 2-1 in order of prevalence. Of these, Piah was the most commonly grown variety on deep-water land and Intan Belian on dry land. Data for 1970/1971 show that fifty-two households grew Piah on a total of 274 plots (*keping*), representing 54 percent of the total number of plots planted that year, while twenty-seven households grew Intan Belian on 108 plots, representing 21 percent of the total. Together the two varieties accounted for 75 percent of the total number of plots planted. Of the two varieties planted in upland fields, Pok

Table 2-1
Paddy Varieties and Number of Plots Planted (1970–1971)

Variety	Characteristics	No. of Plots
Piah	Suitable for *Tanah Dalam*	274
Intan Belian	Suitable for *Tanah Darat*	108
Pok Dut	Upland Rice	33
Pak Amat	Suitable for *Tanah Dalam*	24
Segupal	Suitable for *Tanah Dalam*	18
Anak Ikan	Suitable for *Tanah Darat*	6
Ali Loghat	Suitable for *Tanah Darat*	6
Merak Siam	Suitable for *Tanah Dalam*	5
Padi Kedah		5
Mahsuri	New Variety	3
Lembu Basah + Piah		3
Nalong		2
Ria	New Variety	2
Maya Batil		2
Glutinous Rice		1
Bidor	Upland Rice	1
Unknown		12
Total		505

Dut was planted in 33 fields, making it the third most commonly grown variety. Forty-one households planted only one variety, while the remaining thirty households planted a combination of two or more. The most frequent combination was Piah and Intan Belian. In some cases, different varieties were used in neighboring plots because of slight differences in elevation. Although new varieties such as Mahsuri and Bahagia were common where irrigation projects made double-cropping possible, they were not grown in Galok. The three plots listed in Table 2.1 that are planted with Mahsuri were plots in the double-cropping zone across the river inherited by a Galok farmer.

Only seventy-one households grew paddy, a much smaller figure than the number of households that own paddy land. This discrepancy is caused by two factors; the renting or neglecting of land inherited by one or both spouses, and the renting of very small holdings to other farmers. The total area of paddy, including upland rice, cultivated by owners or tenants in 1970/1971 was about 100 acres (40.5 ha) which amounts to roughly 1.4 acres (0.57 ha) per household. Of this, about 23 acres or 23 percent was farmed by tenants, while the remainder was farmed by the owners. Nineteen households rented land, of which thirteen also owned paddy land, while only six rented all the land they farmed.

The entire one hundred acres (40.5 ha) is not necessarily cultivated every year. Rather planted area varies annually depending on the amount of rainfall at transplanting time. The planted area in 1970/1971 was only about 81 acres (32.7 ha), and in the previous year it was an even smaller 64 acres (25.9 ha) because of a severe water shortage. Figure 2-2 illustrates the planted area in 1970/1971 in comparison with the total potential wet paddy area per household. As can be seen, only some households reduced their planted area.

The yield per unit of planted area is also lower in years with less rainfall. From a survey of each farm household, I computed the average paddy yield to be 220 *gantang* per acre in 1970/1971 and only 124 *gantang* per acre in 1969/1970, both significantly less than the 309 *gantang* per acre expected in a "normal" year. The latter is equivalent to about 1.4 tons of unpolished rice per hectare.

Due to the small scale of farms and the low yield per acre, the amount of paddy produced is often insufficient for home consumption. Even if the average plot were planted to full capacity and a yield of 309 *gantang* per acre obtained, each household would still only produce 433 *gantang* (710 kg of polished rice), barely enough to feed an average family of 5.6 members. Because of the unstable yields, people tend to store any surplus grain produced during a good year to guard against a poor harvest the following year. Only thirty-two of the paddy-growing households produced enough rice in 1970/1971 for home consumption, representing 45 percent of paddy-growing

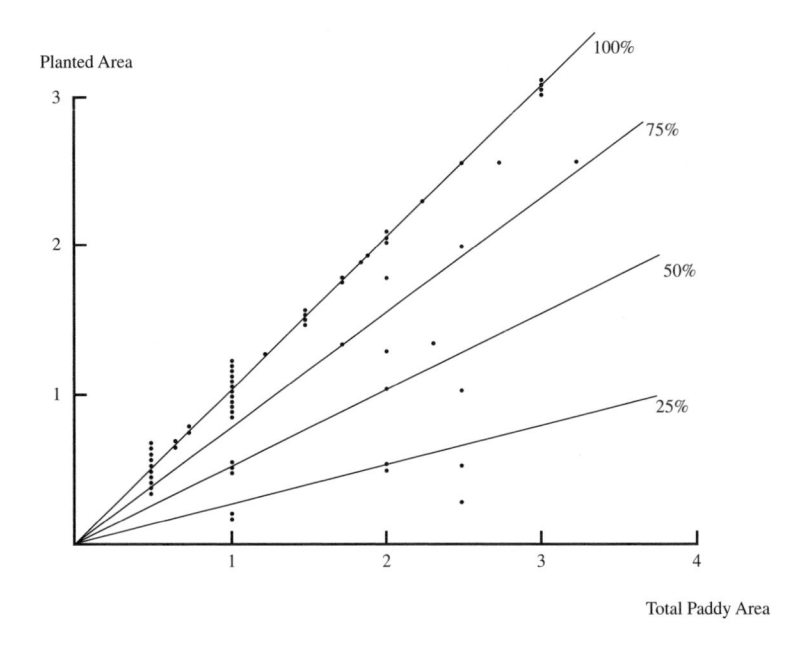

Figure 2-2. Total Paddy Area and Planted Area (1970/71)

households and 22 percent of all households. Self-sufficient food production, which was once a basic characteristic of settlements opened in the last century, was already disappearing from Galok at the time of the study.

2.3. Simple Farm Implements

Rudimentary equipment is used to cultivate rice for home consumption, the main implements being animal-drawn plows, hoes, sickles for harvesting, and threshing tubs. All are generally of simple construction, and not every farm household has all of them. Ownership of the main implements is shown in Table 2-2 and the different methods of obtaining them and their cost are described below.

Plows are made of four wooden parts; the *igu, nangar, nayer* and *penolok*. The farmer either makes them himself or asks a skilled person like a village carpenter. The tip of the blade is also made of wood, although it is sometimes reinforced with an empty tin can or other piece of metal. More than half of those who owned plows at the time of the study period (21 out of 38) made their own. Those who did not most frequently asked someone in Galok, although a few asked people in the neighboring villages of Atas Beting and

Table 2-2
Ownership of Main Farming Implements

Implement	Households by Number of Implements Owned						Percentage of Households Owning At Least One Implement	Average Number Owned Per Household
	0	1	2	3	4	Total		
Plow	33	38				71	53.5	0.54
Hoe	5	27	25	10	4	71	93.0	1.75
Sickle	10	31	20	7	3	71	85.9	1.48
Threshing Tub	29	42				71	59.2	0.59

Paya Mengkuang. In Galok, a carpenter, Salleh bin Samat, received the most orders and payment was usually RM10. (The Malaysian ringgit is abbreviated as RM; in 1970 the exchange rate was 120 yen per ringgit, or 3 ringgit per US dollar.) Plows reportedly last about five or six years, but some farmers used theirs for over ten years, repairing them when necessary. Harrow attachments (*gerap*) for the plow consisting of simple teeth embedded in the wooden blade were also usually made by the farmers themselves. When made by others, payment ranged from RM1.5 to 3.5.

Owned by 93 percent of paddy-growing households, the hoe (*cok*) was the most common implement, yet as many as five households did not have one. Farmers generally bought the metal blade at one of the places shown in Table 2.3 and made the handle themselves. Half were bought in Pasir Mas for a standard price of RM3.5–4, while the next most common point of purchase was a store in a neighboring village. Hoes generally last four to five years.

Table 2-3
Places Where Hoes and Sickles are Purchased

Place of Purchase	Hoe		Sickle	
	No.	(%)	No.	(%)
Local Shop	9	(7.3)	0	
Neighboring Village	33	(26.5)	10	(9.5)
Peddler	0		20	(19.0)
Pasir Mas	62	(50.0)	32	(30.4)
Tanah Merah	11	(8.9)	5	(4.8)
Other Place in Kelantan	0		24	(22.9)
Kedah State	0		7	(6.7)
Unknown	9	(7.3)	7	(6.7)
Total	124	(100.0)	105	(100.0)

Eighty-six percent of households possessed one or more sickles (*sadat*), a slightly lower distribution than for hoes, and the average number owned per household was also a little lower. Although fine saw-toothed sickles are designed for harvesting rice, some farmers used sickles designed for cutting weeds. As shown in Table 2-3, compared to hoes, fewer sickles were purchased in Pasir Mas or in neighboring villages. Instead many were bought from peddlers or from double-cropping districts in Kelantan or in Kedah and other states where farmers from Galok traveled to work during the harvest season. The standard price was RM2–2.5, and they generally last from four to five years. Eight households also owned a combined total of 14 special knives (*tame*) that were used in lieu of, or in addition to, sickles for harvesting. The iron blades were bought in Pasir Mas for about 20 sen (RM1 = 100 sen), and were attached to wood and bamboo handles which the farmer made himself.

A little fewer than 60 percent of farm households owned threshing tubs (*tong*). Many of those who did not own one borrowed from others at need. Eighteen of the 42 tubs in the village were made by the owners. For the farmers who made their own, the materials cost about RM4, while those who ordered tubs from someone else paid about RM10, including materials. The tubs last about five or six years.

2.4. Family-based Paddy Farming

Labor for paddy farming in Galok is characterized by the lack of communal labor organizations and the predominance of the family work force. The number of people available for paddy work per household is shown in Table 2-4. The most common labor unit is a man and a woman, a pattern found in half of all households, followed in descending order by a man and two women, two men and two women, and two men and one woman. It is very rare for members of just one sex to be engaged in paddy work, with one example of a man working on his own and another of two women. As will be discussed below, the head of the household and his wife provide most of the labor, although children are expected to help with transplanting and harvesting when they grow old enough. If a husband or wife cannot work because of illness or pregnancy, they must depend upon hired help. This also applies when a couple becomes too old to farm or when a spouse is lost through death or divorce. In some cases when a couple grows too old to farm, they may rent their land to other farmers.

Division of labor by sex is not always strictly observed as flexibility is not only easier but essential when relying solely on labor within the family unit. In direct contrast with the custom of all-women transplanting groups in Kedah

Table 2-4
Household Work Force

	WOMEN					
MEN	0	1	2	3	4	TOTAL
0			1			1
1	1	35	11	3		50
2		6	7	2		15
3		3	1			4
4		1				1
Total	1	45	20	5	0	71

and other places, the men of Galok even assist with transplanting which is considered to be women's work. In the following section, I will describe the main work involved in paddy cultivation using data primarily from the year 1970/1971, adding some explanations of the methods involved.

2.4.1. Nurseries

In the case of rain-fed paddies, work begins in the nurseries in July when the amount of rainfall gradually increases. Although nurseries are sometimes located in places where water collects easily, they are more often located in dry fields. Once the seed paddy has been prepared, it is sown (*menabor*) without disinfecting or otherwise treating the seed rice. The majority of seed rice is produced and stored by each household without special treatment of any kind. An average of 10.9 *gantang* (12.3 liters/10 ares) of seed is used per acre cultivated. This is significantly more than necessary and is intended to compensate for poor germination or losses caused by birds or water buffalo. Although in some cases fences are put up around the nursery to keep out water buffalo or ducks, this is not the general practice. The amount of seedlings transplanted in the main paddy fields is equivalent to 7.7 *gantang* (8.7 liters/10 ares), a figure corroborated by the Agricultural Officer of Kelantan in Kota Bharu, who estimates that about 8 *gantang* of seed rice (9 liters/10 ares) is used per acre of paddy. The amount the Department of Agriculture considers sufficient is only 3 *gantang*. The number of seedling bundles also exceeds the amount recommended by the Department and seedlings tend to be planted very densely. It is evident from this that paddy cultivation in the area is subsistence-oriented rather than profit-oriented. It also shows that farmers do not want to risk the possibility of lower yields. Preparation and seeding of a nursery is generally carried out by the head of the household working alone, although the work is done by one female for every four males. The majority of people make their nurseries on their own land, but very occasionally they may purchase seedlings or give their seed rice to a neighbor or relative to plant in their nursery.

2.4.2. Preparation of Main Fields

Repairing the bunds and plowing the paddy plots is also the work of the male of the household. Water buffalo (*kerbau*) or oxen (*lembu*) were traditionally used for plowing, but by 1970 the number of people hiring tractors had significantly increased. Methods used for plowing are shown in Table 2-5. Forty-seven households (66 percent) used draft animals, while 22 households (31 percent) hired tractors. The remaining two households used neither because they cultivated upland rice on land too steep to plow. Of those who plowed with animals, 40 households did the work themselves, while the remaining seven employed somebody else or received voluntary assistance.

Only one water buffalo is needed to pull a plow as opposed to two oxen, but the latter are used about twice as commonly as water buffalo. The first plowing (*galah beloh*) is carried out before the field is inundated, followed by a second plowing (*gala balek*, or *gala lumat*) after the field has been flooded. Subsequently, the field is harrowed (*gerap*) twice. When draft animals are used, field work usually takes place between seven and ten in the morning at a pace of one or two plots a day, depending on their size. Larger tracts of land may be plowed prior to seeding the nurseries.

Table 2-5
Use of Draft Animals and Tractors for Paddy Land Preparation

Source of Labour	Source of Draft Power	Source of Draft Animals	Number of Households
Family	Ox	Family	21
		Family + Pawah	2
		Family + Sewa	2
		Pawah	1
		Sewa	1
	Water Buffalo	Family	10
		Free Loan	1
		Pawah	1
		Sewa	1
Voluntary Help	Ox		2
Hired Help	Ox		3
	Water Buffalo		2
	Tractor		22
Upland Rice, Land not Plowed			2

Those farmers who do not own draft animals may use animals borrowed under one of two forms of agreement. The first is known as *pawah*, under which the borrower takes care of the animal for a long period on the conditions that he has the right to use the animal during that time and that any offspring will be shared. The second is called *sewa*, under which the farmer rents the animal, usually for a single season. Payment for the latter is generally made in paddy after the harvest, and amounts to 40 or 50 *gantang* for an ox and about 80 *gantang* for a water buffalo.

A farmer may also employ (*upah*) an operator with draft animals to plow for him. In four of the five examples of this in Galok, the farmers employed a kinsman. In all instances the area involved was small, 0.6 acres (0.24 ha) on average, and payment ranged from RM10 to 20 per job. At about RM21 per acre, this amounted to about RM2 per day. In addition, two farmers had their fields plowed for free, both by immediate relatives. One was the husband's father and the other the wife's younger brother.

The average cultivated area of the 22 households that hired tractors for plowing was 1.2 acres (0.48 ha), twice as large an area as the households employing an operator and draft animals. Ten of the households did not own water buffalo or oxen, 3 owned only one ox, while another 3 owned an ox too young to draw a plow. One farmer owned two oxen, but his brother who owned a tractor plowed his fields free of charge, and another owned paddy in the double-cropping zone across the river where tractor use is common. Thus only four households hired a tractor to plow their fields even though they owned the necessary draft animals for plowing themselves. No one in Galok owned a tractor, which had only recently been introduced at that time. Tractors were hired from owners in Chekok and other nearby villages, and a driver was employed to carry out the plowing. Although the standard fee for such services was reportedly RM30–35 per acre, farm households in Galok only paid an average of RM17 per acre. Although different methods of payment, such as RM3 per plot or RM8 per hour, were arranged by verbal agreement, the average payment was generally as stated above. The amount paid by individual households ranged from a minimum of RM8 to a maximum of RM 40.

2.4.3. Transplanting

Transplanting is done about forty days after the seeds are sown. The task of uprooting seedlings from the nursery and making them into bundles (*cabut semai* or *menyambut*) is in principle women's work, and, as shown in Table 2-6, is done mainly by the wife of the household, sometimes with some help from her daughters or husband. In ten cases, the husband helped, accounting for 17

Table 2-6
Division of Labor for Bundling

Source of Labor	Work Force	Number of Households	
Family	Wife	31	
	Wife + Daughter(s)	9	
	Wife, Daughter(s) + Husband	3	
	Wife, Daughter(s) + Mother	1	
	Wife + Husband	7	58
	Wife + Mother	2	
	Wife + Sister(s)	2	
	Wife + Other Kin	1	
	Mother	2	
Family + Hired Help	Wife + Hired Help	2	
	Wife, Daughter(s) + Hired Help	1	
Hired		4	
Seedling Bundles Bought		1	
Upland Rice, Broadcast Seeding		5	
Total		71	

percent of those households who did their own bundling. The seedlings were bundled from seven in the morning (*pagi*) until noon and from two or three in the afternoon (*petang*) until five. In a full morning's work twenty bundles, each one large enough to be grasped in both hands, can be prepared, and 30 to 40 bundles are prepared for each paddy plot. Seven households hired someone else to bundle the seedlings, but only 4 relied solely on hired labor, while one household bought seedlings. Hired helpers were paid 5 sen per bundle, while seedlings cost 8 sen per bundle.

Once prepared, the bundles of seedlings are carried to the field bund, where the tips of the leaves are trimmed, a procedure which is thought to prevent the seedlings from lodging in high winds. The bundles are then placed at convenient spots around the field and the workers plant them by hand in bunches of 5 to 7 seedlings, replenishing their supply from the bundles as they move along. As far as possible, hills are spaced at intervals of about 30 centimeters in straight rows, although no tools are used to align them.

In principal, transplanting (*cedong*) is women's work. As shown in Table 2-7, however, the husband and wife commonly work together, sometimes with help from their daughters or sons. The married couple transplanted the seedlings in thirty-three households, representing 46 percent of paddy-growing households and 57 percent of households that transplanted their own fields.

Plate 2-1. Plowing with a water buffalo. A rubber grove can be seen in the background.

Significantly, in as many as nine households the husband carried out the work alone, and in another six the wife did the same. In eight cases, a son assisted with the work, and in another eight cases, a daughter. As mentioned before, there is no communal organization of labor, and therefore someone must be hired if there are not enough family members to perform the work. In two cases, the husband was assisted by hired labor, and in six cases, the work was completed entirely by hired labor.

The amount of time it takes to transplant seedlings is similar to that for bundling, the standard being twenty bundles per person in the morning and seven to ten bundles in the afternoon. It takes one or two days for a person working alone to transplant one plot. Usually two people work together, transplanting one or two plots a day. The average rate for hired labor is 5 sen per bundle. No intertillage, weeding or supplementary fertilizing is undertaken after transplanting.

2.4.4. Harvesting

The rice crop is harvested (*cerut*) during the dry season from February to early March, between 150 to 200 days after sowing the seeds. At the time of my fieldwork in 1970, almost everyone used sickles for harvesting, but ten years previously many still used a harvesting knife (*tame*).

Table 2-7
Division of Labor for Transplanting

Source of Labor	Work Force	Number of Households
Family	Husband + Wife	23
	Husband, Wife + Son(s)	3
	Husband, Wife, Son(s) + Daughter(s)	3
	Husband, Wife + Daughter(s)	1
	Husband, Wife + Mother	1
	Husband, Wife + Sibling(s)	2
	Husband	12
	Husband + Son(s)	1
	Husband + Daughter(s)	1
	Husband + Mother	1
	Wife	6
	Wife + Daughter(s)	3
	Wife + Son(s)	1
Family + Hired Help	Husband + Hired Help	2
Hired		6
Upland Rice, Broadcast Seeding		5
Total		71

Stalks are cut about 30 centimeters from the ground and laid on top of the stubble in small bundles. To thresh the grain, workers grasp several of these in both hands and strike them (*memukul*) against the rungs of a wooden ladder-like structure set in the top of a threshing tub. The paddy is sun-dried in the field and, later in the day, winnowed in the wind by placing it in a shallow bamboo container and dropping it from shoulder height onto a mat (*tikar*) spread on the ground. The winnowed paddy is placed in jute sacks and carried home on people's backs or by bicycle and stored in the granary (*baloh*) or in large bamboo baskets.

The basic work force is the family, centered on the husband and wife. Normally labor is divided according to sex, with the women cutting the grain and the husband threshing it, but men sometimes cut paddy as well. The division of labor for harvesting and threshing is shown in Table 2-8. When the work force within the family is inadequate, or when one or more of the family members is unable to work, someone is hired (*upah*) or close friends or kinsmen help (*tulong* or *pinjam*). The amount of time required for harvesting is about the same as that for bundling and transplanting. A husband and wife without other help can harvest between 20 and 50 *gantang* in a morning's work.

Table 2-8
Division of Labor for Harvesting

Source of Labor	Work Force	Number of Households
Family	Husband + Wife	27
	Husband, Wife + Child(ren)	15
	Husband, Wife, Child(ren) + Grandchild(ren)	1
	Husband, Wife + Sibling(s)	3
	Husband, Wife + Mother	1
	Husband, Wife, Father + Mother	1
	Husband, Wife + Other Kin	1
	Husband	1
	Husband + Child(ren)	1
	Wife + Child(ren)	4
	Wife, Father + Mother	1
	Wife + Father	1
	Wife	1
Family + hired help	Husband, Wife, Child(ren) + Hired Help	3
	Husband, Wife + Hired Help	4
	Husband + Hired Help	2
	Wife + Hired Help	2
	Wife, Mother + Hired Help	1
Hired		1
Total		71

Thirteen households hired workers to help with harvesting. Although this exceeds the number hired for transplanting, only one household relied solely on hired help. Payment for harvesting is in paddy, but the amount is not fixed. In one case, for example, a three-member team consisting of the husband's sister-in-law, her husband and her daughter were paid 40 *gantang* of rice for 15 days' work. In this case, however, bed and board were also provided. Although those who assist with harvesting in Salor, the double-cropping district across the river, are paid a standard sum of 5 *gantang* per day, in Galok workers are paid for the job rather than per day, and the rate generally ranges from 5 to 15 *gantang*. People usually hire kinsmen or neighbors, although in some cases immediate family members such as parents or siblings are hired. In the latter case, the element of assistance outweighs that of employment even though some remuneration is made. Winnowing is generally considered women's work, and it is almost always performed by the housewife. The bags of rice are carried by men, sometimes with the assistance of the wife or children. Although husking and milling may be done at home with a wooden mortar and pestle, by 1970 most people took small quantities of rice to one of

Plate 2-2. The use of a knife (*tame*) to harvest rice has become very rare in Galok.

three mills in a neighboring village. Payment for milling was about 5 sen per *kati* (1 *kati* equals about 600g).

2.4.5. Upland Rice

Upland rice (*padi tugalan*) is commonly planted on slightly elevated land where less water collects. It is possible that a larger area was planted to upland rice before the introduction of rubber, but that was a long time ago. In 1970/1971, only nine of the paddy-growing households planted upland rice, accounting for just 7.4 of the 100 acres mentioned earlier. Five of the nine grew only upland rice, while the other four also grew wet rice. The main difference between the two methods is that upland rice is sown directly, a few seeds being dropped into holes made in the soil with a dibble, a method known as *tugal*. Weeds grow profusely with upland rice, making weeding necessary, and the heavy growth of weeds coupled with damage by birds, insects and disease means lower yields in comparison with wet rice. The average yield in 1970/1971 was 118 *gantang* per acre, a little more than half the average annual yield of 220 *gantang* per acre for paddy.

2.5. Changes in Paddy Farming

Paddy growing in the Galok region with its strong emphasis on subsistence and its unstable yields is unlikely to undergo any major improvements. Yet, even in 1970 some changes were clearly taking place as described below.

2.5.1. Selection of Varieties

Subsistence farmers dependent on rain-fed paddy are far from indifferent when it comes to selection of the varieties they plant. Piah, the most widely used variety in Galok, was developed by a farmer of Chinese stock and was introduced to Galok from the district of Salor across the river where it is known as Padi Ketip. Another variety brought back from Kedah by a migrant worker was being planted under the name of Padi Kedah. This free substitution of names makes it difficult to identify the spread of a particular variety. In addition, some varieties previously planted quite widely had become less common by the time of my fieldwork. One of these is Lembu Basah the popularity of which declined because of its susceptibility to disease. However, because seed rice is usually obtained directly from one's own harvest, sudden changes in variety are unlikely.

2.5.2. Use of Tractors

As previously shown, a little less than one third of farmers at the time of the survey plowed with hired tractors. The increasing use of hired tractors is directly related to the introduction of tobacco farming, which will be discussed later. At the same time, however, most of those who used tractors did not own draft animals. Raising buffalo and cattle was in itself profitable and as long as it remained so, it seemed unlikely that tractors would be adopted for plowing on a wide scale.

2.5.3. Chemical Fertilizers

At the time of the survey, twenty-one households, or 30 percent of paddy-growing households, applied chemical fertilizers, two of them on paddy fields across the river. The remaining nineteen used an average of 1.6 eighty-pound (36.3 kg) bags per acre. This is half the amount of 3 bags recommended by the Department of Agriculture. Cash income from tobacco cultivation made it easier to purchase chemical fertilizers. Also, the government's subsidy of chemical fertilizers allowed a farmer to buy an eighty-pound sack for RM6.72 instead of the usual RM9.50, by presenting his land grant deed and identity card at the *penggawa*'s office (the *penggawa* is a local government administrator) in the neighboring village of Chekok to the south of Galok. It is interesting to note that the people living in the southern half of Galok, nearer to the *penggawa*'s office, make up more than 70 percent (14 out of 19) of households using chemical fertilizers. Moreover, some residents in the northern half were unable to buy fertilizer because they did not know the dates or time when purchase was possible.

2.5.4. Harvesting Methods

As mentioned previously, the majority of people at the time of the survey harvested with sickles, whereas formerly people had used a special knife, a practice still continued in other areas of Kelantan. The adoption of the sickle may have been prompted by people who traveled to Kedah to work during the harvest there. This has resulted in the disappearance of a harvest ritual called *padi semangat* in which a woman cut seven ears of rice and reverently placed them in the granary.

At the end of 1977, six years after the survey, I conducted a simple follow-up survey of fifteen households randomly selected from paddy-growing households. Of these, fourteen were there during the 1970/1971 survey, while the other was a new addition. Potential paddy-growing area of the sample households was 29.75 acres of which 8.5 acres or 28.6 percent was rented. The average planted area was 2.0 acres and the average rented area was 0.6 acres. Nine of the sample households rented all or part of their paddy land to tenants. Of the fourteen households that had been part of the original study, eight households rented land in 1977 compared to 5 in 1970/1971. Land purchases

Plate 2-3. Harvesting and threshing work.

and a tendency towards renting out land holdings had caused an increase in the average paddy area and in rented land during the interval between the two studies, factors that point to a decrease in the number of paddy-growing households in the area. Tenant contracts have traditionally been by verbal agreement and this trend continued, with payment in paddy, usually half the yield, to the landowner.

A comparison of the varieties planted by the fourteen households present in both 1970/1971 and 1976/1977 is shown in Table 2-9. Piah remained the dominant variety and use of Intan Belian also continued, but Pot Dut, Segupal, Pak Amat, Padi Kedah, Merak Siam, and glutinous rice are no longer planted and have been replaced by Ali Loghat, Padi Pau, Morak, and Padi Paku. Only three households had made no changes in rice varieties during the interval between the two surveys.

The most noticeable change in technology and labor was the increased use of hired tractors. Eleven of the sample households (73 percent) hired tractors from outside the village to plow their paddy in 1976/1977, and six of these used tractors despite the fact that they owned draft animals. Thus it seems that

Table 2-9
Number of Plots Planted, by Variety, in 1970/1971 and 1976/1977

Variety	1970/1971	1976/1977
Piah	9	9
Pok Dut	4	
Intan Belian	2	2
Segupal	2	
Pak Amat	1	
Padi Kedah	1	
Merak Siam	1	
Glutinous Rice	1	
Ali Loghat		3
Padi Pauh		3
Morak		1
Padi Paku		1

Data are for 14 households. Some gave multiple responses.

livestock raising was no longer a deterrent to the spread of hired tractors. Moreover, the practice of hiring draft animals and operators for plowing or preparing fields had been completely replaced by hired tractors. Only three of the fifteen households (20 percent) applied chemical fertilizers that year and it is thought that many people did not purchase fertilizer because of water shortages. The average yield per acre of the sample households in the same year was only 162 *gantang*. In 1970/1971, 11 percent of households relied partly or entirely on hired labor for bundling seedlings, 12 percent for transplanting, and 18 percent for harvesting. In 1976/1977, 13 percent of households sampled employed someone for bundling, 40 percent for transplanting and 20 percent for harvesting. The use of hired labor for transplanting has particularly increased. Despite the above, however, paddy cultivation continues to be subsistence farming, illustrated by the fact that none of the sample households in 1976/1977 sold any of their rice during that period.

In the 1980s, cheap, delicious, good quality Thai rice began to supplant locally grown rice in Kelantan. A large proportion of rice sold in the Pasir Mas market was produced in Thailand, most of which was smuggled across the border in large quantities by truck, or in small quantities by couriers using the railroad that joins the two countries. As a result, deep-water paddies even in irrigated areas of Kelantan were abandoned, and a large proportion of plots were left untilled. Another factor behind this phenomenon was the exodus of farmers looking for work in Singapore or Kuala Lumpur. Paddy farming in Galok was similarly affected, aggravated by the unstable yields of rain-fed paddy.

Paddy cultivation recovered remarkably with subsequent government restrictions on the influx of Thai rice and protective measures for domestic paddy production. Even rain-fed paddy farming in Galok showed some degree of recovery. In 1991, thirty-six households were involved in paddy cultivation, half the number in 1970/1971. It is difficult to judge whether this figure represents a preference among local farmers for traditional rain-fed paddy production or a gradual movement toward its disappearance. In view of the increase in alternative sources of income and the low contribution of paddy production to overall income, it may represent a tendency among farmers to cling to tradition that exists alongside their tolerance of change.

3
Rubber Tapping and Tobacco Cultivation

3.1. Small-scale Rubber Tapping

As mentioned previously, rubber tapping in Kelantan began in the early part of the twentieth century, shortly after the area around Galok was first opened, and in comparatively new settlements like Galok, it can be considered a traditional occupation like wet-rice farming. A comparison of land taxes (*hasil tanah*) makes it obvious that the state government regards rubber holdings to be more profitable than paddy. Land tax for rain-fed paddy land in 1970 was only RM2 per acre, whereas that for rubber was four times higher at RM8 per acre. This was still the norm in 1992 (when the exchange rate was 50 yen per ringgit), with land taxes for non-irrigated paddy land set at only RM10 per hectare (about RM4 per acre), versus RM25 per hectare (about RM10 per acre) for rubber holdings.

Plate 3-1. A rubber grove. Trees are not necessarily planted in straight rows.

At the time of the study, eighty-eight households in Galok owned rubber holdings amounting to a total area of 158 acres (63.8 ha), and the average area owned per household was 1.8 acres (0.73 ha). Twenty-seven, or 18.5 percent, of the village households owned neither paddy nor rubber land, thirty-one households (21.2 percent) owned paddy but no rubber land, and twelve households (8.2 percent) owned rubber but no paddy land. In contrast, seventy-six households (52.1 percent) owned both, making this the most common land ownership pattern in the village (Table 3-1).

Some of the rubber holdings were located in Ulu Kelantan on a state land development project while still others were situated in jungle areas farther from the river such as Sungai Keladi. The trees on 51 acres (20.6 ha) or 32 percent of the total number of rubber holdings were too young to tap. Moreover, a little under 10 acres (4 ha) or 6 percent, had been cleared of old trees but not replanted, a trend particularly prevalent among elderly smallholders. Thus, only about 97 acres (39.2 ha) of the total area of rubber holdings were actually being tapped. Tapping was carried out by the owners or by share-tappers from Galok or elsewhere, and some villagers in Galok worked rubber holdings rented from people in other villages. In total, seventy-four households had at least one member employed in rubber tapping, and the average area operated per household was 1.4 acres (0.57 ha).

Forty-four households (30.1 percent) did not engage in either paddy farming or rubber tapping, while thirty households (20.5 percent) were involved in rubber tapping alone, twenty-eight (19.2 percent) in paddy farming alone, and forty-four (30.1 percent) in both. Compared with land ownership patterns, there was a stronger tendency to specialize in either rubber tapping or paddy farming, with only about one third of village households involved in both.

As pointed out previously, fewer households owned rubber holdings compared to the number that owned paddy land. And just as the number of households that actually cultivated paddy was less than the number of households that owned paddy, so too the number of households involved in rubber tapping was less than the number of smallholders. The difference, however, is not as noticeable as that for paddy-owning households (Table 3-2). Whereas paddy farming as a traditional village occupation had declined considerably by the time of the study, rubber tapping which generates some degree of cash income however small, was still being continued. Both men and women tap rubber, and the fact that, unlike paddy farming, women can tap rubber on their own may contribute to the comparatively larger number of households that had a member engaged in this occupation. As with paddy farming, the *pawah* system, under which earnings are divided equally between the owner and the share-tapper, was applied when renting rubber holdings. If

Table 3-1
Number of Households Owning Paddy and/or Rubber Land by Size of Holding

Rubber (acres)	0	0.1–0.5	0.6–1.0	1.1–1.5	1.6–2.0	2.1–2.5	2.6–3.0	3.1–3.5	3.6–4.0	4.1–4.5	4.6–5.0	5.1–5.5	5.6–6.0	6.1–6.5	6.6–7.0	Total
0	27	11	8	3	3	3	2								1	58
0.1–0.5	6	8	7	2	1	1										25
0.6–1.0	1	9	6	2	1	1	3									23
1.1–1.5	1	1	2	2	1		1	1								8
1.6–2.0	1	1	1	1			1		1							6
2.1–2.5	1		4	1	3											9
2.6–3.0	2				1	1										4
3.1–3.5							1									1
3.6–4.0					1					1						2
4.1–4.5		1														1
4.6–5.0			1			1										2
5.1–5.5																0
5.6–6.0			2	1			1									4
6.1–6.5																0
6.6–7.0		1		1												2
7.1–					1											1
Total	39	32	31	13	12	7	8	1	1	1	0	0	0	0	1	146

Table 3-2
Number of Households Engaged in Paddy Growing and Rubber Tapping by Scale of Operation

Rubber (acres)	Paddy (acres)									Total
	0	0.1–0.5	0.6–1.0	1.1–1.5	1.6–2.0	2.1–2.5	2.6–3.0	3.1–3.5	3.6–	
0	44	7	11	3	3	2	1		1	72
0.1–0.5	10	3	5	1	1					20
0.6–1.0	12	4	6	3	1		2			28
1.1–1.5		1	1	1		1				4
1.6–2.0	3		2		1	2				8
2.1–2.5	2	1					1			4
2.6–3.0	2		1		1		1			5
3.1–3.5	1									1
3.6–4.0		1				2				3
4.1–4.5										0
4.6–		1								1
Total	74	18	26	8	7	7	5	0	1	146

the tapper himself purchased the acid for coagulating the latex, however, he was entitled to keep the scraps washed from the coconut shells used as receptacles.

Like paddy cultivation, the scale of rubber tapping operations was extremely small. Of the seventy-four households engaged in tapping in 1970/1971, forty-eight (64.9 percent) operated areas of less than one acre. Tapping was carried out mainly in the dry season because trees cannot be tapped when the bark is wet. The flow of latex, however, greatly decreases during part of the dry season when the trees shed their leaves, and trees were only tapped for 180 to 200 days a year. Work began at seven in the morning when trees were tapped for about one hour. After a thirty-minute interval, another hour was spent collecting the latex in buckets or other containers. This was then carried home, transferred to pans or oil cans that had been cut in half, and coagulated by adding acid. By the end of the morning, the milky white rubber had been rolled into sheets. Extremely small amounts of latex such as that yielded by ten to fifteen trees, or scraps left in the containers, were rolled into balls called *pot*. One acre yields three to four *kati* of rubber per day.

Equipment used for rubber tapping was very simple: a tapping knife, half coconut shells for receiving the latex, buckets for carrying it home, oil cans cut in half to make coagulating pans, and simple manually operated rollers. The latter cost about RM150 and are thought to last about seven or eight years, but the cost for other equipment was negligible. Twenty households had their own rollers, and forty-five brought their latex to roll at households which had rollers, paying a monthly rental fee of one day's yield. The nine remaining households did not use rollers.

Rubber sheets were not smoked in this area, but were dried naturally under the house if it had a raised floor, or in the shade. The finished product, yellowish in color and with a distinctive odor, was sold to a Chinese rubber dealer in the neighboring village of Chekok, or to one of the Malay middlemen who went from house to house on their bicycles. Some households sold their rubber as often as every day or as infrequently as once a month, but most sold three to five times a month.

Rubber tapping was once an extremely profitable occupation. From 1960 to 1962 the fourth or fifth grade rubber produced in Galok sold for 70 or 80 sen per *kati*, but by the time of my study, the price of rubber had fallen to 30 or 40 sen per *kati*. Because of the low price of rubber and the greater profitability of tobacco cultivation, a significant number of people gave up tapping during the tobacco season.

During a follow-up survey on a random sample of households in 1976/1977, the price of rubber had risen to between 60 and 78 sen per *kati*, and rubber

Plate 3-2. Rubber tapping.

tapping was somewhat more profitable than in 1970/1971, even after taking inflation into account. Of the twenty-four sample households, thirteen (54 percent) were involved in tapping and the average area was 2.2 acres, slightly larger than that for the previous study. Forty-six percent of those engaged in tapping (six out of thirteen households) were share-tappers, a larger proportion than the 32 percent recorded in 1970/1971 (twenty-three out of seventy-four households). The system of payment for renting rubber holdings, and the technology and equipment used in rubber tapping remained unchanged.

By 1991, however, the total number of households engaged in tapping was only fifty-three, and although not as great a decline as that for paddy farming, this is still a noticeable drop.

3.2. The Rapid Development of Tobacco Cultivation

In 1968, the M.T.C. (Malayan Tobacco Company) established a station in Galok under the auspices of the state government. Similar stations equipped with several work areas and a brick tile barn for curing were built in more than ten rain-fed paddy and coastal locations in Kelantan. Centered around these focal points, tobacco became a secondary crop cultivated during the dry season. This had a significant impact on traditional occupations in Galok, bringing about changes on a scale that had not been seen since the introduction of rubber.

Plate 3-3. Adding acid to the collected latex to make it coagulate.

Plate 3-4. Tobacco plants starting to grow after transplanting.

I will begin by describing conditions in Galok in 1970/1971 around the time when tobacco cultivation was being introduced.

At the beginning, M.T.C. assigned the number of plants to be planted per season and provided technical instruction. Communal nurseries were prepared in February near the end of the paddy season when the amount of rainfall decreased, and seedlings were raised under the guidance of M.T.C. advisors. Around the same time, the fields designated for cultivation were plowed into ridges about nine inches (23 cm) in height. Although occasionally people used draft animals, the use of tractors for plowing was significantly higher than for paddy cultivation because the ground is much harder in the dry season. The cultivation of 1,000 tobacco plants requires one-seventh of an acre of land (5.8 ares). Most people used their own land, but those whose land was far away or who did not own land used other farmers' fields. Rental fees were usually not required because only a portion of the paddy field was used and many owners willingly lent their land to others in the belief that part of the chemical fertilizer applied to the tobacco crop remained in the soil.

Transplanting took place forty days after sowing. The work usually began at eight in the evening and finished around three in the morning, and it took two people about three nights to transplant 1,000 seedlings. After transplanting, one bag of fertilizer provided on credit by M.T.C. was applied per 1,000 seedlings. At first, some farmers substituted cheaper fertilizer intended for paddy cultivation, but although the leaves grew to the same size, they were easily

Plate 3-5. Seasonal workers at a tobacco station (1971).

Plate 3-6. Weighing tobacco leaves brought to the station.

distinguished by their inferior color. Tobacco plants must be carefully tended from start to finish to prevent disease. Although they do not need much water to grow, if it did not rain for two weeks farmers had to haul water from nearby wells to water their fields. Some even dug wells specifically for this purpose.

About one month after transplanting, the leaves can be picked every other day starting from the bottom of the plant. To avoid direct sunlight, picking was done from late afternoon to early evening starting about four in the afternoon and continuing until six-thirty. Harvested leaves were carried to the M.T.C. station the next morning where the farmer graded them himself and clerks assessed their quality and weighed them.

The tasks carried out by the cultivators are as described above. Bundling the leaves, placing them in the curing barn, removing and separating the bundles for further grading, and packing were all done by seasonal workers employed by the station. Work at the station was broken down into five tasks—bundling the leaves, drying, unbundling, grading, and packing—and the work areas for these tasks were linked together by porters. Fifteen regular staff were employed to manage the station, all of whom commuted from outside the village and wore uniforms. During the four-month buying season from mid-May to mid-September, many seasonal contract workers were also employed. In 1971, there were 74 men and 698 women. Twenty of these (2 men and 18 women) were employed as office workers and most of them had secondary school diplomas and came from places like Pasir Mas rather than Galok. The majority of other workers were employed from the surrounding villages including Galok and almost all of those who worked at the station were Malay.

At first each household was, in principle, allowed to cultivate 1,000 plants per season, but this was gradually changed so that by 1971, each adult was allowed to plant 1,000 plants. The planting season was divided into three parts and initially Galok was assigned only the first period. In 1971, however, villagers in the southern half of Galok were also allowed to plant in the third period. Changes in the number of plants cultivated per household in the four-year period from 1968 to 1971 are shown in Table 3-3. The fact that 27 percent of households cultivating tobacco planted over 2,000 plants in the first year when only 1,000 plants were allotted per household suggests that quite a few people manipulated information concerning household members. The number of households growing tobacco nearly doubled in the four years after its introduction, rising to about 85 percent of village households, far exceeding the number of households involved in either paddy growing or rubber. By 1971/1972 tobacco cultivation had become the most lucrative occupation in Galok and the number of plants cultivated per household had increased 2.9 times. Total tobacco production in Galok had likewise increased 5.5 times in four years.

Table 3-3
Changes in the Number of Households Cultivating Tobacco

Number of Plants Cultivated	1968	1969	1970	1971
500	1	1	1	
1,000	46	60	45	16
1,000	12	21	43	19
2,000	5	10	17	22
4,000		2	6	24
5,000			1	20
6,000				14
7,000				4
8,000				2
9,000				1
10,000–				2
Total	64	94	113	124
Average No. of Plants Cultivated Per Household	1,328	1,494	1,864	3,891

Table 3-4
Number of Households by Year Cultivation Started, and Sex and Age of Household Head

Sex of Household Head	Age of Household Head	Year Tobacco Cultivation Started					Total
		1968 (1st year)	1969 (2nd year)	1970 (3rd year)	1971 (4th year)	No Cultivation	
Male	20–29	9 (37.5)	3 (12.5)	3 (12.5)	6 (25.0)	3 (12.5)	24(100)
	30–39	12 (34.2)	8 (22.9)	8 (22.9)		7 (20.0)	35(100)
	40–49	15 (57.8)	5 (19.2)	4 (15.4)	1 (3.8)	1 (3.8)	26(100)
	50–59	15 (68.3)	5 (22.7)	1 (4.5)		1 (4.5)	22(100)
	60–	9 (56.2)	5 (31.3)	2 (12.5)			16(100)
Female	20–29				1(100.0)		1(100)
	30–39					1(100.0)	1(100)
	40–49		1 (20.0)	1 (20.0)	1 (20.0)	2 (40.0)	5(100)
	50–59	2 (25.0)	2 (25.0)	1 (12.5)		3 (37.5)	8(100)
	60–	2 (25.0)	1 (12.5)		3 (37.5)	2 (25.0)	8(100)

3.3. Changes in the Composition of Tobacco Cultivators

A more detailed analysis of the changes in tobacco cultivators during the four-year period from 1968 to 1971 clearly reveals the extent to which Galok farmers responded to this new crop. Table 3-4 presents the age and sex of household heads who were engaged in tobacco cultivation for each year. Sixty-eight percent of male household heads who were in their fifties in 1970/1971 became involved the year tobacco was first introduced versus only 30 percent of those in their twenties and thirties. Rather than indicating any greater degree of ambition among the older generation, however, this reflects the fact that a higher percentage of middle-aged men owned paddy land.

Table 3-5 cross-tabulates the data in Table 3-4 according to the added element of ownership versus non-ownership of paddy land. When women are eliminated from the calculations because of their small number, it becomes clear that the percentage of paddy-land owners who became involved in tobacco cultivation

Table 3-5
Number of Households by Year Cultivation Started, Sex and Age of Household Head, and Land Ownership

Sex of Household Head	Age of Household Head	Land Owner-ship	1968 (1st year)	1969 (2nd year)	1970 (3rd year)	1971 (4th year)	No Cultivation	Total
Male	20–29	O	6 (66.7)	1 (11.1)	0 (0.0)	0 (0.0)	2 (22.2)	9 (100)
		N	3 (20.0)	2 (13.3)	3 (20.0)	6 (40.0)	1 (6.7)	15 (100)
	30–39	O	12 (42.8)	7 (25.0)	4 (14.3)		5 (17.9)	28 (100)
		N	0 (0.0)	1 (14.3)	4 (57.1)		2 (28.6)	7 (100)
	40–49	O	14 (60.9)	4 (17.4)	4 (17.4)	0 (0.0)	1 (4.3)	23 (100)
		N	1 (33.3)	1 (33.3)	0 (0.0)	1 (33.3)	0 (0.0)	3 (100)
	50–59	O	14 (70.0)	5 (25.0)	1 (5.0)		0 (0.0)	20 (100)
		N	1 (50.0)	0 (0.0)	0 (0.0)		1 (50.0)	2 (100)
	60–	O	7 (53.8)	4 (30.8)	2 (15.4)			13 (100)
		N	2 (66.7)	1 (33.3)	0 (0.0)			3 (100)
Female	20–29	O			0			0
		N			1 (100)			1 (100)
	30–39	O				1 (100)		1 (100)
		N				0		0
	40–49	O		1 (33.3)	0 (0.0)	1 (33.3)	1 (33.3)	3 (100)
		N		0 (0.0)	1 (50.0)	0 (0.0)	1 (50.0)	2 (100)
	50–59	O	2 (28.6)	2 (28.6)	0 (0.0)		3 (42.8)	7 (100)
		N	0 (0.0)	0 (0.0)	1 (100)		0 (0.0)	1 (100)
	60–	O	1 (20.0)	1 (20.0)		2 (40.0)	1 (20.0)	5 (100)
		N	1 (33.3)	0 (0.0)		1 (33.3)	1 (33.3)	3 (100)

O = Owner   N = Non-owner

from the first year is greater than the percentage of non-owners in every age group of householder except those in their sixties. Moreover, the discrepancy shown in Table 3-4 between the different age groups is no longer as obvious when evaluated within the common category of paddy-land owners. In particular, the percentage of paddy-owning male household heads in their twenties who became involved in tobacco cultivation from the first year was almost the same as the percentage of those in their fifties. Although a significant number of male household heads in their twenties and thirties did not become involved despite owning paddy lands, this was because they had regular, better paying jobs. Five were store managers and two were elementary school teachers.

The number of non-paddy owning young men participating in tobacco cultivation increased from the second year. An investigation of men in their twenties and thirties who commenced tobacco cultivation in the second year revealed that they could not have started sooner because none of them were independent householders in the year that tobacco was introduced. Eleven were dependent on their parents or other people for their livelihood, and five were living in other villages (Table 3-6). It was tobacco cultivation that gave them an opportunity to establish their own households or to move back to Galok, and accordingly, the response of the younger generations to this new source of income was particularly enthusiastic. Due to the small number of female household heads, it is difficult to evaluate their response, but it seems to have been less dramatic than for men. By the fourth year of the project, the percentage of female household heads who did not participate in tobacco cultivation remained high at 34.8 percent, in contrast with only 9.8 percent of males.

Although not included in the above figures, the number of people returning temporarily to the village for the tobacco season also began to increase from 1971. There were seven that year lodging in different households, all of them under 30 years of age. Two were married with children, three were married with no children and two were single. Outside the tobacco season, five of them were

Table 3-6
Male Household Heads Aged 20–39 who Began Tobacco Cultivation after the First Year

Living Situation	Year Cultivation Started		
	2nd Year	3rd Year	4th Year
Recently Independent Household Head	3	4	3
Living With Parents But Economically Independent	0	1	0
Returned From Another Village	0	2	3

engaged in rubber tapping under *pawah* contracts in the interior, and two resided with kin in another village. This is another example of the positive response of the younger generations towards tobacco cultivation.

From the above observations, the development of tobacco cultivation in Galok can be summarized in three consecutive, though slightly overlapping stages. In the first stage, household heads who owned paddy land and had no better opportunity to generate income began growing tobacco. In the second stage, young men who did not own land and were economically dependent on their parents seized this opportunity to establish themselves as independent household heads, borrowing land to grow tobacco. In the third stage, people who had left the village returned permanently or temporarily to engage in tobacco cultivation.

3.4. Seasonal Contract Work

Although seasonal contract work at the M.T.C. station was available only for about four months of the year, it had as great an impact on the villagers' lifestyles as tobacco cultivation. Workers came from surrounding villages and the number of people employed at the station in 1971 categorized by sex and age is shown in Table 3-7. Women outnumbered men seventy-three to thirteen, because the majority of men were generally involved in cultivating tobacco, while it was the women who processed the harvested leaves. Sixty-four women were in their mid-thirties or younger, comprising 74.4 percent of the total number of workers. Moreover, the number of 15–19-year-old girls was equivalent to 72.1 percent of the entire population for that age group, a remarkably high ratio of employment. The percentage of women between 25 and 28 years of age was somewhat lower compared to other age groups because they were at the child-bearing and child-rearing stage.

Although seasonal contract work at the station was an entirely new type of employment opportunity for the village women, in Kelantan women have traditionally been very active in the economy. In contrast to Malay women in other states, they have played a central role in selling rice, produce, cloth, and other goods at the marketplace, and women in fishing villages have handled the marketing of the daily catch. It is difficult to find the segregation of the sexes typical of Islamic society in these traditional roles. It must be pointed out, however, that women involved in such commercial activities are almost always married, the participation of single women being so rare that it would demand special mention. Similarly, men and women working at the station do not perform their tasks together, and because contract work for men is restricted to specific jobs, there are far fewer men than women employees. Although men of 15–19 years of age have the highest rate of employment for men at the

Table 3-7
Age And Sex of Contract Workers at M.T.C. Station and the Percentage of the Population of the Same Age Group

Age	Male Number	(Percent of Population)	Female Number	(Percent of Population)
10–14			10	(22.2)
15–19	6	(16.7)	31	(72.1)
20–24	3	(13.0)	8	(33.3)
25–29			5	(27.8)
30–34	3	(16.6)	10	(45.5)
35–39	1	(5.9)	4	(28.6)
40–44			2	(9.1)
45–49			2	(13.3)
50–54				
55–59			1	(2.4)
60–64				
65–69				
Total	13	(6.9)	73	(29.8)

station, their actual number represents only 16.7 percent of the male population of the same age.

In the four years following the introduction of tobacco cultivation, the number of people engaged in contract work at the station rapidly increased. Almost no one gave up a job at the station once they had started. In 1971, only three men and three women who had previously worked at the station were not working there that year. The women left their jobs to have children, while the men's job of stoking the fire in the curing barn was eliminated by the installation of propane gas. Some of the men also left their jobs to cultivate tobacco instead. Of the 146 households in Galok in 1971, 47 had one member, 17 had two members and 2 had three members seasonally employed at the station, for a total of 66 households (45.2 percent) with one or more members engaged in contract work.

3.5. Tobacco Surpluses and their Effect on Income

Tobacco cultivators were paid each time they took the harvested leaves to the station, and payment varied depending on the quality of the leaves, ranging from a maximum of 30 sen to a minimum of 10 sen per *kati* (1 *kati* equals about 600 grams). Net income at the beginning of the buying season was only about RM1 until the cultivators had paid back credit owed to M.T.C. for various items including RM1.30 for seedlings, RM15.60 for fertilizer and RM3.80 for agrochemicals per 1,000 plants cultivated. Although quality was the basis for determining price, the standards for judging quality varied considerably depending on the time period. Quality inspections were most severe during the peak of the tobacco season from late June to early July when the harvest exceeded the capacity of the curing barn, and sometimes leaves of poorer quality were rejected altogether.

The M.T.C. had no contract with the cultivators to buy the leaves they picked and therefore, if the company refused to buy on the grounds that the leaves did not meet their inspection standards, the cultivator had no choice but to comply. In another village, this policy caused a dispute between the company and the workers and, as a result, the M.T.C. station in that area was closed. In Galok, however, this type of tension was curbed by the establishment of tobacco stations run by rival companies in neighboring Chekok and other villages. These stations tended to be smaller in scale with a more flexible management style compared to the bureaucratic M.T.C. Some resorted to guerila tactics, buying leaves from farmers that worked under M.T.C. instead of employing their own cultivators. Despite the mitigating effects of such competition, however, M.T.C.'s buying price for tobacco leaves at the peak of the season in 1971 dropped to as low as 15 sen per *kati*.

I computed the average annual income per 1,000 plants cultivated from 1968 to 1971 based on interviews with cultivators as shown in Table 3-8. Although M.T.C. staff claimed that income for a normal yield was RM250 per 1,000 plants, the figure obtained from the interview survey was much lower. This can partly be explained by the farmers' tendency to state a sum lower than their actual income and by losses from drought or disease; but the gap between predicted income and reported income is too great to be explained solely by these factors, and I must therefore conclude that the reported RM250 figure was merely an ideal, not a reality. Moreover, even if the figures cited by farmers' were lower than reality, the income they reported per 1,000 plants for each year decreased relative to the preceding year, indicating that their profits did indeed decrease. There were several reasons for this. The first was reduced yields caused by heavy rains in the second year, and drought in the third and fourth years. Another was a decline in yield and quality caused by a shortage of people to properly tend the increasing number of plants cultivated. The involvement of people who did not have sufficient skills also resulted in poorer yield and quality. Finally, these factors coupled with a steady increase in the overall amount of tobacco cultivated resulted in stricter selection standards at the M.T.C. station.

Despite the decline in income per plant, households managed to increase their overall annual income by increasing the number of plants they cultivated.

Table 3-8
Changes in Average Income Per 1000 Tobacco Plants

Year	Average Income (RM)
1968	162.0
1969	148.6
1970	125.1
1971	101.4
⎰ 1st period	⎰ 88.8
⎱ 3rd period	⎱ 123.4

As shown in Table 3-9, annual income from tobacco cultivation per household rose from RM214 in the first year, to RM221 in the second and RM234 in the third. In the fourth year it leapt dramatically to RM384. If we assume that it takes four months of labor to grow tobacco only during the first period and six months for both the first and third periods, monthly income was RM54 for the first year and RM55 and RM59 for the second and third years, respectively. In the fourth year, overall income for the first period was noticeably low so that those who cultivated only during this period made just RM42 a month as opposed to RM 80 for those who planted during both periods. Although these

Table 3-9
Household's with Income from Tobacco Cultivation

Income (RM)	Year			
	1968	1969	1970	1971
–99	3	11	34	11
100–199	27	28	26	10
200–299	19	23	14	21
300–399	5	13	9	14
400–499	3	9	7	14
500–599	3	5	8	14
600–699	1	2	5	11
700–799	1		4	3
800–899			4	3
900–999				2
1,000–1,099				1
Unknown	2	3	2	20
Total	64	94	113	124
Average Income (RM)	214	221	234	384

monthly incomes are not particularly high, they provided sufficient incentive for village residents to adopt the new crop when compared with the extremely small and unreliable incomes from previous occupations.

Contract work at M.T.C. was either paid by the hour or on a piecework basis, depending on the type of work. Transport, packing, and security were the main jobs for men, for which they were paid an hourly wage of 45 sen. Most of the jobs that women performed were paid by piecework, and these included bundling leaves for curing at a wage of 2 sen per bundle, undoing the bundles once they had been cured for 1 sen per bundle, and sorting for 4 sen per pound. Additional jobs for women included checking sorted leaves, transport, and cleaning for which they were paid an hourly wage of 40 sen. Wages were paid in a lump sum every two weeks.

In the case of hourly wages, a man working eight hours a day twenty-five days a month would earn RM90 and a woman RM80, but due to fluctuations in the number of leaves purchased and a surplus of available workers, working hours were not always steady and actual income was considerably lower. Although security staff regularly earned RM80–90 a month because their work was not affected by the number of leaves purchased, other workers earned only RM40–60 a month. The same is true for those paid on a piecework basis. Although they were assured a minimum of RM1 a day, they often spent part of the day waiting for work to arrive and their wages were around the same or even lower than those paid by the hour.

3.6. The Impact of Tobacco Cultivation

3.6.1. A Decline in Traditional Occupations and a Rise in Commercial Activities

I have already discussed some of the changes caused by the introduction of tobacco cultivation in Galok. In this section, I will summarize its effects on traditional occupations.

Because tobacco is a secondary crop cultivated during the dry season after paddy cultivation is finished, traditional occupations undertaken during the same period were most affected. Rubber tapping was the most important of these, but it was almost impossible to find enough time to tap rubber while engaged in tobacco cultivation or station work. By 1971 only 15 percent of households normally engaged in rubber tapping continued this occupation during the busiest part of the tobacco season because, although wages for tobacco related work were certainly not high, they surpassed the income that could be made from rubber. In 1971, a person would have needed to operate a rubber holding of 1.6

to 2.8 acres in order to make RM50 in a twenty working-day month with an estimated per acre rubber yield of 4 *kati* at 40 sen per *kati* for the former, and a yield of 3 *kati* at 30 sen per *kati* for the latter. As noted previously, very few people in Galok owned that much rubber land. And if a person rented land under the *pawah* system in which he paid the owner half of his yield, he would have to work twice as large an area. This far exceeds the estimated 400 trees, or 2.2 acres that one person can tap per day. Moreover, tapping is suspended for part of the dry season when trees shed their leaves and the flow of latex declines. Many people suspended tapping for a period of one to four months to protect the trees and resumed tapping towards the end of the tobacco season.

Another traditional occupation greatly affected by tobacco cultivation was coconut-sugar making (*penyadap*). The sugar is made by collecting sap in bamboo pipes from the flower stalks of eight to twenty-five coconut palms, boiling it down in an iron pot, and solidifying it in thin sheets. Income ranged from a minimum of RM1.50 per day for eight trees, to a maximum of RM3–5 per day depending on the number of trees. Although this is higher than the income obtained from rubber with its sluggish market, the worker must climb the tall coconut palms twice a day, a strenuous task especially for older people. Formerly, fourteen households in Galok were engaged in sugar making, but eight of these ceased entirely after the introduction of tobacco. Although one stopped because the household head passed away, the other seven switched to tobacco cultivation. All of the latter were over 40 years of age with the exception of a 34-year-old man who began running a shop at the same time. Of the six who continued sugar making, one was in his fifties, another in his forties and the remaining four in their thirties. Two of those in their early thirties suspended sugar making temporarily during the tobacco season to grow 5,000 tobacco plants each.

Occupations other than rubber tapping and sugar making were also similarly affected by the introduction of tobacco cultivation. People either quit these jobs altogether or temporarily suspended operations during the tobacco season. As fewer people were involved, and the economic activity was more irregular, it is difficult to determine the degree to which they declined, but in 1971, the number of people involved in migrant work of every type clearly decreased, and some middlemen dealing in rubber or poultry and charcoal-makers suspended work temporarily during the tobacco season.

Although several traditional occupations began to decline after the introduction of tobacco, different types of small businesses sprang up as individuals took advantage of new opportunities presented by the tobacco station. Before the introduction of tobacco, there were four general stores and two coffee shops in the village. In 1971, in addition to these, four general stores and five coffee shops had opened near the M.T.C. station, three of which were only open during the tobacco season, and a new coffee shop had opened at the edge of village. During the tobacco season, stalls selling cloth, miscellaneous goods, meat, fish, fruit, and drinks lined the road near the station. Most of the stallholders came from other villages, but in 1971 two fried banana vendors, two fish dealers and one lunch vendor were from Galok.

Because paddy was grown after the tobacco season was over, there was no need to adjust the work schedule or labor force for paddy cultivation and accordingly, the impact of tobacco cultivation was more indirect. The main change was the adoption of hired tractors for plowing and preparing paddy plots. Cash income from tobacco made it easier to hire a tractor and operator, and also to buy chemical fertilizer. Other aspects, however, changed very little because paddy farming had always depended upon the family work force rather than on communal work organizations.

3.6.2. Youth Stay in the Village

I have already discussed the fact that tobacco cultivation made it easier for the younger generations to remain in the village or for those who had already left to return permanently or temporarily. This fact is reflected in Figure 3-1, which shows the composition of the population in 1971 by age and sex, excluding those who had returned only temporarily. If the youth and their families who were able to permanently return and those who never had to leave because of tobacco cultivation were excluded from the population, the figure would become hourglass-shaped, the neck representing the generations forced to leave in order to find work. Thus the introduction of tobacco, coupled with the decreased attraction of rubber tapping in the interior due to falling rubber prices, checked the exodus of the younger generations from Galok, at least temporarily.

3.6.3. Changes in Dress and Diet and Purchase of Durable Consumer Goods

Cash income from tobacco cultivation and contract work at the station brought about changes in both clothing and diet. Previously, the main staple of the village diet had been a mixture of rice, salted dried fish, and *budu*, a sauce of salted fish. But with meat and fish readily available at stalls in front of the station during the tobacco season, and a cash income, no matter how small, there was a noticeable increase in the consumption of these items. Moreover, young women working at the station and free to spend their earnings as they wished, bought more cloth and other commodities. In general, most villagers tended to make or buy new clothes during the tobacco season, and the income of a dressmaker located between Galok and the neighboring village of Chekok doubled during this period.

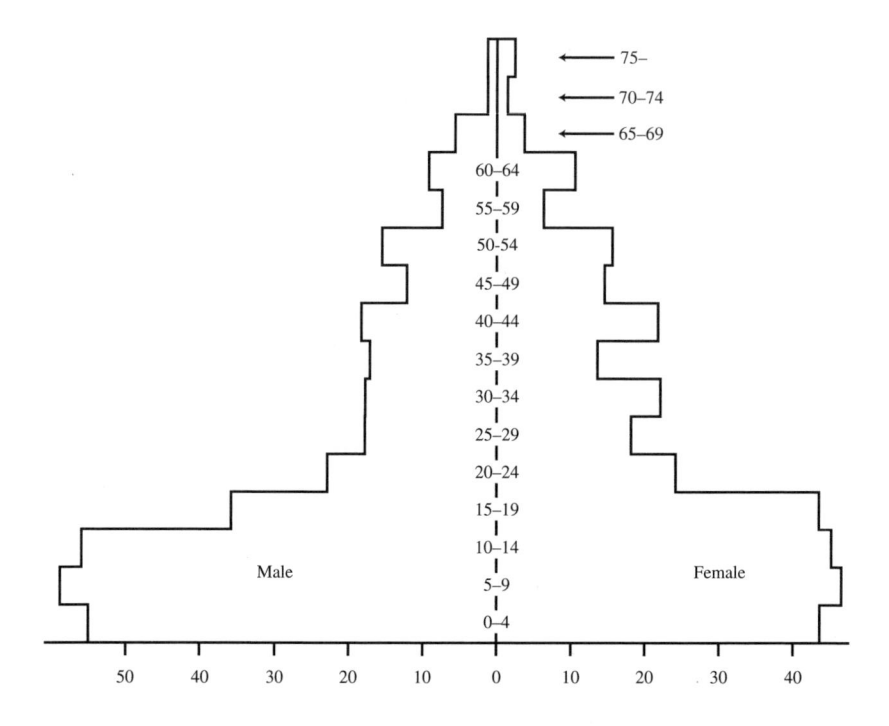

Figure 3-1. Composition of Galok Population by Age and Sex

The purchase of certain durable consumer goods similarly increased, and there was a particularly dramatic rise in the number of bicycles in the village. Not only were bicycles convenient for commuting short distances, they were also useful for carrying tobacco leaves from the field to the station. In 1971, 77 (52.7 percent) of the 146 households in Galok owned a total of eighty-eight bicycles. The period at which they were purchased is shown in Table 3-10. Sixty, or more than two-thirds of the total, were bought after the introduction of tobacco. Twenty-four of these were new, thirty-five were second-hand, and one was given to the owner.

The purchase of transistor radios after the introduction of tobacco was also very noticeable, although ownership was not as high, remaining at only 30.1 percent. Ownership of sewing machines was even lower, and the impact of tobacco cultivation on this commodity appears to have been negligible. It seems that income from tobacco was not sufficient to buy such an expensive item.

In addition to the above, there was a marked increase in the number of people installing suction pumps, driving pipes directly into the ground to draw water essential for both drinking and bathing. Seventeen pumps, each costing between RM80 and 100, had been installed in the village by 1971, the majority

Table 3-10
Number of Bicycles, Radios and Sewing Machines
Purchased by Year

Number of Years Since Purchase	Bicycle	Radio	Sewing Machine
Less than 1	13 ⎫	8 ⎫	1 ⎫
About 1	23 ⎬ 60	5 ⎬ 24	1 ⎬ 6
2	10 ⎪	5 ⎪	2 ⎪
3	14 ⎭	6 ⎭	2 ⎭
4	4	4	2
5	6	5	1
6	2	5	2
7		2	1
8	1		2
9			
10	9		8
11			1
12	2		
13	1		2
14	2		
Over 15	1	1	8
Unknown		3	1
Total	88	44	34

of them after the introduction of tobacco. Most of them were owned by individuals, although there were some communal pumps as well. Even those owned by individuals, however, were used by neighbors so that the pumps served a total of about forty households. The working life of these wells is relatively short, and sometimes they must be replaced after only two or three years. For this reason, several people dug new wells in 1971 which they line with precast concrete casing at a cost of RM140–200.

3.7. The End of the Tobacco Boom

Tobacco cultivation peaked a few years after its introduction and then began to decline. From 1970 other companies set up small-scale tobacco stations, first in the neighboring village of Chekok and then in other parts of Kelantan, competing to buy tobacco leaves. The main company, M.T.C., found that the tobacco it had trained the local people to produce was being bought up by smaller stations or middlemen. In 1975, it closed its station in Galok, and the cultivators in the village had to sell their harvest to small-scale stations in other villages.

Of the twenty-four sample households in the follow-up survey conducted in 1977, seventeen (70.8 percent) grew an average of 5,676 plants each. It seems that the individual cultivator's scale of operation increased, while those who cultivated on a very small scale dropped out. Although the price for tobacco that year ranged from 10 to 37 sen per *kati*, the average buying price was higher than in previous years. The income per 1,000 plants was RM210, and the average income per household derived from tobacco was as high as RM1,191. Formerly cultivators did not pay rental fees for paddy lots used to grow tobacco during the dry season, but in 1977, some people paid RM10 per 1,000 plants under the *sewa* system. With the closing of the M.T.C. station, opportunities for contract work greatly diminished except for a few hired by a small station in nearby Chekok. Of the sample households, only two men were employed at the Chekok station, working as porters for six to ten months for RM120–140 a month.

Since then, the center of tobacco cultivation in Kelantan has shifted to coastal areas such as Jajahan Tumpat, where the sandy soil is more suitable. As a result, fishing in those areas has rapidly been replaced by tobacco from December to April. Yet the villagers of Galok did not totally abandon tobacco, continuing to cultivate from April to August on the alluvial soils around the village.

A tobacco station run by a 62-year-old Chinese man and his two sons in nearby Padang Hangus remains in operation. Formerly located on rented land in Chekok, in 1990 they bought the present site of over 3 acres of land for RM24,000. A total of 150 households in the vicinity cultivate 700,000 tobacco plants a year, and 200 people are employed during the tobacco season for RM15–20 a day. Some work three days a week bundling uncured leaves while others work daily processing cured leaves.

The number of households engaged in tobacco cultivation in Galok in 1991, however, had dwindled to 40, and the average number of plants grown had similarly dropped to 3,444 per household. The estimated pure profit earned was 45 sen per plant, much lower than the 70 sen earned in areas with sandy soil. Eventually, tobacco cultivation in Galok will probably be recorded as just an experiment in the state government's rural policy.

4
Other Income Sources and Changes

4.1. Increased Regular Employment

The villagers of Galok engage in various other occupations in addition to those described in the previous chapter. Many have several different jobs, some of which I will describe in this chapter. In 1971, many villagers worked regularly for a salary or wages, and they can be broadly divided into three main categories: those who worked all through the year for a monthly salary or daily wage, those who worked all through the year for a commission, and those who did seasonal work for either hourly payment or a commission.

A total of twelve villagers fell into the first category. There were three elementary school teachers receiving a monthly salary of RM150–370, three people employed in malaria eradication at monthly salaries of about RM100, an adult education teacher with a monthly salary of RM52, a soldier who sent home RM110 every month, a Department of Irrigation and Drainage worker whose salary was RM130 a month, a coffee shop employee earning RM60 a month, a truck driver earning about RM100 a month, and a permanent employee at the tobacco station with a monthly salary of about RM50. In the second category there were three taxi drivers earning between RM50 and 100 a month. Most of the villagers in these two categories worked outside Galok. Villagers in the third category were employed by the tobacco station as was discussed in the previous chapter.

By 1991, twenty years later, the number of regular employees had further increased. The most noticeable and symbolically significant increase occurred in the number of teachers. There were eighteen teachers living in Galok at this time, four of whom were women, whereas in 1971 all of the teachers living in Galok were men. Moreover, none of them were native to Galok, but were only residing there temporarily because it was close to their place of work. The promotion of education in the intervening period and the availability of scholarships under a government policy favoring Malays made it possible for people from rural areas such as Galok to further their education at teacher training colleges or universities, and many Galok villagers became teachers.

At least twenty-eight who lived in Galok in 1971, nineteen men and nine women, had become teachers by 1991. Of these, six men, a little less than one-third, and two females had returned to work in Galok. The remaining ten teachers resident in the village, including temporary residents, were outsiders. One couple, both teachers, built a modern home of brick and concrete blocks on village land that they had purchased, and hired a neighbor as a nanny so that both the husband and wife could work. They had chosen Galok as their home because of its convenient location between Tanah Merah and Pasir Mas, and the power and water supply.

The most common form of regular employment was day labor at the lumber mill near Tanah Merah. Sixteen young men in their twenties were employed here, but the work was irregular and their income unstable.

4.2. From Agricultural to Urban Migrant Work

Before the introduction of tobacco cultivation, migrant work provided an extremely important source of income for the villagers. Although this may seem an unlikely characteristic of villages like Galok which were cleared for development, they are often the most readily transformed into migrant working societies because of the very nature of their establishment.

In 1970/1971, migrant workers were characteristically young people involved in farming, including rubber tapping, although the same people did not always go every year. As stated previously, the number of workers leaving Galok decreased remarkably after the introduction of tobacco, but even so ten people went elsewhere for temporary work in 1970/1971. The most important type of migrant work was rubber tapping under *pawah* contract, for which many people went to Pahang State. In 1970/1971, half of the migrant workers (five people) went to Pahang for periods of twenty days to three months, and the earnings they brought back ranged from a low of RM20 to a high of RM200. One person went to the rubber belt in the interior of Kelantan state and in the past, people even went to Thailand for rubber tapping, although by 1970 they no longer did so.

Formerly, the paddy harvest in Kedah was an important source of migrant work. Located on the west coast of the Malay peninsula, the rainy season arrives earlier here than in Kelantan on the east coast, and consequently, harvesting in Kedah took place from November until January. Workers in Kelantan took advantage of the difference in the harvest season, travelling across the border of Thailand around to the other side of the peninsula by train. With the introduction of double cropping in Kedah, however, the harvest season changed to February and August, overlapping with the harvest in Kelantan. At the same time, the introduction of tobacco cultivation in Kelantan

Plate 4-1. Using a roller to press rubber into sheets.

created work opportunities at home, and the flow of migrant workers declined remarkably. Only one person went to Kedah during the 1970/1971 study period, staying about a month and bringing back RM60. A few people worked harvesting in paddy-growing areas in Kelantan, mainly the Salor area across the river in Pasir Mas. In 1970/1971 three people went, staying for a week or ten days and earning five *gantang* of paddy per day.

In 1977, migrant work increased once again due to the closing of the M.T.C. tobacco station and the decline in the tobacco market, but there were major changes in the destination of the workers and in the types of jobs they performed. Urban centers became an important source of work, and the most common destination was Singapore, although visa restrictions prevented workers from staying very long. They usually worked from two weeks to two months, mainly as construction workers, earning from 9 to 12 Singapore dollars a day, with one Singapore dollar being almost equivalent in value to the Malaysian ringgit. If a worker spent 5 dollars a day on food, he could still take home RM150 in one month. Five of the twenty-four sample households had at least one member who had worked in Singapore during the previous year. By applying this ratio to the entire village, we can estimate that approximately thirty people in Galok went to Singapore to work. According to the *penghulu* (*mukim* head), about one hundred people a year from Mukim Jabo Timor, including Galok, were going to Singapore to work.

During the same period, two people from the sample households went to work in Pahang, indicating that more people worked there in 1977 than in 1970/1971. One of the two worked tapping rubber under *pawah* contract, while the other worked about four months processing palm oil. Three people from the sample households also traveled to the double-cropping paddy area in Salor, and accordingly, the number doing so is assumed to have increased in Galok as a whole. Payment remains the same at 5 *gantang* of paddy per day, but the length of working period is longer, ranging from ten days to one month. A truck is hired to carry home paddy received in payment for home consumption.

People still traveled to Singapore for work in 1991, and a total of twenty-eight villagers obtained part or all of their income from migrant work there that year, about the same number as in 1977. In addition to the men, who ranged in age from their teens to their forties, there was one 34-year-old woman who worked as a cook. A night bus to Singapore left daily from Pasir Mas. In Singapore, migrant workers generally lived in bunkhouses and worked on construction sites under a Chinese *tauke* or headman, and a remarkable system of mutual assistance existed among people from Kelantan. Due to visa restrictions, the length of stay was short, rarely exceeding three months in duration, and most people relied on friends or acquaintances while living there. But even if a worker did not know anyone, as long as he met someone from Kelantan at the bus terminal, he would be all right. In addition to those mentioned above, thirty other villagers, six of whom were men in their fifties, had worked in Singapore some other year. Thus a total of fifty-eight people from Galok were working or had worked as migrant laborers in Singapore.

4.3. Other Occupations

The villagers of Galok are involved in a variety of occupations other than those described above. Here I will briefly describe those identified in 1971.

4.3.1. Business

People engaged in business in 1971 can be divided into three main categories. The first consisted of those whose store or coffee shop was part of their house, the second of stall holders with temporary shelters, and the third of dealers with no fixed place of business.

In the first category there were eleven general stores which handled mostly sundries, dry goods, and foodstuffs, and four coffee shops. The latter, known as *kedai kopi*, usually had earthen floors and simple tables with long benches, yet they were an indispensable part of daily life in Kelantan. In most cases, they were run by a sociable married woman ranging from her late twenties to early forties who served refreshments and chatted with the customers. The price of coffee or tea was between 10 and 20 sen. The number of stores and coffee shops in 1970/1971 exceeded the needs of the village population because new ones had been opened to cater to the workers that gathered around the station during the tobacco season. Turnover varied widely, ranging from RM3 to 50 a day depending on the scale of operation and the location, and was highest in the tobacco season. General stores had an average profit of 20 percent, while that for coffee shops was 30–50 percent.

Ten street stalls fell in the second category, eight of which operated only during the tobacco season. Three of these eight were run by shopkeepers. Two stalls operated at other times of the year, including the tobacco season, one of which sold meat. The owner slaughtered about ten cattle a year, with a turnover of about RM10–20 per animal. The butchered meat was sold in front of his home in a stall that was only open when he had slaughtered one of his animals. The other year-round stall was owned by a woman who sold vegetables and cakes in front of her house, making RM20–30 a day with a profit of about 20 percent.

The third category was comprised of ten people: three rubber dealers, one cattle dealer, one poultry dealer, a poultry and fish dealer, a poultry and coconut-sugar dealer, a fish dealer, a cloth dealer, and a handyman who also procured radios and other goods for villagers. Unlike the stallholders, some of them suspended work during the tobacco season. The rubber dealers made the rounds of the rubber tappers by bicycle and usually made a profit of 1 sen per *kati*, earning RM20–70 per month. The cattle dealer, who also ran the meat stall, handled about a hundred cattle a year and made about RM10 per head in his transactions. The other dealers worked either daily or several days a week, making RM2–10 per day.

Plate 4-2. A rubber dealer who travels from house to house by bicycle.

Plate 4-3. Weaving roof thatch (*atap*) from palm fronds.

4.3.2. Carpenters and Artisans

Two carpenters, one gold- and silversmith and a bicycle repairman, among others, fall in this category. The carpenters earned RM3–3.5 per day with the client providing the lumber, etc. However, as work was irregular, annual income was only about RM200. The gold- and silversmith earned about RM30 a month, while the bicycle repairman could earn about RM3 a day, but because of the limited number of bicycles in the village, his work was also irregular.

4.3.3. Seamstresses

Three people in the village used sewing machines to make clothes and mattresses (*lembek*). Although villagers usually slept on matting (*tikar*) laid directly on the floor, the number of people using mattresses was gradually increasing. One of the seamstresses was a 32-year-old male transvestite or *pondan*, a phenomenon occasionally seen among Malays. He earned about RM30–40 a month and was particularly skilled at wedding apparel, often traveling some distance to attend marriage ceremonies. *Pondan* are generally thought to be naturally gifted in this field. Of the remaining seamstresses, one was a 60-year-old woman who made RM10–30 a month, and the other was the wife of a school teacher who made about RM5 a month working from her home.

4.3.4. Barbers

There were three barbers in the village and they used very simple implements. A barber usually set up a wooden chair for his customers outside his house, and charged 50 sen for adults and 30 sen for children, earning RM30–40 a month.

4.3.5. Trishaw Drivers

Four people drove three-wheeled pedicabs known as *teksi*, consisting of a bicycle with a compartment for passengers or freight set in the front. Although in Pasir Mas *teksi* drivers had to be licensed, registration was not required anywhere outside of the town, including Galok. They operated mainly during the tobacco season, and carried both passengers and freight, including tobacco leaves. Income during the off-season was only 50 sen to RM2 per day, whereas during the tobacco season it was as much as RM10 or more. Three of the four drivers had their own *teksi*, while the other borrowed his and split the profits with the owner.

4.3.6. Native Healer

There was one native healer (*bomoh*) who used traditional Malay healing methods. Payment was about RM1 per session although occasionally it might be as much as RM5, and the healer earned RM30–40 a month.

Plate 4-4. A fruit and vegetable stall.

Plate 4-5. A meat stall.

4.3.7. Midwives

There were two midwives (*bidan*) called *bidan kampung* meaning "village midwife." They had no formal training and were paid RM1–4 per birth, earning RM30–40 a month. In addition, parents of the children they delivered gave them one *gantang* of rice, or the equivalent in cash (RM1.2), at the end of the month of fasting.

4.3.8. Koran Teachers

Two people in Galok taught children to read the Koran. Both had a group of about ten pupils each and received one *gantang* of rice, or RM1.2, once a year as *fitrah*, a kind of charitable donation under Islamic law.

4.3.9. Cake Makers

Three women made Malay style cakes. Of these, two worked three or four times a week during the tobacco season only, making about RM1 each time. The other made a small amount almost every day and sold them to the coffee shop run by her neighbor, earning about 30 sen a day.

4.3.10. Vegetable Farmers

There were four vegetable farmers who sold vegetables, watermelons and other produce to the villagers. Two of these earned from RM150–200 a year, while the other two farmed sporadically on a very small scale and earned only RM15 to 20 a year.

4.3.11. Firewood and Charcoal Makers

A parent-and-child team burnt wood in a hole they dug in the ground to make charcoal, which they sold in Pasir Mas. They grossed RM90–190 each time, spending RM10–15 on materials, but in 1970/1971 their total earnings from charcoal were only RM120 because tobacco cultivation took precedence and they made just one batch of charcoal. The same pair also earned RM100 cutting firewood for the curing barn at the M.T.C. station.

In 1977, many of the stalls and some of the stores had disappeared because the M.T.C. station had closed, while the turnover of some of the remaining shops had significantly increased, particularly those handling lumber and meat. The increased incomes of the villagers had resulted in a greater demand for lumber to build new homes and additions, as well as in a better diet. I was unable to make a detailed study of changes in the occupations of peddlers or middlemen in 1977, although I found that one former rubber dealer had switched to selling *duku*, a type of fruit, from which he was earning more than he had from rubber in 1971. As *duku* is a seasonal crop, this work was not year-round.

The nature of village occupations was still varied in 1991, but the content had changed. Non-agricultural work in urban areas and elsewhere outside the village was common, and people showed greater mobility. Whereas peddlers had formerly carried their wares on bicycles, in 1991 many were using vans. The various jobs were not mutually exclusive: people might engage in paddy growing, tobacco cultivation and rubber tapping; or they might combine migrant labor in Singapore with tobacco cultivation or with work at the sawmill. In contrast, teachers and public servants with regular salaries tended to have only one job and a single source of income. Thus while specialization had progressed on one hand, on the other, the pattern of diverse and multiple occupations persisted.

In 1991, I noticed that the villagers frequently referred to their work as "village work" (*kerja kampung*). This term was used for both farm work and for paid labor or independent businesses and included all the miscellaneous jobs associated with farm related labor such as paddy, rubber tapping, tobacco, etc., as well as small-scale contracting work such as bicycle and motorcycle repair, and the quarrying and sale of sand and gravel. Few households were solely dependent upon agriculture and the number of households making their living from "village work" was also gradually decreasing.

4.4. Other Sources of Income

4.4.1. Revenue from Renting Land or Housing

Although no one in Galok owns enough land to be called a landlord, people frequently rented very small plots of land. There are several reasons for the extremely small scale of land rentals. The trend towards equalized inheritance resulted in very small individual holdings, the lack of rules governing postmarital residence meant that one or both spouses might own land located some distance from where they lived, and the household structure centered around a married couple made it difficult for the elderly to cultivate their own land. In 1971, 39 households rented paddy fields, and 17 gave tenants permission to tap rubber on their land. In principle, payment for paddy rental was by *pawah* contract, and in 1970/1971, landowners received anywhere from a minimum of 5 *gantang* to a maximum of 400 *gantang* of paddy in payment. As for rubber, the share-tapper or the landowner sold the rubber and they split the proceeds, ranging from a minimum of RM15 to a maximum of RM735 each.

In 1971, four people rented rooms to schoolteachers and tobacco station workers residing temporarily in Galok. Rent ranged from RM5 to 12 per month. Three villagers built small tin-roofed shacks or simple stalls outside their homes and rented these to people from town who came during the tobacco season. Rent for the former was RM10–20 per month, while that for the latter was about 30 sen per day. Another person received RM30 a year in rent for land that someone used to open a store.

Revenue from housing and room rental closely connected to the establishment of the tobacco station declined abruptly when the station closed. In 1991, almost no one rented rooms, despite the fact that homes were much larger than in 1970/ 1971. The only example was a divorced man living alone who rented a room to an unmarried schoolteacher. One person built a small house on *pondok* land adjacent to his own property, and rented it to a working couple comprised of an office worker and an elementary school teacher, and another person from Kota Bharu rented a house in Galok. But such room or house rentals were the exception. Most people who came to live from outside the village borrowed land from kin or friends free of charge and constructed their own homes on the property. This suggests that the rental of housing or rooms was a temporary phenomenon that occurred during the tobacco boom. At the same time, it should be noted that land was beginning to be regarded as a cash commodity. One couple, both elementary school teachers, and a pensioner had bought land in Galok on which they built homes.

Plate 4-6. A fruit and vegetable stall.

4.4.2. Sale of Fruit

The most important of the commercially valuable fruits are *duku* and *durian*. The trees are mainly grown in the compounds, and the fruits are sold to dealers during the season. Coconuts and bananas are also sold occasionally, but as most are grown for home consumption cash income is minimal. In 1970/1971, nine people sold *duku* and two sold *durian*, their incomes ranging from RM20 to RM250 for *duku* and RM15 to RM50 for *durian*. The fruit trees planted, however, are not improved varieties, and sometimes may not bear fruit for several consecutive years. This was still the situation in 1991, and although, in a good year, a significant income can be made, it is very unreliable.

4.4.3. Oxen and Water Buffalo

In 1970/1971, oxen (*lembu*) and water buffalo (*kerbau*) were not only used for farming, but were also raised for their meat. Households normally kept one or two animals, and at most four or five including young calves. Although a stable may be built near the house, they were traditionally raised in the ground floor of the owner's home while the family lived in a loft. New animals are usually offspring of the owner's stock, but they may also be obtained through the *pawah* system in which the person keeping someone else's animal gains possession of one of its offspring. In a few cases, young cattle are purchased and raised for profit, as a calf can be bought for RM50–100, and a grown ox sold for RM130–200 or even RM 300–350 for an exceptionally large bull. Young water buffalo fetch RM170–200 and adults RM300–350. Although there is a fairly wide variation in the amount of profit made when negotiating a sale, it is said that a profit of 20 to 30 sen per day can be made per head. In 1970/1971, sixteen people sold cattle and four sold water buffalo. As both the wet paddy and tobacco harvest of the previous year were poor, animal sales were higher than in normal years, probably because they represent a source of cash in times of need.

In 1977, tractors were widely used in paddy cultivation and as a result the number of water buffalo had significantly decreased. Of the twenty-three sample households, two had owned a total of four water buffalo during the 1970/1971 survey, yet by 1977, none of the households in the sample were raising any. Changes also occurred in cattle raising, but in a different direction. Although the number of households raising cattle in the sample had decreased from sixteen (69.6%) to twelve (52.2%), the total number of cattle remained constant at forty head. This represents a decrease in the number of households raising cattle and an increase in the number of cattle raised per household, reflecting a shift away from raising livestock as draft animals to raising them for meat.

By 1991, there were almost no water buffalo in the Galok area, and although there were cattle, there was nothing to indicate that cattle-raising had increased in importance since 1977.

5
Income and Lifestyle

5.1. Problems in Assessing Income

It is difficult to assess accurately the income of the villagers of Galok, particularly at the level of the individual household, because of their dependency on several sources of income. This situation is further complicated by the following factors:

(a) **Instability of income.** As mentioned previously, the dependence of farming in this region on rainfall results in large fluctuations in paddy yields from year to year. Similar fluctuations occur in fruit production, while the price of rubber also has noticeable ups and downs. Thus income from a specific source in any one year does not represent income from that source in the average year.

(b) **Irregular frequency of income.** The villagers have frequent opportunities to receive cash payments whether from rubber tapping, tobacco cultivation, work at the tobacco station, shop keeping, carpentry or other work, and the amounts they receive vary widely depending on the season. As the villagers have limited literacy and arithmetic, they cannot be expected to keep a comprehensive record or to remember all these payments.

(c) **Diversity and continuity of income sources.** Sources of income in Galok are quite diverse and many are intermittent. Moreover, most households have several sources of income. Even a checklist of the major items is no guarantee that the informant will offer exhaustive information about his or her own sources of income.

(d) **Dependence of fee on circumstances.** Even when standard fees for work exist, they are subject to change in accordance with individual circumstances or as a result of discussion between the parties involved.

(e) **Indeterminacy of home consumption.** Although the estimated value of vegetables, fruit, coconuts, cassava, betel leaves, chickens, ducks, eggs, goats, sheep, and other items which are produced and consumed domestically, should be added to income, this is practically impossible.

(f) **Difficulty of precise calculation.** Considering farm accounting methods and other factors, it is almost impossible to adopt a method of income calculation that includes depreciation.

5.2. Villagers' Incomes by Source

While recognizing the existence of the above problems, I assessed the approximate income of the residents of Galok from November 1970 to October 1971 through oral surveys of each household conducted on an average of four occasions. Although this time period may seem somewhat unusual, October 1971 corresponds with the end of the tobacco season in the fourth year after tobacco cultivation began. My thirteen-month stay in Kelantan ended in September 1971, and the interviews concerning income obtained from tobacco cultivation in the third period were conducted by my assistant, Wan Junoh bin Wan Jusoh, in the field.

The total village income for each income source calculated from the results of interviews is shown in Table 5-1. Income from payment in paddy was converted to cash at a value of 50 sen per *gantang*. Consumption of goats, sheep, chickens, ducks, eggs, coconuts, cassava, vegetables, and fruits were

Table 5-1
Total Village Income, by Source (November 1970–October 1971)

Source	Income (RM)	Percent	Trend
Tobacco Cultivation	48,304	31.0	+
Regular Employment	36,766	23.6	+
⎰ For M.T.C.	⎰ 16,230	⎰ 10.4	+
⎱ Other	⎱ 20,536	⎱ 13.2	+
Business	24,711	15.9	+
Rubber Tapping	16,847	10.8	–
Paddy Growing*	7,044	4.5	±
Rent (land and houses)*	5,365	3.4	±
Coconut-sugar Making	4,353	2.8	–
Sale of Oxen and Water Buffalo	3,370	2.2	±
Carpentry and Other Trades	2,070	1.3	±
Sale of Fruit	1,120	0.7	±
Migrant Work	565	0.4	–
Employment in Paddy Work*	499	0.3	±
Other	4,943	3.1	–
Total	156,017	100.0	

*Payment in paddy has been calculated as 1 *gantang* = 50 sen

not calculated for each household and they are therefore not included in the table. Even with a generous estimation, their total value would only amount to RM8,800. The most important source of income was from tobacco cultivation, which accounted for approximately 30 percent of total income. This combined with 10.4 percent of income derived from work at the M.T.C. tobacco station, means that 41.4 percent of the villagers' income was directly related to tobacco. Moreover, the introduction of tobacco cultivation also substantially boosted the income of shopkeepers and stallholders.

Incomes from rubber tapping, coconut-sugar making, and migrant work among other occupations declined in both relative importance and absolute amount because the price of rubber dropped and because the villagers shifted to tobacco cultivation. The three occupations listed above had a relative weight of only 10.8, 2.8 and 0.4 percent, respectively. The income generated by the introduction of tobacco cultivation far outweighed that lost through the abandonment of traditional occupations. Total income from paddy cultivation when payment in kind is converted to cash amounted to only 4.5 percent, and although paddy yield in 1970/1971 was particularly low compared to normal years, it is still clear that by this time paddy cultivation contributed very little to the villagers' income.

5.3. Household Income

Before presenting the results of interviews on the income for each household, I must first describe the characteristics of households and families in Galok. As will be detailed later (sections 7.7. and 9.3.), the typical household is centered around a married couple into which temporary or additional members can be readily incorporated to form the basic unit of livelihood. If the independent household is defined as a group that keeps a separate budget even though it may share a residence with others, then it has an average of 4.7 members, an average 2.4 of whom earn an income from some kind of work. The flexibility of the family group in Galok gives rise to the following difficulties in assessing household income.

(a) Income other than that from communal family labor is regarded as the individual's property. In many households unmarried children in particular contribute only occasionally to the household budget. Thus the household income shown here is simply the total of the incomes of the household members.

(b) There is noticeable movement of household members due to divorce and adoption of children or aging parents, and this can lead to abrupt changes in household income.

(c) Household income depends on whether a young couple returns to reside with one set of parents. In their early marriage the young couple will probably belong to the parental household, but after a few years, even if they continue to live in the same house, they will establish an independent budget. The income of each of the newly separated households will be very different from that of the joint household just before separation, although the standard of living of the people involved will show little change.

(d) Some elderly people receive partial or full financial support from their children yet live independently in a separate house on *pondok* or other land and keep a separate food budget.

(e) In polygynous families, it may be impossible to separate the household accurately because the wives maintain separate kitchens but share a common income, a fact which somewhat complicates the concept of household. For convenience, polygynous families that live together but maintain separate kitchens were treated as a single household, and as a result, the total number of households was reduced from 146 to 145.

The average annual income per household calculated from total village income was RM1,076, and the average monthly income was RM90. This figure combined with RM60, the estimated cash value of goats, sheep, chickens, ducks, eggs, coconuts, cassava, vegetables and fruit consumed by a single household gives a total income of RM1,136 per household and a monthly income of RM95. If we take into consideration possible unreported income, annual income likely exceeded RM1,200 while monthly income was slightly more than RM100. This is equivalent to an annual income of 144,000 yen and a monthly income of 12,000 yen at the exchange rate of that time.

While recognizing the difficulties in assessing income and the problems in the concept of the household, I have drawn up the distribution of household incomes according to household size, as shown in Table 5-2. I have excluded, however, the home consumption of everything except paddy in my calculations. The most notable characteristic of income distribution is the absence of households with extremely high incomes. The highest annual income recorded for any household was only RM4,585 (about 550,000 yen at the exchange rate of the time) and only five households, including this one, had an annual income of over RM2,500, the majority of which consisted of the salaries of primary school teachers (two households) and business earnings (three households). Because of the extremely small scale of landholdings resulting from the trend towards equal division of inheritance since Galok was first opened, the ordinary farmer of the 1970s could not expect to achieve a high income as long as his livelihood remained dependent on the land. The second characteristic of

Table 5-2
Number of Households by Income and Size

	NUMBER OF HOUSEHOLD MEMBERS				
INCOME (RM)	1–2	3–4	5–6	7–	TOTAL
–499	13	15	4	1	33
500–999	7	18	15	5	45
1,000–1,499	2	12	12	13	39
1,500–1,999		4	5	3	12
2,000–2,499			4	7	11
2,500–2,999		1			1
3,000–3,499		1		2	3
3,500–3,999					
4,000–4,499					
4,500–4,999				1	1
Total	22	51	40	32	145
Average Income (RM)	RM 506	RM 918	RM 1,171	RM 1,616	RM 1,076

Table 5-3
Number of Households by Income and Number of Working Members

	NUMBER OF WORKING MEMBERS					
INCOME (RM)	1	2	3	4	5	TOTAL
–499	12	17	3	1		33
500–999	3	28	11	3		45
1,000–1,499	1	18	11	7	2	39
1,500–1,999		5	5	2		12
2,000–2,499		3	4	3	1	11
2,500–2,999		1				1
3,000–3,499		1	1		1	3
3,500–3,999						
4,000–4,499						
4,500–4,999	1					1
Total	17	73	35	16	4	145
Average Income (RM)	596	1,009	1,263	1,293	1,964	1,076

household income was that it rose to some extent with increases in household size. This tendency appears even more marked if the five households with the highest incomes are omitted. A large household usually means a large work force and consequently a high total income, as shown in Table 5-3. The fact that income is dependent on the size of the labor force rather than on land is indicative of an urban rather than a rural economy. The introduction of tobacco cultivation seems to have reinforced this trend.

In Table 5-4 household incomes are classified according to the sex and age of the householder. Average annual incomes of more than RM1,000 are seen in households where the household head is a male ranging in age from his thirties to his fifties or a female in her thirties. Incomes of less than RM500, the lowest income bracket, are noticeable among households with male heads over sixty and female heads in their fifties, and are particularly prevalent in households with an elderly and/or female household head. This phenomenon can also be in part explained by the dependency of household income on the size of the work force. Households with younger heads also have noticeably lower incomes as the wife's earning power may be limited by pregnancy, childbirth, and raising children, or because the householder may not own any land, the basis of livelihood. In view of this last factor, it is clear that income is not determined solely by the size of the work force. Households with middle-aged heads and both land and labor power tend to have higher incomes, while

Table 5-4
Number of Households by Income and Sex and Age of Householder

Income (RM)	Male					Female					Total
	20–29	30–39	40–49	50–59	60–	20–29	30–39	40–49	50–59	60–	
–499	7	3	2	2	6			1	6	6	33
500–999	11	10	6	8	4			1	2	3	45
1,000–1,499	6	8	13	7	2		1	2			39
1,500–1,999		5	5	1	1						12
2,000–2,499		4	1	3	3						11
2,500–2,999		1									1
3,000–3,499		2		1							3
3,500–3,999											
4,000–4,499											
4,500–4,999		1									1
Total	24	34	27	22	16		1	4	8	9	145
Average Income (RM)	818	1,543	1,138	1,230	992		1,004	873	336	396	1,076

those in the youngest and oldest age groups, which lack either land or working members, tend to have very low incomes. This demonstrates a link between household income and the stage of family development.

As will be discussed in more detail in chapters 6, 10 and 11, the residence pattern in Galok is one of groups of households with parent-child or sibling ties occupying the same or neighboring compounds, and of single households with no kin resident in the immediate vicinity. The latter are established through inheritance or purchase of a compound, or through leasing land (or part of a house) from an unrelated person, either free of charge (*tumpang*) or for a rental fee (*sewa*). Table 5-5 shows household income according to type of residence. It is notable that 75.8 percent of households with an income of less than RM500 and 84.6 percent of those with an income of less than RM299 were resident in a shared compound. These are in most cases old people or young people who have just become independent, and most rely, to some extent, on the kinsmen with whom they share the compound and this type of living arrangement supplements their low incomes.

5.4. Income from Payment in Kind

As has been explained, paddy is cultivated on such a small scale in Galok that it often does not feed even the families that produce it. Moreover, yield varies widely depending on the amount of rainfall in a given year. For these reasons, harvested paddy is almost never sold, and even if yield exceeds the amount

Table 5-5
Number of Households by Residence and Income

| INCOME (RM) | SHARED HOUSE OR COMPOUND | INDEPENDENT RESIDENCE | | | | TOTAL |
		INHERITED	PURCHASED	*TUMPANG*	*SEWA*	
−299	11		1	1		13
300–499	14	3	1	1	1	20
500–999	33	7	1	3	1	45
1,000–1,499	28	4	3	4		39
1,500–1,999	6	3	1	1	1	12
2,000–2,499	8	1	2			11
2,500–2,999	1					1
3,000–3,499	1		1		1	3
3,500–3,999						
4,000–4,499						
4,500–4,999				1		1
Total	102	18	11	10	4	145

needed to sustain the family that year, surplus grain is stored against possible crop failure the following year. In 1970/1971, there was only one instance in which a household sold paddy and the amount was just 100 *gantang* of a total yield of over 500 *gantang*. Households that do not grow their own may receive paddy as a sharecropping fee or as remuneration for harvesting work. In the past, paddy was usually distributed and consumed without ever being converted to cash.

Table 5-6 presents the amount of paddy obtained by each household from cultivation, rent, and labor wages, or a combination of these. It is noteworthy that paddy formed part of the income of 111 households, 76.6 percent of all households in the village. On average, however, the amount was only 190 *gantang*, which is barely sufficient to feed two adults. As mentioned earlier, the villagers planted just 81 percent of the total paddy area in 1970/1971, and the yield per plot was only 71 percent of that normally expected. If we assume that the amount of paddy used as payment in kind is comparable to the amount of rice harvested per year, the amount of paddy received in payment from various sources in a normal year would be enough to feed only three or four adults, and even this amount cannot be expected every year. Moreover, in 1970/1971, 23.4 percent of households received no paddy for home consumption at all. Thus paddy supply in Galok is chronically deficient, and must be supplemented by purchasing at the Pasir Mas market polished rice from the lower reaches of the Kelantan River or from Thailand. Traditionally, the villagers of Galok tended as far as possible to conserve

Table 5-6
Number of Households by Source and Amount Obtained in Paddy

Source	-49	50-99	100-199	200-299	300-399	400-499	500-599	600-699	700-	Total	Average (Gantang)
Paddy Growing	6	3	12	22	10	2	2	1	1	59	236
Rent	8	7	4	8	1					28	111
Labor Wage	5	4	1		1					11	70
Paddy Growing + Rent			3	3		2	1			9	281
Paddy Growing + Labor Wages			2							2	180
Labor Wages + Rent			1							1	120
Paddy Growing + Labor Wages + Rent				1						1	290
Total	19	14	23	34	12	4	3	1	1	111	190

their limited supply of cash by receiving payment in paddy for home consumption.

5.5. Conditions in 1977

5.5.1. Changes in Income

Prices in Malaysia rose considerably between 1970/1971, when the study was conducted, and 1977. According to data from the Bank Negara Malaysia (Central Bank of Malaysia) based on a 1967 value of 100, the consumer price index rose from 101.3 in 1970 to 154.8 in 1977. The price index for foodstuffs rose particularly steeply with a value of 169.4 in 1977 compared to 101.3 in 1974. The most important indicator for the villagers' daily life is rice. In 1970/1971 villagers generally considered one *gantang* of paddy to be equivalent to 50 sen in cash, but in 1977 that figure had doubled to RM1. Charitable donations called *fitrah*, which are collected by the imams on behalf of the Kelantan state government at the end of the month of fasting, were designated as one *gantang* of polished rice per person. These donations were usually given in cash, and the amount increased about 1.7 times, rising from RM1.20 per person in 1971 to RM2 in 1977.

Keeping in mind the above, let us compare the income of villagers for the two periods in time. Of the sample twenty-four households surveyed in 1977, twenty-three were independent households at the time of the original study in 1970/1971. While recognizing changes in household members due to aging or other factors, the sample was divided into fourteen paddy-growing households and nine non-paddy-growing households, and overall income and average incomes from the main sources of income were compared as shown in Table 5-7. Overall income increased 2.9 times for paddy-growing households and 2.5 times for non-paddy-growing households, both of which exceed the increases in the consumer price index and the price of paddy noted above. The largest contributor to this increase for paddy-growing households was regular employment followed by tobacco cultivation and rubber tapping. Income from paddy cultivation (estimated by cash conversion), on the other hand, increased 1.2 times, which in fact represented a reduction. The largest factor contributing to the increase in income for non-paddy-growing households was various types of business enterprise followed by rubber tapping and rent.

The increase in income was not evenly distributed among all households. The income of five of the twenty-three households (two paddy-growing and three non-paddy-growing) increased by less than 1.5 times, while the income of seven households (four paddy-growing and three non-paddy-growing)

Table 5-7
Changes in Average Income by Income Source 1970/1971–1976/1977

	Paddy-Growing Households (14)				Non-Paddy-Growing Households (9)			
	(1) 1970/71	(2) 1976/77	Increase/ Decrease	(2)/(1) × 100	(1) 1970/71	(2) 1976/77	Increase/ Decrease	(2)/(1) × 100
Income Source	(RM)	(RM)	(RM)		(RM)	(RM)	(RM)	
Paddy Growing	93	112	+19	121	50	0	−50	0
Rubber Tapping	176	439	+263	250	169	526	+357	312
Tobacco Cultivation	498	1,025	+527	206	338	522	+184	155
Seasonal Employment	86	133	+47	155	80	133	+53	167
Regular Employment	111	914	+803	820	0	267	+267	-
Migrant Work	0	139	+139	-	8	55	+47	692
Business	94	139	+45	149	548	1,036	+488	189
Rent	5	212	+207	4,128	32	378	+346	1,169
Fruit Selling	4	30	+26	842	4	24	+20	550
Other	171	452	+281	264	32	145	+113	455
Total	1,237	3,595	+2,358	291	1,261	3,037	+1,776	245

tripled. The household with the greatest rise in income saw an increase of 11.2 times, largely due to the combined incomes of the daughter, a nurse, and her husband, a soldier. The household with the greatest reduction in income was a paddy-growing household that did not cultivate tobacco and their income dropped by 58 percent compared to the previous study period. This indicates the emergence of class differences defined by income discrepancies among the residents of Galok who had formerly belonged uniformly to the low-income bracket. Such discrepancies arose more from differences in labor force than from land ownership.

5.5.2. Durable Consumer Goods

Table 5-8 presents a comparison of data concerning the ownership of beds, radios, bicycles and sewing machines by the twenty-three sample households for which data could be obtained from both 1970/1971 and 1977. Although some households that had owned such durable consumer items no longer did so in 1977, in general, data showed an increase in the number of owners for each item. Bicycles had the highest ratio of ownership, and the number of households that owned two or more increased, while the total number of bicycles owned by the twenty-three sample households increased from fifteen to twenty-five. The number of motorcycles in the sample also increased, doubling from two to four in total. In 1970/1971, a married couple generally retired with their small children to the bedroom to sleep while other family

Table 5-8
Ownership of Specific Durable Consumer Items in 1970/1971 and 1977

A. BED			1970/71		
		OWN	DO NOT OWN	TOTAL	PERCENT
1977	Own	7	6	13	56.5
	Do Not Own	2	8	10	43.5
	Total	9	14	23	
	Percent	39.1	60.9		100

B. RADIO			1970/71		
		OWN	DO NOT OWN	TOTAL	PERCENT
1977	Own	5	7	12	52.2
	Do Not Own	3	8	11	47.8
	Total	8	15	23	
	Percent	34.8	65.2		100

C. BICYCLE			1970/71		
		OWN	DO NOT OWN	TOTAL	PERCENT
1977	Own	14	4	18	78.3
	Do Not Own	1	4	5	21.7
	Total	15	8	23	
	Percent	65.2	34.8		100

D. SEWING MACHINE			1970/71		
		OWN	DO NOT OWN	TOTAL	PERCENT
1977	Own	5	3	8	34.8
	Do Not Own	2	13	15	65.2
	Total	7	16	23	
	Percent	30.4	69.6		100

members spread matting (*tikar*) and one or two pillows on the floor in other parts of the house. Very few people owned beds. By 1977, however, the number of beds had significantly increased and mattresses were gradually replacing *tikar* for sleeping on the floor. Some people had also begun covering themselves with blankets instead of wrapping themselves in a sarong. In 1977, six out of the twenty-three households used blankets. The use of mosquito nets had also increased. Although I did not investigate the number of people who owned wristwatches in 1970/1971, by 1977, members of fifteen (62.5 percent) out of twenty-four households owned a total of twenty-three wristwatches.

5.6. Conditions in 1992

In the 1992 survey, I did not interview each household concerning their income. This was partly due to the limited length of the survey period, but also to the increased awareness of privacy accompanying the rise in income which made it more difficult to ask people personal questions about how much money they made. Although it was not impossible to determine the approximate income of household members who received a salary, it was very difficult to estimate that of other wage earners, including migrant workers, because of the irregular nature of their work, and it was even more difficult to estimate the income of those who ran their own businesses or contract workers. Moreover, the number of people depending on income from these types of employment had markedly increased.

The basic lifestyle of people in Galok had undergone major changes. Electrical service was introduced around 1988, and telephone lines were installed in 1991. This was followed by the installation of a water system in 1992. The main road running through the middle of the village was widened and traffic had increased. Some households even owned cars and the automobile had begun to play a major role in daily village life. Vans were used to transport and sell fresh fish and other foodstuffs on a regular basis, changing the role of stores in the village. The introduction of electricity likewise brought changes, and the spread of televisions, refrigerators and electric fans was particularly noticeable.

Here I will describe the ownership patterns of some consumer items in 1992. Although 75 of the 211 households in Galok in 1992 owned bicycles, this represents only 35.5 percent of the total, less than the percentage of households that owned bicycles in 1970/1971. This can partly be explained by the increased use of motorcycles and cars in place of bicycles with 74 households (35.1 percent) owning motorcycles and 33 (15.6 percent) owning cars. Furthermore, 123 households (58.3 percent) owned at least one of these three items. At the same time, the decline in tobacco cultivation meant that bicycles were no longer needed for transporting tobacco, and the construction of an Arabic school beside the *pondok* in 1981 and a secondary school (*sekolah menengah*) in nearby Chekok in 1985, made it easier to get to and from school without a bicycle.

Plate 5-1. A house on stilts with wooden siding and tiled roof (1971).

Plate 5-2. A house on stilts with thatched roof and woven bamboo walls (1971).

Plate 5-3. The house of a teacher who moved to the village and bought land.

Plate 5-4. A new bungalow-style house made of concrete blocks and brick.

Forty-nine households (23.2 percent) owned sewing machines which merely reflects the increase in the number of households. It may be that this lack of change is due to improved access to clothing stores in larger towns and peddlers who sell door to door, which facilitate the purchase of ready-made clothes.

As for water and fuel, the installation of a water system and the use of motorized pumps greatly affected daily life. By 1992, a large number of homes had finally been connected to the water system. The number of people using propane instead of wood for fuel had also increased. As far as I could determine, 111 households (52.6 percent) were connected to the water system or had motorized pumps, and 108 (51.2 percent) used propane for fuel. As mentioned above, electrical lines connected the village to a power supply making the use of electrical appliances possible, and 119 households (56.4 percent) had televisions, 100 (47.4 percent) had electric fans, 50 (23.7 percent) were using refrigerators, and 16 (7.6 percent) had washing machines.

One noticeable change in daily village life is the increasing use of footwear. Previously it was common to place a water container at the foot of the stairs leading to the front door of the house so that people could wash their feet before entering, but now the use of rubber sandals and of shoes and socks has spread, making this custom increasingly unnecessary. In 1970/1971, paddy work was done barefoot, but now a significant number of people wear rubber boots.

In the past, there was a distinct difference between town and village life, and even the wealthier village households could never hope to possess television sets, refrigerators or washing machines. This discrepancy has been rapidly eliminated, a major reason that town dwellers attracted by the low cost of land have moved to the village. The difference in lifestyle, at least in material terms, has changed from a difference in quality to a difference in quantity. At the same time, the lifestyle patterns of some households within the village remain unchanged, creating visible discrepancies in lifestyle and class divisions within the village.

6
Land and Residence

6.1. Inheritance and Individual Ownership

In pioneer villages like Galok, land was the basis of the people's livelihood. As this was still the case in 1970/1971, I will begin this chapter with a description of the villagers' relationship to land up until that point.

Apart from the communally owned land for the mosque and the cemetery, all village land was privately owned, and most of it was either bought or acquired through inheritance. Although the state government's development plan awarded people land in jungle areas on condition that they cleared and cultivated it, the acquisition of land in this way was unusual. In its land register, the District Land Office (*pejabat tanah*) classified land into several different categories on the basis of land use such as paddy land (*padi*), rubber land (*getah*), and fruit groves (*dusun dan macam macam*), in addition to the communally owned land mentioned above. The land taxes (*hasil tanah*) referred to in 3-1 basically follow the system that was established during the period of British colonial rule, and the sum is quite low because, although land was the main source of the people's livelihood, it was not necessarily the main source of tax income for the rulers. In 1990, land tax had changed very little in the twenty years since the study, and in fact, the amount had decreased when considered in relation to increased income and inflation.

The concept of individual ownership is remarkably strong, and the husband's and wife's lands are clearly and consciously distinguished. Although land purchased jointly by the couple is registered under only one name, it is considered joint property over which they have equal rights. The concept of family land does not exist, although children often view their parents' land as one entity to be divided after both parents have died rather than separately after the death of each parent. Land ownership for each household consisting of the area owned by a married couple, and sometimes this combined with that of other coresident kin, has already been presented in Table 3-1 for paddy and rubber land, the basis of the villagers' livelihood. Of the 144.3 acres of paddy land owned by the villagers, 80.5 acres (55.8 percent) was inherited and 63.8 acres (44.2 percent) was purchased, while of the 158.2 acres of rubber land, 71.9 acres (45.4 percent) was inherited, 64.5 acres (40.8 percent) was purchased, and 21.8 acres (13.8 percent) was granted by the government in return for opening the land. The latter was located in remote areas of Ulu Kelantan and other regions far from Galok, and the area owned per person was quite large. Only six people in the village had acquired rubber land in this way, whereas a very high proportion had obtained paddy and rubber land through purchase, an important point, which will be discussed later. In this section I will focus on the subject of inheritance.

As Muslims, the Malays may apply either Islamic law or customary law (*adat*) in the division of inheritance. Islamic law contains a body of detailed legislation governing inheritance that is administered by the Islamic court. Under Islamic law, when a man dies his widow usually receives a portion and the remainder is divided up among his children—siblings of the same sex receive equal shares, but sons receive twice as much as daughters. Under customary law, on the other hand, sons and daughters, in principle, receive an equal share. In Galok, the complicated calculation methods employed under Islamic law are rarely used for division of land inheritances. The villagers tend to choose customary law, although the principle of equal division is often tempered to suit particular circumstances.

Based on the assumption that the majority of inheritance passes from parent to child, let us examine the data more closely for a clearer picture of how inheritance is distributed among the heirs. Table 6-1 presents data concerning land inherited from parents obtained from interviewing the household heads or their spouses whose parents had already died (103 households). More than 90 percent of inherited land for both paddy and rubber was bequeathed from parent to child, and most of the rest was passed down from grandparent to grandchild. In cases where siblings were born to the same father but a different mother, or to the same mother but a different father, the method for dividing inheritance and the sex of the inheritor were classified from a comprehensive perspective. For example, in a family with eight children where five children had the right to inherit from the father and three from the mother, it was treated as a case of equal inheritance if the father's property was distributed equally among the five and the mother's equally among the three.

Sixty-four landowners had sons and daughters amongst whom property was divided. In only 28 cases, less than half the total, however, did all of the children receive equal shares. Of the remainder there were 19 cases in which distribution of inheritance was not governed by any particular principle and in many of these the portion of one child, whether male or female, was greater. In some instances, one or more siblings renounced their right to inherit. There were also 14 cases in which sons received more than daughters, a fact that suggests the influence of Islamic law. In none of these cases, however, was the son's share twice as much as the daughter's. This preferential treatment of males seems to have been most common in families where there was only one son among several daughters. When all the children were the same sex, equal division was most common with seven out of eight cases being so divided. There were also five cases of an only child who inherited everything.

As can be seen from the above, the principle of equal inheritance is not strictly adhered to, yet at the same time it is the predominant trend. Under such a system of equal division of inheritance, an increase in population naturally causes fragmentation of lands into smaller and smaller holdings. Theoretically, if land owned by the parents is evenly divided between an average of two children, the holding of each child when combined with that of a spouse will be about the same size as their parents' holding. In actual fact, however, the average area owned per person in the parents' generation compared to the average area inherited by their children was 2.7 to 1 for paddy and 1.8 to 1 for rubber land for villagers whose parents had both died. If inheritance were the only means of acquiring land, the recent decline in the death rate would have resulted in severe fragmentation of holdings.

With the increasing population and the lack of new lands to open in the area, the fragmentation that accompanies the equal division of inheritance can be checked by the migration of landowners from the village and the use of their lands by those who remain. The effectiveness of this recovery mechanism is manifest in the fact that among the present generation of householders in 1970/1971, the total area of land purchased was only slightly less than the total area inherited.

The price of land near Galok varies slightly according to certain factors, but around 1970 it ranged from RM800 to RM1,500 per acre for both paddy and rubber land. This was quite a large sum for Galok residents who could live on only RM50 a month, and land purchase was taken very seriously. The relationship between parties to the sale of paddy and rubber land is shown in Table 6-2. About 25 percent was purchased from parents or siblings for both types of land, and more than 50 percent from a kinsman of some kind including immediate family. Some villagers have told me that they feel it is undesirable to let land inherited from parents pass into the hands of strangers, and, although economic factors do not always permit it, this preference for sale to relatives is borne out by the figures. At the same time, it is important to note that the villagers have sufficient detachment to conduct such cash transactions between parent and child and between siblings.

Table 6-1
Inheritance of Parents' Land

Inheritance/ No Inheritance	Siblings	Method of Division	Number of Cases			
Inheritance	Both Sexes	Equal Division	28			
		Other	33		64	
		No Sexual Discrimination*	(19)			
		Males Given Preference	(14)			77
		Land Sold and Proceeds Divided	3			
	Same Sex Only	Equal Division	7		8	
		Other	1			
	Only Child		5			
No Inheritance	Property Disposed of Before Death		4			
	Parents Had No Property		17			
Unclear			5			
Total			103			

*Includes four cases where one sibling bought land from the other siblings.

Table 6-2
Relationship of Sellers to Buyers of Land

Seller	Paddy Land		Rubber Land	
Parent	8		5	
Grandparent	1		0	
Sibling	8	35 (55.5%)	6	25 (53.2%)
Aunt or Uncle	5		3	
Cousin	5		4	
Other Kin	8		7	
Unrelated	26	(41.3%)	22	(46.8%)
Unknown	2	(3.2%)	0	(0.0%)
Total	63	(100.0%)	47	(100.0%)

6.2. Changes in the Number of Landowners from 1957 to 1992

Using the land register at the district office in Pasir Mas, I investigated changes in the number of landowners in Galok from 1957 to 1992, in consideration of population increase, the tendency toward equalized inheritance, and the comparatively frequent sale of land. The section on Galok did not contain all the land in the village but only ownership of the central 166.6 acres (67.5 ha), including 65.5 acres of paddy, 63.9 acres of rubber and 37.2 acres of fruit orchard and residential land. The register currently in use was first started in 1957 and changes in the number of landowners during the 35-year period from that year until 1992 are presented in Table 6-3. Because legal proceedings for inheritance may take place a considerable time after the death of a parent, the timing of changes in land ownership may not be wholly accurate, but neither are such proceedings delayed indefinitely. The number of paddy landowners increased from 85 to 100, the number of rubber landowners from 85 to 105, and the number of fruit and residential landowners from 48 to 65. This increase in the number of landowners is evidence of the fragmentation of landholdings, but it is still a relatively low rate of increase in comparison with the rise in population. Thus the fragmentation process appears to have been somewhat arrested by such mechanisms as the relinquishing of inheritance rights by some children and by combining inheritance with land purchase. It shows that once landholdings have been divided to a certain extent, the possibility of fragmentation beyond that point becomes much lower. It also reflects the fact that the villagers' livelihood is no longer as dependent on land as it was in the past.

6.3. Land Ownership and Postmarital Residence

Newly married couples live for a short time with one set of parents and in due course build themselves a house on one of their parents' land or on some other property if they can purchase land elsewhere. The choice of residence in a bilateral society is inevitably influenced by factors other than the legal dominance of one set of kin and thus, newlyweds will live with the side most attractive in economic, geographic and human terms. For farmers, economic attraction consists of a greater potential to raise production. Geographic attraction lies in greater convenience of location and human attraction in such things as the greater desire of one set of parents to have the couple live with them. In theory, the balance of these three factors determines where the couple takes up residence, though in 1970/1971, ownership of land, the means of production, carried the most weight in the decision making process, a fact borne out by analysis of the data.

Postmarital residence of married couples for 112 household heads was examined by comparing land ownership of the husband and wife for paddy and rubber land combined, organizing the data into three different categories—the husband owns more land than his wife, both own similar amounts of land or none at all, and the wife owns more land than her husband—and the choice of postmarital residence was compared as presented in Table 6-4. As the table clearly shows, couples tended to choose virilocal residence when the husband's landholding was larger and uxorilocal residence when the wife's was larger.

Table 6-3
Changes in the Number of Landowners Listed in One Land District of Central Galok, 1957–1992

( ) = number of women

Year	Paddy	Rubber	Fruit/Residential	Year	Paddy	Rubber	Fruit/Residential
1957	85 (39)	85 (53)	48 (28)	1975	89 (38)	87 (55)	55 (33)
1958	85 (39)	83 (53)	48 (27)	1976	89 (37)	88 (56)	55 (32)
1959	84 (38)	86 (53)	51 (27)	1977	88 (37)	89 (57)	55 (32)
1960	84 (38)	86 (53)	51 (27)	1978	88 (37)	94 (56)	55 (31)
1961	82 (37)	86 (53)	50 (27)	1979	88 (37)	97 (61)	54 (31)
1962	82 (37)	86 (53)	50 (27)	1980	91 (41)	97 (62)	55 (31)
1963	82 (37)	86 (53)	50 (27)	1981	92 (41)	99 (62)	57 (32)
1964	78 (37)	85 (53)	50 (27)	1982	93 (41)	97 (61)	56 (32)
1965	80 (38)	85 (53)	54 (29)	1983	95 (43)	97 (59)	56 (32)
1966	80 (39)	86 (53)	53 (29)	1984	96 (44)	97 (64)	59 (34)
1967	81 (37)	86 (53)	53 (29)	1985	100 (44)	103 (66)	60 (34)
1968	82 (37)	88 (53)	55 (30)	1986	102 (46)	103 (66)	62 (36)
1969	82 (36)	88 (53)	55 (30)	1987	103 (49)	103 (67)	62 (36)
1970	83 (36)	88 (52)	55 (31)	1988	102 (49)	103 (66)	63 (35)
1971	83 (35)	87 (52)	54 (32)	1989	100 (47)	103 (66)	63 (34)
1972	84 (35)	87 (53)	54 (32)	1990	100 (46)	105 (67)	65 (34)
1973	84 (34)	87 (54)	54 (32)	1991	100 (47)	105 (67)	65 (34)
1974	87 (38)	87 (54)	55 (33)	1992	100 (47)	105 (67)	65 (34)

Paddy 65.5 acres (43 plots), rubber 63.9 acres (34 plots), fruit/residential 37.2 acres (21 plots)

Table 6-4
Postmarital Residence According to Relative Scale of Land Held by Husband and Wife

Postmarital Residence	Scale of Landholdings			Total
	Husband's > Wife's	Husband's = Wife's	Husband's < Wife's	
Virilocal	40 (70.1%)	6 (27.3%)	6 (18.2%)	52 (46.4%)
Neolocal	12 (21.1%)	10 (45.4%)	6 (18.2%)	28 (25.0%)
Uxorilocal	5 (8.8%)	6 (27.3%)	21 (63.6%)	32 (28.6%)
Total	57 (100.0%)	22 (100.0%)	33 (100.0%)	112 (100.0%)

The relatively higher rate of virilocal residence over uxorilocal residence is related to the difference in the scale of lands obtained by men and women through inheritance and purchase.

The table also shows that there are exceptions to the general trend: six couples reside virilocally although the wife's landholding is larger, and five couples reside uxorilocally although the husband's landholding is larger, for a total of 11 cases or 9.8 percent of the total. In four of the former cases, the husband is not dependent on the land for his livelihood. One is engaged in coconut-sugar making, one is a shopkeeper, one works for the Drainage and Irrigation Department, and one is a poultry dealer. As for the other two, the wife of one inherited the land recently and until then they had relied on the husband's land for their living, and the landholding of the other was almost the same size as his wife's. In the five cases of uxorilocal residence despite the husband's larger landholding, the husbands of two couples were employed in coconut-sugar making while another bought land for their house from his father-in-law and had taken up neolocal residence. In the two remaining cases, the husband owned rubber land and the wife paddy land and as the wife's land was nearer the road, it was considered a more convenient place to live. These exceptions indicate that when land does not provide the main source of income, the location of residence is determined by economic factors other than the size of landholding (6 cases), that when the husband's and wife's lands are of equal productivity, conditions other than economic ones may be considered (3 cases), and that the time at which an inheritance is received can influence the decision (1 case).

The permanent residence of a couple who are of working age is not finally determined until both have received their inheritances and finished buying their own land. Of course, in many cases, residence is decided on the expectation of inheritance, but it must be borne in mind that the preceding data include many people at a transitional stage, particularly young couples, who will move in future. Despite the growing dependence on wage income in 1970/1971 reported in earlier chapters, the influence of land ownership on the selection of postmarital residence was clearly evident, but as people's livelihood became less dependent on the land, other factors came to carry more weight. It may be that the importance of land ownership on livelihood and the selection of postmarital residency among Malays was a transitional phase that occurred in the recent past when the value of land was at its highest.

6.4. Residential Kin Groups

If only one child's nuclear family remains resident in the parental compound, and the other children either live with their spouses' families or newly acquired land, the parental compound will not be divided. If on the other hand, the nuclear families of two or more children remain on the parental compound, as time passes the coresident siblings, or aunts and uncles, nieces and nephews, become the compound householders, and finally their children, cousins to each other, will succeed. During the early period of settlement when lands were first being opened there was plenty of both residential and agricultural land, and residential kin groups were easily formed.

In 1970/1971, there were thirty-six groups comprising two or more households of related families resident in the same or neighboring compounds, with an average of 2.9 households in each group. Of the 146 households in the village, 101 (69.2 percent) belonged to such a group. Three of the groups had been formed recently through the purchase of neighboring land rather than on existing landholdings, and these have therefore been omitted from the analysis. The remaining 33 groups have been classified according to the relationship between the householders as shown in Figure 6-1. Sixteen groups (types I–IV), about half of the total were comprised of the parents' and one or more of their children's households. Of these, the five groups classified as type IV included the households of two or more children, and the five groups classified as type III were the independent household of one child and the parental household in which another married child is coresident. In these ten cases, it is possible that in future the siblings will divide the compound between them. The future is less clear for the four groups classified

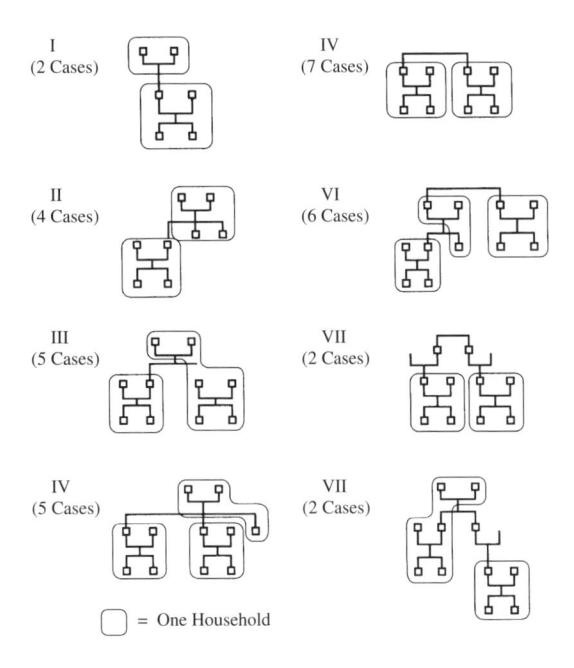

Figure 6-1. Types of Neighborhood Kin Groups

as type II comprised of one child's household living in the parental compound along with the parents' unmarried child or children. The only residential kin groups where there is no possibility of the compound being divided in future are the two groups classified as type I, consisting of the parents' household and the household of one child's family and no unmarried children. In the other fifteen groups (types V to VII), the compound has already been divided among the siblings, or is presently jointly owned but expected to be divided in future, or in addition to these, is shared by the siblings' children's families. The remaining two groups (type VIII) are somewhat exceptional, comprising a temporarily extended family household including the householders' parents, together with the household of the child of one of his siblings who has left the compound.

Because these compound household groups are not formed on the basis of a particular individual's rights or obligations to remain in the compound, they are not necessarily permanent or stable. Nevertheless, they do constitute the nuclei of neighborhood kin groups, and it is generally hoped that children will, in future, live near each other if there is room in the compound or surplus arable land. Immediately after the area was opened for settlement, every family had some land to spare and neighborhood kin groups were easily formed. However, the subdivision of land that has taken place with the passing of generations restricts their expansion.

The expansion of a neighborhood kin group may be followed by its dissolution. In some cases the relationship between kin may be weakened by one or more siblings selling their share of a compound to someone unrelated. Conversely, the continued expansion of a kin group resident in one compound may give rise to general poverty in the compound or to excessive dependence on one kinsman. In 1970/1971, some of the compounds in Galok contained a cluster of shabby houses, while others contained one ordinary house surrounded by huts.

Table 6-5
Ownership of Residence in Independent Households

Type of Ownership		Number of Households	(%)
Owned	Inherited	19	(42.2)
	Purchased	12	(26.7)
Rented	Without Charge (*tumpang*)	10	(22.2)
	With Charge (*sewa*)	4	(8.9)
Total		45	(100.0)

6.5. Independent Residence

Forty-five households in Galok have no kin living in the same or in neighboring compounds. These single households are another aspect of the common residence pattern described above where the parents share their compound with the household of one child. In some instances, the child's household has been left on its own in the parental compound for some reason, while in others a new independent residence has been formed by a child who left the parental compound. Ownership patterns of independent households is shown in Table 6-5 and the individual cases are described below.

6.5.1. Residence on Inherited Land

Nineteen single households (42.2 percent) resided on land inherited from their parents. In two cases, the heir was an only child, unmarried at the time, who inherited all the parents' land. In twelve cases, the heir's siblings and their families had left the parental compound, leaving only the heir and his or her spouse. All of the above fourteen cases can be viewed as a temporary phenomenon falling into type I of the classification in Figure 6-4. In the remaining five cases, the child had built a new residence on land owned by the parents or grandparents.

6.5.2. Residence on Purchased Land

Twelve independent households (26.7 percent) had purchased the land for their residences. In eight of these, at least one spouse was a native of Galok while the remaining four came from nearby villages. The household heads ranged in age from 32 to 65. In four cases, the land had been purchased from kin while in eight cases it had been purchased from non-kin. There is a possibility in all twelve cases that the parents' and children's households may reside together in one compound in future, but not all the properties have sufficient space.

6.5.3. Renting Free of Charge (Tumpang)

An owner who does not occupy a residence may allow another person to use it free of charge (*tumpang*). When the arrangement is temporary, the tenant often builds a shack small enough to be carried on people's shoulders. These arrangements are made quite easily, and in 1970/1971 ten households had built a home on land rented under the *tumpang* system. All of the householders had lived outside Galok at least once, eight in a neighboring village and two in a village some distance away. Both of the latter had some connection with Galok— the husband in one family and the husband's father in the other were born there. Six of the ten households rented land from kin and four from non-kin. In all cases, a close personal relationship existed between the tenant and the landlord

Plate 6-1. A village residence (1971).

that made the arrangement possible. Seven of the household heads were relatively young, ranging in age from 23 to 27, with an average age of 29, and they had very clear reasons for moving to Galok. For some, tobacco cultivation enabled them to make a living without owning land while others took advantage of Galok's convenient location along the road to find work in such occupations as taxi driving and bicycle repair. They were attracted by the improved living conditions in Galok. This type of residence would not have been possible when the villagers' livelihood depended entirely on rainfed paddy cultivation and rubber tapping. As for the other three households, the heads were comparatively older and their reasons for moving to Galok were more temporary and circumstantial in nature, although all of them were influenced by its location along the road. One worked mainly as a charcoal maker near Galok, another was a carpenter who was temporarily living with his second wife because she did not get along with the children of his previous wife, and one was an elderly woman who wished to live closer to her children's families.

6.5.4. Rented Land or Rooms (Sewa)

In 1970/1971, four households were renting for a fee (*sewa*) and although three rented part of a house, only one of them rented land. As all other land was rented free of charge under the *tumpang* system, this case can be considered an exception. The wife, a native of Galok who started a store in front of the

M.T.C. station struck up an agreement with the landowner who lived across the street to rent the land for RM30 a year. All three of the remaining households were temporarily renting a portion of a large house. Two were elementary school teachers while the third worked as a night watchman at the station, and all three came from outside Galok. Rent ranged from RM10 to 12 a month. These households also represent a new category of residence that did not exist formerly in Galok.

6.6. The Mode of Life among Kin and Neighbors

From the preceding sections it can be inferred that the lives of the villagers center on the neighborhood kin groups of parents and children or of siblings that are formed in response to the circumstances of the members. Although the members of the group are in close daily contact, each household tries to manage an independent budget and children try to secure their living expenses independently by sharecropping (*pawah*) paddy or rubber land belonging to their parents, grandparents, other kin, or other people, by engaging in migrant work, or by growing tobacco. Although independence is the general rule, some degree of dependence naturally arises when children are too young or parents are too old to support themselves entirely. Also, on occasion, the compound kin group may include individuals with a mental handicap or illness, or more distantly related elderly kinsmen who lead a semi-independent life under the protection of parent, siblings or other kin.

As mentioned earlier, when children marry they may remain in the parental compound, move to their spouse's compound, or move to a new compound. When marriage or relocation involves leaving the village, the question may arise of the disposal of land inherited from parents, which must either be sold, rented or lent, to kinsmen or other villagers remaining in the village. The basic form of renting is sharecropping (*pawah*) in which the landowner and the sharecropper divide the harvest equally. The relationships between landlords and tenants of paddy and rubber lands in Galok for 1970/1971 are shown in Tables 6-6 and 6-7. The data are recorded from the perspective of landlords and tenants resident in Galok and include both land in Galok owned by village residents and sharecropped by outsiders, and land owned by non-Galok residents that is sharecropped by village residents. In over 70 percent of cases for both paddy and rubber land, landlords resident in Galok leased their land to kinsmen, while in over 50 percent of cases, tenants resident in Galok rented their holdings from kinsmen. A higher degree of mutual trust appears to exist between landlord and tenant when they are kin than when they are not and the method of paying rent differs accordingly. In rubber tapping, for example, when the sharecropper and landlord were kinsmen, the sharecropper sold the finished rubber sheets himself in over 70 percent of cases, whereas when they were unrelated, the landlord sold the rubber and divided the money with the sharecropper in every case.

The parent-child centered kin groups occupying the same or adjoining compounds are not large, normally comprising only two to four households, and of course, single, independent households have no kin living in the immediate vicinity. Thus relationships with neighboring non-kinsmen are also very important in the villagers' lives. As paddy is rainfed, there is no need for communal management of irrigation, and since paddy is grown only

Table 6-6
Relationship of Tenants to Landlords (For Landlords Resident in Galok)

Tenant	Paddy Land		Rubber Land	
Parent	2		5	
Aunt or Uncle	2		0	
Sibling	11		0	
Child	7	43 (74.1%)	3	17 (70.8%)
Grandchild	4		0	
Cousin	2		2	
Nephew or Niece	6		6	
Other Kin	9		1	
Unrelated	15	(25.9%)	7	(29.2%)
Total	58	(100.0%)	24	(100.0%)

Table 6-7
Relationship of Landlords to Tenants (For Tenants Resident in Galok)

Landlord	Paddy Land		Rubber Land	
Grandparent	2		2	
Parent	1		1	
Aunt or Uncle	0		2	
Sibling	2	8 (50.0%)	4	15 (57.7%)
Cousin	2		1	
Other Kin	1		5	
Unrelated	8	(50.0%)	11	(42.3%)
Total	16	(100.0%)	26	(100.0%)

on a small scale primarily by the married couple for home consumption, communal farm work is rare. Similarly, rubber tapping is basically carried out by the individual and does not require communal labor. The communal aspects of the neighborhood are thus most manifest in daily life rather than in work activities.

Cooperation in every day life in the 1970s was well illustrated by the use of wells and pumps. Water for drinking, laundry and bathing is very important, and in the past, homes were rarely far from rivers because of the need to obtain water easily. Some villagers can still remember using sections of bamboo with the inner nodes knocked out as vessels to carry water to homes located at a distance from the river. When the road connecting Pasir Mas and Tanah Merah was made, people settled alongside it and wells became indispensable. Villagers began to drive pipes directly into the ground to pump up water. Those with a well or pump in their compound used it themselves, but also often shared with villagers who did not have their own. While sharing and joint ownership among kin is to be expected, cooperation extended to non-kinsmen and covered a wide area. In 1970/1971, as many as nine households shared the same well. In the nineties, individual use became much more common when a water supply system was installed, although some people still shared taps.

Another form of cooperation was the communal feasts (*baewah*) held on important annual festivals and rites of passage. The annual festivals frequently accompanied by feasting were the month of Prophet Mohamed's birth (Bulan Maulud), the month of fasting (Bulan Puasa) and the celebration of the end of the fast (Hari Raya Puasa), while the most important rites of passage are weddings and funerals. Wedding and funeral feasts are major gatherings with guests from the same and neighboring compounds, kinsmen who live further away, neighbors, and many acquaintances. In contrast, the feasts given in the month of fasting and for rites of passage other than weddings and funerals are mostly small gatherings attended by the compound kin group or kin from an adjacent compound, kin within easy walking distance, and neighbors. Usually ten to twenty guests are invited, and they fall within the closest circle of cooperation in every day life. At memorials for the dead or feasts during the month of Prophet Mohamed's birth, this group will be joined by a few others including the religious teacher (*To' guru*) from the *pondok* (residential religious school).

For house building or relocation, assistance is enlisted from a larger circle of people and those who happened to be there at the time usually offer to help. People's relationships with the midwife (*bidan*) and the Koran teacher also extend beyond the confines of the neighborhood. Thus the neighborhood circle of cooperation forms the nuclei for wider circles of interaction in daily life.

6.7. The Village as a Series of Neighborhood Circles

The term for village in Malay is *kampung,* and from what I observed of Galok, the *kampung* consist of a series of overlapping neighborhood circles. Village boundaries are not always distinct and the villages have no well-defined organizations as can be seen from the characteristics described below.

6.7.1. Village Boundaries According to the Land Register

Galok lies along the road and is bordered to the north and south by paddy fields, which at first glance appear to mark its boundaries. According to the land register, however, the *pondok* school and a nearby group of houses at the south end of the village actually lie outside Galok, while the east side of the road is part of the village Jabo and the west side of Padang Hangus. Again, in the central part of the village, land belonging to the villages of Hutan Mala and Jabo dovetails with that of Galok. The boundaries in the land register are arbitrary, probably reflecting to a large extent the residence or birthplace of the landowners at the time the register was compiled. This shows that Galok was not originally a single village. Some people refer to Galok as two separate villages: Galok Hulu (*hulu* meaning "upstream") and Galok Hilir or Hujung Galok (*hilir* meaning "downstream" and *hujung* meaning "beginning" or "end"). This may give the impression that the long narrow village was later divided into an upper and lower village, but it is also quite conceivable that it was originally two villages that more recently merged into one joined by the road.

6.7.2. Consciousness of Community Boundaries

The villagers themselves are vague about the location of village boundaries. For example, when the people at the northern end of Galok say "here," they include not only Galok but also the neighboring village. Moreover, as some people who live near the river away from the road did not originally call their settlement Galok, it can be assumed that the name was only gradually adopted for that area. Similarly, Kubang Kelian, a *kampung* comprised of only seven households west of Chekok is sometimes referred to as part of Chekok.

6.7.3. Residence of the Mosque Congregations

At each end of Galok is a mosque (*masjid*). Previously this area was served by only one mosque located in the village of Chekok to the south along the road. Around 1962 this mosque was relocated at the southern end of Galok and named Masjid Kubor because of the cemetery (*kubur*) beside it. Around 1965 or 1966, another mosque, Masjid Hujung, was constructed at the northern end of Galok, receiving its name from its location at the entrance to the village. In 1970/1971 only one *imam* had been appointed by the state government to serve the *mukim* or administrative unit of which Galok was a part, and he ran the older mosque at the southern end while his deputy ran the newer one in the north. For Friday prayers, villagers generally attended the mosque nearer to home, together with people from surrounding villages. Thus, Masjid Kubor was supported by half of the Galok residents, half of the Jabo residents, and by residents of such villages as Chekok, Kampung Tengah, Padang Hangus, Kuek, and Kubang Kelian, while Masjid Hujung was supported by the other half of the Galok population, the other half of the Jabo population, and by villagers from Atas Beting, Paya Mengkuang, Hutan Mala, and other villages,

6.7.4. Administration

In Kelantan, the administrative unit below the district (*jajahan*) is the subdistrict (*daerah*), and below the subdistrict is the *mukim*. Galok is part of Mukim Jabo Timor in Chetok subdistrict. The *mukim* is the lowest administrative unit, headed by a *penghulu,* who is appointed by the state government and under the jurisdiction of the *penggawa*, the head of the subdistrict. Formerly, there were about twenty *penghulu* in Chetok, but by 1970/1971 the subdistrict had been reorganized and their number reduced to five. By 1992, this number had been reduced further to three. In 1970/1971, the *penghulu* for Mukim Jabo Timor was responsible for 16 villages (*kampung*), large and small, none of which had its own headman. Paya Mengkuang was one of the 16 villages under Mukim Jabo Timor, but part of this *kampung* was also under the jurisdiction of neighboring

Plate 6-2. A compound in 1991. Bricks are used for a part of the traditional wooden house.

Mukim Chetok, indicating that administrative boundaries sometimes divide *kampung*.

6.7.5. School Districts

The primary school for the area began as a public school in 1949 and was handed over to the government as a national school (*sekolah kebangsaan*) in 1959. It is located in nearby Chekok and serves several villages in the area including Chekok, Galok, Jabo, Padang Hangus, Jintan, Kuek, and Pasir Parit. Thus again, the villages do not have their own organizations but are included in a larger overlapping unit that centers on the school.

As can be seen from the above, villages called *kampung* comprise a simple series of overlapping neighborhood circles revolving around various units of daily life and without any fixed framework or organizations. Their size varies according to their location and the circumstances surrounding their settlement. Mukim Jabo Timor, for example, has one village, Kubang Kelian, of only seven households and other villages as big as Galok. Villages with very few households may consist of only one or two groups of kinsmen, or otherwise have a high degree of group unity, but this overall unity is naturally less well defined in larger villages.

6.8. Summary

Among the Malays of this region, the selection of postmarital residence, the inheritance or purchase of land, and migration to open new land appear to be determined mainly by economic factors. In a new settlement on recently opened land, there is more space than in an older settlement, and as the population increases, the next generation naturally expands into new territory. When land area is sufficient, more than one child can remain in the parents' compound or a neighboring kin compound, but with each successive generation, available land within the compound shrinks in size and more children are forced to leave the compound and take up residence elsewhere, thereby preventing further expansion of the number of households within the compound. Fragmentation of land is somewhat retarded by land purchase and rental, but in 1970/1971 it was expected that despite this recovery mechanism, fragmentation would continue to progress. The residential kin group organization has its greatest potential in the first generation of a new settlement. This is the process by which residential groups in Malay farm villages were formed.

In areas dependent on paddy and rubber for their livelihood, the relationships within compounds shared by the households of parents and children, or siblings and their families, and the relationships with the neighborhood comprised of more distant kin were an important part of daily life. Outside this inner circle there existed weaker, overlapping circles in which the villagers shared some common aspects of daily life, and beyond that were more scattered relationships with relatives and acquaintances living further away.

The village and its adjacent paddy and rubber lands were cleared and settled in the recent past, a process which is thought to have occurred quite rapidly from the end of the 19th century to the early 20th century. Villages like Galok are assumed to have developed from the families of numerous settlers that each formed a separate nucleus, rather than from the gradual increase in the population of a few central pioneer households. This factor may account for the greater lack of village organization. Although this makes it easier for the government to establish arbitrary administrative boundaries, inevitably, communication within these newly created frameworks is not as smooth as it might otherwise be.

In this chapter I have focused on the role that residential land plays in the villagers' lives, but this role has changed significantly. As the villagers came to depend increasingly on migrant work and other forms of employment, the meaning of land changed. The concept of the village as a place of production was largely lost, replaced instead by the concept of the village as primarily a place of residence, and consequently, the influence of ownership of paddy or rubber land on the choice of postmarital residence greatly diminished, and kin groups living in the same compound entered a new phase. These changes will be further discussed in a subsequent chapter.

7
Marriage and Divorce

7.1. Marriage

Marriage is one of the greatest transitions in the life of a Malay. As will be discussed below, although matrimonial ties are not always stable, sexual relations between men and women are only sanctioned within the context of marriage, and any form of sexual relations outside that context brings both religious and social condemnation. There was no strict prohibition against social intercourse between single men and women among the Malays of Kelantan and the segregation of male and female, a fundamental principle of Islam, was not practiced. For a man and woman to live together without marrying, however, was viewed as a severe transgression against social conventions and as marriage contracts could be easily made, people conformed to the outward norms of Islamic society.

In this section, I have outlined the marriage procedure among the upper stratum of village society in Galok in 1970/1971, although the lack of noticeable social divisions meant that greater complexity was the only noticeable difference. It is difficult to determine the degree to which traditional practices for marriage were followed at that time because new fashions and trends inevitably found their way even into rural areas.

The first official step towards marriage was initiated by the parents of a young man of marriageable age who played the more active role in the selection of a spouse, delegating a kinsman or friend to approach the parents of a suitable girl. The girl's parents then consulted with their daughter who, in most cases, knew the suitor by sight. Often the boy and girl were in love and marriage was simply the natural result, although occasionally the parents of a daughter might be so eager for an early marriage that the girl did not even know her husband-to-be.

If the intermediary received an affirmative response from the girl's parents, he inquired about the desired marriage payment (*belanja*) and engagement gifts (*meminang*), and reported back to the boy's family. The boy's parents and relatives then visited the girl's home, bearing the engagement gifts which included, among other things, a gold necklace worth about RM80 or a gold ring worth about RM50, cloth for three garments worth about RM12 each, shoes worth about RM6, cosmetics, condensed milk, sugar, and bananas. The girl's family reciprocated with gifts usually amounting to half the value of those received, including a ring, traditional Malay garments, condensed milk and sugar. The date of the wedding was decided at this meeting.

Wedding ceremonies were often held just after the rice had been harvested. The third and twelfth months (*Rabi'ul Awal* and *Dzulhijah*) of the Islamic calendar were also popular, while the second month (*Safar*), which was considered unlucky, and the month of fasting (*Ramdzan*) were usually avoided. School holidays might also be taken into consideration. Wedding dates were thus determined on the basis of several different calendars—agricultural, Islamic and academic—and as some were lunar and others solar calendars, the number of weddings held in a given month differed every year.

Malay-Muslim marriage involved two ceremonies: *bernikah,* the signing of the marriage contract (*nikah*), which had religious and legal significance; and *peratur,* which had social and traditional significance.

The *bernikah* was usually held at the bride's parents' home, with the imam officiating at the signing of the marriage contract by the bridegroom and the bride's guardian, usually her father, before two witnesses and the couple's relatives. First, the imam solemnized the marriage by pronouncing the *akad*

Plate 7-1. Wedding presents from the groom's family for the bride. Money constituting the marriage payment has been folded and assembled into a decorative arrangement.

nikah, a formula specifying the names of the parties entered into marriage and the amount of the marriage payment. The groom then accepted the *akad nikah* by repeating the formula in a single breath: "Bearing marriage payment of (amount), I wed (name), the daughter of (name)." These words must be uttered loud and clear enough for the imam and the witnesses to hear. Should the groom falter, the imam would have to repeat the solemnization until the groom responded in the required manner.

Following the solemnization, the marriage payment was made. Prepared in advance, red RM10 notes or blue RM50 notes might be folded and arranged, for example, in the shape of flowers. For families in the upper stratum, the payment was usually about RM500, of which the entire sum became the property of the bride. A registration fee of RM13 was paid to the imam, 40 percent of which was his fee.

The *peratur* was the centerpiece of the wedding reception, usually held at the bride's parents' home the day after the *bernikah*. Invitations indicating the date and time were delivered to guests in advance. The bride's family slaughtered a cow or water buffalo the day before the reception to prepare a feast (*baewah* or *kenduri* in standard Malay). Close relatives and neighbors helped with preparations, and in some cases, villagers known for their culinary skills were employed. The cost of the most magnificent feasts could rise as high as RM1000, and the number of guests might exceed a thousand if the bride's family was wealthy and actively involved in society. If there was not enough space in the house to accommodate everyone, marquees or temporary shelters consisting of a roof on posts were erected outside. The guests began to arrive around noon in twos and threes, forming small groups of either men or women, and left once they had eaten. Close relatives or friends might bring gifts such as cloth or glasses, but most guests gave cash amounting to RM1 or one or two *cupak* of rice (about 1/4 *gantang*). The bride's family thus recovered between 70 and 80 percent of the cost. After the feast, the guests were given a boiled egg in a basket or on a bamboo skewer, or cake or biscuits to take home.

The groom and his relatives arrived in a procession at about four o'clock in the afternoon for the *peratur* (also *beratur,* meaning "to line up;" or *bersanding*). This was the central part of the reception and consisted of the enthronement of the bride and groom, garbed like Indian royalty or in white Muslim-style clothes, side by side on decorated chairs or a bed. The groom's family brought cooked glutinous rice (*pulut semangat*), colored boiled eggs (*telor semangat*), Malay style cakes, bananas, condensed milk, cloth, women's shoes, cosmetics, etc. arrayed on large brass stands. The rice and eggs were divided into two equal portions, and half was returned to the groom's family.

The groom's relatives stayed for one or two hours, and when the meal was finished, returned home leaving the groom behind.

The groom stayed at the bride's house for about one month and then returned to his parents' home accompanied by his bride (*sambut menantu*). His parents held a feast, equivalent in scale to the reception, to which they invited their relatives and other villagers, as well as some of the bride's family.

Weddings between the majority of villagers were usually much simpler. In the decade preceding 1971, marriage payments in Galok were mostly around RM200 and the average was RM229 (Table 7-1) The ceremonial signing of the marriage contract was always carried out, but the *peratur* was frequently omitted from the reception. Guests were invited in person rather than by invitation card, and instead of slaughtering an animal, the meat for the feast might be purchased. The cost of a small feast was about RM200, of which about 50 to 60 percent was recovered from the guests.

7.2. Early Marriage and the Universality of Marriage

Marriage in Galok was characterized by the young age at which women married for the first time, and the fact that very few people remained single for their entire life. Data for 1970/1971 on the ages of men and women when they first

Table 7-1
Marriage Payments For First Marriages

Payment (RM)	From Interviews With Husbands	From Interviews With Wives
22.5	1	1
32	1	1
100	1	6
150	3	2
200	19	18
250	1	1
300	5	6
400	4	5
500	1	2
Unclear		1
Total	36	43
Average	RM 229	RM 229

These amounts were for marriages in the 10-year period prior to 1971. The slight difference in the amounts given by the husbands interviewed versus the wives is because of cases in which one spouse was absent due to death, divorce, or other reasons.

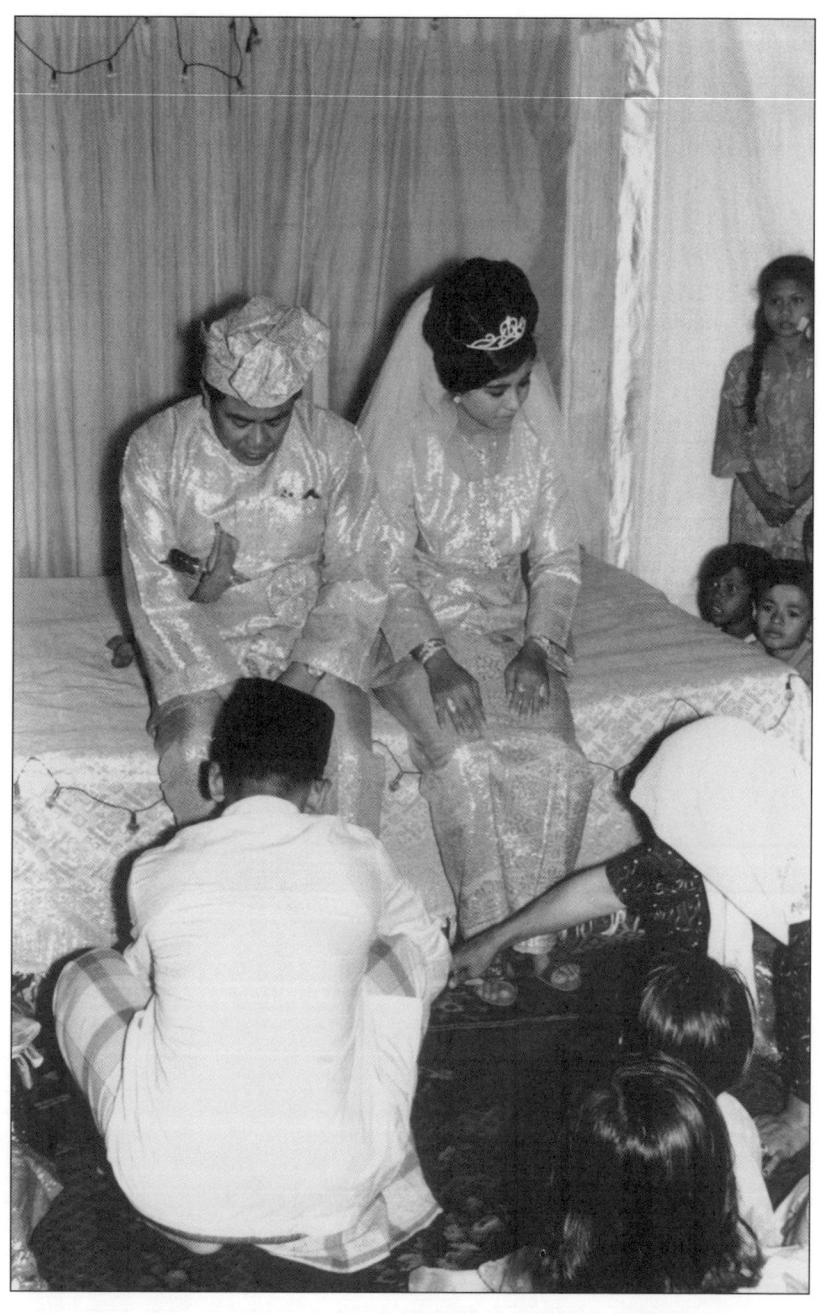

Plate 7-2. The bride and groom seated upon a decorated bed.

married are presented in Table 7-2. The average age of women was 16.5 and the modal age was 15. Only 6 percent of women were over 20 when they first married, a very low figure. There is a broader age range for men at first marriage due to the influence of economic factors, but even so, the average age was 20.5 and the modal age was 20. It must be borne in mind, however, that at that time, the villagers' responses concerning their own age were not always reliable which may explain the concentration of people aged 15 and 20, two relatively easy numbers to remember.

Almost all men and women of marriageable age were married. Marriage was practically a certainty for women and every woman in the village had at least been married once by the time she was 25. Although some men married later than others, the overwhelming majority of them did marry. Even those for whom marriage would seem impossible, such as the mentally handicapped

Table 7-2
Age at First Marriage

AGE	MALE	FEMALE
11		1
12		7
13		10
14	1	16
15	5	41
16	2	19
17	3	26
18	15	17
19	9	5
20	39	6
21	9	1
22	8	1
23	6	
24	2	
25	10	1
26	2	
27	2	
28		
29	1	
30	6	
31 or over	1	
Total	121	151
Average Age	21.5	16.5

Ages are for ever-married residents of Galok.

(*bodoh*), sometimes married. In Galok, one 40-year-old man who lived with his older brother because delayed mental development made it impossible for him to live independently, had been married when he was twenty. His wife was an older woman from a neighboring village who had been married before, but, unable to stand the marriage, she asked for a divorce six months later. She had a son by this marriage and raised him herself after the divorce.

Although, in principle, everyone marries, a small minority remain single. Known as *pondan*, men who dress in women's clothing can be seen sometimes in farm villages. There were two *pondan* in Galok in 1970/1971, both of whom were 32 years old. One had left to become a dancer in Kuala Lumpur but when police began stricter law enforcement, he returned to live with his parents and help with their business. The other worked as a seamstress. People with mental illnesses (*gila*) are also debarred from marriage and there was one 23-year-old man in Galok who remained single for this reason.

7.3. The Range of Intermarriage

Prohibitions against intermarriage in Islam cover a comparatively narrow range, including parents and children, siblings, uncles and aunts, nephews and nieces, grandparents and grandchildren, step-parents and step-children, and foster parents and foster children. Cousins and more distant relatives may intermarry, and no further restrictions exist in customary law. Because the villagers have closer daily contact with kin than with other people, there is a greater chance that they will find a spouse through this channel, but in actual fact, this was not always the case.

Details of marriages between kin are shown in Table 7-3. For men, first cousins (*sa-pupu;* or *se-pupu*), second cousins (*dua-pupu*), and the children of first cousins (*anak sa-pupu*) are the most common types of kinswomen married, and these combined with marriages to more distant kin account for 16.6 percent of all marriages. For women, first cousins, second cousins, and parents' first cousins (*pak sa-pupu*) are the predominant kinsmen married, and marriage to all types of kin account for 13.9 percent of marriages. No men married parents' first cousins (*mak sa-pupu*) and no women married children of first cousins, indicating a tendency to avoid marrying men to women of an older generation. Marriages between cousins, whether cross cousins or parallel cousins, were not particularly favored, accounting for only 3.7 percent of marriages for men and 3.1 percent of those for women. Against the background of the high divorce rate, which will be discussed later, there were arguments both for and against marriages between cousins. Some people claimed that cousins should marry because it is easier for them to establish stable marital relations while others claimed that if the marriage failed, the relationship between the couple's parents, siblings to one another, would deteriorate.

If anything, there was a trend towards community endogamy, or more specifically, marriage to people living close by, including neighboring villages, because the villagers did not have a clear concept of *kampung* boundaries. In this sense, intermarriage between Galok residents accounts for only a portion of all marriages, 22.3 percent for men (61 out of 241 marriages) and 22.5 percent for women (75 out of 294), whereas marriages to people in both Galok and neighboring villages comprise 56 percent of all marriages for men (135 out of 241) and 56.8 percent of all marriages for women (167 out of 294).

7.4. Divorce

Although divorce is frowned upon under Islam, the Koran stipulates provisions for divorce and recognizes it as legally permissible. Although divorce proceedings are based on the Koran, there is a great deal of variation depending on the locality and the times. In 1970/1971 the following types of divorce were recognized.

(1) *Talak*: A husband can divorce his wife by notifying her of *talak*, a special word denoting repudiation that is equivalent to a declaration of divorce. He must inform the imam or the religious judge (*kadhi*) residing in the district of his declaration, in return for which he is issued certificates for a fee of RM12. This sum is sent to the Islamic court and 40 percent is returned to the imam as payment. The declaration is followed by a prescribed period of waiting, three months

Table 7-3
Kinship between Spouses

Relationship To Spouse	Men		Women	
First Cousin (*sa-pupu*)	9		9	
Second Cousin (*dua-pupu*)	10		10	
First Cousin's Child (*anak sa-pupu*)	7	40	0	41
Parent's First Cousin (*pak sa-pupu*)	0		7	
Other Kin	14		15	
Non-Kin	194		252	
Unknown	7		1	
Total	241		294	

For all marriages of Galok residents.

and ten days for older women, and until the end of the third menstrual period for younger women, or, if pregnant, until delivery. During this period, the husband can revoke the divorce if both he and his wife agree. The revocation is called *rojok* and costs RM2 to obtain. A husband may twice revoke *talak*, but after a third repudiation of the same wife, he can only remarry her after she has been legally married to someone else and subsequently divorced.

(2) *Pasah*: The judge of the Islamic court has the authority to grant a divorce. Although it is classified as a divorce procedure, it is actually a type of annulment, and is applied in cases where the husband's whereabouts are unknown.

(3) *Tebus talak*: Literally, "to buy *talak*," this method is used when the wife seeks a divorce through a judge of the Islamic court. If the husband is at fault, the wife returns RM100 or 200 of the marriage payment to him, but if the husband is not at fault, she must return it in full and sometimes pay even more.

(4) *Ta'alik*: If a husband breaches any of the conditions written on a separate piece of paper appended to the marriage contract signed at the marriage ceremony, the religious judge can, at the wife's request, demand that he repudiate the marriage. The appended conditions usually stipulate that a husband may not be absent for over three or four months, beat his wife until she bleeds, or fail to support the family. The wife must produce two witnesses to the husband's behavior in all of the above cases.

Of the four methods described above, *talak* was almost the only one used for divorces in Galok. Two cases of divorce by *pasah* were recorded, but both were for women whose husbands died in Japanese labor camps in Burma during the Second World War, and neither *tebus talak* nor *ta'alik* had ever been used.

Although in form *talak* is initiated by the husband, in a far greater number of cases, it was actually the wife who wanted a divorce as shown in Table 7-4. When a wife sought divorce, a husband rarely opposed her and instead declared *talak*.

Using the figures for the total number of marriages from Table 7-3 and for the number of divorces from Table 7-4, 41.5 percent of marriages for men and 39.8 percent of marriages for women ended in divorce. This is a very high divorce rate, particularly when one considers that the number of *talak* divorces revoked by *rojok* were not counted, and that current marriages may disintegrate in the future. As evidenced by the greater number of wives instigating divorce, this trend does not derive from any characteristic of Islam, but rather, it is connected with the native Malay outlook on the family and matrimony. The main

Table 7-4
Person Seeking Divorce

Person	For Men	For Women
Husband	19	17
Wife	38	49
Both Husband and Wife	11	25
Wife's Father	1	
Unclear	31	26
Total	100	117

Table 7-5
Number of Ever-Divorced People and their Percentage Relative to Ever-Married People

	Men			Women		
Age	Ever Married	Ever Divorced	Percentage	Ever Married	Ever Divorced	Percentage
10–19				11	1	9.1
20–29	31	3	9.7	40	8	20.0
30–39	33	9	27.3	34	13	38.2
40–49	30	14	46.7	38	19	50.0
50–59	22	15	68.2	23	12	52.2
60–	16	10	62.5	19	8	42.1
Total	132	51	38.6	165	61	37.0

Table 7-6
Ever-married People by Number of Times Divorced

Number of Times Divorced*	Men	Women
0	80	103
1	29	31
2	9	12
3	6	12
4	3	4
5	1	2
6	3	
Unknown	1	1
Total	132	165

*Excluding the two cases of *pasah*

causes cited for divorce were incompatible character, conflict over postmarital residence, and discord with the spouse's family. In most cases, comparatively minor conflicts quickly led to divorce. It is impossible to ignore the fact that the high divorce rate is in part encouraged by easy divorce procedures; however, the divorce rate differs in other parts of the Malay peninsula despite the fact that almost exactly the same laws are applied, suggesting that the attitude of those responsible for implementing divorce laws in Kelantan is a closely related factor. This point will be further discussed in 8-2 and 8-3.

When a couple divorced, each spouse retained the property they acquired by inheritance, and any jointly purchased property was divided equally. In one case, a couple divorced after planting a tobacco crop and divided the rights to the crop equally between them, and in another case, a house was divided up and part of it moved to the property of the former spouse.

The percentages of people who had been divorced compared to those who had been married are shown in Table 7-5, including the two cases of *pasah*. The percentage of married or once married men who had been divorced was 38.6 percent, very similar to that for women which was 37 percent. Except for those aged 60 and over, for whom data were incomplete, the divorce rate increased with age. Rather than indicating an increased tendency towards divorce for longer marriages, this trend was a result of the gradual decrease in the divorce rate, which appeared as a difference in the divorce rate among the age groups.

Table 7-6 presents the number of people who have been divorced grouped by the number of times they were divorced. The number of those who had never been divorced exceeded the number who had, and most had divorced only once. The significance of repeated divorce, however, cannot be ignored as the number of people divorced two or more times was only slightly smaller. The greatest number of divorces per person was six for men (three people) and five for women (two people). These facts show that divorce had become commonplace in the daily life of the villagers.

The number of divorces grouped according to the duration of the marriage and the number of children is shown in Table 7-7. Fifty percent of divorces for men took place within a year of marriage, and 85 percent within five years. For women, 40.2 percent of divorces took place within a year of marriage and 78.6 percent within five years. These figures included some divorces that occurred almost immediately after marriage; in fourteen cases each for men and women (14 percent and 12 percent of divorces, respectively) the marriage lasted less than three months. In contrast, the number of divorces after ten years of marriage was very low with only eleven for men (11 percent) and nine for women (7.7 percent).

Table 7-7
Number of Divorces by Duration of Marriage and Number of Children
(not including pasah)

	Number Of Children													
	For Men							For Women						
Duration	0	1	2	3	4	5+	Total	0	1	2	3	4	5+	Total
< 6 months	20	1					21	17						17
≈ 6 months	1	1					2	5						5
< 1 year	3	1					4	6	1					7
≈ 1 year	19	4					23	13	5					18
2 years	7	7					14	10	9					19
3 years	3	5	1	1			10	4	8	1	1			14
4 years	1	5	1	1			8	2	1	1				4
5 years	1	1	1				3	4	3	1				8
6 years		1					1	7			1			8
7 years		1		1			2		2	1	1			4
8 years		1					1	1						1
9 years							0		1	2				3
10 years			2		1		3		2	1	1			4
11 years							0							0
12 years							0							0
13 years							0		1					1
14 years							0							0
15 years +			2		1		3	1		2			1	4
Unknown	3	1	1				5							0
Total	58	28	8	4	1	1	100	70	33	9	4	0	1	117

Table 7-8
Custody of Children After Divorce

Guardian	For Husbands	For Wives
Wife	22	32
Husband	10	2
Wife's Mother	4	7
Shared between Husband and Wife	3	3
Husband's Sister		1
Wife's Sister		1
Move Back and Forth	1	
Already Grown Up	2	1
Total	42	47

The comparatively high proportion of divorces in the early stages of marriage is also reflected in the number of children at the time of the divorce. Fifty-eight men (58 percent) and 70 women (59.8 percent) had no children when they divorced. Moreover, in close to 70 percent of cases with children, the couple had only one child at the time of the divorce. Due to the flexibility of family ties which will be discussed in more detail later, there were no fixed rules governing the custody and care of children after a divorce. Table 7-8 shows who took care of the children following their parents' divorce. Even allowing for the fact that some of the divorced parties had left the village and were not interviewed, there were noticeable discrepancies between the replies given by the wife and the husband, and therefore the figures are not completely reliable. Nevertheless, the following percentages are worthy of note. In 52.4 percent of cases in the husbands' responses and 68.1 percent of cases in the wives', the mother took care of the offspring, whereas the husband took care of the offspring in only 4.3 percent of cases in the wives' responses and 23.8 percent of cases in the husbands'. Moreover, in 9.5 percent of cases for

Table 7-9
The Relation of Kinship To Marriage And Divorce

RELATIONSHIP	MEN			WOMEN		
	MARRIAGES	DIVORCES	PERCENTAGE	MARRIAGES	DIVORCES	PERCENTAGE
Kin	40	16	40.0	41	17	41.5
Non-kin	197	79	40.7	252	100	39.7
Unknown	7	5		1	0	
Total	244	100	41.5	294	117	39.8

Table 7-10
Number of Divorces for All Marriages Compared to Those for Inter-Galok Marriages

		MARRIAGES	DIVORCES	PERCENTAGE
Men	All Marriages	241	100	41.5
	Marriages between Galok Residents	61	18	29.5
Women	All Marriages	294	117	39.8
	Marriages between Galok Residents	75	21	28.0

Excluding the two cases of *pasah.*

husbands and 14.9 percent of cases for wives, the maternal grandmother took care of the offspring. Overall, the wife and her family had a much more noticeable presence, a fact directly related to the large number of divorces that took place soon after marriage when the children were still young.

Data was tabulated in Table 7-9 to determine whether kin relationship to one's spouse influenced the number of divorces. Very little difference was found, however, between the number of divorces for kin and non-kin, and thus kinship between spouses does not appear to affect the rate of divorce. Of the nine cases of first cousin marriage for both men and women, six ended in divorce, showing rather a higher divorce rate.

Table 7-10 shows the relationship between community endogamy and the divorce rate. Although, as has been mentioned, the villagers' concept of community is often vague, extending to include relations with neighboring villages, I have only compared marriages with residents of Galok to the total number of marriages. The divorce rate for the former is noticeably lower, probably due to the lower likelihood of conflict over the location of post marital residence. A considerable number of divorces result from the unwillingness of one partner to leave their own community and live in the spouse's community.

7.5. Remarriage

Frequent divorce is accompanied by a high rate of remarriage. As sexual relations between men and women are only sanctioned within the institution of marriage, if the divorcee is comparatively young, it is considered only natural that he or she should remarry. The same is true for bereaved spouses, and no virtue is attached to remaining single for the rest of one's life. Occasionally people wait for their children to reach adulthood before remarriage. The formalities for remarrying are simpler than for the first marriage. Divorced or widowed men can remarry at any time, but women must observe a prescribed period of waiting—that for divorcees three months and ten days or three menstrual periods while that for widows is four months and ten days. The wishes of the couple play a greater role in the selection of a spouse than in the first marriage. The signing of the marriage contract in accordance with Islamic law is indispensable, but the grand feast accompanying the *peratur* is omitted. The marriage payment for a woman remarrying is also less. In the decade preceding 1970 the average payment was RM125 and the standard payment was RM100, half the usual amount for a first marriage.

Table 7-11 presents the number of marriages contracted by people who were or had once been married in 1970/1971, and 38.6 percent of men and 41.2 percent of women had married two or more times. For women, these figures all represented remarriages, but for a few of the men they represented polygynous marriages. Table 7-12 presents the ages at which people remarried. Unlike those for first marriages, the ages are more diverse with an average age of 32 for men and 27.1 for women. The interval that elapsed from the time of divorce or bereavement to the time of remarriage for those who remarried is shown in Table 7-13. The average period was 1.5 years for men and 1.8 years for women, and about one fourth remarried within six months of their divorce or bereavement.

The combination of spouses according to the number of times each had married is shown in Table 7-14. Unions between people who had never been married and between people who were remarrying were most common, but there were exceptions. Although it was slightly more common for a girl marrying for the first time to wed a previously married man than for a man marrying for the first time to marry a widow or a divorcee, but the difference is very slight, indicating the weakness of the concept of male superiority.

In its ceremonial aspects, remarriage is less important than first marriage, but its social significance is just as high. When the first marriage fails, people try to redeem the situation through a second marriage, many of which are successful. When they are not, however, the divorced parties can try again in a new marriage.

7.6. Polygyny

Under Islamic law, a man is permitted to marry four wives, provided he treats them all equally. In 1970/1971, polygynous unions accounted for 5.4 percent of all marriages for men (13 out of 241) and 7.1 percent for women (21 out 294), and there were no cases where a man had more than two wives simultaneously. In terms of quantity, then, they were not a very important aspect of marriage in Galok.

Six men in the village had made polygynous marriages, of whom two still had more than one wife at the time of the study. One man was a 52-year-old farmer whose first marriage ended in divorce, and who remarried at the age of 30. At the age of 35 he took another wife, five years younger than the first, creating a polygynous union. Both wives had been married and divorced once. They lived in the same house but in separate wings, each with its own kitchen. It was unusual, however, for two wives to live in the same building in polygynous unions in this area. The second case was a 39-year-old primary school teacher who had rented a room at his new place of appointment in Ulu Kelantan, while his two wives lived in separate houses in Galok. He had made a previous polygynous marriage at the age of 30 but this had ended in divorce

Table 7-11
Ever-married Persons by Number of Marriages

Number Of Marriages	Men		Women	
1	80		96	
2	22		37	
3	16		12	
4	6		11	
5	2	51 (38.6%)	6	68 (41.2%)
6	2		1	
7	2		1	
8	1			
Unknown	1		1	
Total	132		165	

Table 7-12
Number of Marriages by Age at Remarriage

Age At Remarriage	Men	Women	Age At Remarriage	Men	Women
13		1	33	2	1
14		3	34	2	1
15		2	35	9	8
16		4	36	3	5
17	1	2	37	2	2
18	1	8	38	2	
19		5	39		2
20	4	12	40	1	4
21	5	9	41	2	
22	4	6	42	2	3
23	3	5	43		1
24	5	5	44	2	1
25	7	3	45	4	1
26	6	4	46	1	
27	6	3	47	3	1
28	3	5	48		
29	2	3	49		
30	8	9	50+	4	1
31	2	2			
32	3	2	Unknown	10	5

Average age of remarriage: 32.0 years for men and 27.1 years for women.

Table 7-13
Interval between Divorce or Death of Spouse and Remarriage

	MEN			WOMEN		
INTERVAL	REMARRIAGE AFTER DIVORCE	REMARRIAGE AFTER DEATH OF SPOUSE	TOTAL	REMARRIAGE AFTER DIVORCE	REMARRIAGE AFTER DEATH OF SPOUSE	TOTAL
< 6 months	18	3	21	26	4	30
≈ 6 months	2		2	5	1	6
< 1 year	6	1	7	2	1	3
≈ 1 year	21	5	26	24	5	29
2 years	15	1	16	16	4	20
3 years	7		7	13	2	15
4 years	3		3	3	3	6
5 years	2		2	1		1
6 years	1		1		2	2
7 years	1		1	1		1
8 years	1		1	1		1
9 years						
10 years				1		1
11 years +					1	1
Unknown	7	4	11	6	7	13
Total	84	14	98	99	30	129

Table 7-14
Couples by Number of Marriages

	REPORTED BY HUSBANDS							REPORTED BY WIVES						
NUMBER OF MARRIAGES BY WIFE	NUMBER OF MARRIAGES BY HUSBAND							NUMBER OF MARRIAGES BY WIFE	NUMBER OF MARRIAGES BY HUSBAND					
	1	2	3	4	5+	UNKNOWN	TOTAL		1	2	3	4	5+	UNKNOWN	TOTAL
1	113	17	8	3	1		142	1	139	13	8	2	1	1	164
2	13	23	9	2	9		56	2	12	41	9		5	1	68
3	2	9	4	4	3		22	3	4	17	4	1	3	2	3
4	2	1	2	2	1		8	4	2	6	6	2	2	1	19
5			4	1	1		6	5		5	3	3			11
Unknown	2	1	1	1	1	1	7	Unknown					1		1
Total	132	51	28	13	16	1	241	Total	157	82	30	8	11	6	294

after one year. He entered his second polygynous union when he was 32. For his first wife, this was her first marriage, but the second wife, two years her junior, had been divorced four times. In both cases the wives were on comparatively good terms, which is regarded as exceptional. The four other men who had had polygynous unions were married to a second wife only briefly before the first wife, unable to tolerate the situation, asked for a divorce. In one case the polygyny lasted only five days, while in another it lasted only ten. In every case the second wife was younger than the first, and for two of them it was their first marriage, while for the other two it was a remarriage.

For eight of the women who had had polygynous marriages, it was their first marriage, while for thirteen it was their second. All of the second wives had been married before. Six of the first wives subsequently divorced, and the other two were the wives of the men just mentioned who continued their polygynous unions. Nine of the second wives subsequently divorced, two became monogamous through the divorce of the other wife, and the remaining three were still married in 1970/1971. Two were the second wives of the two men mentioned above, and the husband of the other was living outside Galok. Of those who had been a first wife, 75 percent were divorced, slightly greater than the 69.2 percent of those who had been a second wife who divorced. The difference, however, is insignificant.

Polygyny, then, is likely to occur in connection with remarriage, and often leads to divorce. As divorce was easily obtained, it was difficult to maintain a polygynous union and it would seem that polygynous marriages were not an established part of family life for Malay villagers.

7.7. Household Composition

As can be surmised from the frequency of divorce, the marital bond is weak. Despite this, however, the married couple is the nucleus of the family unit, as is supported by the fact that children of a previous marriage are sometimes separated from the new household when the parent remarries. As a unit, the couple is quite independent, and rarely do two or more couples share a household. A newly married couple will sometimes live with one set of parents, but this is understood to be a temporary arrangement, and sooner or later they will become independent. Only when one of the parents has died does the likelihood increase that a young couple will share a residence and household with the remaining elderly parent (usually the mother). Although in a conventional system of classification such a household would be termed an extended family, in Kelantan this type of structure does not arise from any particular principle of family composition.

Although one married couple is the nucleus of the family unit, this does not preclude other people from joining the household. Rather it makes it much more flexible and therefore easier to integrate other members within the same household, particularly adopted and foster children. At the same time, the parents and their unmarried children are not seen as an indivisible unit, and the children can be easily adopted by another household. Likewise, a divorcee can easily return to her parental home with her children, and when she remarries can either take her children with her or leave them in their grandparents' care. The flexibility of the family bond functions as a buffer, absorbing the painful repercussions of divorce. As described above, the village household in Galok is a flexible group, which shares the same residence and which, although it is centered on one married couple, easily accommodates changes in members.

The family unit in Galok could be taken as a nuclear family and the family cycle viewed accordingly. In some families, however, a married child continues to live with one or more parents, a phenomenon most commonly seen when one of his parents is widowed. Moreover, even when a married couple has achieved an independent means of livelihood, they may build their home within the same compound as the parents. In such cases, although both the parents' and the children's households are economically independent, many other aspects of their daily lives are closely interrelated, and in this sense, they cannot be viewed as truly independent nuclear families. Accordingly, the family cycle in Galok is not accurately represented by the simple nuclear family mode; rather a diversity of family patterns may arise from a child's marriage and in this sense it is practically meaningless to assume the existence of a typical family cycle in Galok.

As children marry, the parental family pattern will alter depending on whether the parents have (1) a married child living in the same house; (2) a married child living in the same compound; (3) both (1) and (2); or (4) only the unmarried children remaining as the married ones have left. At each stage of family development from the time the first child marries to the time when all the children have married and one spouse has died, these options produce a variety of family patterns. In addition, divorce can abruptly change the household composition at any stage. The absence of rules concerning the children's place of residence, together with the length of childbearing age, produce a wide variation in the age difference between parents and the children living with them. In Figure 7-1, I have attempted to organize the diverse data to establish how the basic family structure changes. The arrows connecting each stage in the family cycle indicate the possibility of change in the family composition.

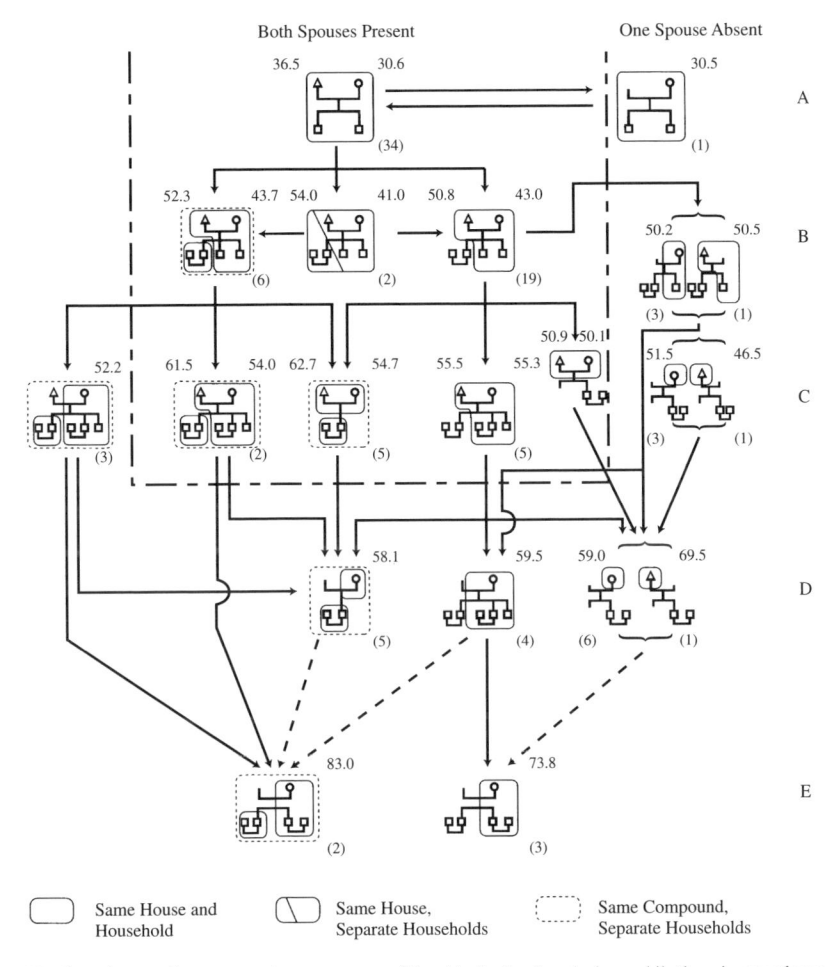

Figure 7-1. Development of Household Composition

Numbers above each pattern are the average ages of the older husbands and wives, while those in parentheses are the number of cases

An elderly wife, or sometimes husband, who has been widowed, will attempt to continue supporting herself as long as she is physically able. Of the sixteen elderly villagers at stage D, fifteen of whom were women with an average age of about 60 and one of whom was a man nearing 70, only four were living with their children. Although they did maintain their independence, the others were not entirely isolated. Five had married children living in the same compound, while six of the remaining seven lived with grandchildren. In contrast the elderly for all five cases at stage E who were no longer able to support themselves lived with their children. In stage E, the child has become the household head, and the parent lives in the care of the child's family. This type of composition can also arise when an elderly person who formerly lived alone is taken into a child's household.

A nuclear family comprised of a young couple may temporarily be formed in a parental compound by the early demise of the parents. In other cases, they are formed by a couple that has left the parental residence at some stage in family development. Leaving home can mean simply moving into the parental compound or it may mean moving onto other land that happens to be available at the time. The above organization of data according to stages in family composition represents a cross-section of the family compositions observed in 1970/1971. How they actually changed over time is recorded in a subsequent chapter.

7.8. Divorce Trends in Kelantan

In this section, I will extend the range of observation to make a statistical assessment of divorce trends for the entire state of Kelantan, identifying changes in attitude towards divorce and the position of Pasir Mas district, including Galok, within the state. The number of marriages and divorces among Muslims in Kelantan state for the 42-year period from 1948 to 1990 are shown in Figure 7-2 and Table 7-15. Values for 1948 through 1957 are from Shirle Gordon (n.d.), who published data she had collected for each state in *Intisari*, a journal then based in Singapore. Values for 1957 through 1970 were obtained from the Kelantan state religious court (Mahkamah Shariah) during the 1970/1971 study period, those for 1973 to 1983 were obtained from the state *kadhi* court (Mahkamah Kadhi) during the follow-up survey in 1984, and those for 1984 through 1990 were obtained from the Pejabat Qadhi Besar office in Kelantan in October 1991. There are no data for 1971 and 1972 because these years fell between two periods of data collection, and records were not preserved. In fact, the series of chronological data presented here can no longer be obtained in Kelantan State.

In 1950 and the preceding year, the divorce rate was exceedingly high with about 90 divorces for every hundred marriages. This rate gradually declined thereafter, dropping to about 50 divorces per 100 marriages around 1970. In 1979, the divorce rate began to decline noticeably once again, and this gradual reduction was due, in part, to the spread of education, particularly secondary education, and the related rise in the age at which people first married. In 1984, there was a sudden drop in the number of divorces with only 17.9 divorces per one hundred marriages, half the number of the previous year, and the rate

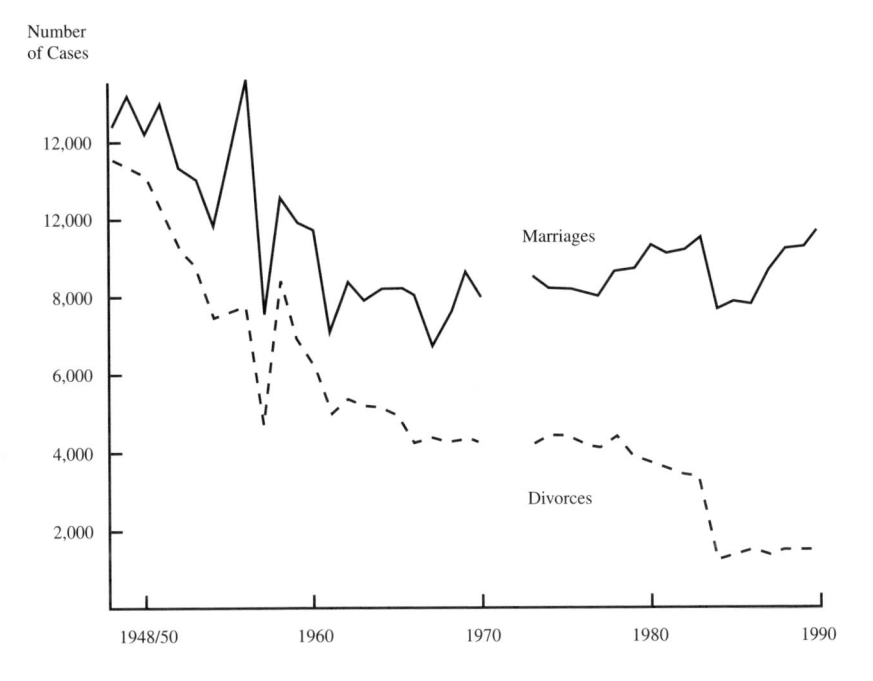

Figure 7-2. Changes in the Number of Marriages and Divorces in Kelantan

continued to remain low. This phenomenon was the result of revisions in family law concerning Muslims implemented mainly in 1982 and 1983, which were aimed at making it more difficult to apply for divorce. The revisions required the divorce applicant to apply through the religious judge (*kadhi*) of the Islamic court rather than through the imam as was formerly done.

When the divorce rate was at its highest, the overall number of divorces revoked by *rojok* (also known as *rujuk*) never exceeded 10 percent. This was followed by a period of irregular fluctuation, however, and around 1970/1971, it hovered at slightly above 10 percent. From 1979 to 1983, when the divorce rate was gradually declining, the proportion of *rojok* was higher, rising to 15 percent in 1980. But with the sudden drop in divorces in 1984, cases of *rojok* decreased correspondingly and the proportion dropped to as low as 7 percent, indicating that it was becoming more difficult to obtain divorce.

Regional differences in divorce rates for Muslims living in Kelantan State for 1970 and 1990 are presented in Table 7-16 and Figure 7-3 according to the percentage of divorces per 100 marriages for each district. In 1970, the districts of Tumpat, Kota Bharu, and Pasir Mas situated along the coast and near the mouth of the Kelantan river, a region considered to be the traditional center of

Table 7-15
Marriage and Divorce in Kelantan (1948–1990)

YEAR	MARRIAGES	DIVORCES	Rojok	DIVORCES PER 100 MARRIAGES
1948	12,488	11,625	683	93.1
1949	13,256	11,384	1,007	85.9
1950	12,326	11,163	768	90.6
1951	13,131	10,247	923	78.0
1952	11,391	9,298	805	81.6
1953	11,092	8,777	657	79.1
1954	10,003	7,549	681	75.5
1955	11,639	7,660	702	65.8
1956	13,830	7,846	749	56.7
1957	7,611	4,747	467	62.4
1958	10,723	8,530	644	80.0
1959	10,054	6,856	738	68.2
1960	9,810	6,363	668	64.9
1961	7,176	5,068	514	70.6
1962	8,399	5,463	517	65.0
1963	7,987	5,278	1,477	66.1
1964	8,264	5,270	584	63.8
1965	8,275	5,052	519	61.1
1966	8,177	4,395	810	53.8
1967	6,933	4,489	458	64.8
1968	7,703	4,423	419	57.4
1969	8,668	4,518	546	52.1
1970	8,163	4,352	583	53.5
1971				
1972				
1973	8,705	4,480	579	51.5
1974	8,419	4,602	572	54.7
1975	8,275	4,637	609	56.0
1976	8,220	4,459	518	52.2
1977	8,165	4,309	556	52.8
1978	8,851	4,557	550	51.5
1979	8,869	4,118	588	46.4
1980	9,540	3,912	588	41.0
1981	9,307	3,780	530	40.6
1982	9,421	3,552	481	37.7
1983	9,711	3,566	528	36.7
1984	7,915	1,419	153	17.9
1985	8,065	1,608	159	19.9
1986	7,996	1,738	125	21.7
1987	8,989	1,604	113	17.8
1988	9,502	1,671	117	17.6
1989	9,536	1,686	117	17.7
1990	10,225	1,696	133	16.6

Sources 1948–1957: Shirle Gordon, 'Marriage/divorce in the eleven states of Malaya and Singapore,' *Intisari* 2, no.2 ; 1957-1970: data from Mahkamah Shariah, Kelantan State; 1973–1983:data from Mahkamah Khadi, Kelantan State; 1984-1990: data from Pejabat Qahdi Besar.

Kelantan, had a relatively low divorce rate of less than 50 per 100 marriages, while the districts of Tanah Merah and Ulu Kelantan in the upstream Kelantan river area had a high rate of over 70 divorces per 100 marriages. Ulu Kelantan, the district with the highest rate, had the following characteristics in 1970. (1) The main occupation was rubber tapping and women were able to earn their own living easily. (2) Transportation infrastructure was minimal and communities were small, making family life very important, but at the same time, creating a situation in which tensions within the family could easily arise. (3) Large numbers of migrants came to open new land, many of whom considered life harder than in their native region. (4) The level of education was low and modernization least advanced. Although Pasir Mas in which Galok is located had one of the lowest divorce rates, the divorce rate in Galok itself was almost as high as that in Tanah Merah, second only to Ulu Kelantan, and it had a very strong inland character compared to the rest of Pasir Mas district. Galok can therefore be considered to be located in a region of Kelantan with a relatively high divorce rate.

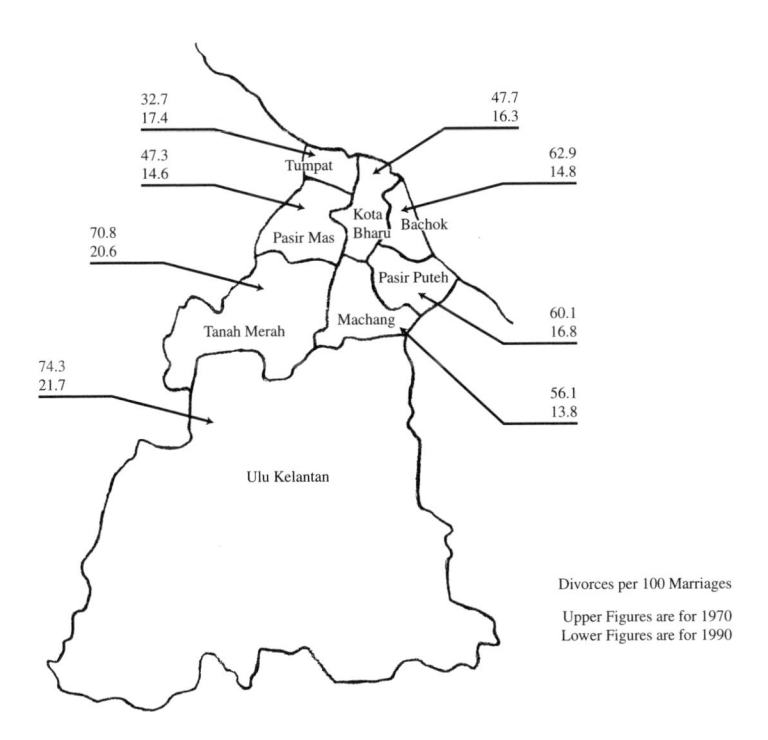

Figure 7-3. Divorce Rates for Each District in Kelantan

In 1990, the overall divorce rate had decreased, and regional differences were less noticeable. Even so, Ulu Kelantan, which had by then been divided into Jajahan Gua Musang and Jajahan Kuala Kerai, continued to show the highest divorce rate in the state, with 17.7 divorces per 100 marriages for the former district and 23.1 for the latter, and an overall divorce rate of 21.7.

Table 7-16
Number of Marriages and Divorces in Each District of Kelantan

DISTRICT (*Jajahan*)	1970			1990		
	MARRIAGES	DIVORCES	DIVORCES/100 MARRIAGES	MARRIAGES	DIVORCES	DIVORCES/100 MARRIAGES
Kota Bharu	2,321	1,107	47.7	3,079	503	16.3
Pasir Mas	1,311	620	47.3	1,266	185	14.6
Pasir Puteh	1,050	631	60.1	1,032	173	16.8
Machang	644	361	56.1	820	113	13.8
Bachok	838	527	62.9	802	119	14.8
Tumpat	805	263	32.7	991	172	17.4
Tanah Merah	677	479	70.8	945	195	20.6
Ulu Kelantan	490	364	74.3	(867)	(188)	(21.7)*
(Kuala Kerai)				636	147	23.1
(Gua Musang)				231	41	17.7

Sources: 1970, Mahkamah Shariah, Kelantan State; 1990, Pejabat Qadhi Besar, Kelantan State.
*Ulu Kelantan was divided into Kuala Kerai and Gua Musang districts in 1990.

8
Islam and Divorce in Three Malay Villages

This chapter compares the occurrence of divorce in Galok during the 1970/1971 study period with that of two other Malay villages which were studied around the same time (between 1968 and 1972), identifying both the common characteristics of families in villages on the Malay Peninsula and their diversity. At the same time, I will attempt to characterize the rural family of Kelantan within the context of the conditions prevailing in Malay society.

The location and features of the two other rural communities studied are as follows.

(1) Padang Lalang is located about 7.5 km from Alor Setar, the capital of Kedah state, in a fertile paddy-growing area known as the granary of Malaysia. Double cropping was introduced in the latter half of the 1960s with construction of an irrigation canal under the Muda River irrigation project. The village developed along the canal forming a ribbon settlement of 180 households with a total population of 897.

(2) Bukit Pegoh is located on a small, low-lying plain near the coast about 13 kilometers from Melaka city, and the main occupations were paddy farming, rubber tapping and migratory work. The 89 households were concentrated on an island of higher land surrounded by paddy fields and the total population was 481.

The study of Padang Lalang was conducted by Masuo Kuchiba, from 1968 to 1969, and that for Bukit Pegoh was conducted by Narifumi Maeda from 1971 to 1972.

8.1. Kinship Structure, Islamic Law, and Values

Although they differ in various details, the basic features of the kinship structures in the three villages were similar. The husband and wife in the Malay kinship system are in principle equally important. Despite adoption of the patrilineal Arabic naming system whereby the child takes the father's name, in Malay kin consciousness Ego is viewed as the center and the family tree fans outwards from the individual to both older and younger generations. As there are no surnames, the number of generations that one individual can remember is extremely limited. Kin groups formed on the basis of matrilineal, patrilineal or ambilineal principles dictating communal ownership or the succession of rituals or property to subsequent generations do not exist. Although the husband gives the wife a marriage payment when they marry, in principle this transaction takes place between the two individuals and kin are not involved as a group in its delivery or distribution. The average marriage payment for a first marriage in Padang Lalang from 1959 to 1968 was RM551, in Bukit Pegoh from 1956 to 1971 was RM360, and for Galok from 1961 to 1970 was RM229. This is equivalent to 20 percent or 30 percent of the average annual income for residents of each village, which in itself is not an unusually high sum.

Although there was no particular preference for cousin marriage, 18.1 percent of all marriages in Bukit Pegoh were to first cousins, while the figure for Padang Lalang was 9.1 percent and for Galok 3.4 percent. In Bukit Pegoh and Padang Lalang, the percentage of marriages to second cousins was much lower than that to first cousins, but in Galok it was about the same. Marriages to any kin including first and second cousins accounted for 42.5 percent of all marriages in Bukit Pegoh, 20.6 percent in Padang Lalang and 15.1 percent in Galok. There were no rules stipulating community endogamy in any of the three villages. Bukit Pegoh, an agglomerated settlement, had clearly defined boundaries, whereas the borders of Padang Lalang and Galok, ribbon settlements stretching along the irrigation canal and along a road, respectively, were indistinct. The rate of community endogamy was 47.6 percent for Bukit Pegoh, 22 percent for Padang Lalang, and 25.4 percent for Galok.

None of the three villages had any principles governing the selection of postmarital residence, and virilocal, uxorilocal or neolocal residence could be chosen according to one's individual circumstances. In both Padang Lalang and Galok people tended to choose the most advantageous location in terms of the size of paddy and rubber holdings, and virilocal residence was slightly more common than uxorilocal residence as a result of the inheritance patterns described later. In Bukit Pegoh, on the other hand, where there is less dependence on farmland and where other sources of income such as migratory work carry more weight, there was a higher proportion of uxorilocal residence.

Property is owned by the individual, and household property is the sum total of that owned by the husband, wife and other household members. Property jointly acquired by the married couple is, in principle, divided equally at the time of a divorce. In the case of inheritance, property is divided by either Islamic law where sons are awarded twice as much as daughters, or by customary law (*adat*) where all offspring receive equal shares. Although comparatively wealthy families tend to choose Islamic law, it is rarely strictly applied. Instead there is a tendency towards even distribution among both sons and daughters tempered to suit particular circumstances.

The household centers on one married couple and often appears to be nuclear in form. This, however, does not arise from any custom or ideological principle regarding household composition. Malay families are less cohesive than Japanese families, and could rather be viewed as a network of personal relationships. The household consists of the kin within this network who are closely connected to the central married couple, but the members do not always continue to live together. Depending on the circumstances, it is perfectly natural for a child to take one or both parents into his own household or for a grandchild to be adopted into a grandparents' household.

These characteristics of Malay kinship and family structure provided a foundation which facilitated a speedy resumption of family life after a divorce without many of the difficulties usually associated with such an event. At the same time, the lack of stability in personal relationships and the selection of postmarital residence by mutual consent rather than by any clear principle meant that discord between a husband and wife could easily lead to divorce.

Islam is an important foreign element that forms a standard for Malay behavior and influences attitudes towards marriage and divorce. Islamic law is based on the Koran and has regulations concerning all aspects of family life including marriage, divorce, and inheritance. The four methods of divorce stipulated in the Koran—*talak, pasah, tebus talak,* and *ta'alik*—are described in Chapter 7.

Although the application of Islamic law in Malaysia varies slightly from state to state, there were no fundamental differences between these divorce procedures in the three states of Kedah, Melaka, and Kelantan, where the survey villages were located. Islamic law is characterized by a high degree of flexibility in its application, and a few examples concerning marriage and divorce laws are cited below.

- Example 1: The marriage payment is mandatory, but the method for converting it to current monetary values and its relative importance is unclear, and therefore, the actual amount is left to the discretion of the society of the time.
- Example 2: In Islamic law a man is permitted to marry up to four wives but no more. One application of Islamic law allowed a man de facto to acquire more sexual partners by ownership of female slaves. Another application allowed a man to have a continuous series of wives through successive divorces. At the same time, however, a strict interpretation of the stipulation that a polygynous husband must treat

each of his wives equally can be used to support the prohibition of polygyny, because equal treatment is impossible.
- Example 3: *Talak*, or renunciation of the marriage contract, can only be implemented by the husband, regardless of his wife's wishes. Because, in fact, it is often used by husbands in automatically acceding to their wives' desire to terminate the marriage, *talak* makes divorce easy to obtain as long as one or other spouse wants it. Yet when this law is tempered by the Islamic tradition that, in the eyes of God, divorce is the most abhorrent of all the things permitted, it can be a very effective means of keeping divorce in check.

As can be seen from the above, it is possible to arrive at diametrically opposing interpretations of the same law, yet both extremes remain within the framework of Islam and can be supported by citing religious doctrine. The interpretation applied depends upon the customs that existed prior to the introduction of Islam and the effects of contact with other cultures and religions.

As aforementioned, the basic kinship structure of Malay society facilitates divorce, a fact supported by the prevalence of divorce in the proto-Malay Jakun society. Although the Jakun did not accept Islam, their kinship structure is almost identical to that of the Malays. (See Tsubouchi 1969, Maeda 1967, Maeda 1969, Logan 1847, Favre 1848, etc.) The adoption of Islamic law in Malay society may even have made divorce easier, because the individual could justify his actions in the name of God, whereas in Jakun society the authority of the community, kin and the chief remained somewhat more effective. On the other hand, exposure to Christian thought and Christian society which condemned divorce, and contact with European culture which embodied these values, caused the Malays to emphasize similar trends of thought found within the Islamic system. It is unlikely, however, that the latter were spontaneously adopted by the masses. Rather, these ideas were most probably introduced by the intelligentsia or the religious elite, in which case the condemnation of divorce would be carried out in the name of religion.

It seems clear from observations of the three farm villages that Islamic divorce laws in Galok, Kelantan were applied according to the more tolerant Malay interpretation in which divorce was treated as an individual's choice. The imam who registered divorces on behalf of the Islamic court dealt with applications as if they were routine office work. A person who declared *talak* had to pay a fee of RM12 to the Islamic court, 40 percent of which was subsequently returned to the imam as his fee. This sum was more than the average wage laborer made in one day and thus it was a source of income that would be hard for an imam to ignore. In contrast, Malays in Melaka are thought to have been more influenced by other outside forces because their location resulted in frequent contact with

Europeans and Chinese. In 1960 the state established a Department of Islam (Jabatan Ugama Islam) to integrate the proliferation of Islamic court judges under one religious administration, and it began a statewide campaign to reduce divorce. In addition, a popular religious teacher living in the Bukit Pegoh area preached against divorce. The Islamic courts and their representatives, the imams, who registered divorces, tried to persuade couples seeking divorce to reconcile. The attitude towards divorce in Kedah at this time was somewhere between that in Kelantan and Melaka, though perhaps slightly closer to Kelantan. Here, too, however, religious leaders took every opportunity to raise public awareness concerning the excessive number of divorces.

8.2. Divorce Features

Data on marriage and divorce in the three states where the study villages are located are presented in Table 8-1. Some of the data presented previously for Kelantan have been reused here, while much of the data for Kedah are missing. Data for Melaka are from 1930 to 1971. Judging from the ratio of divorces to marriages, Kelantan had the highest divorce rate of the three states, followed by Kedah and lastly by Melaka. It is impossible to determine whether this trend existed prior to 1948 because earlier data for Kedah and Kelantan were unobtainable. If we assume that the divorce rate in every state in the past was never lower than that in the early 1950s, it follows that the divorce rate for Melaka even at the beginning of the 1930s was lower than that for the other two states. The number of divorces per 100 marriages in Melaka from 1931 to 1935 was 38.8. From 1951 to 1955 it was 31.1, while in Kedah it was 61.4 and in Kelantan, 76. The ratio of divorces in Melaka sharply increased in 1945 and 1946, partly as a result of the sudden rise in the number of marriages in the preceding years, which indicates that some fluctuations probably occurred in the divorce rate in the past as well, rather than there being a consistently higher divorce rate prior to 1930.

Keeping the above qualifications in mind, it appears that the divorce rate in Melaka state has been lower than in other states from early in its history. Moreover, a marked decline began in 1962 and from 1966 to 1970 only 11.8 percent of marriages ended in divorce. In contrast, Kelantan appears to have a traditionally high number of divorces, although it is doubtful whether the extremely high rate of 93.1 divorces per 100 marriages in 1948 and 90.6 in 1950 was normal in preceding years. Rather some fluctuation may also have occurred in this state. Kelantan did not see a sudden decline in the divorce rate until around 1970, several years after that in Melaka. A gradual decrease did occur with the number of divorces dropping to as low as 56 per 100 marriages from 1966 to 1970, but this was still much higher than that for Melaka even at its highest in the early 1930s. Due to insufficient data, it was not possible to clearly identify divorce trends in Kedah state, but the fact that there were only 50.7 divorces per 100 marriages in 1964 indicates that this state also witnessed a gradual decline.

Data for the three states concerning the percentage of *rojok*, or revocations of divorce, reveals several differences. Kedah had the highest number, while Kelantan and Melaka had relatively fewer. Comparing the values for the period from 1951 to 1955, 25.6 percent of divorces were revoked by *rojok* in Kedah (excluding 1953, data for which were missing), 10.9 percent in Melaka, and 8.7 percent in Kelantan. These figures indicate that while a declaration of *talak* in Kelantan was very likely to end in divorce, in Kedah there was a high possibility that it would be revoked upon reconsideration. The decrease in revocations in Melaka, on the other hand, seems to have resulted from more careful consideration of the initial decision to divorce. The difference between Kedah and Melaka, then, was the higher percentage of reflection after the decision was made versus prior deliberation, and perhaps Kedah can be viewed as being in the early stages of a decline in divorce rates and Melaka in the later stages.

Divorce rates in the three study villages similarly differed noticeably. Of all marriages contracted by residents of Galok (Kelantan), 40.6 percent ended in divorce compared to 16.1 percent in Padang Lalang (Kedah) and 10.2 percent in Bukit Pegoh (Melaka). As the same person may marry and divorce more than once, the percentage of married people who divorced was 37.7 percent for Galok, 17.7 percent for Padang Lalang, and 7.2 percent for Bukit Pegoh. This order mirrors that of the divorce rates for each state.

As only 13 cases of divorce were reported for men and women in Bukit Pegoh, I will attempt a slightly more detailed comparison of the occurrence of divorce in Galok and Padang Lalang which had more cases. Table 8-2 presents the percentage of married people who divorced according to sex and age. Although information on the incidence of divorce was unclear for a high percentage of women in Padang Lalang, if we assume that it did not greatly exceed that for men, the percentage of people who divorced is greater in Galok than in Padang Lalang for all ages excluding those in the lower age groups, which had very few divorces. The number of times married people divorced is presented in Table 8-3. A significant number of people in Galok had divorced twice or more. In Table 8-4 and 8-5 data for men and women who have divorced is organized according to the length of time they were married and the number of children. An accurate comparison is difficult due to the amount of unclear data for Padang Lalang, but the general trends are described hereunder. The percentage of divorces that occurred within the first year of marriage is higher in Galok, with 28.4 percent for men and 24.8 percent for women, compared to 13.1 percent for men and 12.5 percent for women in

Table 8-1
Yearly Changes in Marriage and Divorce in Kelantan, Kedah and Melaka

YEAR	KELANTAN			KEDAH			MELAKA		
	MARRIAGES	DIVORCES	Rojok	MARRIAGES	DIVORCES	Rojok	MARRIAGES	DIVORCES	Rojok
1930							1,358	653	97
1931							1,118	548	70
1932							1,233	537	69
1933							1,369	551	66
1934							1,640	526	66
1935							1,549	519	57
1936							1,466	545	74
1937							1,771	595	53
1938							1,576	461	46
1939							1,452	514	57
1940							1,690	629	64
1941							2,063	587	75
1942							1,892	629	75
1943							3,066	940	101
1944							3,223	1,344	166
1945							2,793	1,699	216
1946							1,936	993	87
1947							1,859	759	75
1948	12,488	11,625	683	7,724	5,032	884	1,767	711	52
1949	13,256	11,384	1,007	7,222	4,645	1,116	1,924	670	66
1950	12,326	11,163	768	8,945	5,170	1,117	2,159	729	78
1951	13,131	10,247	923	9,621	4,977	1,323	2,693	805	100
1952	11,391	9,298	805	7,266	4,801	1,061	2,235	633	77
1953	11,092	8,777	657	6,778	4,285		1,943	648	70
1954	10,003	7,549	681	5,789	3,968	1,087	1,871	604	60
1955	11,639	7,660	702	5,814	3,634	984	1,945	632	54
1956	13,830	7,846	749	4,836	3,173	737	2,099	625	69
1957	7,611	4,747	467	6,940	3,924	982	1,939	560	66
1958	10,723	8,530	644				1,969	536	60
1959	10,054	6,856	738				1,977	582	56
1960	9,810	6,363	668				2,003	564	61
1961	7,176	5,068	514				1,865	544	50
1962	8,399	5,463	517				1,441	213	18
1963	7,987	5,278	1,447				1,687	315	9
1964	8,264	5,270	584	5,105	2,589	671	1,633	263	26
1965	8,275	5,052	519				1,773	260	18
1966	8,177	4,395	810				1,672	170	13
1967	6,933	4,489	458				1,813	225	11
1968	7,703	4,423	419				1,772	225	12
1969	8,668	4,518	546				1,860	204	13
1970	8,136	4,352	583				1,908	240	6
1971							2,025	210	4

All data were collected by Jabatan Ugama Islam (Department of Religion), and the published data were subsequently compiled by Gordon (n.d.), Djamour (1959), Umeda (1966), Maeda (1974), Tsubouchi (1972), and others.

Padang Lalang. The percentage of people who divorced after they had children was 42.0 percent for men and 40.2 percent for women in Galok compared to 47.4 percent for men and a much higher 75.0 percent for women in Padang Lalang. The difference in the percentages for men and women in Padang Lalang is due to the fact that women who had been divorced but did not have children declined to admit their divorce in interviews. Thus, it is highly probable that the category of unclear in Table 8-2 includes divorced women without children. A comparison of the data shows that the decline in divorces was accompanied by a reduction in the number of people repeating divorce and in the number of divorces occurring early in marriage.

The relationship between divorce trends and kin marriages for the three villages was investigated with the following results. In Bukit Pegoh 5.6 percent

Table 8-2
Number and Percentage of People Divorced in Galok and Padang Lalang

GALOK (KELANTAN)

Age	Men				Women			
	Ever Married	Ever Divorced	Unclear	Percentage	Ever Married	Ever Divorced	Unclear	Percentage
10–19					11	1		9.1
20–29	31	3		9.7	40	8		20.0
30–39	33	9		27.3	34	13		38.2
40–49	30	14		46.7	38	19		50.0
50–59	22	15		68.2	23	12		52.2
60–	16	10		62.5	19	8		42.1
Total	132	51		38.6	165	61		37.0

PADANG LALANG (KEDAH)

Age	Men				Women			
	Ever Married	Ever Divorced	Unclear	Percentage	Ever Married	Ever Divorced	Unclear	Percentage
10–19					5		1	
20–29	29	3		10.3	57	10	4	17.5
30–39	58	7	1	12.1	61	7	3	11.5
40–49	37	8		21.6	31	6	2	19.4
50–59	23	5		21.7	32	6	7	18.8
60–	26	10	1	38.5	31	7	10	22.6
Total	173	33	2	19.1	217	36	27	16.6

Table 8-3
Number of Ever-married People in Galok and Padang Lalang by Number of Times Divorced

	GALOK		PADANG LALANG	
NUMBER OF TIMES DIVORCED	MEN	WOMEN	MEN	WOMEN
0	80	103	138	154
1	29	31	23	33
2	9	12	7	2
3	6	12	3	1
4	3	4		
5	1	2		
6	3			
Unclear	1	1	2	27
Total	132	165	173	217

Excluding 2 cases of *pasah* in Galok. Figures for Padang Lalang are from Kuchiba's unpublished materials.

Table 8-4
Number of Divorces by Duration of Marriage in Galok and Padang Lalang

	FOR MEN		FOR WOMEN	
DURATION	GALOK	PADANG LALANG	GALOK	PADANG LALANG
< 1 year	27	5	29	2
≈ 1 year	23	7	18	4
2 years	14	7	19	5
3 years	10	5	14	1
4 years	8		4	1
5 years	3	3	8	
6 years	1	1	8	
7 years	2		4	2
8 years	1	2	1	
9 years			3	1
10 years +	6	8	9	
Total	95	38	117	16

Unclear cases (5 men in Galok, 11 men and 23 women in Padang Lalang) are not included.

Table 8-5
Number of Divorces by Number of Children in Galok and
Padang Lalang

NUMBER OF CHILDREN	FOR MEN		FOR WOMEN	
	GALOK	PADANG LALANG	GALOK	PADANG LALANG
0	58	20	70	4
1	28	12	33	11
2	8	2	9	1
3	4	3	4	
4	1	1		
5 +	1		1	
Total	100	38	117	16

Excluding unclear cases (11 men and 23 women in Padang Lalang).

of total kin marriages ended in divorce, much lower than the 13.7 percent of total marriages to non-kin that ended in divorce. In Padang Lalang, 7.3 percent of kin marriages and 19.9 percent of non-kin marriages ended in divorce, and although higher than the percentages for Bukit Pegoh, the relative relationship between the two remains the same. In contrast, 40.7 percent of kin marriages in Galok ended in divorce versus 40.1 percent of non-kin marriages, showing a negligible difference between the two.

The percentage of marriages to first cousins, the most important kin, that ended in divorce was 0 percent for Bukit Pegoh, 1.9 percent for Padang Lalang and 66.7 percent for Galok. Residents of each village studied viewed marriages to first cousins as more likely to be compatible but at the same time as a potential source of conflict between the parents, siblings to each other, should a divorce arise. It is possible to interpret the figures for Bukit Pegoh and Padang Lalang as evidence that first cousin marriages are more satisfying or that reconciliation is more effective if discord arises, but this does not hold true for Galok. Rather, there seems to be a tendency for Galok residents to avoid first cousin marriages because of the potential for divorce. The percentage of first cousin marriages in Galok was significantly lower than for the other two villages and, as if to compensate, there were a greater number of marriages to more distant second cousins.

There was insufficient data to compare the effect of community endogamy on divorce for the three villages, but if we look only at Galok, 28.6 percent of endogamous marriages ended in divorce, which is significantly lower than the 44.6 percent of marriages to people outside the community.

8.3. Comparison and Observations

Although kinship structure in all three villages was basically the same, attitudes towards kin marriages, including first cousin marriages, caused some slight differences. However, the low divorce rates in Padang Lalang and Bukit Pegoh cannot be entirely explained by the high proportion of kin marriages. As was pointed out earlier, the high divorce rate in Galok applied equally to both kin and non-kin marriages, while Padang Lalang's divorce rate was in the middle and Bukit Pegoh was the lowest. The fact that kin marriages in Galok did not act as a deterrent suggests that they do not automatically curb divorce. Moreover, although first cousin marriages seemed to function as a deterrent to divorce in Bukit Pegoh and Padang Lalang, the percentage of first cousin marriages that comprised the total number of marriages was only 18.1 percent and 9.7 percent, respectively, and therefore, the low rate of divorce for these marriages only partly explains the overall low divorce rate in both villages.

Narifumi Maeda also studied Bukit Meta, a village near Bukit Pegoh in Melaka state. First-cousin marriages comprised only 8.1 percent of all marriages in this village, while kin marriages, including first cousin marriages, accounted for 22.5 percent. This proportion is much lower than that for Bukit Pegoh, and is about the same as that for Padang Lalang. The percentage of marriages that ended in divorce in Bukit Meta was only 7.5 percent, while only 5.5 percent of married people had ever been divorced. Both of these rates are lower than those for Bukit Pegoh, indicating that the effect of first cousin or kin marriages in curbing divorce should not be overrated.

Similarly with regards to the controlling effect of community endogamy on divorce, when we compare marriages to people within the same community to those with outsiders, even if there is a lower divorce rate for the former, it is not possible to claim that places with a low proportion of community endogamy will have higher divorce rates or visa versa, a point clearly demonstrated by the low divorce rate in Padang Lalang compared to Galok despite the fact that the former had less community endogamy. In other words, divorce rates for marriages to members of the same community and those to outsiders only relate to relative differences in the divorce trends among the members of a specific community.

From the above observations, it is obvious that the differences in divorce trends among the three villages cannot be explained by differences in social or kinship structure. They can, however, be understood as a manifestation, or even an augmentation, within traditional Malay Islam of the tolerance for divorce inherent within the Malay kinship structure, and as a result of the process of modernization in which Islamic teachings on marriage were reinterpreted.

In this study, Galok is considered to be a typical example of traditional Malay Islam, as described earlier. But was this type of Islam common to all areas of Kelantan at that time? Studies by Raymond and Rosemary Firth of a fishing village along the coast of Kelantan and by Richard Downs of a farm village in Pasir Puteh district both point out the high divorce rates in these

Table 8-6
Marriage and Divorce among Muslims in Singapore, 1921–1991

Year	Marriages	Divorces	Divorces Per 100 Marriages	Year	Marriages	Divorces	Divorces Per 100 Marriages
1921	2,055	1,133	55.1	1957	2,303	1,201	52.1
1922	2,073	1,239	59.8	1958	2,332	1,149	49.3
1923	2,113	1,205	57.0	1959	2,116	577	27.3
1924	3,089	1,285	41.6	1960	1,814	574	31.6
1925	2,616	1,311	50.1	1961	1,560	401	25.7
1926	2,633	1,335	50.7	1962	1,483	447	30.1
1927	2,554	1,466	57.4	1963	1,690	430	25.4
1928	2,556	1,421	55.6	1964	1,698	324	19.1
1929	2,469	1,428	57.8	1965	1,928	366	19.0
1930	2,307	1,366	52.9	1966	1,911	301	15.8
1931	2,177	1,264	58.1	1967	1,894	374	19.7
1932	2,084	1,277	61.3	1968	1,971	200	10.1
1933	2,006	1,260	62.8	1969	1,972	244	12.4
1934	2,163	1,132	52.3	1970	2,272	219	9.6
1935	2,070	1,159	56.0	1971	2,471	241	9.8
1936	2,039	1,182	58.0	1972	2,662		
1937	2,320	1,208	52.1	1973	2,823		
1938	2,065	1,241	60.1	1974	2,895		
1939	2,014	1,145	56.9	1975	3,233	304	9.4
1940	2,213	1,249	56.4	1976	2,946	300	10.2
1941	2,440	1,267	51.9	1977	3,163	377	11.9
1942	2,949	1,139	38.6	1978	3,109	357	11.5
1943	3,582	1,705	47.6	1979	3,677	515	14.0
1944	2,907	2,165	74.5	1980	4,032	505	12.5
1945	2,982	2,046	68.6	1981	4,429	614	13.9
1946	3,095	1,734	56.0	1982	4,822	536	11.1
1947	2,784	1,588	57.0	1983	4,594	711	15.5
1948	2,605	1,545	59.3	1984	4,494	637	14.2
1949	2,516	1,401	55.7	1985	4,563	738	16.2
1950	2,506	1,501	59.9	1986	4,385	786	17.9
1951	2,699	1,526	56.6	1987	4,465	796	17.8
1952	2,658	1,474	55.5	1988	4,801	893	18.6
1953	2,445	1,417	58.0	1989	4,794	907	18.9
1954	2,457	1,357	55.2	1990	4,762	972	20.4
1955	2,472	1,247	50.4	1991	4,806	1,021	21.2
1956	2,414	1,074	44.5				

Sources: 1921–1964, Djamour (1959) p.117 and Djamour (1966) p.129 & p.183; 1965–1968, *Singapore Year Book* 1968, p.80; 1969–1970, *Singapore 1971*, p.262; 1971–1972, *Singapore 1972*, p.63 & p.265; from 1973 to the present, *Year Book of Statistics Singapore* 1981/82, 1985/86, 1991.

areas. In the Firths' study, 82.6 percent of men and 80 percent of women had been married twice or more, and 63 percent of villagers in Down's study had been married twice or more. Because they include remarriages of widows and widowers, these figures are not equivalent to the divorce rate, yet even so they are higher than the rate of remarriage in Galok, which was 38.6 percent for men and 41.2 percent for women. The studies, carried out in 1940 and 1958, respectively, were both in areas some distance from a town. Even considering the higher death rate at that time, we can surmise from these figures that traditional divorce rates were higher than those for Galok in 1970.

On the other hand, as will be shown later, Kubang Bemban, a village adjacent to the town with the district office, had a much lower divorce rate of 26.8 percent for men and 19.4 percent for women at that time despite its location in the same district as Galok. These cases illustrate that Kelantan was also undergoing a gradual transformation, and that differences within the state were already pronounced. The subsequent decline in the divorce rate in Kelantan and the equalization of regional discrepancies have already been discussed. Pronounced regional differences in divorce rates on the Malay Peninsula are considered to have been a temporary phenomenon. Although the period was far from short, it would be erroneous to view the situation as static because the occurrence of divorce declined in correspondence with the reinterpretation of Islamic teachings.

This change was not restricted to Malaysia. The divorce rate among Muslims (mainly Malays) in neighboring Singapore and also among those in Indonesia clearly decreased from the beginning of the 1960s. Changes in the number of marriages and divorces among Muslims in Singapore are presented in Table 8-6. The reduction in the divorce rate was even more organized and systematic than in Melaka consisting of revisions to the divorce law in 1957 that were implemented from the top levels of administration in 1958, and the establishment of a matrimonial court. Divorce laws were further revised in 1966 to curtail divorce even more strictly. The role of Islamic leaders at the local level was less pronounced in Singapore than in Melaka.

The divorce rate among Muslims in Singapore reached its lowest point between 1970 and 1975, when there were only 10 divorces per 100 marriages, but began rising again in 1976 with the number of divorces per 100 marriages exceeding 20 by the 1990s. It should be noted that after the divorce rate had declined due to modern reinterpretations of Islamic teachings, it rose again among the predominantly Malay Muslims in Singapore in correspondence with urbanization. This is similar to changes in divorce trends in Japan from the late 19th century to the present, and in contrast to divorce trends in Europe and North America.

A variety of movements to reduce divorce also arose in Indonesia, and as shown in Table 8-7, a noticeable reduction in the number of divorces began from around 1965. Changes in the number of marriages and divorces in each district of Java are shown in Table 8-8, and a marked decline occurred at an early date in Jakarta and Jogjakarta special districts which include two major political and cultural urban centers of the same names. After 1985, divorce in Jarkarta and Jogjakarta special districts sank as low as Singapore's lowest value ever, and was far below that for Singapore in the same year. The divorce rate in Java remained low thereafter, and the rates in all states for 1990/1991 were far below Singapore's lowest figure. These changes accompanied revisions in legal procedures and like Singapore, were probably temporary in nature.

The kinship structures of the Malays in the Malay Peninsula and Singapore and of the Javanese and Sundanese in Java were characterized by a permissive approach to divorce. Even if Islam had not been introduced into their society, the direct reflection of the indigenous kinship structure is likely to have resulted in a relatively strong tendency towards divorce. The interaction of Islam with this social structure functioned both to encourage and to discourage divorce. Initially the tolerance for divorce within the existing kinship structure was reinforced by the Islamic view that the individual was responsible to God, freeing him from community conventions and allowing him to justify his actions in the name of religion. The deterrent factors inherent in Islam were only activated later by a wave of modernization that caused this aspect to receive more attention and emphasis. These examples give us a glimpse of the flexibility that characterizes Islam. In this chapter I have recorded how Islamic modernization took the form of legal revisions manifested in current national policies. The kinship structure was influenced by these types of changes, resulting in the alteration of some of its forms. Changes in marriage and divorce in Galok must therefore be observed as one phenomenon within the larger context of major changes that were occurring within the contemporary Islamic society of Southeast Asia.

Table 8-7
Marriage and Divorce among Muslims in Indonesia

YEAR	MARRIAGES (× 1,000)	DIVORCES (× 1,000)	Rojok (× 1,000)	DIVORCES PER 100 MARRIAGES	Rojok PER 100 DIVORCES
1950	1,276	629	43	49.3	6.8
1951	1,443	815	61	56.5	7.5
1952	1,310	783	59	59.8	7.5
1953	1,417	723	76	51.0	10.5
1954	1,383	735	56	53.1	7.6
1955	1,313	760	62	57.9	8.2
1956	1,086	584	42	53.8	7.2
1957	1,148	598	40	52.1	6.7
1958	1,242	672	49	54.1	7.3
1959	1,320	697	56	52.8	8.0
1960	1,254	654	55	52.2	8.4
1961	1,162	606	48	52.2	7.9
1962	1,036	593	45	57.2	7.6
1963	1,321	670	56	50.7	8.4
1964	1,130	613	46	54.2	7.5
1965	1,178	578	48	49.1	8.3
1966	1,097	513	37	46.8	7.2
1967	804	325	20	40.4	6.2
1968	1,042	468	24	44.9	5.1
1969	1,099	411	24	37.4	5.8
1970	859	298	11	34.7	3.7
1971	890	276	9	31.0	3.3
1972	989	303	10	30.6	3.3
1973	768	238	8	31.0	3.4
1974	1,180	324	12	27.5	3.7
1975	1,152	303	11	26.3	3.6
1976	935	107	2	11.4	1.9
1977	1,082	169	2	15.6	1.2
1978	1,242	212	3	17.1	1.4
1979	1,125	189	3	16.8	1.6
1980	1,190	199	3	16.7	1.5
1981	1,176	244	3	20.7	1.2
1982	1,150	180	3	15.7	1.7
1983/84	1,158	176	3	15.2	1.7
1984/85	1,110	167	3	15.0	1.8
1985/86	1,249	132	3	10.6	2.3
1986/87	1,227	156	2	12.7	1.3
1987/88	1,179	155	3	13.1	1.9
1988/89	1,276	132	2	10.3	1.5
1989/90	1,211	113	1	9.3	0.9
1990/91	1,338	61	1	4.6	1.7

Data compiled from *Statistical Pocketbook of Indonesia* for each year from 1953 to 1963 and for 1971/72 and 1972/73, and from *Statistik Indonesia* for the years 1976, 1983, 1988 and 1992.

Table 8-8
Marriage and Divorce among Muslims in Java

REGION	YEAR	MARRIAGES	DIVORCES	Rojok	DIVORCES PER 100 MARRIAGES	Rojok PER 100 DIVORCES
West Java	1953	355,170	217,237	17,763	61.2	8.2
	1964	245,081	152,029	13,047	62.0	8.6
	1970	223,457	81,423	2,893	36.4	3.6
	1975	296,871	100,917	4,181	34.0	4.1
	1980	259,181	46,783	1,474	18.1	3.2
	1985/86	493,513	30,358	1,764	6.2	5.8
	1990/91	321,428	12,956	564	4.0	4.4
East Java	1953	451,898	243,163	37,613	53.8	5.5
	1964	244,944	149,109	9,384	60.9	6.3
	1970	265,859	107,533	4,084	40.4	3.8
	1975	333,905	94,439	2,785	28.3	2.9
	1980	320,523	64,438	717	20.1	1.1
	1985/86	275,871	49,177	487	17.8	1.0
	1990/91	294,821	18,412	204	6.2	1.1
Central Java	1953	376,490	187,834	11,433	49.9	6.1
	1964	238,661	137,826	7,383	57.7	5.4
	1970	209,203	77,320	2,539	37.0	3.3
	1975	290,534	75,111	2,141	25.9	2.9
	1980	284,757	57,584	598	20.2	1.0
	1985/86	155,332	27,362	208	17.6	0.8
	1990/91	274,399	19,777	215	7.2	1.1
D.K.I. Jakarta	1953	28,623	11,706	1,194	40.9	10.2
	1964	32,434	12,981	1,397	40.0	10.8
	1970	26,340	4,971	259	18.9	5.2
	1975	29,515	3,030	148	10.3	4.9
	1980	32,794	3,889	110	11.9	2.8
	1985/86	31,142	2,974	62	9.5	2.1
	1990/91	38,240	870	16	2.3	1.8
D.I Yogyakarta	1953	30,933	11,796	460	38.1	3.9
	1964	4,426	3,225	63	72.9	2.0
	1970	19,862	5,284	146	26.6	2.8
	1975	24,811	3,691	100	14.9	2.7
	1980	24,625	2,839	26	11.5	0.9
	1985/86	25,825	2,813	35	10.9	1.2
	1990/91	24,640	2,106	3	8.5	0.1

Sources: 1953, Djamour (1959) p.135; 1964, Nugroho (1967) p.175; 1970, *Statistical Pocketbook of Indonesia, 1970 & 1971*, p.43; 1975, *Statistik Indonesia*, 1976; 1980, *Statistik Indonesia*, 1983; 1985/86, *Statistik Indonesia*, 1988; 1990/91, *Statistik Indonesia* 1992.

9
Changes in Population and Households

9.1. Follow-up Survey Conducted in 1991

A detailed study on changes in population and households in Galok was conducted from September to November 1991. Using the data cards on individual household composition compiled during the first survey in 1970/1971, each household still existing was revisited to determine whether the original household members were alive, and if so, what type of household composition now exists and what types of increases have occurred in kin members both inside and outside the village through marriages, births, etc. Data concerning those who had moved into the village since 1971 were also collected. In the twenty-year period, many household members had established independent households in Galok, and accordingly, duplication of data on the same household or individual was unavoidable. Although overlapping data and discrepancies in the number of children, ages, etc. were eliminated as much as possible when organizing the data, the figures recorded in this chapter are only provisional. Moreover data on household composition from the 1984 survey used to relate data from 1970/1971 with those from 1991 were not entirely reliable, as some information was collected through indirect sources such as interviews with neighbors or kin. It is also possible that some people who moved into the village from outside after 1971 and then either moved away again or died before 1991 were omitted from the data.

9.2. Changes in Population Composition

The population of Galok grew from 690 in 1971 to 1,100 in 1991. This section looks at the form this increase took. Figure 9-1 shows the population pyramid for 1991 superimposed upon that for 1971. It is obvious that the number of people in all age groups except women over 85 had increased by 1991. A comparison of the percentage of the total population in each age group for the two survey years is shown in Figure 9-2. Despite the overall growth shown in

Figure 9-1, no major alterations occurred in the shape of the pyramid. Close observation, however, reveals two slight changes. One is a decrease in the percentage of people comprising the younger age groups, particularly men aged 20–24, but also men in the 25–29 and 30–34 age groups, and women in the 20–24 and 15–19 age groups. Although this change has not yet resulted in a decrease in real numbers, it does reflect a significant increase in the outflow of younger people from the village. The other change is a rise in the percentage of the population comprising the older age groups, excluding men aged 65–69 years and women over 85. This reflects the aging of residents remaining in the village from 1971 due to the lower death rate and other factors. In addition, the number of girls aged 0–4 in the 1991 population pyramid is remarkably low, but whether this was merely a statistical coincidence, a result of the subjects' disregard for girls under five years of age, or a failure to distinguish correctly between boys and girls, is not clear at this time.

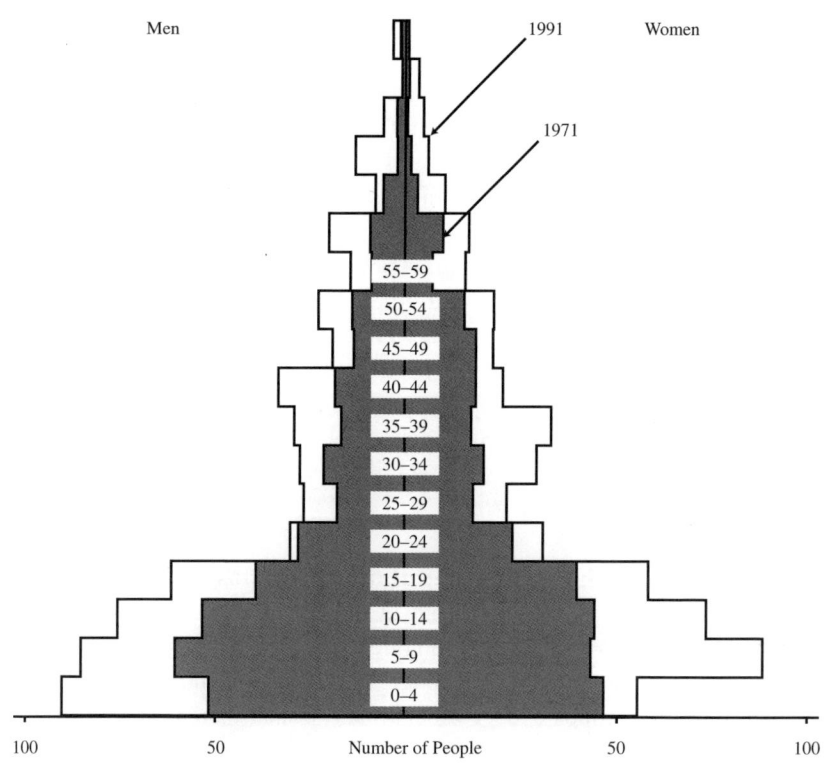

Figure 9-1. Population Pyramids for 1971 and 1991 (Actual Population)

Figure 9-3 presents the population pyramid for 1971 compared to the number of 1971 residents still living in Galok in 1991. The distribution of age and sex in the 1991 population forms a tower rather than a pyramid shape. It must be noted, however, that the significance of the number belonging to the under 25 age groups in 1971 who still lived in Galok in 1991 is different from that of those over 25. The majority of the latter were already married in 1971, and accordingly their spouses were counted as residents of Galok regardless of their native origin. In contrast, many people in the younger age groups were single in 1971 and might since have married a spouse from another village. Thus the shape of the 1991 pyramid with regards to age composition is not particularly meaningful in itself.

If postmarital residence follows virilocal principles then the sex ratio of those still resident in the younger age groups should be quite high, whereas if it follows uxorilocal principles, it should be quite low. In fact, however, neither

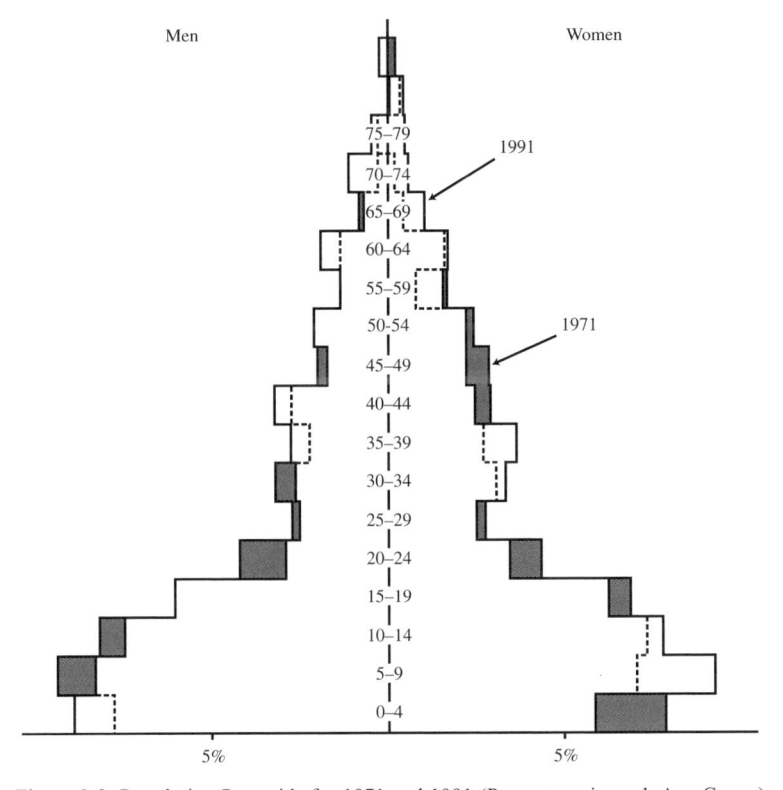

Figure 9-2. Population Pyramids for 1971 and 1991 (Percentage in each Age Group)

of these trends was evident. The sex ratio among still resident villagers was only 0.9, reflecting the common Malay tendency towards the selection of postmarital residence on the basis of bilateral principles and individual circumstances. It also reflects the fact that comparatively fewer men remained in the village than women.

The differences between the population pyramid for 1971 and the pyramid for people remaining in 1991 are the result of deaths and out-migration. In Figure 9-4, the number of those who died, regardless of the place of death, has been added to the data shown in Figure 9-3 on the number of 1971 residents still living in Galok in 1991. It is evident that very few Galok residents who were over 30 in 1971 had moved out of the village in 1991. In contrast, the out-migration of people in the under-19 age groups surpassed the number of those the same age who stayed. Figure 9-5 shows the 1971 population still resident in Galok superimposed upon the population pyramid

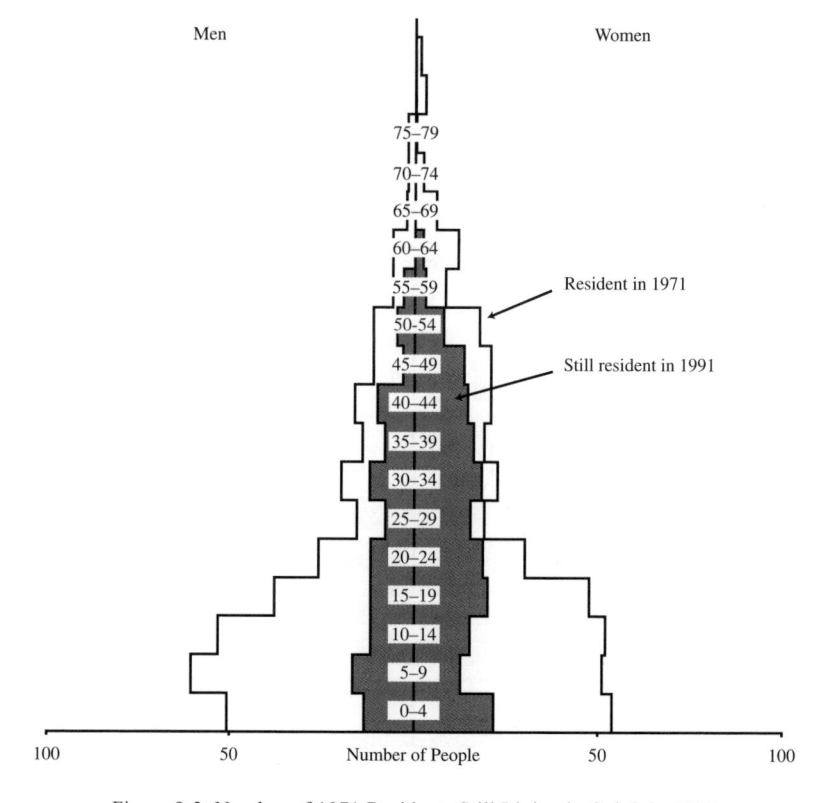

Figure 9-3. Number of 1971 Residents Still Living in Galok in 1991

for 1991. A comparison of Figures 9-4 and 9-5 reveals that the outflow of people under nineteen (aged 20–39 in 1991) far exceeded the inflow of people the same age. This becomes even more obvious if we compare separate diagrams of out-migration versus in-migration as in Figure 9-6. In the over-20 age groups (over 40 in 1991), however, newcomers exceeded outgoing migrants for both men and women, indicating that population growth in Galok can be partly attributed to immigrating couples who established independent households. It also reveals the mobile character of the village population.

The main out-migration destinations of the 1971 population, in other words, their place of residence in 1991, are shown in Table 9-1. As can be seen, they moved to all parts of Malaysia, more than one third (35.7 percent) of them out of Kelantan. It should be noted that the sex ratio of migrants moving out of state is generally high, while that of migrants moving within the state is

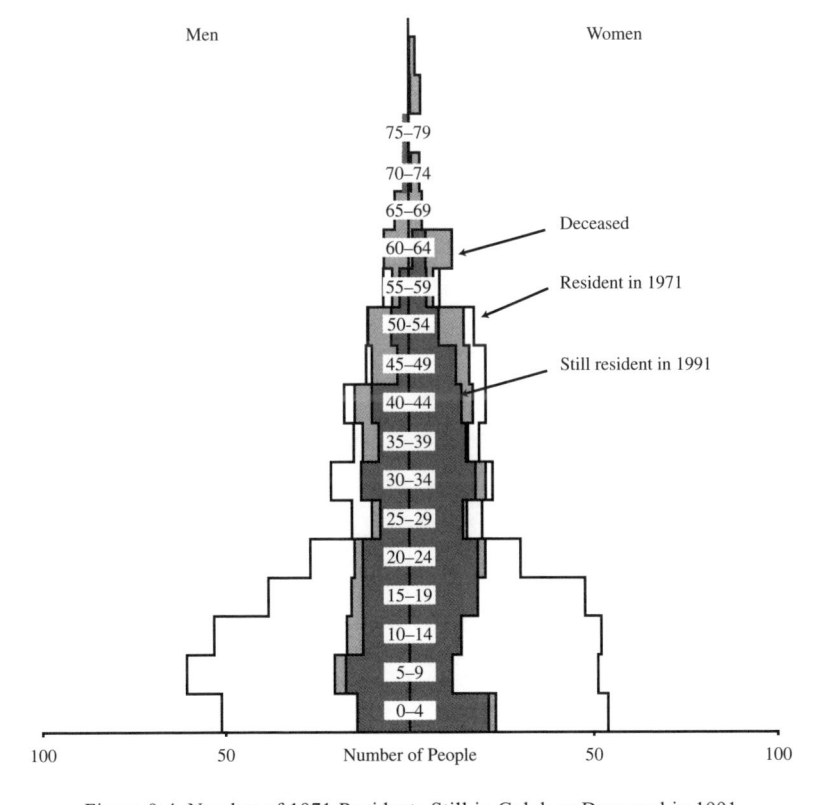

Figure 9-4. Number of 1971 Residents Still in Galok or Deceased in 1991

comparatively low and in some cases the proportion of women is higher. In terms of the sex ratio, migration to Ulu Kelantan district (now divided into Kuala Kerai and Gua Musang districts) resembles out-of-state migration. It is in fact farther away from Galok than other districts, and government and other development projects provide more opportunities for employment. Another notable feature is that out-migration to Kuala Lumpur occurred only among those who were under 19 years of age in 1971. This does not eliminate the possibility that some people at the time of the 1971 survey may already have moved to Kuala Lumpur; however, it does illustrate that migration to the capital rose rapidly among the relatively younger age groups. Although only twenty-six (fifteen men and eleven women) of those aged over 30 in 1971 were resident outside of Galok in 1991, this nevertheless shows that migration was not limited to the young. One major characteristic of their movement, however, was that their destinations were all within Kelantan state.

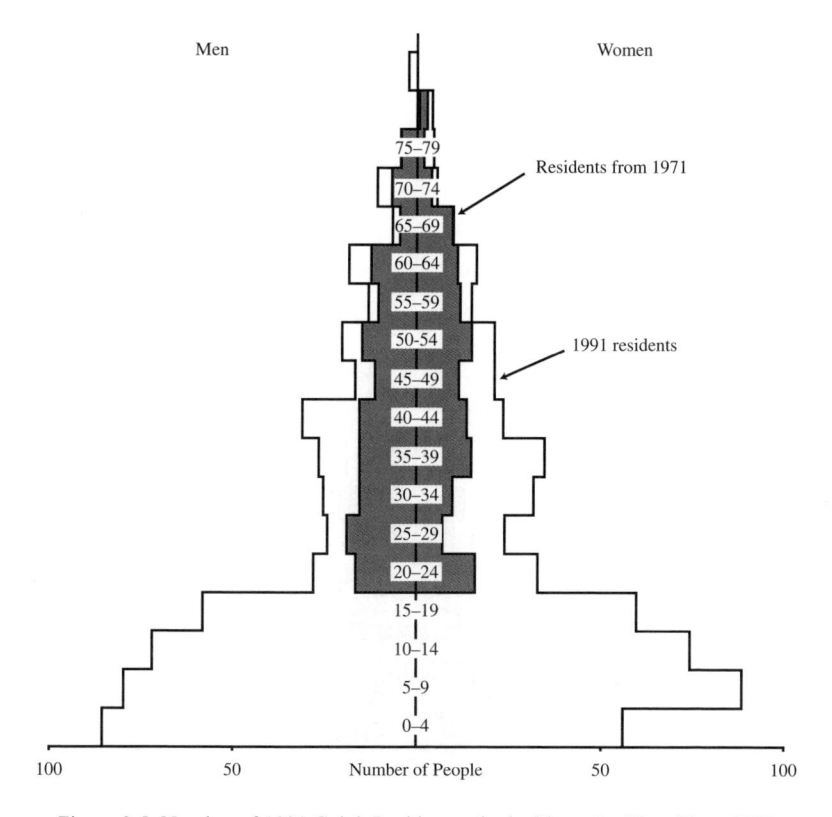

Figure 9-5. Number of 1991 Galok Residents who had been Resident Since 1971

Let us look at the role births, deaths and the resultant natural population increase played in the changes that occurred in the Galok population over the twenty-year period. At the time of the first survey in 1970/1971, family planning had begun to penetrate rural areas of Malaysia, and at least several people in Galok were receiving the Pill. Before family planning could take root, however, there was a change in national policy, and the movement towards population control petered out, at least in rural areas of Kelantan including Galok. With the spread of education, the age at which women first married, around eighteen in 1970/1971, rose noticeably, and this was accompanied by a corresponding decrease in the number of births during a woman's child-bearing years. At the same time, however, a decline in the infant and child mortality meant that the number of children surviving to maturity was almost the same. Here, I have tried to estimate the general trends in population movement during the twenty-year period.

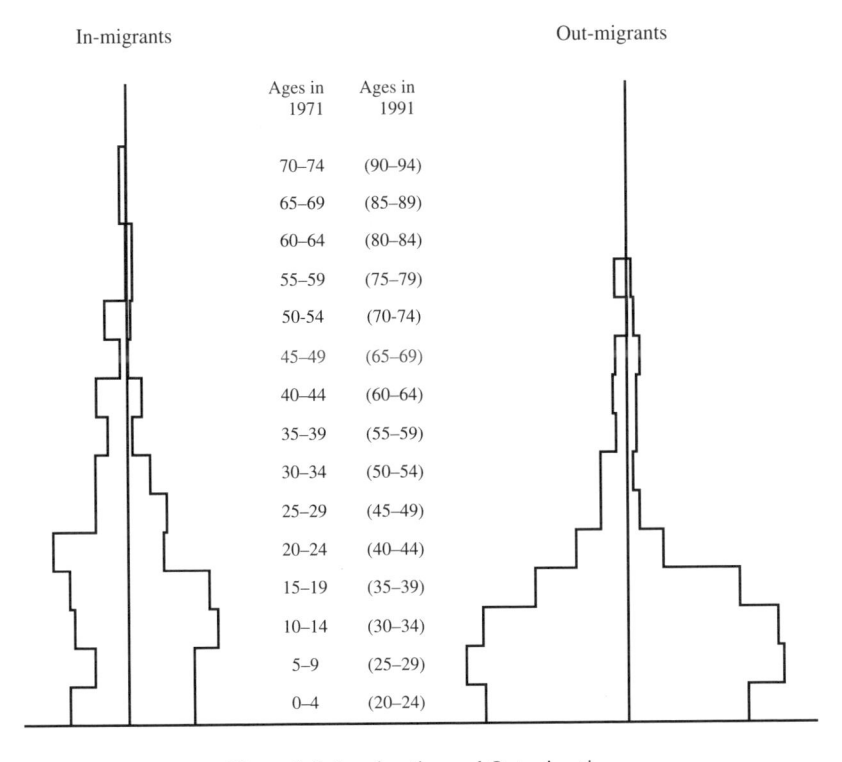

In-migrants	Ages in 1971	Ages in 1991	Out-migrants
	70–74	(90–94)	
	65–69	(85–89)	
	60–64	(80–84)	
	55–59	(75–79)	
	50-54	(70-74)	
	45–49	(65–69)	
	40–44	(60–64)	
	35–39	(55–59)	
	30–34	(50–54)	
	25–29	(45–49)	
	20–24	(40–44)	
	15–19	(35–39)	
	10–14	(30–34)	
	5–9	(25–29)	
	0–4	(20–24)	

Figure 9-6. In-migration and Out-migration

Table 9-1
Destinations for Out-migration from the 1971 Population

AGE IN 1971	KUALA LUMPUR*1		OTHER STATES		ULU KELANTAN		TANAH MERAH		KOTA BHARU		PASIR MAS*2		OTHER*3	
	MEN	WOMEN	MEN	WOMEN	MEN	WOMEN	MEN	WOMEN	MEN	WOMEN	MEN	WOMEN	MEN	WOMEN
0–4	6	6	10	8	6	3	2	5	3	2	5	1	2	3
5–9	8	2	9	12	7	5	4	4	2	4	7	7	2	2
10–14	6	2	11	7	5	2	6	8	2	5	2	9	3	2
15–19	5	3	7	4	3	2	1	3	2	2	4	7		5
20–24			3		2	1	1			1	6	3		3
25–29			2			1		1		1	4			
30–34					1		1		3		1	1		
35–39						1	1						1	1
40–44						1			1		2	1		
45–49							2	3						
50–54								1				1		
55–59					1						1	1		
Unknown							1							
Total	25	13	42	31	25	16	19	25	13	15	32	31	8	16

*1 including Petaling Jaya   *2 excluding Galok   *3 including unclear cases

Age-specific fertility was determined for female residents of Galok from the cumulative number of years spent in five-year age intervals from 15 to 49 years and the number of births in each interval. Table 9-2 shows the results, together with the total fertility rates (TFRs) based on these data. The calculated TFR of 4.860 for 1972-1991 might be underestimated, because some infant deaths that occurred during the twenty-year period may not have been reported. If the figure is revised by adopting the infant motality rate of 64.5 per 1,000 births for girls and 65.2 for boys from the Model Life Tables (Model East: life

Table 9-2
Age-specific Fertility and Total Fertility Rates (1972–1991)

	Age Interval	Number of Births	Cumulative Number of Woman-Years	Fertility (births per woman-year)
1972–1991	15–19	43	651	0.066
	20–24	173	758	0.228
	25–29	180	673	0.267
	30–34	113	564	0.200
	35–39	70	426	0.164
	40–44	13	342	0.038
	45–49	3	340	0.009
			TFR	4.860
1972–1981	15–19	36	431	0.084
	20–24	85	380	0.224
	25–29	70	252	0.278
	30–34	34	190	0.179
	35–39	25	181	0.138
	40–44	5	161	0.031
	45–49	1	160	0.006
			TFR	4.700
1982–1991	15–19	7	220	0.032
	20–24	88	378	0.233
	25–29	110	421	0.261
	30–34	79	374	0.211
	35–39	45	245	0.184
	40–44	8	181	0.044
	45–49	2	180	0.011
			TFR	4.880

expectancy at birth for females, 65.0 years; for males, 63.0 years), then the TFR would be 5.20 or slightly higher. Although this is by no means the maximum limit of fertility, it is typical of the high birth rate that might be expected when no artificial birth control is adopted.

To determine whether any change had occurred in fertility during the twenty-year period, age-specific fertility was calculated for two decades—1972 to 1981 and 1982 to 1991—and the figures are presented with the unrevised TFR values in Table 9-2. Although the 1982–1991 period was not a full decade, because the study in 1991 ended in November, there was little probability of any additional births before the end of the year, and even if some births had occurred, they would have had very little influence on the overall value. In terms of the TFR, the figure for 1982–1991 was slightly higher than that for 1972-1981. In the four groups aged over 30 years, fertility was higher in the later decade than in the earlier, which suggests that the trend towards birth control among the older women that emerged during the 1970s had been reversed due to new movements encouraging the birth of children and a laissez-faire attitude towards birth control. This conclusion should not, however, be accepted without reservation, because birth records for the earlier decade may be less complete than those for the later decade, particularly with regard to higher infant mortality in the earlier period. In this case, perhaps the only conclusion to be drawn is that there was no marked reduction in fertility over the two decades.

Using genealogical records, I evaluated the extent by which the 1971 population had grown by 1991, and the proportion of residents who stayed in the village and who left. Although the objective was to measure the proportional increase in the 1971 population over the two decades, some adjustments to the computation methods were necessary in order to account for out-migration for marriage and other reasons. First, I identified the number of men resident in Galok in 1971 and the number of their direct male descendents born between 1971 and 1991 who were still alive in 1991, and on the basis of these figures, computed the average annual rate of increase. I also identified the number of the above who were residents of Galok in 1991 and computed the rate of increase within the village. The same calculations were carried out independently for women living in Galok in 1971 and their female descendents born during the twenty-year period.

There were 349 men resident in Galok in 1971. When combined with their male descendents, the total number is 582, of whom 285 live in the village. The overall male population increased 1.67 times during the twenty-year period at an annual rate of 2.59 percent, but the male population that stayed in the village decreased at an annual rate of 1.01 percent. As for women, there were 342 resident in Galok in 1971 and these combined with their female descendents numbered 622 in 1991 of which 283 lived in the village. The overall female population multiplied 1.82 times during the twenty-year period at an annual rate of 3.04 percent, but the female population remaining in the village decreased at a rate of 0.94 percent. The lack of noticeable difference between the rates of increase and decrease for men and women remaining in Galok is due to the bilateral kinship structure of Malays and its effect on the selection of postmarital residence. The fact that the number of people who are genealogical residents of the village decreased while the overall population increased provides an interesting contrast and is due to in-migration as discussed below.

To investigate the relationship of population growth to trends in mortality, I identified how many male and female residents in each five-year age interval in 1971 were still living in 1991, checked the degree of compatibility with the survival rate calculated from the Model Life Tables for a projected twenty years later, and selected the average life expectancy with the highest degree of compatibility, as shown in Table 9-3. From the four models in Coale and Demeny's Life Tables, the average life expectancy for men is estimated to range from 58.6 years (Model South) to 63.8 years (Model North), and that for women from 62.5 years (Model South) to 67.5 years (Model West and Model North). When the difference between the theoretical and actual values for each age set are compared, Model East has the highest compatibility for men and women, followed by Model West, Model South and Model North. If Model East is applied, the average life expectancy for men is 63 years and that for women is 65 years. Although all of these values are much lower than those for more developed nations, they are also not extremely low.

The mean annual rate of decline in the number of men resident in Galok in 1971 was calculated from the number who were still alive in 1991. Although this could be used as the death rate, using an unreplenished population group to

Table 9-3
Average Life Expectancy Estimated from the Model Life Tables

	MEN		WOMEN	
ORDER OF COMPATIBILITY	MODEL LIFE TABLE	AVERAGE LIFE EXPECTANCY	MODEL LIFE TABLE	AVERAGE LIFE EXPECTANCY
1	East Level 20	63.0	East Level 19	65.0
2	West Level 20	63.6	West Level 20	67.5
3	South Level 18	58.6	South Level 18	62.5
4	North Level 20	63.8	North Level 20	67.5

Source of data for Model Life Tables: Coale, A.J. & P. Demeny, *Regional Life Tables and Stable Populations*, 2nd ed., Academic Press, 1983

calculate mortality causes distortion. Accordingly, the Model Life Table mortality levels for each age interval (Model East Level 20 for men and Model East Level 19 for women) were used to find the theoretical number of deaths and estimate the death rate. The annual average death rate thus obtained was 7.3 for the entire population, 6.5 for men and 8.1 for women. This high rate for women was influenced by the high death rate among the three women over eighty in 1971. Using the simple formula that the rate of population increase equals the difference between the birth and death rates, the estimated values of birth rate are high: 32.4 per 1,000 based on the male population and 38.5 based on the female population.

9.3. Changes in Household Composition

According to 1971 observations, the basic household in Galok was nuclear in appearance, but it was quite common for non-nuclear kin to be adopted into the household or for core members of the nuclear family to reside with other kin. Frequent divorce and remarriage further complicated household composition. Table 9-4 analyzes the family composition of Galok households in 1971 in relation to the stages of the family career presented in Figure 9-7, showing the number of cases in which members of the core nuclear family— the couple's unmarried children, one spouse's unmarried children, or a spouse—are absent, and the number of cases in which extra members—one spouse's unmarried children, adopted children, parents, divorced daughters, grandchildren, or collateral kin—are present, as well as model cases with no additional or absent members. Data on household composition in 1991 have been categorized in the same way in Table 9-5. The similarities and differences between 1971 and 1991 are described below.

The high number of both additional and absent members remained unchanged. In that sense, no fundamental transformation has occurred in the flexibility of household composition or in the lack of fixed principles governing it. However, in 1991 the number of normal households with no absent or additional members had slightly increased, and it is evident that a change of direction was taking place.

The first point of note is the decline in the percentage of very small households. Households classified as type III, nuclear families with unmarried children, increased 1.83 times, while type V households consisting of nuclear families in which some children have married and left home, increased 1.7 times. In contrast, households comprised of a single person living alone (type I), a young couple (type II), an elderly couple (type VII), and an elderly person living alone (type VIII) showed little or no increase and in the case of type II, actually decreased. This decrease in newly independent households comprised of a young

Table 9-4
Family Composition of Households in 1971

			ABSENT MEMBERS			ADDITIONAL MEMBERS				
STAGE OF FAMILY CAREER	TOTAL NUMBER OF HOUSEHOLDS	HOUSEHOLDS WITH MODEL COMPOSITION	COUPLE'S UNMARRIED CHILD	ONE SPOUSE'S UNMARRIED CHILD	ONE SPOUSE	ONE SPOUSE'S UNMARRIED CHILD	ADOPTED CHILD	PARENT	DIVORCED DAUGHTER	GRANDCHILD	COLLATERAL KIN
I	3	2						1			
II	6	3	1					2			
III	59	41	7	10	2	6					1
IV											
V	30	12	1	1	4	4		1	5	12	
VI	18	5			10					7	
VII	14	6						3	1	5	1
VIII	16	8					1			7	
Total	146	77	9	11	16	10	7	1	6	31	2

Polygynous marriages are counted as two households because the husband is counted twice.
Source: Kuchiba, Tsubouchi, and Maeda (1976), p. 202.

Table 9-5
Family Composition of Households in 1991

			ABSENT MEMBERS			ADDITIONAL MEMBERS				
STAGE OF FAMILY CAREER	TOTAL NUMBER OF HOUSEHOLDS	HOUSEHOLDS WITH MODEL COMPOSITION	COUPLE'S UNMARRIED CHILD	ONE SPOUSE'S UNMARRIED CHILD	ONE SPOUSE	ONE SPOUSE'S UNMARRIED CHILD	ADOPTED CHILD	PARENT	DIVORCED DAUGHTER	GRANDCHILD	COLLATERAL KIN
I	3	1									2
II	1	1									
III	108	71	13	1	12	2	1	11			7
IV	5	3	2								
V	51	26	4	1	12	2		3		10	
VI	10	1	1		3					7	1
VII	15	10							1	5	
VIII	18	12							2	4	1
Total	211	125	20	2	27	4	1	14	3	26	11

Polygynous marriages are counted as two households because the husband is counted twice.

couple was accompanied by the emergence of a new pattern in which newlyweds resided with their parents (type IV), although such households were few. These changes resulted from a trend towards the construction of larger, more permanent dwellings in place of the small, simple houses of the past and consequent the

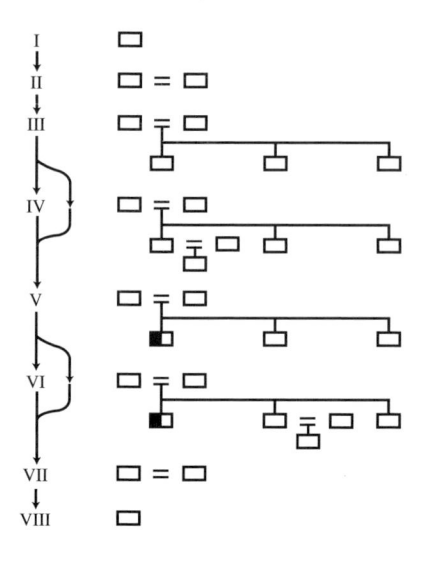

Figure 9-7. Stages of the Family Career

decline in the number of young and old villagers living in independent houses that might better be termed huts. Concerning young people, it should also be noted that their absolute number resident in the village did not increase. The increase in the average number of members per household from 4.7 in 1971 to 5.2 in 1991 also, at least in part, relates to the change in house size.

A decrease in the number of households in type VI, which consist of married children residing with parents, appears to contradict the above-mentioned trend, but this decline can be accounted for by the number of parents included as additional members in households categorized as type III. Whereas only one household in 1971 included a parent as an additional member, in 1991 the number had increased to fourteen. This change in the way of viewing household members corresponds to changes in occupation in Galok and the accompanying shift in the identity of the household's primary breadwinner.

A closer look at the identities of absent and additional members makes the nature of changes in household composition more apparent. First let us look at cases where the couple's unmarried children are absent. In 1971 there were only nine households missing such members, but this had increased to twenty by 1991. The latter included a new phenomenon of unmarried children moving to attend school or work in distant locations. Here I have only counted the number of children under 18, but due to the rising age of first marriage, the number of unmarried children over 18 had greatly increased and if these were added to the above, the total number of unmarried children absent from the parents' household would be even greater.

The number of absent unmarried children of a spouse has noticeably declined. Although in some instances a spouse's unmarried children were counted as additional members, such cases had also markedly decreased. This is thought to be mainly related to the decrease in the number of remarriages resulting from the lower divorce rate. The number of households which included an adopted child as an additional member dropped from seven to one in 1991. It seems that the trend towards household composition being based on kin relationship is becoming stronger. The number of households which included a divorced daughter similarly decreased from six in 1971 to three in 1991, also due to the lower incidence of divorce.

The increase in the number of absent spouses is difficult to explain from the premise of fewer divorces; however, it may be due to the lower incidence of remarriage among bereaved or divorced spouses. Moreover, some spouses live separately because of the distance from the workplace, a new phenomenon which will be described in more detail below.

The number of households which included grandchildren dropped from thirty-one in 1971 to twenty-six in 1991, which at first glance seems to indicate a declining trend. However, eleven type III households in 1991 included a parent or parents as opposed to zero households in 1971. If we consider the fact that the children of the householder are the householder's parent's grandchildren, then the actual number of households which include grandchildren have increased. The number of co-resident grandchildren has particularly decreased in type VIII households consisting of a single elderly person. In 1971 seven households of this type had co-resident grandchildren, versus only four in 1991. Moreover, in one of the latter, a divorced daughter was also co-resident. Thus only three 1991 households had pure alternate generation residence patterns compared to all seven cases in 1971. This change indicates that it is no longer considered desirable for grandchildren to live with an economically weaker alternate generation grandparent. As mentioned before, there was only a slight increase in the number of type VIII households which center on a single elderly person, and the percentage these comprised of total households dropped from 11 percent in 1971 to 8.5 percent in 1991. This relative increase reveals a stronger trend towards single elderly people living alone as opposed to coresidence with a grandchild or grandchildren.

The number of households which included collateral kin as additional members increased from two in 1971 to eleven in 1992. This represents a movement away from nuclearization of the family and towards the formation of stronger living units based on kin relationships. This includes cases in which a grandparent who formerly took in grandchild now resides with the grown grandchild's family.

9.4. Various Aspects of Change in Household Structure

9.4.1. Tracing Married Couples Resident in 1971

Following the comparison of changes in household composition in the previous section, I carried out a more detailed analysis of change in the family with regard to several elements of the household. Deaths and divorces that had occurred by 1991 among the 126 married couples that lived in Galok in 1971 are presented in Table 9-6 according to the husbands' age. From an overall viewpoint, 53 marriages were terminated by death or divorce in the twenty-year period, while 73 couples remained married to the same partner. That far more marriages ended with the death of a husband (26) than with the death of a wife (6) is considered a natural consequence of the differences in the spouses' ages and in average life expectancy.

There were a total of twelve cases of divorce, but only one to three cases each occurred in seven of the eight age groups between the ages of 20 and 59. In the 1970/1971 study, the younger generations had a higher possibility of divorce, and the divorce trend decreased markedly the longer a couple were married. If this trend continued after 1971, then the highest number of divorces would occur in the 20–24 age group. In reality however, of the sixteen couples in that category, only one divorced, a fact related to the sharp decline in divorce trends accompanying changes in people's ideas on marriage and revisions of divorce law and application procedures. That early divorce, so common in the past, should decrease this markedly, is worthy of our attention. Moreover, of the seventy-three couples still married in 1991, ten had moved out of the village. Although the majority of out-migrants were young people in their twenties in 1971, some were also in their early forties.

Remarriage after divorce or the death of a spouse is shown on the right hand side of Table 9-6. If we compare this with the number of deaths and divorces, we find that remarriage was higher among divorced spouses than among widowed spouses, and higher among men than women. After remarriage, more men and women lived outside than inside the village. A total of sixteen people who remarried left the village, which is almost equivalent to the ten couples (20 people) still married from 1971 who moved out. Of those who remained in Galok after remarriage, two were husbands and two were wives, accounting for only 20 percent of all remarried couples. Remarriage tends to change not only one's place of residence but also one's lifestyle.

Table 9-6
Present Situation of Married Couples Resident in 1971

Age of Husband in 1971	Present Situation of Couple					Remarriage				Residence after Remarriage			
	Both Deceased	Husband Deceased*	Wife Deceased*	Divorced	Both Living	Husband		Wife		Husband		Wife	
						After Death of Spouse	After Divorce	After Death of Spouse	After Divorce	Galok	Other	Galok	Other
20–24					15 (4)								
25–29			1	3	7 (3)		1				1		2
30–34		2	2	2	14 (1)	2	2	1	2	1	2	1	3
35–39		5		1	10 (1)		2	1	1				
40–44	1	2	1	2	13 (1)			1	1		1	1	1
45–49		6			6								
50–54	1	5	1	1	5		1			1	1		
55–59			1	2	3	1	1				1		
60–64	4	3											
65–69	2	2											
70–74	1	1						1					1
Total	9	26	6	12	73 (10)	4	7	4	5	2	9	2	7

Figures in brackets indicate number of living outside Galok. *Does not include deaths after divorce.

9.4.2. Separate Residence of Spouses

Next let us look at cases in which spouses live separately, a phenomenon that had become quite conspicuous in 1991.

- Case 1: The wife (30) is from Galok and the husband (age unknown) from Tondong in Pasir Mas district. In 1984, both worked as teachers and were living together in Kuantan in Pahang state. In 1991, the husband had enrolled as a student at the Universiti Teknologi Malaysia and was living in Johor, while the wife lived in her parents home in Galok with her daughters aged one and three, and worked as a teacher in the neighboring village of Chekok.
- Case 2: The wife (35) is from Galok and works as a teacher, while the husband, who is about the same age as his wife, is from nearby Padang Hangus and also worked as a teacher. The two lived and worked together in Kuantan, but after the wife's father died, the husband returned to Galok ahead of her and was living with her mother (65). Of the couple's six children, the oldest two, a daughter aged nine and a son aged seven, returned to Galok with the father, while the other four, three sons aged six, three and one, and one daughter aged five, remained with their mother in Kuantan.
- Case 3: The wife (41), a native of Galok, married a man (43) from Pahang. They have two daughters and two sons, the eldest being their 19-year-old daughter and the youngest their three-year-old son. The husband is a public servant employed by the Department of Fisheries. Formerly he worked in Kelantan, but three years ago he was transferred to Kuala Lumpur. His wife lives in Galok with her mother (67) and four children, and runs a coffee shop. The husband returns occasionally to visit.
- Case 4: Both the husband (39) and wife (30) are from Galok. The husband works for the military intelligence bureau and lives in Ulu Kelantan, while the wife lives in Galok with their three boys and one girl ranging from nine to three years in age. The husband returns home once a week.
- Case 5: The wife (31) is from Galok, while the husband is from Trengganu. The husband presently lives in Gua Musang, where he works for the Federal Land Development Authority (FELDA), and visits his wife and two children, a nine-year-old daughter and seven-year-old son, once a week.
- Case 6: The wife (23) and their two-month-old son live in Galok with her mother and father-in-law. The husband (24), a soldier, is stationed in Tanah Merah but has not yet been granted a house.
- Case 7: The husband (37) a native of Galok, is presently a migrant worker in Pahang. The couple's house is under construction in Galok

but is only half-completed. The wife (age unknown) and their two sons aged three and one are living in Rantau Panjang with the wife's mother.
• Case 8: The wife (35) is from nearby Jabo Hilir and her husband is from Chetok, also nearby. As the wife's elder brother lives in Galok, they built a home ten years ago near his house where the wife lives with their three sons and two daughters the eldest of whom is ten. The husband lives in Kuantan and runs a coffee shop with his relatives. He returns home once a month.

Judging from the above cases alone, the factor which most commonly results in spouses living apart appears to be the wife's continuation of her relationship with her native home. The spread of education and increased employment opportunities for women mean that both husband and wife have independent sources of income, which makes living separately easier. In Case 2, both spouses wanted to return to Galok but the husband happened to receive a transfer before his wife. Although long-term separations are most common among people earning regular wages, people frequently travel to Singapore and other places as migrant workers and thus the temporary separation of married couples for work reasons is regarded as commonplace.

Couples that move out of Galok may each maintain separate residences elsewhere in which case their children sometimes reside in the village with their grandparents. Cases of this type are described below. From the perspective of

Plate 9-1. A village family (1971).

Galok residents, the grandchildren are extra members added to an existing household and thus would fall under the category of grandchildren in the column for additional members of Table 9-5 on the family composition of households. This can be seen as a new type of situation in the adoption of grandchildren.

- Case 9: The wife (34), a native of Galok, was working as a midwife at a clinic in nearby Jabo but was transferred to Tanah Merah. The husband (33) works in Ulu Kelantan, his native district. They have a four-year-old son and a one-year-old daughter but the former lives in Galok with the grandfather (54) and grandmother (55).
- Case 10: The husband (28) is from Galok and has been working in a lumber mill in Gua Musang for four years. The wife (26) is a nurse from Ulu Kelantan and is in training for one year in Kuala Lumpur. Their three-month-old infant is being cared for by the grandfather (49) and grandmother (45) on the husband's side and the wife comes home once a month.

9.4.3. Households of Newcomers to Galok

As I have mentioned, the influx of new residents into Galok has resulted in an increase in the overall population, despite the decrease due to out-migration in the population of people born and raised there. Identification of the newcomers should allow a clearer characterization of the village.

In Table 9-7, data on village households have been organized in a simple fashion to illustrate reasons for living in Galok. The majority are households whose member(s) have been continuous residents since 1971. Such households numbered 142 in 1991 comprising 67.3 percent of the total. Theoretically, this figure could include households with a spouse that had moved in after 1971 due to the death of a former household member or the establishment of separate residence, or new households established by people born in Galok after 1971 who continued to live there. In actual fact, however, there were only two cases of the former. Despite the general continuity of household composition, replacement of household members due to such factors as out-migration and return migration is not uncommon.

Thirty-three households (15.6 percent) were established by persons who had left the village and then returned. Of these, 14 were living in Galok at the time of the 1971 study but left to establish their own household elsewhere and later returned with their families, while 19 had left before 1971 but had returned to establish their own households by 1991. These households, which were all established by natives of Galok, combined with the 142 households of residents who stayed in Galok amount to 175 households, outnumbering the 146 original households in 1971. This increase resulted from return migration of former Galok residents. Although Galok had lost its attraction as a place of agricultural production, to many of those who returned its attraction as a place of residence had increased, representing a kind of U-turn phenomenon.

The most common place of residence for out-migrants was Pahang state. Seven Galok residents migrated there, including one to Kuantan. As for more distant locations, there were three cases of villagers moving to Thailand, one to Sabah, three to Trengganu, two to Pinang, and two of soldiers with no fixed residence. Within Kelantan, in addition to two cases in Ulu Kelantan and two in Kota Bharu, out-migrants also lived in the neighboring villages of Atas Beting, Hutan Mala, Padang Hangus, and Kampung Tujoh.

Rubber areas have undergone comparatively recent development in Pahang, Thailand and Ulu Kelantan where Galok residents have traditionally migrated to work. There were several teachers among those who returned from Sabah, Trengganu and Pinang and, although they had accepted postings to work in distant places, they never stopped looking for an opportunity to return to Galok until their hopes were finally realized. As for those who returned from neighboring villages, this was probably a result of comparing the living conditions in their villages with those in Galok. In addition to the above, one woman returned after a divorce and established her own household.

In seven cases, in-migrants had kin in Galok, and they were able to rely on these connections to settle in the village. Some returned to property inherited from their parents, Galok natives, and one woman, widowed by her first husband, moved onto his land. Others were lent land for their homes free of charge from kin. There were only two cases where the person moving in relied on acquaintances, and although there are some similarities between these and households who relied on kin, their residence pattern was more unstable. One householder came from Kota Bharu and as his wife's elder sister lives in Galok,

Table 9-7
Households in 1991 by Reason for Living in Galok

REASON	NUMBER OF HOUSEHOLDS
Continued Residence by a Household Member (Including a Deceased Member)	142
Return to Village After Temporary Absence	33
Kin are from Galok	7
Moved to Galok Through a Friend	2
Moved from a Nearby Village	22
Purchased Land in Galok	5
Total	211

he was able to rent a house there. The other household came from Thailand, and built a simple wooden house on land rented free of charge. They earn their living working as day laborers and at other jobs.

As many as twenty-two households moved in from neighboring villages. The majority of them were attracted by amenities available in Galok. Land conveniently situated along the road, however, is already monopolized by original residents. Many of the newcomers live in a newly formed group of houses located down a narrow road so that the owners of adjacent properties can get maximum use out of their land. In-migrants include former residents from villages surrounding Galok such as Jabo, Jintang, Atas Beting, Hutan Mala and Chetok. The number of households and population are noticeably declining in villages such as Jabo built along the river bank (*tepi sungai*), which once had a high population density and were the first areas settled along the middle reach of the Kelantan river.

Five households purchased land in Galok to live on. Two of these households had been living in Pengkalan Chupa near Kota Bharu where both parents and children did contract work, and the relationships they developed when they went to work in Galok just happened to lead to the purchase of land. A teacher working in Tanah Merah and a driver for the government Veterinary Department also purchased land in Galok and moved there. One resident of nearby Jintang moved to Galok after purchasing land from a villager living in Kota Bharu. In all of the above, those who purchased land in the village previously had no direct connection with Galok. There were at least two people among those who returned to the village after a temporary absence who purchased land in Galok before moving back. If we add up the number of households that relied upon acquaintances, those who moved in from nearby villages, and those who purchased land, a total of twenty-nine new households moved into the village. This figure is very close to the thirty-three households of those who returned to the village after a temporary absence, demonstrating that the village community is not exclusive.

9.5. A Summary of Changes in Population and Households

Many Galok residents moved out of the village, and many others moved in, illustrating the mobile nature of Galok residents. A superficial look at the in-migrating and out-migrating populations might give the observer the false impression that the population of Galok will be completely replaced over time. The reality, however, is quite different. Many of those who leave the village return when their circumstances change, and the majority of the 1991 population was still comprised of people born in Galok. People from outside the village are accepted, but their reasons for moving to Galok are similar to those of Galok natives returning to the village. If living in Galok was not attractive enough to lure native villagers back, it would hardly appeal to outsiders. Although the village is not exclusive, at the same time, it does not accept outside elements at a rate that would cause a rapid change in its members. The predominance of families that remain in the village indicates that continuity is maintained.

Return migration may be a temporary phenomenon in response to improved living conditions in Galok, which now has electricity, running water, telephones and opportunities for income from sources other than agriculture. Without these changes it is likely that the population and number of houses in Galok would have decreased, as have those of other villages along the river, despite the natural population increase resulting from the high birth rate. In fact, if we look at the population residing in Galok in 1971, the number of people migrating out of the village exceeded the natural increase. At the same time, different evaluations of living conditions in Galok that are dependent on individual circumstances seem to exist, as evidenced by there being both an inward and an outward flow of population. The fact that people are moving into the village suggests that something was lacking in their former place of residence when compared to Galok. Similarly, the out-migration of youth is a choice based on a the same criteria. Even if we look solely at economic factors, this is not a simple push and pull relationship but rather a dual structured push and pull.

Selection of residence has an economic orientation on the one hand, and a kin and community orientation on the other. The former takes into consideration profitability, while the latter is concerned with joint participation. Those returning to the village were influenced equally by economic and community considerations, while teachers who returned were able to satisfy both orientations.

With more permanent, larger dwellings being built, households in Galok are beginning to establish themselves as independent units of daily life. In this process, the number of more dependent units such as households comprised of a grandmother and grandchild decrease, and the only alternate generation households that will survive are comprised of younger, more economically independent grandparents. The remaining weaker units become more reliant upon money sent from children who have left the village.

The kin composition of households appears to have become purer in terms of kin relations due to fewer adoptions and fewer children from previous marriages because of the lower divorce rate. In the past, household composition in Galok centered on one married couple, to which members were frequently added or subtracted. Emphasis on kin purity leads to elimination of unrelated elements from the household, and an increase in purely nuclear families. It would be natural to find a trend towards nuclear families in Galok. On the contrary, however, the previously mentioned trend to form consolidate the independent unit of daily life has resulted in households with an extended family type of composition. This dual orientation towards both nuclear families with the goal of purer kin relationships and extended families with the purpose of consolidation, seems contradictory. Yet the reality of the Galok household can be found within this balance of contradictions. The nuclear family has not become an ideology, but merely fulfills a role as a centripetal part of household composition, while the consolidation of kin bonds can be identified as a fluctuating component of the principles governing household composition.

In this analysis, I have not looked at the relationships between kin living in close proximity to each other. In the past, weaker household units were sustained by this type of neighborhood kin group, and the limited amount of land available for production imposed natural restrictions on increases in the number of households. If the focus of land use becomes residential, then the possibility of changes in residence patterns will naturally arise. This subject will be dealt with in the following chapter.

10
Multihousehold Compounds: Changes over Twenty Years and their Significance

10.1. Changes in the Population of Multihousehold Compounds

Kin living in neighborhood groups are generally considered to form the basic unit of daily life in Southeast Asian villages. The term "multihousehold compound" was used by Koichi Mizuno to define this type of neighboring kin residence pattern. In his study on Don Daeng, a village in Northeast Thailand, Mizuno reported that one or more children remained in the compound of their parents, building separate dwellings and establishing their own households but sharing production and consumption. If we focus solely on the location of postmarital residence, a similar phenomenon can be found, at least superficially, throughout Southeast Asia. Because the households are in close proximity, daily contact is frequent, and if we consider the kin relationships that create this type of residence pattern, they can be viewed as one type of kin group. Due to the bilateral principle governing postmarital residence in Malay villages which allows the couple to select virilocal or uxorilocal residence depending upon individual circumstances, kin relationships within the group are more diverse and the degree of cooperation and sharing is more varied. Mizuno emphasized the elements of communal ownership and cooperative labor within the multihousehold compound, illustrating the compound's corporate nature. In the case of Malay villages, however, the corporate character is weaker, and in that sense, the term kin-neighborhoods would be a more accurate description. I have used the term multihousehold compounds here, with the clear understanding that it is within a broader context that takes into consideration the existence of similar phenomena occurring throughout Southeast Asia.

When sorting the composition of multihousehold compounds into different categories it becomes obvious that composition changes and develops over time. By grouping multihousehold compounds according to time periods, we can identify the various stages of development, but we cannot always clearly define the process that leads to the dissolution of a compound. Multihousehold compounds established on a limited area of land, can continue indefinitely as long as each household remains nuclear in composition and only one child establishes an independent household within the compound. In Mizuno's study area, for example, the typical composition was one household consisting of the parental couple and the youngest daughter and her husband, and a separate household established within the compound by another married daughter and her husband, and the two daughters and their spouses are destined to create the next multihousehold compound after their parents' death. As long as the area of land remains limited, however, this will be difficult, and migration will act as an essential, intrinsic mechanism to prevent overcrowding and fragmentation. The problem of limited land applies not only to the compound but also to cultivated land. Although in the case of the latter, this may be somewhat alleviated by exploiting undeveloped land or by improving yield, in villages like Don Daeng that are basically collective in form and where compounds border directly on one another, a solution such as migration is more urgent.

Malay villages often develop along canals or roads, forming ribbon settlements. In paddy-growing areas, land available for compounds is comparatively restricted, but it is not impossible to expand the area by reclaiming paddy land. In areas where rubber and fruit groves are interspersed with dry paddy fields, it is easier to establish a compound because, unlike more favored areas along roads, land is not as crowded and each household can choose their own site. When adjoining rubber estates are divided among siblings, some may set up their households immediately adjacent to one another, while others may set them up as much as fifty meters apart. Or they may originally build their houses close together, only to move them further apart when they rebuild. In these cases, the concept of the compound has become indistinct, and the group would more appropriately be termed a kin neighborhood, yet it still has not entirely lost the characteristics of a multihousehold compound.

In this chapter, I will attempt to record and analyze the types of changes that occurred in multihousehold compounds in Galok over the passage of time, focusing on 1971 and 1991 and pursuing the changes that occurred in the intervening twenty years. Data for 1991 were obtained during the follow-up survey from September to November as well as from an additional survey conducted from July to August 1992. In 1984, an attempt was made to briefly grasp changes that had occurred in multihousehold compounds, but as the consideration of these here would make interpretation too complicated, I have restricted data to the above stated two points in time. For this reason, as in the previous chapter, members of multihousehold compounds who joined after 1971 and left before 1991 are excluded from the data.

The population increase in Malay villages in Kelantan state was marked, and Galok was no exception. As stated in the previous chapter, the population of Galok increased 1.59 times, rising from 690 in 1971 to 1,100 in 1991, which represents an annual rate of increase of 2.36 percent. The male population which numbered 349 in 1971 had risen to 582 by 1991, a figure obtained by adding the number of male descendants born in the twenty-year period and subtracting those who died, and of this number, 285 remained in the village. While this represents a natural increase in the total male population of 1.67 times at an annual rate of 2.59 percent, the population of males that remained in the village actually decreased at an annual rate of 1.01 percent. Similar calculations were applied to the female population, which increased from 342 in 1971 to 622 in 1991, of which 283 remained in the village. The annual rate of natural increase was 3.04 percent but the female population that remained in the village decreased at an annual rate of 0.94 percent. The increase in the village population, therefore, was not based upon an increase in the 1971 resident population, but rather was sustained by in-migration, including the return of villagers that had left Galok prior to 1971.

In 1971, 95 households resided within multihousehold compounds, representing 65.5 percent of the total of 145 households, and their population numbered 474, equivalent to 68.7 percent of the total population (690). From the fact that multihousehold compounds comprised two-thirds of both village households and village population, it is easy to surmise that the population trends mentioned above were largely determined by changes in the members of these compounds. However, this must be verified through examination of actual multihousehold compounds, highlighting any trends that are revealed in sharper relief within that context.

The number of households comprising each of the thirty-six multihousehold compounds in 1971 are compared with the numbers in 1991 in Table 10-1 to identify any changes. In 1971, the average number of households was 2.64, and in 1991 it was 2.72, exhibiting little difference. The number of households remained the same in thirteen of the thirty-six compounds, increased in twelve and decreased in eleven. In other words, one-third exhibited no change, while the remaining two-thirds changed to some degree. These facts indicate that although the expansion of multihousehold compounds is restricted, their internal structure is changing constantly.

The average number of households in multihousehold compounds that expanded during the twenty-year period increased from 2.42 in 1971 to 3.84

in 1991, while for those that shrank in size, it decreased from 2.91 in 1971 to 1.64 in 1991. These figures indicate that there was a tendency for compounds smaller than average to expand and for compounds larger than average to shrink. It must be noted that in the process of the reduction in size, a total of seven compounds with two households lost one household and thus ceased to be a multihousehold compound. In the village as a whole, this type of dissolution was occurring on the one hand, while on the other, new multihousehold compounds were being formed, although in this analysis multihousehold compounds newly formed during the twenty-year period have been excluded from the observations.

The same method as that applied to the village population was used to observe changes in the number of people living within multihousehold compounds over the twenty-year period, except that members of the above mentioned seven compounds were included, while members of recently formed compounds were not. In 1971, the male population living in multihousehold compounds numbered 241. With the addition of male offspring born during the twenty-year period and the subtraction of men who died, this population had increased to 390 by 1991 of which 143 were still residing in the same compound. This represented a natural increase of 1.62 times, equivalent to an annual rate of increase of 2.44 percent, while the population of those who remained in the compound decreased annually at a rate of 2.58 percent. Applying the same method of calculation, the female population rose from 233 in 1971 to 419 in 1991, of which 196 remained in the same compound, representing a natural overall increase of 1.80 times at an annual rate of 2.98 percent, and a decrease in the female population remaining within the compound at an annual rate of 0.86 percent.

Table 10-1

Number of Households in 1991 in Multihousehold Compounds of 1971

NUMBER OF HOUSEHOLDS IN 1971	NUMBER OF HOUSEHOLDS IN 1991										TOTAL
	1	2	3	4	5	6	7	8	9	10	
2	7	9	7	1							24
3		2	2			1					5
4		2	1	1	1						5
5											0
6						1				1	2
Total	7	13	10	2	1	2	0	0	0	1	36

The rate of natural increase for both male and female populations was only slightly lower than that calculated for the village population as a whole, and the difference is considered to be insignificant. The percentage of the original population and their descendants who remained in the same compound decreased for both male and female populations. For women, the difference was negligible compared to that of the village as a whole, although it may have been slightly sharper. The decrease in the number of men remaining in the compound, however, was noticeably greater than the decrease in the number of men remaining in the village. In other words, no noticeable difference was discerned between the decrease in the male and female populations when looking at the overall population, but when this was compared within multihousehold compounds, a clear difference became apparent. In the case of women, 196 people, 46.8 percent of the 1991 population that resulted from natural increase (419), remained in the compound whereas only 143 men, or 36.7 percent of the total male population (390), remained. Of the ninety-five households residing within a multihousehold compound in 1971, thirty-three were uxorilocal residence, whereas by 1991, the proportion of uxorilocal residence had increased to forty-eight out of ninety-eight households.

Although the above gender difference can be explained as a result of the bilateral principles governing selection of residence, it still indicates a slightly stronger tendency for women to remain in the same compound. This corresponds to a relatively stronger tendency for men to leave, showing that women are slightly more likely to perpetuate the multihousehold compound than men. It must be noted, however, that this mechanism is not evident within the context of the village as a whole, possibly because of two phenomena. Men residing in multihousehold compounds tend to leave the compound to establish independent households within the village and men from independent households also have a high tendency to remain in the village, whereas this trend is lower for women. The number of men and their male descendants who resided in a compound but subsequently established independent households within the village was thirty-five. Even when these were included within multihousehold compounds, this population decreased at an annual rate of 1.5 percent, exceeding that for women. In contrast, after adding the number of living male descendants to the original population of 108 men in 1971, and subtracting those who died, a total of 107 men (0.991) who did not live in compounds remained in the village in 1991, exhibiting an annual rate of decrease of only 0.05 percent.

When the same observations were conducted on the female population, the total number of women, including their female offspring who once lived in multihousehold compounds but are now members of independent households

Plate 10-1. A village family (1971).

within the village was 16, slightly lower than the figure for men. In 1971, 109 women were not members of multihousehold compounds, whereas today their number combined with that of their female offspring has decreased to as low as 71, with an annual rate of decrease of 2.12 percent. Thus, while women are seen to have a stronger tendency to remain in multihousehold compounds, men are more likely to comprise or perpetuate independent households. In other words, men have a stronger orientation towards independence, while women have a stronger orientation towards dependence. However, this appears only as a slight gender difference in residence patterns within Galok, and the principle of women remaining and men leaving may not have extended beyond the confines of the village.

10.2. Changes in the Composition of Multihousehold Compounds

Here I will attempt to uncover aspects not shown in the above quantitative analysis by giving a concrete description of the kind of changes in the members comprising multihousehold compounds. I followed changes that occurred during the twenty-year period for all thirty-six multihousehold compounds existent in 1971, but as it would be very complicated to present all the cases here, I present only the more striking cases below.

- Case 1 (Figure 10-1): In 1971, two households lived in the compound, that of the older brother, then 47 years old, and that of the younger brother, then 39, but during the twenty-year interval the older brother and his eldest son died. In 1991, the older brother's second son (38) was working for the Department of Commerce in Kuala Lumpur and was married with three children. The older brother's widow (60) was living in the compound with her 20-year-old daughter. The younger brother (59) and his wife (51) continued to live in the compound but their children, apart from one daughter, had moved to Kota Bharu, Kuala Lumpur, and Jeli in Tanah Merah. Two of the younger brother's sons, aged 31 and 27, were already married. The eldest daughter (26), who was their third child, lived in the same compound in a house behind her parents' house and her husband (30) worked at a bank in Pasir Mas. (In 1992, this daughter and her family moved to Trengganu, leaving only her parents in the compound.)
- Case 2 (Figure 10-2): The scale of the multihousehold compound in this case was larger than that described above. Six households resided in the compound, three of which were the core households formed by three sisters, aged 47, 37, and 30 at the time, while the other three were the households of their children. In 1991, the household of the

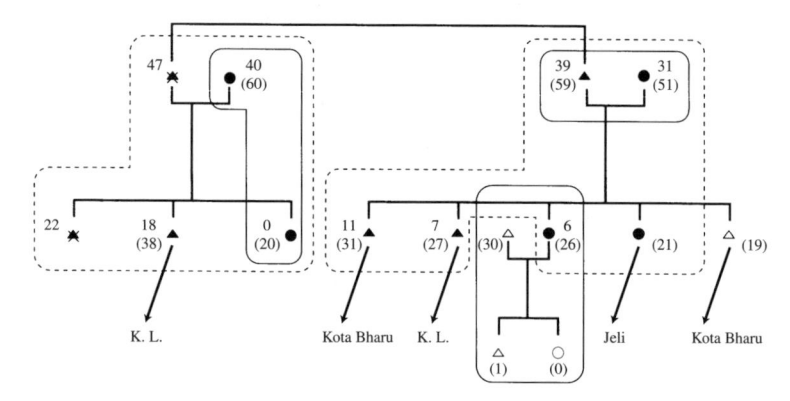

▲● Resident in 1971. Numbers show age in 1971; those in parentheses, age in 1991.
✶◼ Died between 1971 and 1991. Number is age in 1971.
△○ Born or in-migrated after 1971. Number in parentheses is age in 1991.
⎯ Household of 1991 (resident in Galok).
⋯ Household of 1971 (resident in Galok).

Figure 10-1. Changes in Multihousehold Compounds: Case 1

eldest male offspring (47) returned after temporarily residing in Sungai Durian in Ulu Kelantan district and set up residence in another part of the village, and in his stead, his younger sister (39) set up a new household within the compound. The population of the compound increased slightly from twenty-seven in 1971 to thirty-two in 1991. In 1971, the parents' household was comprised of an average of 5.7 people, while the children's households were comprised of an average of 3.3 members, but in 1991, these figures were reversed with an average of 2.3 members in the parents' household and 8.0 in the children's. During this process, many male and female offspring of the parents left the compound, two going to Kuala Lumpur (male, 33; female, 27) and others to destinations both in and out of the state. The fact that children left the compound and lived elsewhere is similar to Case 1. In this compound, offspring of children who had lived in an independent household within the compound were adopted by the grandparents after the children left the compound, and in 1991, there were two living with the grandparents. One of these was the seventh of their ten grandchildren, the daughter (10) of the eldest male offspring (47) mentioned above who had lived in Ulu Kelantan but returned to set up a household outside the compound. The other was the eldest female offspring (8) of the grandparents'

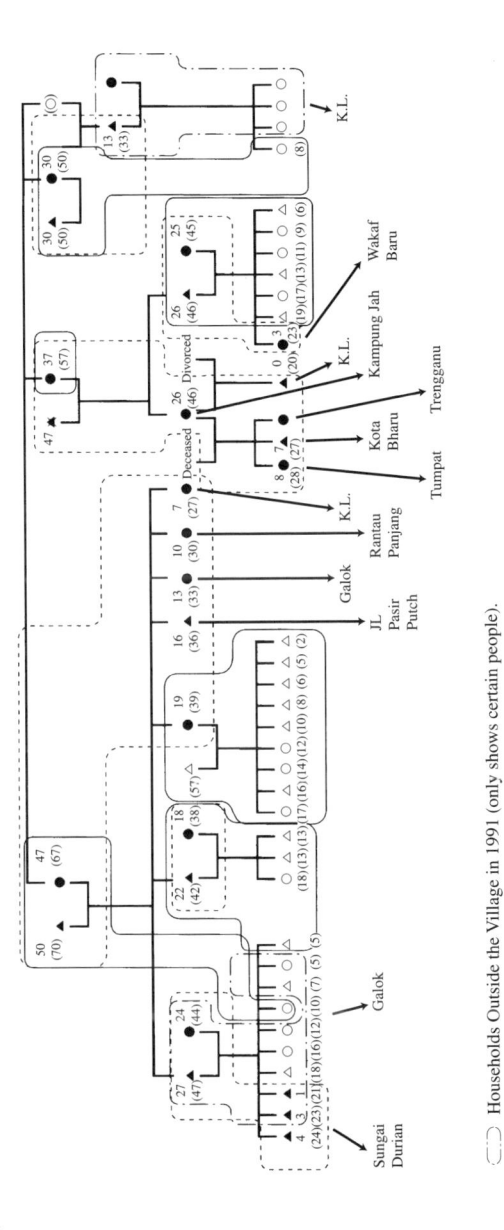

Figure 10-2. Changes in Multihousehold Compounds: Case 2

daughter who lived with her family in Kuala Lumpur because her husband worked for the air force.

The two cases described above are contrasting examples. In the former, the sons were expected to remain in the compound whereas in the latter the daughters were expected to remain. This shows the absence of any fixed rule governing the composition of Malay multihousehold compounds as both sons and daughters may build a house and remain within the compound. Although a slightly higher percentage of daughters remain, this is not a rule but rather a result of selecting residence according to individual circumstances, and merely represents a statistical manifestation of a small tendency.

- Case 3 (Figure 10-3): This compound was comprised of the households established by one brother (52) and three sisters (62, 42 and 40) in 1971, but by 1991 all four of them had died. Almost all of their children had left the village and formed their own households. The most common place of migration was a development area in Ulu Kelantan upstream along the Kelantan river. In 1991, one daughter (30) and one son (22) of the youngest sister had established their own separate households in the same compound. The son who was not yet married lived on his own and worked in Tanah Merah at a sawmill. His older sister who lived in the same compound had been widowed once and remarried. Her second husband was the son of the second brother of the original four siblings that had lived in the compound in 1971. He had returned to Galok from Thailand twelve years earlier and married his first cousin. His wife had also temporarily lived outside the village in Pahang with her former husband. The child of her former marriage lived temporarily with his grandmother in the compound. From the above, it is clear that the person who remains in the compound is decided within the context of very changeable circumstances. The person considered most suitable to remain does not always do so, yet the one who does remain is not merely left behind because others move out.

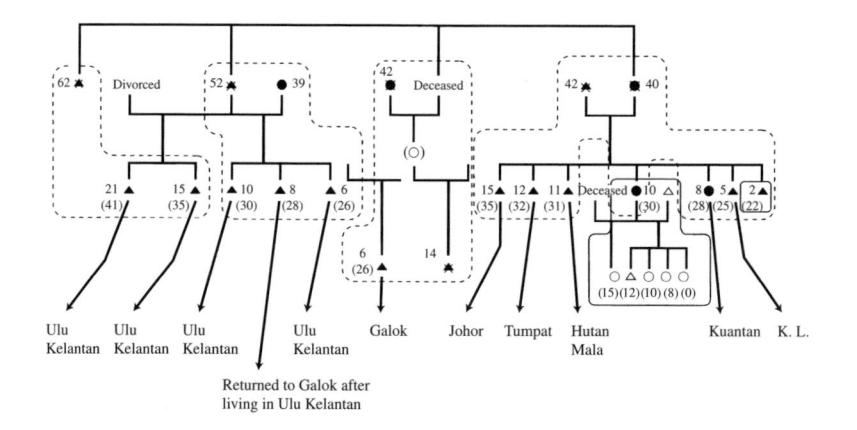

Figure 10-3. Changes in Multihousehold Compounds: Case 3

- Case 4 (Figure 10-4): In 1971, the compound consisted of the parents' household (father 41, mother 35) and the household of the eldest son (22). In 1984, the eldest son's household moved to the native village of his wife, Hutan Mala, where they lived with their five children, three of whom were born in Galok and two in Hutan Mala. In place of the son's household, the household of the eldest daughter (35) resided in the compound. This daughter had been living in Hutan Mala, her husband's home, with her three children, but returned to Galok some time after her brother left to live in her parents' compound. During the interval, the compound temporarily consisted of only one household of five people, comprised of the parents' and their unmarried children. It is worthy of note that the multihousehold compound did not merely result from children staying in the compound, but went through a process in which one child's household left the compound and the village and after an interval of time, was replaced by another child's household that had left and then returned. The parents' second son (31) and daughter (24) were both married and living in Kuala Lumpur, while their unmarried sons (26 and 22) were living in Kota Bharu and Gua Musang, respectively.

Cases 3 and 4 indicate that the formation of multihousehold compounds includes cases of in- and out-migration.

- Case 5 (Figure 10-5): In 1971 this multihousehold compound was comprised of a 70-year-old mother living with her daughter, who was

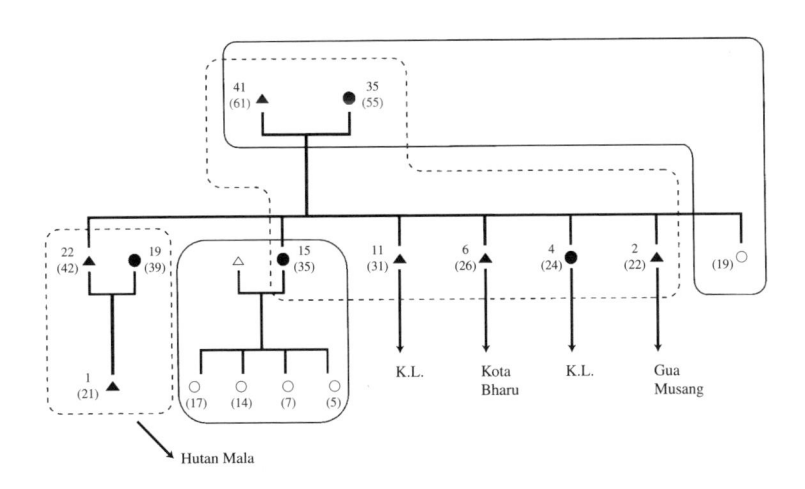

Figure 10-4. Changes in Multihousehold Compounds: Case 4

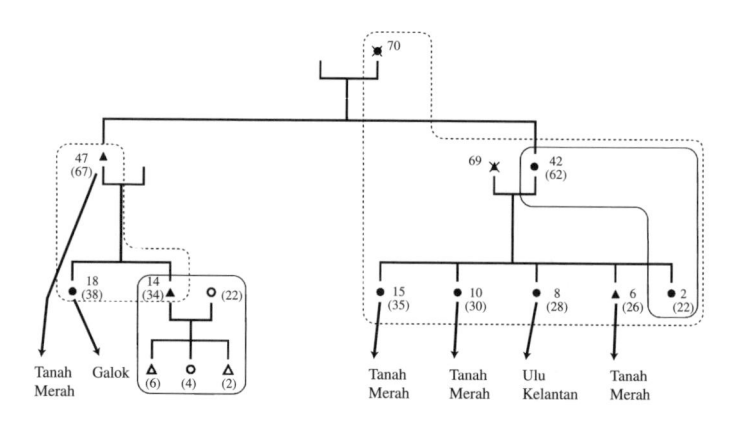

Figure 10-5. Changes in Multihousehold Compounds: Case 5

42 at the time, and her family, and the household of her 47-year-old son who was divorced. The mother died soon after, and the daughter's husband, who was almost the same age as her mother, died in 1981. From 1971 to 1991, the children who had been living with the daughter moved to Tanah Merah and Ulu Kelantan, establishing their own households, and only one unmarried girl (22) remained. During this time, the second girl (30) divorced and remarried, and of the two children, one girl and one boy, born during her first marriage, the boy, who was the youngest, temporarily resided in his mother's sister's household in the compound. The divorced son who was the head of the other household remarried and moved to Tanah Merah district in around 1975. Of his two children, his daughter (38) married in Galok and resides in her husband's compound, which is relatively close. His son who was fourteen in 1971 (34 in 1991) married, divorced and remarried and lives with his three children in the compound, and is occupied in paddy growing, rubber tapping, and tobacco cultivation. It should be noted that in this case the household head left the compound, while his child remained.

- Case 6 (Figure 10-6): In 1971, the compound consisted of the parents' household (father 57, mother 47) and the daughter's household (20). As they lived in separate dwellings within the same compound, they formed a multihousehold compound, but in 1991 the two households had been combined into one. During the intervening twenty years, two children (a daughter, 36, and a son, 30 in 1991) had married and moved to Pasir Puteh and Johor, respectively, to form their own households,

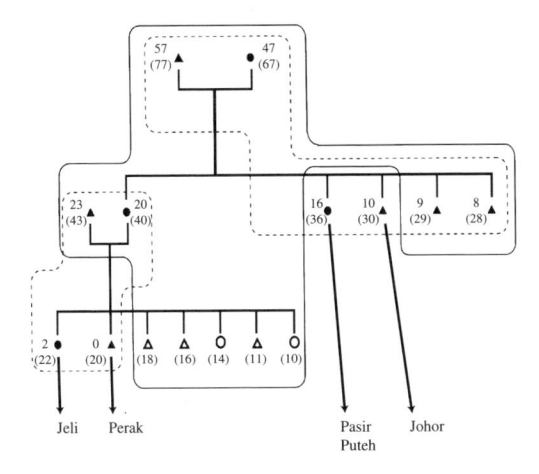

Figure 10-6. Changes in Multihousehold Compounds: Case 6

leaving two unmarried sons (29 and 28) in the parents' household. Meanwhile, the first child of the daughter's household, a girl (22), married an employee of the Public Works Department and moved to department housing in Juli, Tanah Merah district. They have two children. The daughter's second child, a boy (20), moved to Perak three years ago and is working as a prison guard.

10.3. Summary and Observations

The changes observed in the multihousehold compounds in Galok have undoubtedly been influenced by the changes in occupation in recent years. The factors bearing upon the formation of multihousehold compounds in a period when land is significant for production, whether paddy growing or rubber tapping, are naturally different from those operating when income is obtained outside the village or through non-agricultural occupations. When land was a place of production, its productivity determined the size of the village population, and the expansion of multihousehold compounds was limited by the requirement to keep land in production. The introduction of tobacco cultivation created a situation in which work force rather than land area was decisive, but the low profitability of tobacco cultivation relative to the labor invested, its seasonal nature, and the inferior quality of the tobacco produced compared to that grown in coastal areas inevitably reduced tobacco cultivation to a secondary or supplementary source of income. As migrant work and both regular and irregular employment became the main sources of the villagers' income and the village's significance as a place of residence came to the fore, it became possible for residential compounds to accommodate more households than previously and for paddy and rubber lands to be converted to residential use.

The increased potential for expansion of the multihousehold compound, however, was offset by the migration of household members in search of employment, and accordingly, as noted previously, the actual increase was not that remarkable. The trend towards building larger more permanent homes in recent years also checked increases in the number of households within the compound. Although the standards that govern surplus population and overcrowding are not easy to define, if we use chronic overpopulation and declining income as the criteria, overcrowding has never been serious in Galok, despite the fact that relative income has remained chronically low. This is due to the incorporation of migration as an integral part of the villagers' daily life and an inherent feature in the continuation of the multihousehold compound. Changes in occupation therefore do not seem to have affected the essential components of multihousehold compounds, instead merely causing slight variations. Unfortunately, too much time has passed for this to be verified by an additional survey.

The fact that women showed a slightly stronger tendency to remain in the compound is a relative phenomenon, merely reflecting the slightly higher percentage of men leaving the compound within the decreasing population trend for both men and women in multihousehold compounds. In terms of the village unit, the tendency for men to leave the compound is offset by the increase in the number of men setting up independent households within the village. The delicate balance of mutual interchange between multihousehold compounds and independent households is an inherent feature of the changes that occur in multihousehold compounds. The pattern that emerges is a higher orientation among men towards independence, and among women towards dependence in the selection of residence. This pattern, however, represents a trend rather than a manifestation of an underlying principle of behavior.

If sex and order of birth are the only standards used to evaluate each individual multihousehold compound, it is virtually impossible to predict who will remain and who will leave. The first born and the last born, regardless of sex, appear to have a comparatively greater chance of remaining in the compound than their siblings, but birth order is not a determining factor, as there is always a possibility that they will move out of their own accord.

Judging from changes that occurred in this twenty-year period, it is impossible to identify the development cycle of multihousehold compounds. What I have attempted to describe in this chapter is rather the unpredictable nature of Malay multihousehold compound composition. At the same time, however, the principle of living together in the same compound clearly exists, and perhaps this could be termed a tendency towards the formation of irregular kin groups.

The formation of multihousehold compounds played a very important role in establishing a community base in many areas of Southeast Asia when new settlements were being opened. Once past the formative period, the multihousehold compounds set down roots and moved into a period of succession, and the irregular nature of their composition became more pronounced. When membership in multihousehold compounds during this period was based on specific kin relationships, even if they were not cyclical, there was a greater possibility of predicting succeeding members. In Galok compounds, however, this type of principle does not exist. Multihousehold compounds are formed by the selection of their members. The word selection implies a positive action, but the people making the choice are, for the most part, unaware of it, and the members who comprise the household seem to be less a result of choice than of simply remaining behind. In either case, the most important point is that no particular value is given to the continued existence of the multihousehold compound.

In addition to the lack of principles governing membership, the unpredictability of multihousehold compound composition in Galok is caused by the movement of member households, particularly the out-migration of the parents' household and its replacement by a child's household. This phenomenon is particularly noticeable in the later period of succession rather than in the formative period.

In conclusion, let us consider the possibilities for the future based on an extension of this unpredictable character. Although multihousehold compounds comprised of multiple households exist, any child may freely leave the parental compound to live elsewhere. If all the children decide to move, very little resistance is made and it is therefore possible that some day only the households of the elderly will be left in the compound, as opposed to Japan where the principle of lineal descent demands that the eldest son remain. On the other hand, there is also a possibility that living close to one's kin will be highly valued, and the multihousehold compound will be maintained without disintegrating. Observation of the present situation in the village reveals the existence of both situations; elderly people living alone on the one hand, and on the other, multihousehold compounds that have continued through successive generations and independent households that have converted into compounds. At this point, however, no significant change has occurred in Galok.

11
Life in a Minor Pondok and Changes, 1970–1992

11.1. *Pondok* of Kelantan

The Malay word *pondok* literally means "hut," but it also refers to a type of religious boarding school comprised of the house of the teacher (guru) and the school building (*madrasah*) in the center surrounded by many huts where the guru's followers live, cooking their own meals, and study his teachings. The small huts of the students are all called *pondok*, but so is the entire school complex. This type of religious school can be found throughout the states in the northern part of the Malay peninsula and in southern Thailand, and has provided Malays with religious education. *Pondok* in the Malay peninsula were the subject of numerous studies in the 1960s and 1970s (for example, Rauf n.d., Fraser, 1960; Fujimoto, 1966; Yano, 1970; Winzeler, 1970; Winzeler, 1974; Awang Had, 1977). With the introduction of the modern education system in the 1980s, however, research on traditional education seems to have declined, although I was able to discover at least one comparatively recent report (Cf. Surin, 1985). Rather than focussing on the educational function of the *pondok*, I will look at the relationship between the *pondok* system and the lives of Malay villagers in an attempt to trace changes that have occurred in the *pondok*.

As a *pondok*'s fame is directly related to the knowledge of the guru and his charisma, which is sometimes viewed as a supernatural power, such schools should potentially last only one generation, terminating with the death of their founder. In fact, however, many *pondok* are passed down from father to son. With the introduction of the elementary school system and especially after the spread of lower secondary education in the latter half of the 1960s, a noticeable decline occurred in the number of youth studying at *pondok*. Some *pondok* responded by renovating their facilities or reorganizing their educational system by providing Arabic language instruction and creating ties with universities in Saudi Arabia, Egypt and other countries, while striving to maintain a balance between tradition and modernization. With the growing influence of the Islamic Party in Kelantan politics, some of these *pondok* were able to send representatives to the state assembly or national parliament, and some received financial assistance from the state government to improve their buildings and grounds and were visited by the Sultan. Thus, education in *pondok* schools did not die out, but rather began to serve a new role in society.

Upon visiting several *pondok*, I noted that their grounds contained huts for the elderly and houses occupied by ordinary villagers in addition to the huts or dormitories for young people. Part of one *pondok* had even been transformed into a type of welfare facility. With help from its supporters, a row of apartments with a raised floor and connecting corridor was constructed to serve as a home for elderly villagers without kin who lived on RM30 a month in subsidies from the Social Welfare Department. By taking in elderly residents, the *pondok* were able to achieve a transformation in their function.

The third category of residents in the *pondok* is ordinary families. The family and kin of the religious teacher or guru naturally live on the grounds, but in addition to these, distant relations or acquaintances who are in some way connected to the guru build their homes and live within the *pondok* which preaches the acceptance of others as a religious obligation.

The predominant change in minor *pondok* was the declining number of young students and the increasing number of elderly residents taking their place. This trend had already been observed in many *pondok* as early as 1970, and by 1992 it had become well established. Here I will compare study results for the minor *pondok* adjoining the village of Galok obtained in 1971 with the results from the follow-up survey conducted in 1992 to determine what changes occurred in this minor *pondok*, and to attempt to elucidate the relationship between lifestyles in the farm village and the *pondok*.

11.2. Establishment of a Minor *Pondok* and Transitions

This *pondok* was opened in 1937 on a little over one acre of land adjoining the southern end of Galok owned by the father of a guru in Jabo. According to the results of interviews carried out in 1971, the guru's year of birth is recorded as 1919, which would have made him 18 years old at the time the *pondok* was opened. This information is questionable, however, and considering the year of his marriage and the age of his eldest son, it seems likely that 1919 was mistaken for 1909. If this is the case, he would have been 28 at the time the *pondok* opened. Although he studied at *pondok* in Pasir Mas and other places, he has never stayed a long period in Mecca, travelling there only once on an ordinary pilgrimage in 1953.

When the *pondok* first opened, there were few students, but the number increased gradually reaching as many as fifty several years later. It was not until 1949 that a private elementary school (*sekolah rakyat*) was established in the area, and thus the *pondok* was the main source of education for children before the opening of the secular school. The elementary school was repaired by the government in 1953, and in 1959 it came under government jurisdiction and

Table 11-1
Pondok Experience by Age (For Men in Galok)

Age in 1971	Total Population	Number with *Pondok* Experience	Percentage
20–24	22	2	9.1
25–29	18	3	16.7
30–34	19	5	26.3
35–39	17	4	23.5
40–44	18	6	33.3
45–49	12	6	50.0
50–54	15	11	73.3
55–	23	7	30.4
Total	144	44	30.6

Table 11-2
Literacy of Pondok Pupils in 1971 by Period of Stay (For male residents of Galok who had received only pondok education)

Period of Stay	Literacy					Total
	Illiterate	Can Write Name Only	Can Read Only Jawi	Can Read Only Rumi	Can Read Both Jawi And Rumi	
< 1 year	1					1
1 year	3	2	1			6
2 years	2					2
3 years	5		2		1	8
4 years	1					1
5 years	2		2		1	5
6 years			1			1
7 years			1			1
8 years <		1	1		1	3
Total	14	3	8	0	3	28

was made into a national school (*sekolah kebangsaan*). Around 1960, the number of youth living in the *pondok* decreased to about twenty, but in their stead the number of elderly, and particularly of elderly women, increased, exceeding the number of youth by the mid-1960s. In January, 1965, a lower secondary school was opened in Kankong about four miles away, resulting in further development of school education, and the number of young students living in the *pondok* had decreased to only five by 1971.

The proportion of male Galok residents at the time of the 1970/1971 survey who had stayed at a *pondok* (not necessarily the one in Galok) during their youth is shown in Table 11-1. The highest rate, 73.3 percent, occurred in the 50–54 age group, indicating that *pondok* education was at its peak in the 1930s. In the older age groups, the proportion of those who had attended *pondok* remained around 30.4 percent, indicating that *pondok* education was not a long established tradition, but rather peaked at a certain period. The rate of attendance among those aged 20–24 was only 9.1 percent, and the decline in young students living in the *pondok* was already marked. Table 11-2 shows the reading and writing ability of those who received only *pondok* education, and it is obvious that it did not ensure literacy. This may be one reason why the *pondok* were so readily replaced by the public school system.

When the founding guru died in 1986, his eldest son, born in 1934, an imam who had been living in Paloh in Tanah Merah district, returned with his family and began teaching religion at the *pondok* while working as an instructor at an Arabic school in nearby Padang Hangus. This guru has since retired, and now teaches religion only once a week on Thursdays. Although the *pondok* continues to exist, it has lost any aspirations for expansion or development.

11.3. Location of Houses and Living Conditions

In 1971, the *pondok* consisted of fifty-seven large and small buildings including the *madrasah* or school building in the center with an adjacent well. The locations of these buildings are shown in Figure 11-1. The guru's house was built facing the road and was connected to the *madrasah* at the back. Five of the small huts were unoccupied. All of the buildings had raised floors, and while the larger homes had an area of about 81 square meters or more, the huts were only 9–13.5 square meters. As was typical of buildings in Kelantan, the larger structures, including the guru's residence and the *madrasah*, were roofed with slate and wood was used at least partially for the walls. The huts (*pondok*), which comprised the vast majority of buildings on the grounds, had thatched roofs and woven bamboo walls. Houses of ordinary size were built much like those in the nearby village, but the construction of the huts was much simpler.

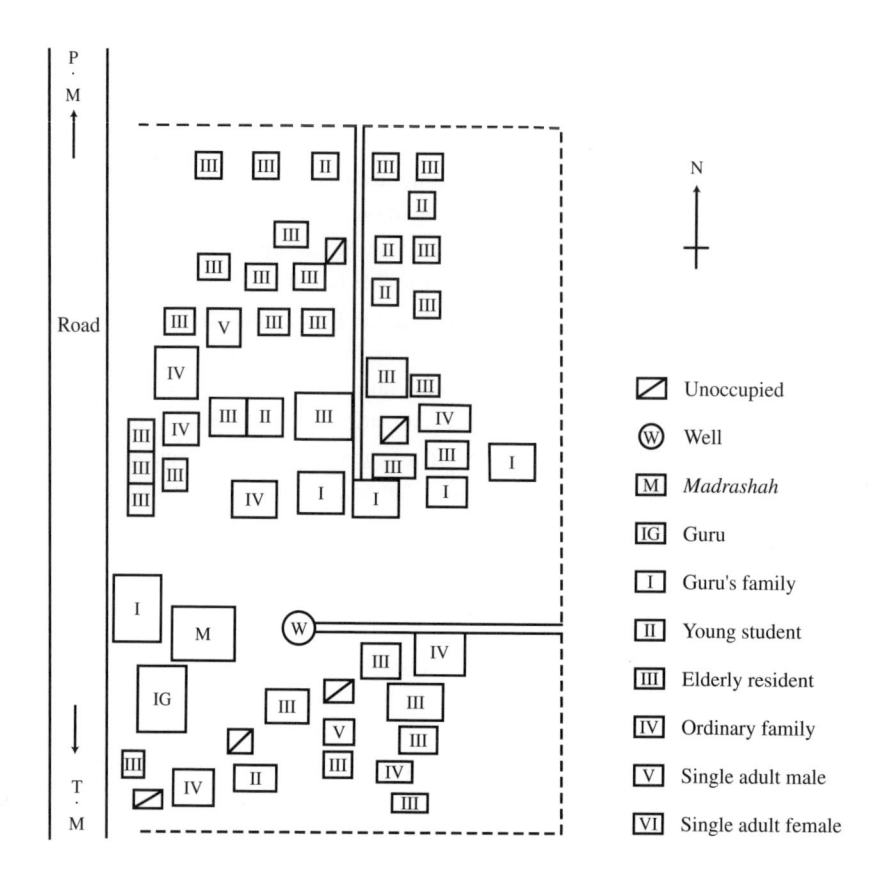

Figure 11-1. Location of Buildings in the *Pondok* (1971)

Houses of ordinary size belonged to the person living in them. Huts were likewise considered to be the property of the individual who built them or who received them directly from the former occupant. When the occupant died and a hut remained unoccupied, however, it was considered communal property (*wakaf*), and its management was entrusted to the guru. In 1971, none of the houses were equipped with toilets, and the residents used the nearby bush for this purpose as was true for the residents of the surrounding villages. All of the *pondok* residents obtained water from the well at the entrance of the *madrasah* in the center of the grounds. A concrete cistern had been built beside the well, and one of the *pondok* residents received RM10 (about 1,200 yen at the exchange rate of that time) per month from the guru to fill the tank with well water daily. Used to perform ablutions before worship services, *pondok* residents paid 30 *sen* a month to the guru for the use of this water. *Pondok*

Plate 11-1. View of the pondok in 1971; no. 1.

Plate 11-2. View of the pondok in 1971; no. 2.

residents also paid the guru RM1 a year for the lamp oil used in the *madrasah* as the area did not yet have electricity. There were no other obligatory fees besides those listed above.

By 1992, living conditions had changed radically. The locations of buildings in the *pondok* grounds are shown in Figure 11-2. The road through the *pondok* connecting Pasir Mas and Tanah Merah had been widened and households located along the road, including that of the guru, were awarded compensation and moved several meters back, at which time the buildings were either renovated or new ones built in their place. The paddy fields behind the grounds were filled in, extending the *pondok*'s land area. The number of houses and huts with thatched roofs and woven bamboo walls had greatly decreased, and those with roofs of sheet metal or new materials and wooden walls had

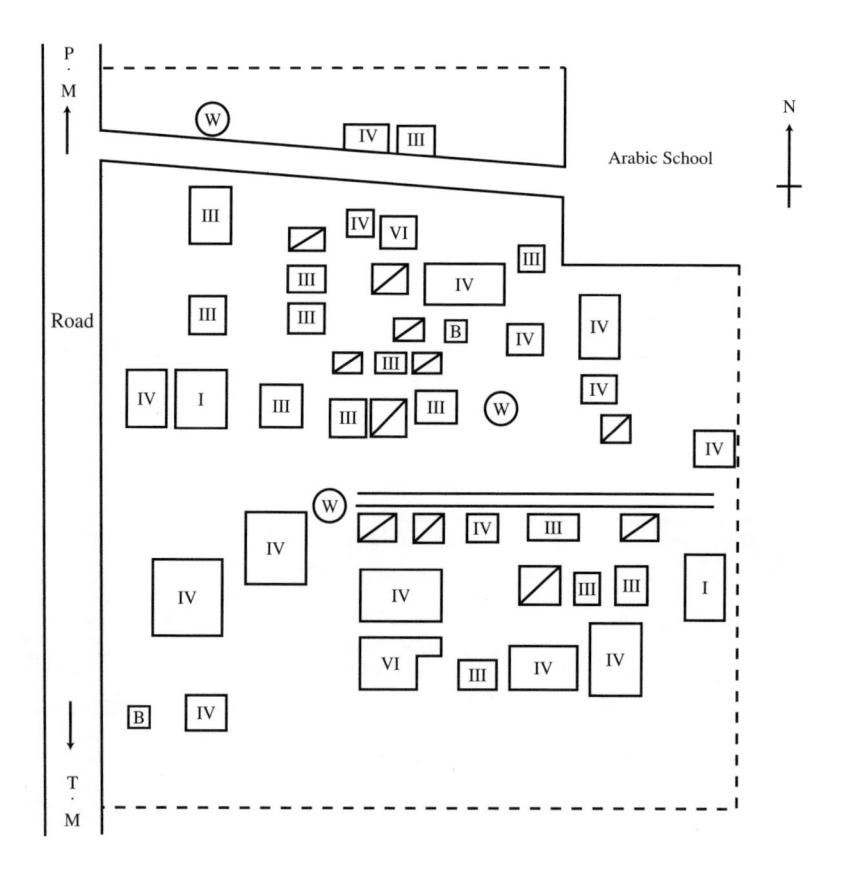

Figure 11-2. Location of Buildings in the *Pondok* (1992)

increased. The floor area per home had also expanded. Ten years had passed since the extension of electric power to Galok and some houses even had running water by 1992. The number of wells had increased to three. An electric pump was now used to pump water from the central well into the cistern, and the residents of the *pondok* paid the guru RM1 per month for the electricity. A considerable number of toilets had been constructed within the grounds. Housing conditions had considerably improved compared to 1971, but were still not on a par with that of ordinary residences in the village. Drainage was poor in some parts of the grounds, and puddles several centimeters deep formed in these places. In both outward appearance and living conditions, the *pondok* remained backward compared to the surrounding village.

Households in the *pondok* in 1971 and 1992 were classified according to composition category and period of stay, as shown in Table 11-3. In 1971, there were fifty-three households in the *pondok*, including single person households, but this number had decreased to thirty-three in 1992. Although residences grew

Table 11-3
Number of Households in The Pondok by Category and Period of Stay,
1971 and 1992

Period of Stay	Guru's Family and Kin	Young Person	Single Elderly Person	Family	Single Adult Male	Single Adult Female	Total
< 1 year			3 (2)		2	(1)	5 (3)
1 year			6				6
2 years		2	2	(1)			4 (1)
3 years			2 (2)				2 (2)
4 years			5 (1)				5 (1)
5 years		1	3	(1)			4 (1)
6 years		2	1 (1)	(1)			3 (2)
7 years			1 (1)	(1)			1 (2)
8 years			2	(2)			2 (2)
9 years	1						1
10 years	2		3 (1)	1			6 (1)
11 years			(1)				(1)
12 years							
13 years			2	(1)			2 (1)
14 years			(1)				(1)
15 years <	4 (3)		2 (5)	5 (6)		(1)	11 (15)
Unknown				1			1
Total	7 (3)	5	32 (15)	7(13)	2	(2)	53 (33)

Numbers in parentheses are for 1992.

in size, as described above, this does not sufficiently explain the decrease in the number of households. In 1971, there were only five empty houses, while in 1992 there were as many as twelve. We cannot ignore the fact that the number of actual buildings, including the *madrasah*, decreased from fifty-nine to forty-six, but in the increasing number of empty houses we can see the decline of the *pondok*.

11.4. The Guru's Family and Kin

In addition to the guru's family, there were a total of seven households living in the *pondok* in 1971 that were family or kin of the guru, including the guru's father (80), his father's half-sister (62), his older brother (62), the mother of his previous wife (70), his younger sister (50), and his son by his previous wife (32). The relationships between these households are shown in Figure 11-3. The ages of the guru's family shown in the figure are not entirely reliable, although they are somewhat more accurate than that of the guru. As has been discussed before, residency of close kin within the same compound was a common phenomenon, although the number of relations living in the same place was somewhat greater than usual in this case. Of the kin households listed above, the first five no longer existed in 1992 due to the natural deaths of the household heads.

The household of the guru in 1971 was comprised of the guru, his 19-year-old wife and their 1-year-old son. The guru had been married four times before. He divorced his first wife after three or four months, his second wife died after bearing him three children, his third marriage ended in divorce after a year and a half, and his fourth wife died after ten years of marriage. For a short period of time, his marriages to his third and fourth wife overlapped in a polygynous union. He had married the spouse of 1971 in 1969, but this union ended in

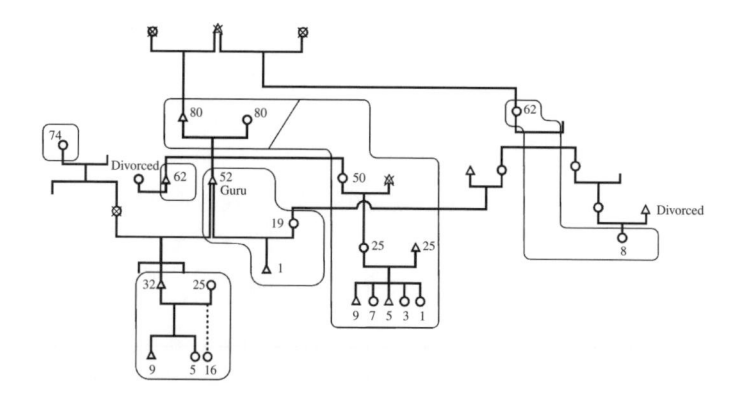

Figure 11-3. The Guru's Kin Living in the *Pondok*

divorce after four years of marriage and his wife left with the children for Pahang where she remarried. The guru then married a woman who was over thirty from Kota Bharu district. This last wife returned to her native home after the guru's death. The mother of his second wife, as mentioned above, was living in the *pondok* in 1971. At that time, the eldest child of his second marriage, a son (37) was living in Paloh in Tanah Merah district cultivating paddy and teaching the Koran. The second child, another son (32), had opened a combined tailor shop and general store along the road in front of the *pondok*, and the third child, a daughter (30) was married and lived in Galok.

In 1971, the guru did not cultivate his own land (1.5 acres of paddy and 4.75 acres of rubber land, of which 1.5 acres had been replanted and could not be tapped), but instead rented it to tenants. He had purchased the majority of this land thirteen to thirty years earlier from his cousin, a nephew and others. Due to the poor paddy harvest and falling rubber prices, income from this land in 1970/1971 was only about 200 *gantang* in paddy and RM300 in cash. For the guru's household of three people, 200 *gantang* of paddy was sufficient for one year. In addition to this, he received about 50 *gantang* of paddy from the village at harvest time as a form of Islamic tax called *zakat*, and at the end of the fast, he received cash, with a portion in rice, equivalent to about 40 *gantang* of polished rice from some of the *pondok* residents and villagers as *fitrah*. He was also invited to offer prayers at the cemetery (*tunggu kubor*) for funerals, prayers of supplication (*sembahyang hajat*), etc., for which he received RM1 each time from which he earned about RM100 annually. On such occasions he would often be invited for meals and frequently participated in wedding feasts (*baewah*). Although his lifestyle was not particularly affluent, neither was he poor.

The guru's son earned more than RM700 a month from the tailor shop which measured about six meters by three and was equipped with three sewing machines, while his income from the general store ranged from RM300 to RM400 a year. This combined with income from a total of 7 acres of rubber land and 2.5 acres of coconut land acquired in 1958 gave him a total annual income of close to RM2,000, much higher than the income of most Galok residents. The guru's younger sister's household cultivated paddy and tobacco, and derived cash income from the daughter's husband's job as a trishaw driver, and from renting 1.5 acres of rubber land, giving an annual income of 200 *gantang* of paddy and RM900 in cash. The guru's mother and father lived in the same house as his younger sister, but their households were separate. Because of their advanced age, their sole income was derived from renting paddy (1.75 acres) and rubber land (1.5 acres), amounting to a total of about 150 *gantang* of paddy and RM200 in cash. The guru's older brother had divorced six months earlier, and was living alone, and in addition to tapping his father's rubber land under the *pawah* system, he also rented out rubber (2 acres) and paddy land (1.5 acres) of his own, making about 150 *gantang* of paddy and RM300 in cash. The guru's aunt lived on support sent by her daughter and son-in-law who lived in Tanah Merah. The mother of the guru's previous wife was supported by her five grandchildren, three grandsons and two granddaughters, one of whom ran the tailor shop in the *pondok*. The economic status of the guru's kin living in the *pondok* was varied and not always particularly affluent, with some members dependent on financial support.

Five members of the guru's kin living in the *pondok* including the guru himself had been on pilgrimage to Mecca at the time of the 1971 survey, a much higher percentage than that for ordinary villagers. In 1950, the guru's father and younger sister went using money from land that they sold, in 1953 the guru went using his savings, and in 1960 the guru's aunt and his previous wife's mother went, generating funds through the sale of land to their children and grandchildren, and travelling with the guru's eldest son who at that time lived in Tanah Merah.

By 1992, the guru's son had returned to Galok from Tanah Merah as aforementioned accompanied by his wife and three children and they were living at the southern end of the *pondok* grounds near the road. He had six other children, but the two eldest were married and living in Tanah Merah and Trengganu, while the remaining four had left home and were studying at Universiti Kebangsaan Malaysia and other institutions. There were only two households comprised of the guru's kin remaining in the *pondok*. Of these, the former guru's younger sister's household had shrunk to four people, including the younger sister and her husband and half sister, while the five grandchildren had all left. The present guru's younger brother, who in 1971 had lived along the road in front of the *pondok*, had moved to reclaimed paddy land at the very back of the *pondok* where he built a concrete-block bungalow. Whereas before he had run a shop and a small tailor business, he now provided sand for construction purposes. His household included himself (53), his wife (46), six sons and two daughters, the eldest of whom was his second daughter (17). His eldest son (29) and daughter (25) were married and living within Kelantan, while another son (19) was studying at Universiti Teknologi.

11.5. Residents of the *Pondok*

11.5.1. Young men

As I have mentioned, five young men studying religion lived in the *pondok* in 1971. Although some *pondok* took young girls as students, segregating them from the men, this *pondok* only accepted young men. From eldest to youngest, their ages were 22, 21, 19, 14, and 13. The 22- and 19-year-old had each lived in the *pondok* for six years, the 21-year-old for five years, and the 14- and 13-year-olds for two years. Their native villages were mainly within about a two-mile radius (2 *batu* = 3.2 km) of the *pondok*, all of them located in areas relatively far from a road. The 22-year-old and 14-year-old's parents were neighbors and the younger followed the older one to the *pondok*, living in the same hut.

The older students had their own income. The 22-year-old borrowed land and cultivated tobacco as well as working at the tobacco station in Galok, earning over RM600 a year. The 21- and 19-year-olds also borrowed land from relatives or other people for tobacco cultivation making about RM500 a year. The 22-year-old was almost entirely independent, but the other two received supplements of rice from their parents. They also attended funerals and other ceremonies with the guru, receiving from 50 *sen* to RM1 as a tip, amounting to an income of about RM5 a month. The younger two resided in the *pondok* solely to learn about the Koran and religion, and each received about two to four *gantang* of paddy and RM2 to RM4 in cash every month from their parents. Viewed from this perspective, the lifestyles of youth in the *pondok* were quite varied.

In 1992, there was not a single youth residing in the *pondok* to study religion. This was in contrast to more famous *pondok*, which improved both their facilities and curricula and still have many young students even today.

Plate 11-3. View of the pondok in 1971; no. 3.

11.5.2. Elderly Residents

In 1971, three-fifths of *pondok* residences, including small huts, were occupied by older people. The majority of these were women, with only two men, one of whom lived with his wife and the other with his grandchild. Almost all the elderly residents came from villages within a radius of ten miles (16 km) of the *pondok*, including the guru's native village of Jabo (ten people), and other nearby villages such as Chekok, Galok, Padang Hangus and Kampung Tengah (a total of six people). According to the land register, the *pondok* is located in Jabo, but geographically it is also easily accessible to residents from both Galok and Chekok, which are located along the road. Despite this, natives of the guru's home village of Jabo were dominant among *pondok* residents indicating that the majority of the guru's and his parents' personal connections were concentrated there.

Some of the elderly residents had income from work at the tobacco station in Galok or in stores, while others received rent for property they own. Still others received partial support, while those with no income were totally dependent upon outside assistance. Income earned in 1971 is shown in Table 11-4. The highest income did not exceed RM800 and almost 90 percent made less than RM300, while more than one-third had no income at all. It is clear from this table that those with higher incomes received proportionately less financial support from others. No one particular child was responsible for supporting those elderly residents who required financial assistance. Rather, all their children, regardless of gender, sent money or food when they had some to spare. When asked which child should be responsible for supporting their parents, villagers frequently said their sons, but in reality, the ratio was two males to one female. In some cases, grandchildren sent an allowance. Where there were no children or grandchildren, or where they were unable to offer support, the elderly received financial assistance from other kin, from fellow villagers, or from people who came to worship at the *pondok*. Funds sent by children amounted to about RM10 a month at the most, and in some cases several children irregularly sent sums of RM1 to RM2 a month, or small amounts of rice.

Of the thirty-two households comprised of elderly residents, twenty-five (78.1 percent) lived entirely alone, and six (18.8 percent) lived with grandchildren including one great-grandchild. Only one household was comprised of a married couple. It should be noted that four of the six elderly people living with grandchildren, including the great-grandchild, were from Jabo or a nearby village. Three of the grandchildren were male and five were female, and they ranged in age from 6 to 25 years. A more detailed look at the kin relationships with the grandchildren reveals that four were offspring of a

Table 11-4
Situation of Elderly Residents According to Income

SELF-GENERATED INCOME (RM PER ANNUM)	INDEPENDENT	PARTIALLY SUPPORTED	FULLY SUPPORTED	TOTAL
0			11	11
–49		3		3
50–99	1	3		4
100–199	2	4		6
200–299	4			4
300–399	1	1		2
400–499				
500–599	1			1
600–699				
700–799	1			1
Total	10	11	11	32

son whose wife had died (two were siblings), two were children of a daughter who had divorced, one was the child of a daughter who lived with her husband in Tanah Merah, and one was the child of a grand-daughter whose husband had died. Of these grandchildren, a 25-year-old male and 16-year-old girl were cousins raised by their grandmother in the *pondok*, but had married one year previously and continued to live with the grandmother.

If we look at the situation of elderly Galok residents excluding those who lived with their children's families, there were eight cases of elderly people, seven of whom were women, living with their grandchildren as opposed to six who lived on their own, five of whom were women. In comparison, a much greater proportion of the elderly in the *pondok* lived alone. Living with a grandchild relieved the elderly person's feeling of loneliness, and particularly when the grandchild was a girl, meant there was someone there to take care of them. In the village, grandchildren living with their elderly grandparents were able to maintain close contact with other kin living nearby. The typical pattern was an elderly grandparent living with one or two grandchildren, whose parents lived close by. In the case of residence in the *pondok*, however, especially for people who came from villages some distance away, the grandchild was cut off from his kin, a situation most children would not want. Add to this a low income, and the proportion of grandchildren living with their elderly grandparents in the *pondok* is understandably lower.

For elderly people living in the *pondok*, their spiritual relationship with the guru and their personal relationships with other elderly residents is of great significance. For someone who has lost a spouse or close kin at an advanced age, residence in the *pondok* offers emotional support. Some choose to live in the *pondok* even though their children have offered them a place in their home. It must be stressed, therefore, that residence in the *pondok* is not chosen as a last resort, but rather has a more positive meaning.

At the time of the survey in 1971, five elderly *pondok* residents had been to Mecca on pilgrimage, all of them as members of pilgrimage tours organized by the Malaysian government. Each case is described below from the oldest to the most recent. Case 1, a woman (73), sold rubber land for RM3,000 to go on pilgrimage with her husband in 1958. Case 2, a woman (62) saved money made through selling fish, straw matting (*tikar*) and cloth and joined a pilgrimage group on her own in 1961. Case 3, a woman (75), sold about one acre of paddy land inherited from her mother to her cousin for RM1,400 and went on her own in 1963. Case 4, a woman (55), used RM600 obtained from the sale of two paddy fields to her daughter and RM900 in savings and joined a group on her own in 1967. Case 5, a woman (57), sold one acre of rubber land to her son for RM1,200, and using an additional RM200 of her own money, traveled with her daughter-in-law's parents. It is important to note that pilgrimages made by elderly people are connected to the sale of land. Four out of the above five cases sold land to fund their pilgrimage. In many cases, the purchaser of the land is a child or other relative. Interestingly, this reveals the individual character of property ownership and the ways in which children and kin support the elderly.

The number of elderly residents dwindled from thirty-two in 1971 to fifteen in 1992. If we look at the length of residency for both years we find that the period of stay ranges from less than one year to as long as over fifteen years in both cases, showing that although the total number of elderly residents is declining, new residents are still coming in. If we look at the percentage of people according to length of stay, however, those who had resided in the *pondok* for less than three years dropped from 34.4 percent in 1971 to 13.3 percent in 1992, while the percentage of those who had lived there for over fifteen years rose from 6.3 percent in 1971 to 33.3 percent in 1992. This indicates that elderly newcomers to the *pondok* are gradually decreasing in number.

The five elderly residents who had lived in the *pondok* for more than fifteen years in 1992 are described below.

    (1) Female (67): Originally from Kampung Kuek, part of Mukim Jabo, she came to the *pondok* twenty years ago and is a distant relative of the guru. Married but divorced fifteen years ago, she has three daughters who live in Sungai Golok, Jeli, and Hutan Mala. She has no property but works at the tobacco curing plant, earning from RM3 to

RM5 a day. In 1973, she sold five paddy fields she had inherited in Chekok and used the proceeds from the sale to go on pilgrimage to Mecca. She lives in a simple dwelling with 5 m by 4.5 m built of woven bamboo walls and a sheet metal roof, borrowing it free of charge (*wakaf*) after the owner died. It has no electricity and she uses well water.

(2) Female (68): She came from Chabang Empat to live in the *pondok* twenty years ago. She has been married nine times but every marriage ended in divorce. Childless, she adopted her older brother's daughter (18) and they live together. Both of them work at the tobacco curing plant earning from RM3 to RM5 each a day. They live in a building of woven bamboo about 4.5 m by 4.5 m built at their own expense. They have no electricity and use well water.

(3) Female (62): Born in Chekok, she moved to the *pondok* when her mother began living there. She has been divorced four times. Her daughter (38) who was born in the *pondok* has continued to live next-door, and she also has one son and two other daughters. She owns inherited property consisting of one acre each of paddy and rubber land in Sungai Keladi, which she lets to sharecroppers. She is now temporarily residing in a different *pondok* called Pondok Lubuk Tapak in Lemal. In 1985 she went to Mecca on pilgrimage using funds from the sale of one acre of fruit land to her two daughters. She has electricity and uses the running water at her daughter's house next-door.

(4) Female (80): Originally from Chekok, she is the guru's second cousin and fourteen or fifteen years have passed since she came to the *pondok*. She has been married twice and divorced both times. Her 44-year-old daughter and family live a slight distance away within the same *pondok*, and she has two other daughters and one son. She owns two acres of paddy land in nearby Kebang Gendang, which is sharecropped by her nephew. In 1967, she went on pilgrimage to Mecca, raising funds by selling two acres of paddy to her eldest daughter. She lives in a simple hut 3 meters by 3 meters made of woven bamboo with no electricity. She uses well water.

(5) Female (70): Originally from Jabo Hilir, she came to the *pondok* fifteen years ago and is a distant relative of the guru. Her 42-year-old son who studied at this *pondok* when he was 14 lives next door and his eldest son presently lives with the woman. The woman's husband accompanied her to the *pondok* and lived there until he passed away. She owns a general store near the road on the western edge of the

pondok grounds, and lives on this income as well as on support from her son. She went on pilgrimage with her husband by boat. Although she has electricity, she does not have a fan or television, and she uses well water.

The four elderly people described below are relatively recent arrivals who had lived in the *pondok* for three years or less in 1992.

(1) Female (86): Originally from nearby Chekok, she was living in Ayer Lanas with her youngest daughter but moved to the *pondok* about three years ago. Although she has been married five times, every marriage ended in divorce. Two years ago, her eldest daughter (60) moved to a house next-door with her own daughter (30) and grandchildren, and the woman eats her meals in their home. Because she has impaired vision, her daughter often takes care of her. She owns 0.5 acres of inherited paddy land, which she rents out to sharecroppers, and the previous year she earned twenty to thirty *gantang* of paddy in this way. She has no electricity and uses well water.

(2) Female (70): Her husband died three years ago and she has lived in this *pondok* for three years, coming from Jabo along the river. She has no children of her own. Her husband's previous wife's son lives in Chetok but is an invalid. The guru is her distant kin. Her older brother's son (55) lives in a compound adjacent to the *pondok* grounds and he built her hut. She owns two paddy fields in Jabo, which she sharecrops, but the previous year they were not cultivated. She lives on her savings. In 1957 she sold three acres of rubber land and went on pilgrimage with her husband, who died in 1989, to Mecca. She has electricity but no fan or television and uses well water.

(3) Female (55): Originally from Belimbing in Tanah Merah, she lived for eleven years in Pondok Lati, but she moved to this *pondok* one year ago because the steps to the mosque in the other one were too high. She received her *pondok* by *wakaf* from the guru. Divorced, she has four children, three sons and one daughter, all of whom have been adopted into other families. She works in the rubber estate owned by the guru earning 50 sen a day. She has no electricity and uses well water.

(4) Female (60): She moved to the *pondok* from Salak in Tanah Merah four months previously and lives in the same hut as the 55-year-old woman above. She earns 50 sen a day working in the guru's rubber grove. Her husband died seven years ago and she has no children.

The children and families of some of the long-term residents also live in the *pondok*. Of the five people described in this category above, the families of three reside in the *pondok*, indicating that they have become quite accustomed to *pondok* life. Although the lifestyle is not affluent, it has its own organized system. At the same time, however, living conditions are poor and three of the five long-term residents and three of the four newer arrivals live in small huts without electricity. The number of divorcees is outstanding among both types of residents, indicating that the *pondok* takes in people who are thrust into positions of insecurity. Some of the recently arrived elderly women have similar backgrounds to the long-term residents, but the two most recent arrivals lack family support and rather than living in the *pondok* for religious reasons, they use it as a temporary place of residence or as a refuge.

Despite the declining numbers of elderly residents in the *pondok*, the number making a pilgrimage to Mecca has increased even in absolute numbers compared to 1971, with nine of the fifteen people in this category having been to Mecca. Economic development in Malaysia has made pilgrimage easier for many, but it must be pointed out that, even though they lacked financial security, people sold their property in order to go. Despite the knowledge that the sale of land would aggravate their poverty, they placed more importance on pilgrimage, demonstrating that priority is given to religious experience. At the same time, however, five of the nine elderly people who went to Mecca did not sell land to do so, and the number of people who sell land in order to go is decreasing compared to 1971.

11.5.3. Families

There were seven households residing in the *pondok* grounds in 1971 comprised of families that did not have any kin relationship to the guru. All except one of these came from a neighboring village. The one exception was a newlywed couple (23 and 16 years of age) who came from a village less than two miles away. The wife and her grandmother had lived together in the *pondok* and when she married the grandmother had given the couple her hut and returned to her native village. In that sense, the *pondok* was the bride's native home.

These families lived in the *pondok* with the guru's permission, but their relationship to him as his religious followers or pupils was weak. If this type of household increases, a *pondok* will lose its original function, yet it is not unusual in Kelantan for *pondok* to contain some ordinary families. Due to the limited land available, these households were unable to raise oxen for tilling paddy fields, and those who owned paddy land generally rented it to others. In 1970/1971 five of the seven households cultivated tobacco and this was their most important source of income. Other primary occupations were peddling medicine and rubber tapping. Annual household income ranged from RM600 to RM1,200, with an average of RM793, lower even than the mean income of RM1,076 for Galok residents.

By 1992, the number of families living in the *pondok* had increased to thirteen households. In 1971, all the households except one for which data were unclear had resided in the *pondok* for more than ten years, but in 1992, six households (46.2 percent) had a history of less than eight years, showing that families had moved into the *pondok* comparatively recently. These newer residents are described below.

(1) Female household head (40): Born in nearby Kankong, the household head was divorced once, and built a house in the *pondok* with her second husband where they had lived for eight years. Her husband was an imam in Tanah Merah, but in 1992 he went to Mecca with his first wife and died there. After her husband's death, the household head worked at the elementary school cafeteria in Chekok for a daily wage of RM5. She lives with her two sons, aged 8 and 4 years. There is electricity but no fan or television, and she uses well water.

(2) Female household head (43): Born in Jabo, the household head lived in Tok Uban but moved to the *pondok* eight years ago where she lives with her 17-year-old son. Her husband lives with his second wife in Tok Uban. They have three other sons, aged 27, 23, and 19, and a 13-year-old daughter, but the sons live in Sabah, Kuala Lumpur and Johor, and the daughter lives with her grandmother in Galok. The husband has no children by his second wife. The woman lives on income earned from rubber tapping and selling sweets at a nearby coffee shop, with occasional financial support from her sons. She is the second cousin of the previous guru. The house has electricity, a fan and a television, and was connected to the water supply just three months earlier.

(3) Male household head (79): Born in Padang Hangus, the household head used to live in Thailand where he worked as a carpenter. He moved to the *pondok* seven years ago with his wife who is over fifty although her exact age is not known. He has one son and four daughters by this wife, but his son and one daughter live in a rubber area in Pahang state and the other three daughters live in Kelantan. The man owns one acre of inherited paddy land in Padang Hangus, which he rents out to sharecroppers, and his wife makes additional income by working at the tobacco curing plant and selling sweets at a coffee shop. Ten years ago he sold two acres of rubber land in Tok Uban and used the money to go to Mecca. Their home has electricity but no fan or television and they use well water.

(4) Male household head (70): The household head was born in Jabo but lived in Thailand and moved to the *pondok* six years ago. He lives with his 50-year-old wife and two unmarried daughters aged twenty and

eighteen. He has three sons in Thailand who run their own businesses. He also has one daughter (over 40) living in Chekok from his marriage to his first wife, which ended in divorce. In addition to tapping rubber, he also teaches about thirty children the Koran. He was invited to the *pondok* by the present guru for this purpose, and was a follower of the previous guru. They have electricity but no fan or television and they use well water.

(5) Male household head (25): The household head is from Tanah Merah where he works in the office of a hospital, and he lives with his 23-year-old wife and their 1-year-old daughter. His wife who is originally from Bachok, moved to the *pondok* in 1987 borrowing a house on the edge of the grounds and teaching at the adjacent Arabic school. After marrying, they lived in this same house which was built by a villager living near the *pondok* and they pay a rent of RM20 per month. They have electricity, an electric fan and television, and the water supply was connected two months previously.

(6) Female household head (60): The household head came about two years ago from Sungai Keladi and lives with her 30-year-old daughter and four grandchildren. Her husband lives in Sungai Keladi with their son. The husband owns two acres of paddy and 0.5 acres of rubber land. The husband of the daughter is missing and the daughter works in the sawmill in Tanah Merah and makes sweets for sale at a coffee shop. The household head went to Mecca with her husband three years ago. They have electricity but no fan or television and they use well water. The woman's mother (86) moved next door three years ago, and is introduced under section 11.5.2 on elderly residents.

A variety of people are included within these households, and the fact that two had experienced polygynous marriages and two others had lived in Thailand indicates that many of them are not typical families. Nor should we overlook the young couples renting houses within the *pondok* grounds. The *pondok* has recently begun to be called Kampung Pondok, or Kampung Pondok Jabo, as if reflecting the increasing number of families living in it, a phenomenon that should be noted as a response to changes in the character of the *pondok*.

11.5.4. Single Male and Single Female Adults

In 1971, there were two single adult males aged forty-six and thirty-four living on their own in the *pondok*. They had chosen it as a temporary residence. The 46-year-old had a slight mental handicap, and although he had been married several times, his last wife had divorced him one year earlier. He had been working in the Machang rubber area cutting old trees, but came to the *pondok* one month earlier and began cultivating tobacco. He also worked as a water carrier during celebrations such as weddings. The 34-year-old had moved in two months earlier to work at the tobacco station in Galok. He had been living in Chenoh in Pasir Mas district about eleven miles (17.6 km) away, but had lost his wife two years previously. He had two sons aged eight and five but they were living with his wife's grandmother. He returned once a month to his own village and each time gave them RM5. These two men left shortly after, and in 1992, there were no single adult males living in the *pondok*.

In 1992, there were two single adult women residing in the *pondok*, a new category not seen in 1971. One of these was an unmarried girl of twenty-five. She had been living with her divorced mother in the *pondok*, but was left on her own when her mother went to live temporarily in Pondok Lubuk Tapak. During the survey in 1992, she was visiting her older sister's family in Kuala Lumpur, and I was told that she had begun working in a factory there. The other was a 37-year-old woman who had arrived nine months earlier. Born in Atas Beting, she had lived there until her husband married a second wife. When told that this wife was to live in the same house she applied for and was granted a divorce two years earlier. She paid the RM48 for the appeal herself in her haste to get divorced. She had four daughters ranging in age from 7 to 19 who lived with their father and came to visit occasionally. She worked the night shift at the sawmill in Tanah Merah, earning RM7.5 a day. Her hut was new and neatly kept, but had no electricity and she used well water. Of these two cases, the former can be viewed as a result of changes in the family, while the latter used the *pondok* as a refuge.

This was not the first case of women using the *pondok* as a shelter. In addition, one 46-year-old woman originally from Kampung Sirih who had been residing in the *pondok* for fifteen years in 1992, lived on RM40 a month from the Social Welfare Department received for a disability. As she lived with her 17-year-old adopted daughter, her household was classified in Table 11-3 under families. She had two adopted daughters but one of them had been employed for the last two or three years in Kota Bharu making batiks. The girls' parents were too poor to pay rent and the second daughter was born in the woman's home. Soon after, the mother died, followed a short time later by the father. Thirty-four days after the birth of the second child, the woman adopted them. Some people criticized her for adopting children when she herself was handicapped, but she consulted the guru who advised her not to abandon them and repaired a hut for her to live in. The adopted daughter who still lived with her worked four days a week at the elementary school cafeteria in nearby Chekok earning RM5 a day, and commuted to Pasir Mas twice a week to learn sewing. They have no electricity but the water supply was recently connected.

11.6. The Changing Function of the *Pondok*

In this chapter, I have recorded the changes that occurred within a minor *pondok* near Galok. Due to the development of the public school system, youth had already begun to distance themselves from *pondok* education by 1971. This ought to have signaled the disintegration of the local *pondok*. Like other minor *pondok* in Kelantan, however, it sought new opportunities, replacing young students with older residents. The only option left to the guru of that period was to support a *pondok* focussed on the elderly.

As the analysis of household composition in previous chapters shows, parents' households and those of their children in this region are often found within the same compound, although not always within the same house, and this mechanism seems to circumvent serious confrontations between parent and child, as well as preventing the isolation of elderly parents. This indicates that the increase in the number of elderly residents in the *pondok* is not necessarily a result of the villagers' desire for an alternative to caring for the aged members of their community. At the same time, we must acknowledge that the minor *pondok* did come to fill the role of old people's homes.

The changes that occurred in the *pondok*'s function, at least in the case of minor *pondok*, can be seen as a shift from education to social welfare. When the *pondok* was revisited in 1992, the number of elderly residents had decreased, and another aspect of the *pondok*'s role had come to the fore, that of a shelter or temporary residence. People who ran into difficulties living in regular society chose the *pondok* as a refuge, while people who could not find

Plate 11-4. The pondok in 1991.

an appropriate place to live, chose it as a temporary residence. This function was always inherent within the *pondok* as evidenced by the 1971 survey record of a 55-year-old woman with leprosy who had been living in the *pondok* for thirteen years.

The variations in the degree of emphasis placed on each of these three functions can be viewed as part of the process of change over time, and as the specialization of the roles of the different *pondok* during the same time period. In Kelantan today, large *pondok* such as Pondok Sungai Durian in Kuala Kerai district (formerly part of Ulu Kelantan) or Pondok Lubuk Tapak in Pasir Mas district have maintained and even consolidated their role in education. In the minor *pondok*, on the other hand, the role of refuge dominated. Although the function of assisting the elderly was more obvious in minor *pondok*, it was not entirely absent from the more renowned *pondok*. About 300 elderly people resided in Pondok Sungai Durian in addition to about 400 young students. There were differences in scale, but the function of refuge was also common to both. In this sense the specialization of function appears to be a relative phenomenon.

Table 11-5
Pondok Residents by Sex and Age, 1971 and 1992

AGE	MALE		FEMALE		TOTAL	
	1971	1992	1971	1992	1971	1992
0–4	4	5	4	6	8	11
5–9	4	5	8	8	12	13
10–14	6	7	6	7	12	14
15–19	2	4	6	8	8	12
20–24	4			4	4	4
25–29	2	1	3	1	5	2
30–34	2		2	2	4	2
35–39	2		1	4	3	4
40–44	1	3	1	2	2	5
45–49	2	3	2	3	4	6
50–54	2	1	1	4	3	5
55–59		2	12	1	12	3
60–64	2		7	5	9	5
65–69			8	2	8	2
70–74	1	1	4	6	5	7
75–79		1	2	1	2	2
80–84	1		2	3	3	3
85–				1		1
Total	35	33	69	68	104	101

Pondok, including the minor *pondok* described in this chapter, which placed a strong emphasis on the function of refuge in addition to their function as a form of social welfare, could be regarded as the epitome of a rural slum. Such *pondok* cannot conceal their degeneration. As mentioned before, *pondok* can be viewed as having a life span of only one generation based upon the relationship between a specific guru believed to be endowed with supernatural powers and his followers. It is misleading, however, to base one's evaluation solely on such a one-sided view of the ideal *pondok*, as illustrated by the existence of numerous *pondok* operated by a guru from the second generation, and the fact that minor *pondok* such as the one studied in this chapter have been maintained through a process of change.

The changes described above are evident in the age composition of *pondok* residents for 1971 and 1992 as shown in Table 11-5 and Figure 11-4. In 1971,

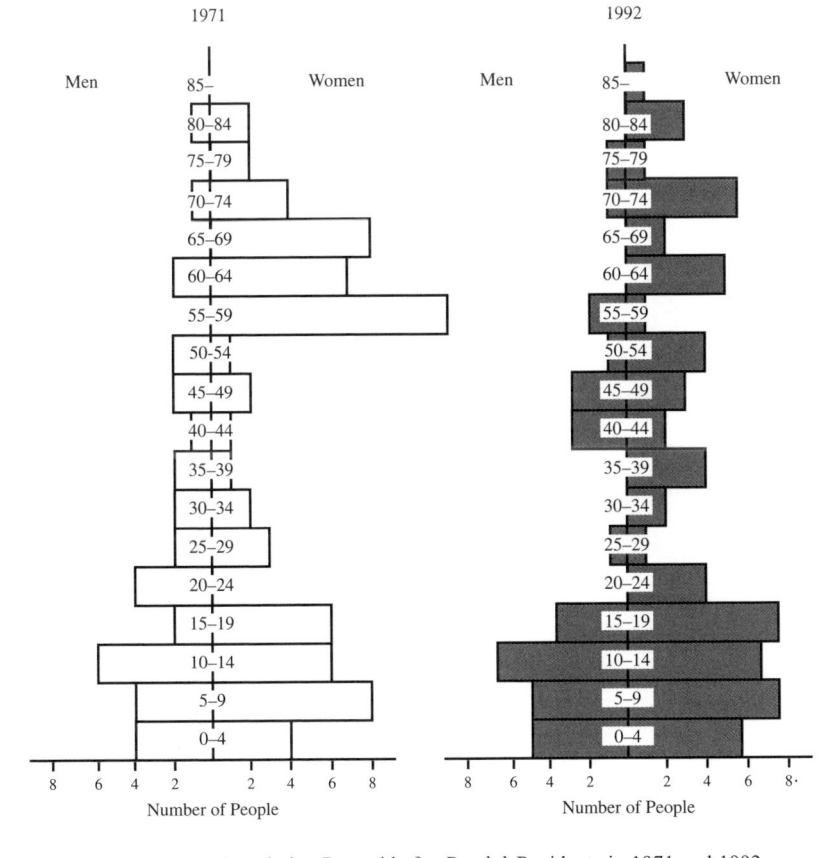

Figure 11-4. Population Pyramids for *Pondok* Residents in 1971 and 1992

older female residents dominated, particularly those in the 55–59 age group, while in 1992, although still noticeable, the difference was less drastic, the population of the 55–59 age group had declined considerably, and the average age of elderly women had increased. Although there were ten male residents between the ages of 20 and 39 in 1971, there was only one in 1992, a dramatic drop in the prime working population. The number of middle-aged women between the ages of 35 and 54, on the other hand, had noticeably increased.

An organization once established takes on a life of its own, and we must remain aware that its dissolution may be a gradual process. One of the reasons the *pondok* is being maintained despite changes is that it is able to take in the destitute in the name of religion. Although poverty remains a reality, the *pondok* as a religious entity can alleviate its negative connotations. In this way, it maintains connections with surrounding villages, including those located some distance away. If minor *pondok* had clung to their educational function, they would have disappeared. By recognizing the potential for change inherent in the nature of the *pondok* and its organization, we can observe the *pondok* with a broader vision over a longer period of time. The *pondok* is an integral part of village and family life and I believe that it will persist for some time to come.

12
A Comparison of Two Villages

Before returning to Japan after completion of the 1970/1971 survey in Galok, I asked Wan Junoh bin Wan Jusoh, my Malay assistant, a youth in his mid-twenties, to take the same questionnaire I had used in Galok and conduct an identical survey in his own village. The village he surveyed was Kubang Bemban, a community of eighty-one households, located about a quarter to half a mile (0.4 to 0.8 km) from Pasir Mas. The purpose of the survey was to identify common elements in Malay farm villages in different locations through a comparison of the two villages, and to determine the direction of change in Malay farm villages through a cross sectional analysis. Kubang Bemban adjoined Pasir Mas and one section of it was incorporated within the administration of Pasir Mas township although it still bore the name of Kubang Bemban. This section of the village was excluded from the present study.

12.1. Occupation and Income

Kubang Bemban's proximity to Pasir Mas resulted in an increasing number of villagers becoming dependent on the town as a source of livelihood. The town is centered around various state and federal government agencies such as the District Office and the Land Office, a train station and a market surrounded by shops. At the time of the survey, however, there were no factories other than a small repair shop, and accordingly, residents of Kubang Bemban who worked in town were mainly engaged in occupations within the commercial and service sectors. The occupations and income source categories for household members in Kubang Bemban and Galok and the proportion of total households with members involved in these occupations are shown in Figure 12-1. The order of occupations is arranged from the highest to the lowest ratio of Kubang Bemban households compared to Galok households. Occupations more common in Kubang Bemban than in Galok (those with a value of 2.0 or more) included trishaw driving, sweet making, carpentry, artisanship, barbering, hairdressing, regular year-round employment, and vegetable growing. In comparison, tobacco cultivation, migrant work, fruit vending, roller rental, coconut sugar-making, rubber tapping, leasing of rubber land, seasonal

CHAPTER 12

1 Trishaw Driving
2 Sweet Making
3 Carpentry, Artisanship, Barbering and Hairdressing
4 Year-round Employment
5 Vegetable Growing
6 Business
7 Paddy Rental
8 House Rental
9 Paddy Growing
10 Sale of Oxen and Water Buffalo
11 Seasonal Employment
12 Rubber Land Rental
13 Rubber Tapping
14 Coconut Sugar-Making
15 Roller Rental
16 Fruit Vending
17 Migrant Work
18 Tobacco Cultivation

Percentage

■ Kubang Bemban   □ Galok

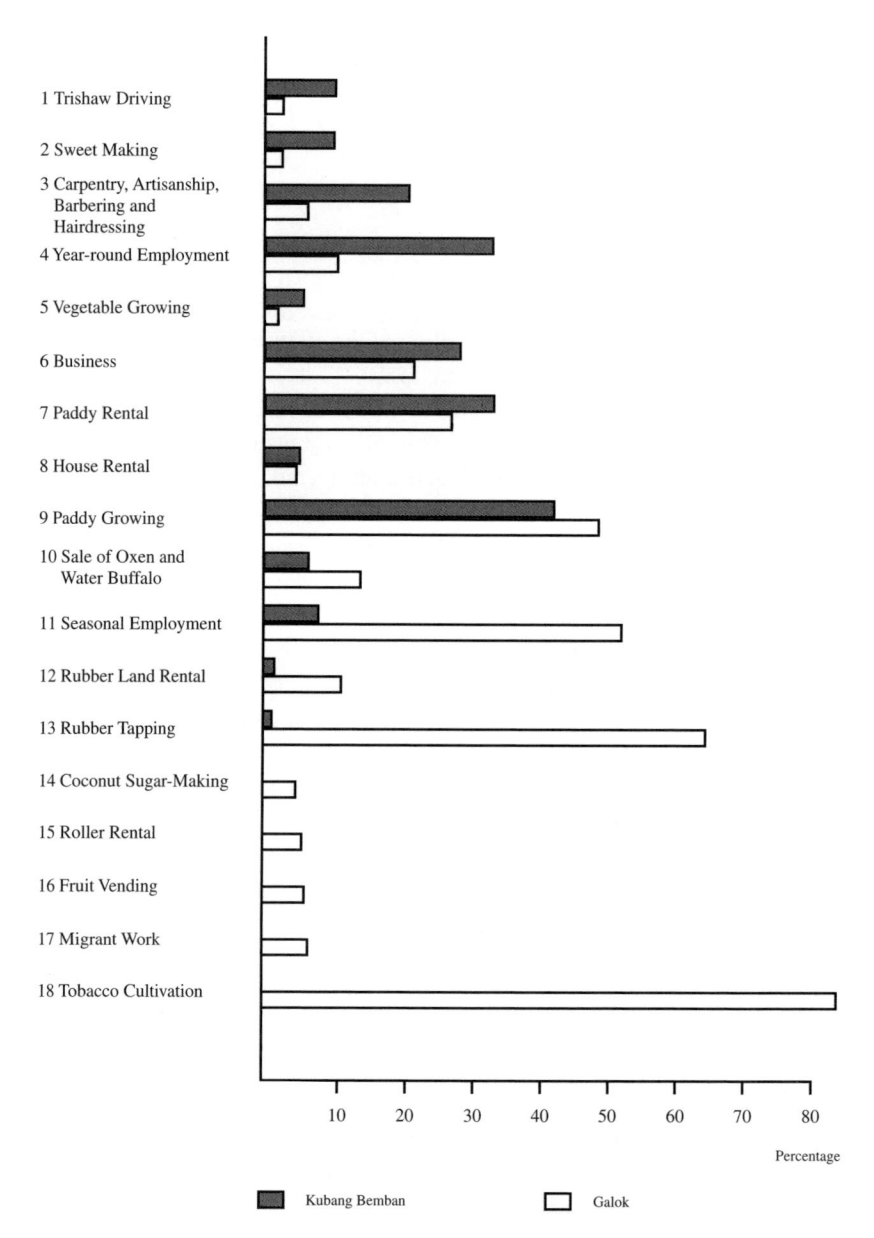

*Proportion of households with members engaged in each occupation to the total number of households, but only showing those with a value of over 3% in either Kubang Bemban or Galok.

Figure 12-1. Proportion of Households Engaged in each Occupation

employment, and sale of oxen and water buffalo were characteristic of Galok. No remarkable differences were observed between the two villages in business, renting of paddy land and houses, and paddy cultivation as occupations or sources of income. Looking at the types of occupation, Galok leaned more strongly towards rubber tapping, while Kubang Bemban was more service oriented, but the diversity of income sources was common to both villages.

Figure 12-2 shows the proportion of total income earned by residents of Kubang Bemban and Galok from each income source. The values were calculated for both villages, and sources of income were arranged from the highest to the lowest ratio for Kubang Bemban as compared to Galok. As mentioned above, trishaw driving, carpentry, artisanship, barbering, hairdressing and year-round employment were the occupations most characteristic of Kubang Bemban, and the combined income from these amounted to 52.2 percent of the

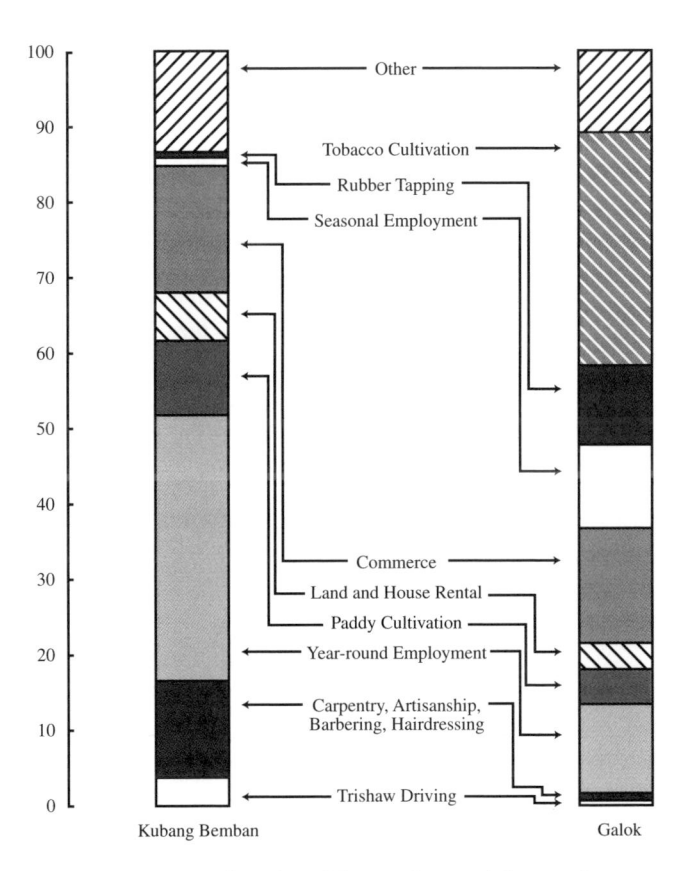

Figure 12-2. Proportion of Total Income from each Income Source

village's total income, a clear indication that land as a unit of production was not as important in Kubang Bemban as it was in Galok. The percentage of households in Galok which owned neither paddy nor rubber land was 18.5 percent, versus 34.6 percent in Kubang Bemban.

As in other Malaysian states, the lifestyle of farmers in Kelantan began losing its structure of self-sufficiency at an early period. Even in Galok, which was located some distance from a town, farmers began small-scale rubber tapping soon after the village was established, becoming accustomed to a cash economy. In that sense, daily life in the more remote villages paralleled life in villages located closer to towns and cities. Moreover, unlike the states along the west coast of Malaysia, Kelantan had few residents of Chinese ancestry, and there were traditionally many opportunities for Malays to become involved in commercial activities.

Residents of both Kubang Bemban and Galok were engaged in paddy cultivation, but while there were some similarities between the two, there were many differences. The small-scale of paddy land ownership, with an average land holding of 1.5 acres in Kubang Bemban and 1.2 acres in Galok, and the family forming the basic unit of labor, with home consumption as the main objective of production, were the main similarities. However, paddy cultivation in Kubang Bemban, which was located near Pasir Mas and blessed with favorable irrigation conditions, and the more remote Galok, which was dependent upon rainwater, differed in the following ways.

First, the ratio of paddy cultivating households to households owning paddy land in Kubang Bemban was lower than in Galok. If the number of land owning households is designated as one hundred, there were only fifty-eight paddy-growing households in Kubang Bemban compared to sixty-six in Galok.

A second difference, related to the first, was the higher proportion of sharecropping in Kubang Bemban. Of the total forty-seven acres (19 ha) of cultivated paddy land, eighteen acres (7.3 ha) or 38.3 percent were sharecropped. In comparison, of the one hundred acres (40.5 ha) of cultivated paddy land in Galok only twenty-three acres (9.3 ha) or 23 percent were sharecropped. Moreover, six of the thirty paddy-growing households (20 percent) in Kubang Bemban sharecropped all of the land they farmed, versus six out of seventy-one paddy-growing households (8.5 percent) in Galok.

Third, double cropping was carried out in thirty-two of the forty-seven acres (68.1 percent) of cultivated paddy land surveyed in Kubang Bemban.

Fourth, with the conversion to double cropping many Kubang Bemban farmers had begun planting Mahsuri, a new variety recommended by the government, and 77.6 percent of all paddy were planted with it. New varieties were not used at all around Galok.

Fifth, the majority of farmers (60.9 percent) in Galok used draft animals to plow their fields, whereas 70 percent of farmers in Kubang Bemban hired tractors.

Sixth, chemical fertilizers were only used by 29.6 percent of paddy-growing households in Galok, while every paddy-growing household in Kubang Bemban applied them without exception. The amount applied per acre also differed, and even if the average is calculated only among those households that used fertilizer in Galok, the average application was just 1.6 bags as opposed to 2.6 bags in Kubang Bemban. The amount recommended by the Department of Agriculture was 3 bags per acre.

Seventh, differences occurred in yield per unit of land, corresponding to the differences described above. Farmers in Galok could expect a yield of 309 *gantang* per acre in a normal year, and in 1970/1971, actual yield was 220 *gantang*. In Kubang Bemban, on the other hand, an annual yield of 970 *gantang* was obtained in double cropped fields and 502 *gantang* in single cropped fields.

These seven differences reveal a fundamental disparity in paddy cultivation between the two villages. In Galok, the objective of paddy cultivation was primarily home consumption, but in Kubang Bemban, the characteristic of paddy as a cash crop was much stronger. This is related to the fact that Kubang Bemban is located further downstream than Galok with more favorable conditions for irrigation, allowing paddy to be cultivated as a commercial crop. In Galok, annual income from paddy cultivation was RM7,044, accounting for only 4.5 percent of total income, whereas in Kubang Bemban income from paddy was RM15,503 representing 9.9 percent of total income. While there was less dependence on land as a unit of production in Kubang Bemban, paddy cultivation was conducted under much more stable conditions. In Galok, kinsmen or neighbors might be hired to help with the harvesting work. Such employment, however, often lacked the character of wage labor where the worker is paid a fixed fee for a specific job. Rather, it was more a form of mutual assistance where those who helped were given a share of the harvest, which the recipient used for home consumption, as an expression of appreciation. In Kubang Bemban, on the other hand, while the unit of labor for the harvest was in principle the family, when outside help was hired, it was a proper business transaction.

The differences in occupation structure described above created differences in household income between the two villages. The distribution of annual household income in Kubang Bemban and Galok is presented in Figure 12-3. In Galok, 53.7 percent of households had an income of less than RM999 whereas only 31.3 percent fell into this income bracket in Kubang Bemban and the highest percentage (37.3 percent) was found in the RM1,000 to RM1,999 income bracket. In Galok, no one made an annual income of more than

RM5,000, but in Kubang Bemban households in this income category accounted for 6.3 percent of the total. Average annual household income in Galok was RM1,076, versus RM1,963 in Kubang Bemban, which is 1.8 times greater than that for Galok. Moreover, whereas the intermediate value of household income in Galok was RM936, in Kubang Bemban it was RM1,520, or 1.6 times higher than that for Galok.

Ownership of items recently introduced into Malaysian homes around that time such as mattresses, beds, transistor radios, bicycles, sewing machines, electric fans, motorcycles and cars reflects the differences in household income described above, and there is an obvious disparity in the rate of distribution between the two villages as shown in Figure 12-4. Kubang Bemban has a higher rate of distribution for all items, although the two villages do not exhibit the same order of distribution. The main differences were the dramatic increase in bicycles in Galok caused by a sudden demand for them as a means of transport for tobacco cultivation, and the absence of electric fans in Galok because there was as yet no electricity.

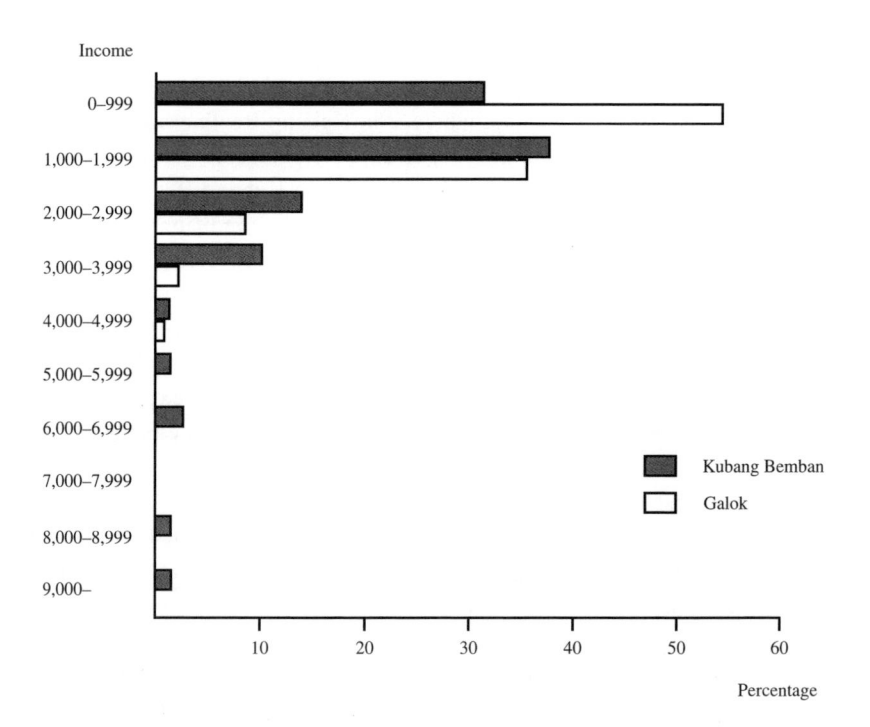

Figure 12-3. Distribution of Household Income

Houses in Kubang Bemban were more attractive in appearance than those in Galok. Figure 12-5 shows the floor area of houses in both villages. Galok generally had a greater number of smaller homes including extremely small structures with an area of only 200 square feet (18.6m^2), but there was basically no great difference between the two villages. In terms of construction cost, however, the amount of money spent to build a house in Kubang Bemban far exceeded that in Galok as shown in Figure 12-6. This factor is related to improvements in appearance and comfort achieved through the use of better building materials such as wooden boards in place of woven bamboo, the installation of doors, windows and ceiling boards, the use of slates rather than thatch on the roof and of concrete blocks as footings to keep wooden posts off the ground, and the replacement of wooden ladders with concrete steps. The average construction cost for a house in Galok was RM1,015 or 0.9 times the average annual income, whereas the average construction cost of RM 2,925 in Kubang Bemban was 1.5 times the average annual income. This shows that the amount of money residents expend on their homes increases dramatically when they acquire some degree of surplus income.

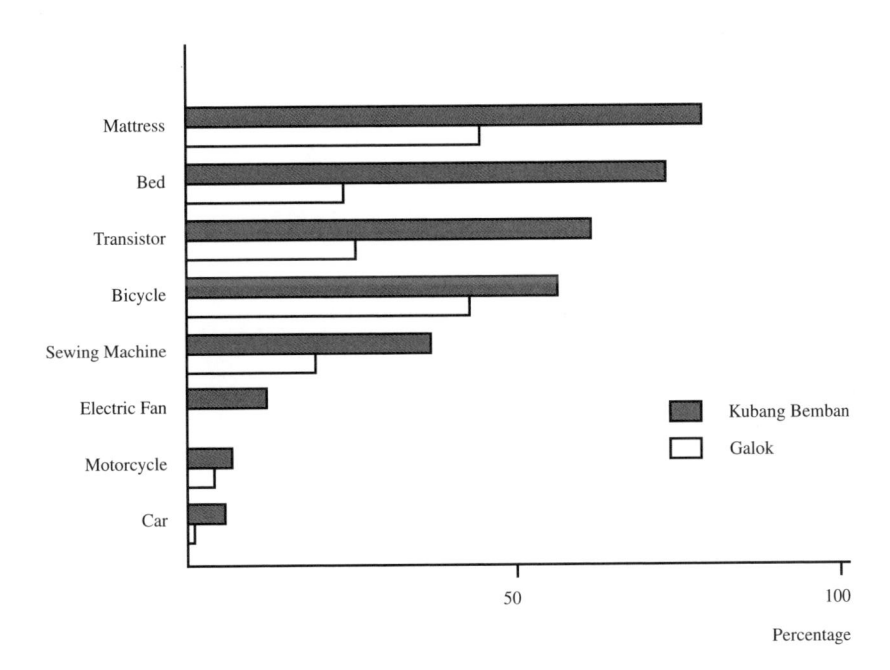

Figure 12-4. Distribution of Household Goods and Appliances

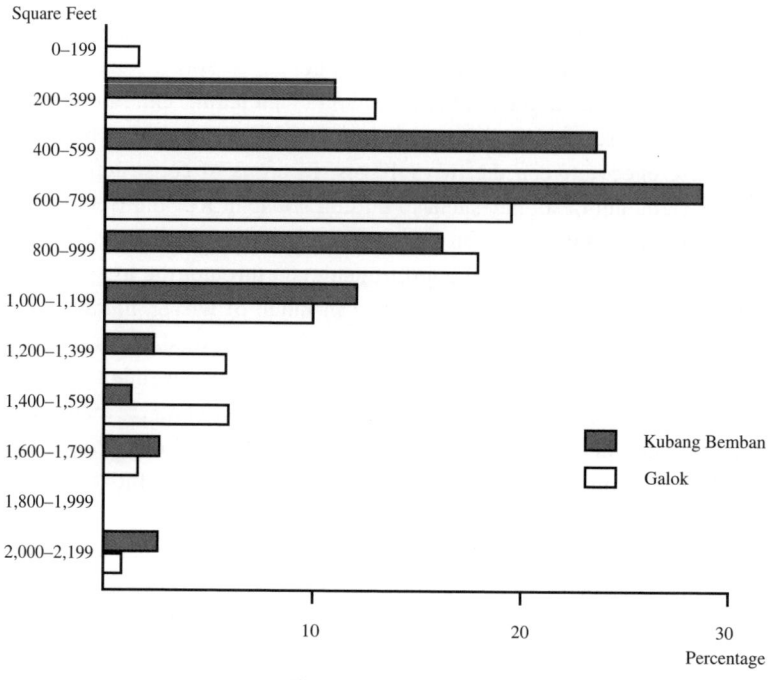

Figure 12-5. Size of House

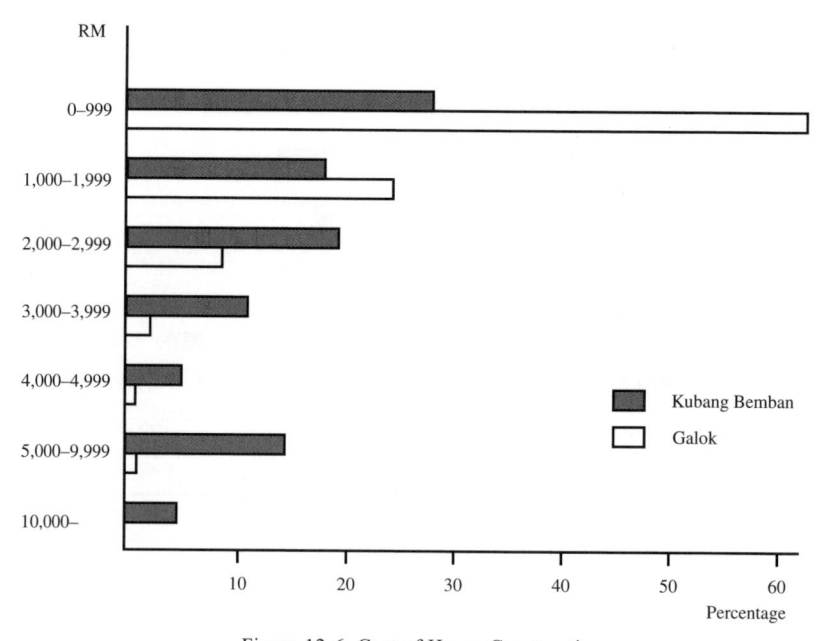

Figure 12-6. Cost of House Construction

12.2. Some Aspects of Family Life

Multihousehold compounds in which the parental household and the household of a child reside within the same compound, and the neighboring kin groups which develop from these have played a crucial role in the life of Malay farmers. As discussed previously, there were thirty-six multihousehold compounds in Galok, with an average of 2.8 households each, and 69.2 percent of all households lived in such a compound. In Kubang Bemban, there were twenty multihousehold compounds with an average of 2.3 households in each, and 56.8 percent of all households resided in a compound. In this sense, the basic structure of daily life was the same in both villages, although it should be noted that the number of residents who did not belong to a multihousehold compound was slightly higher in Kubang Bemban.

Although household composition was generally centered around one married couple, the framework of the family was not firmly fixed, and while some children left before marriage, the household readily accepted additional members as was seen in Galok. Table 12-1 compares the family compositions of households in Kubang Bemban and Galok. The percentage of households with model composition, having neither absent nor additional elements, was 52.7 percent in Galok and 58 percent in Kubang Bemban. Although the latter is slightly higher, the difference is insignificant. Both villages display a similar degree of flexibility in family composition.

Stages IV and VI represent extended or stem family structures, and 12.3 percent of Galok households and 21 percent of Kubang Bemban households

Table 12-1
Family Composition of Households in Kubang Bemban

			Absent Members			Additional Members					
Stage of Family Career	Total Number of Households	Households with Model Composition	Couple's Unmarried Child	One Spouse's Unmarried Child	One Spouse	One Spouse's Child	Adopted Child	Parent	Divorced Daughter	Grandchild	Collateral Kin
I	(3)	(2)					(1)				
II	(6)	(3)	(1)				(2)				(1)
III	26 (59)	21 (41)	2 (7)	(10)	(2)	1 (6)	3				
IV	5	4		1							
V	24 (30)	8 (12)	(1)	(1)	3 (4)	5 (4)	3	2 (1)	2 (5)	7 (12)	
VI	12 (18)	7 (5)			5 (10)		2	1		(7)	
VII	6 (14)	2 (6)					2 (3)		(1)	2 (5)	(1)
VIII	8 (16)	5 (8)					(1)		2	3 (7)	
Total	81(146)	47 (77)	2 (9)	1 (11)	8 (16)	6 (10)	10 (7)	3 (1)	4 (6)	12 (31)	(2)

Figures in parentheses are for Galok.
Polygynous husbands are included twice and the two households are treated separately.

belonged to these. If we look only at those households with model composition, the percentage of extended families, including stem families, was 6.5 percent in Galok and 23.4 percent in Kubang Bemban. Contrary to what one might expect, the village closer to a town had a higher percentage of extended, including stem, families. One factor that might be related to this is the difference in the cost of house construction described above. The homes of as many as 16.4 percent of Galok households were so small that they could only be termed huts and, although they were included within the under RM999 construction cost category in Figure 12-6, they actually cost less than RM200 to build. Moreover, families in stage IV, in which the first child to marry lives in the parental household, were found only in Kubang Bemban. This indicates that, at least in terms of having one's own home, married children in Galok could become independent comparatively easily. It is particularly interesting to note that household composition was influenced by having a house rather than by consciousness of the family bond.

As for marriage and divorce, Figure 12-7 plots the aggregated percentages of ever-married people in the total population against age at first marriage. The earliest marriage among women in Galok was at the age of 11, and half the female population was married by 15. Marriage among women in Kubang Bemban began at 14, and half of the female population was married by the age

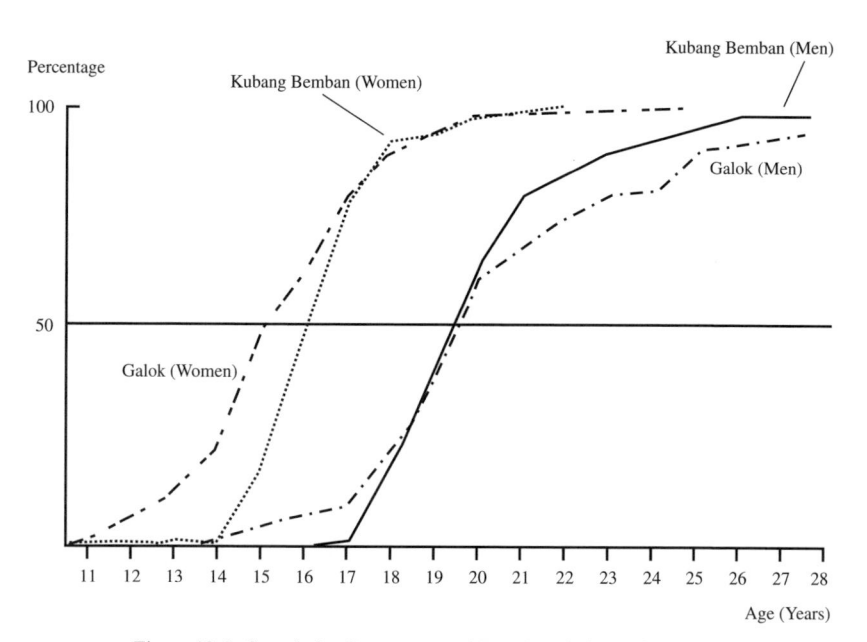

Figure 12-7. Cumulative Percentages of Ever-Married People by Age

of 16. In both villages, 80 percent of women were married by the age of 17 and 90 percent by the age of 18. Although there was some difference in the age at which women first married, in both villages they married young and all women married. Galok had the earliest marriage among men, starting at the age of 14, but Kubang Bemban had a higher proportion of married males aged over 20. The difference in the age of first marriage may to some extent be related to the spread of education, as discussed in a subsequent section.

The most common amount given as a marriage payment from the groom to the bride in Galok during the ten-year period preceding 1971 was RM200, while in Kubang Bemban it was RM300. The average was RM229, equivalent to 21.3 percent of annual income, for Galok and RM319, equivalent to 16.3 percent of annual income, for Kubang Bemban. The absolute value was higher for Kubang Bemban, although this amount represented less of a burden than the amount paid by men in Galok. The ceremony and reception in Kubang Bemban was also more complicated and extravagant than in Galok.

Figure 12-8 shows the number of marriages and divorces among the ever-married population. The proportion of ever-divorced people is lower in Kubang Bemban. In Galok, 38.6 percent of ever-married men divorced, as did 37 percent of ever-married women, versus only 26.8 percent of men and 19.4 percent of women in Kubang Bemban. In particular, the number of people who repeatedly divorced was noticeably lower in Kubang Bemban. The notably high proportion of people experiencing remarriage in Galok is closely related to the high proportion of divorces. The fact that the percentages of women who remarried and of women who divorced are much lower than those for men is

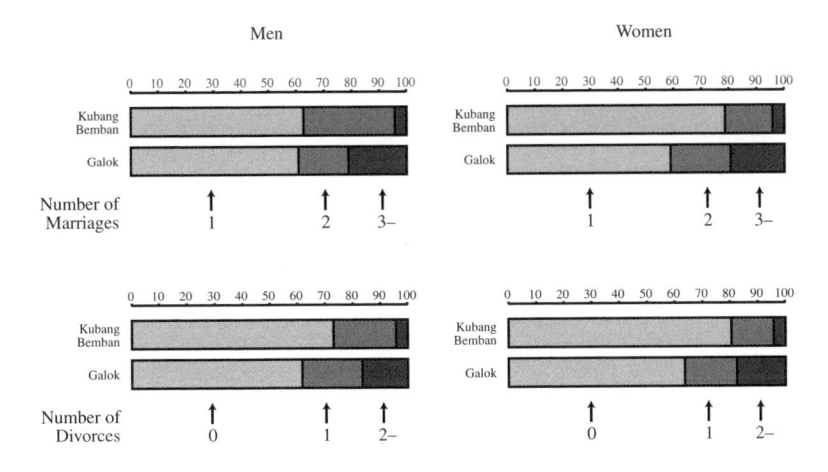

Figure 12-8. Percentages of Ever-married Persons by Number of Marriages and Number of Divorces

thought to be due to inaccurate representation of the facts during the survey rather than a faithful reflection of reality. It may be that women in Kubang Bemban were particularly reluctant to tell non-kin about divorce, or that it was easier for Malay villagers to talk about such a private matter to a foreigner than to a youth from the same village. Figure 12-9 shows the percentage of ever-divorced among ever-married people according to age. Except for men in their forties, the percentage in Kubang Bemban is lower for all age groups. Nine of the fifteen ever-married men in their forties in Kubang Bemban had been divorced, but this exceptional value may have been a chance result of the smallness of the sample population.

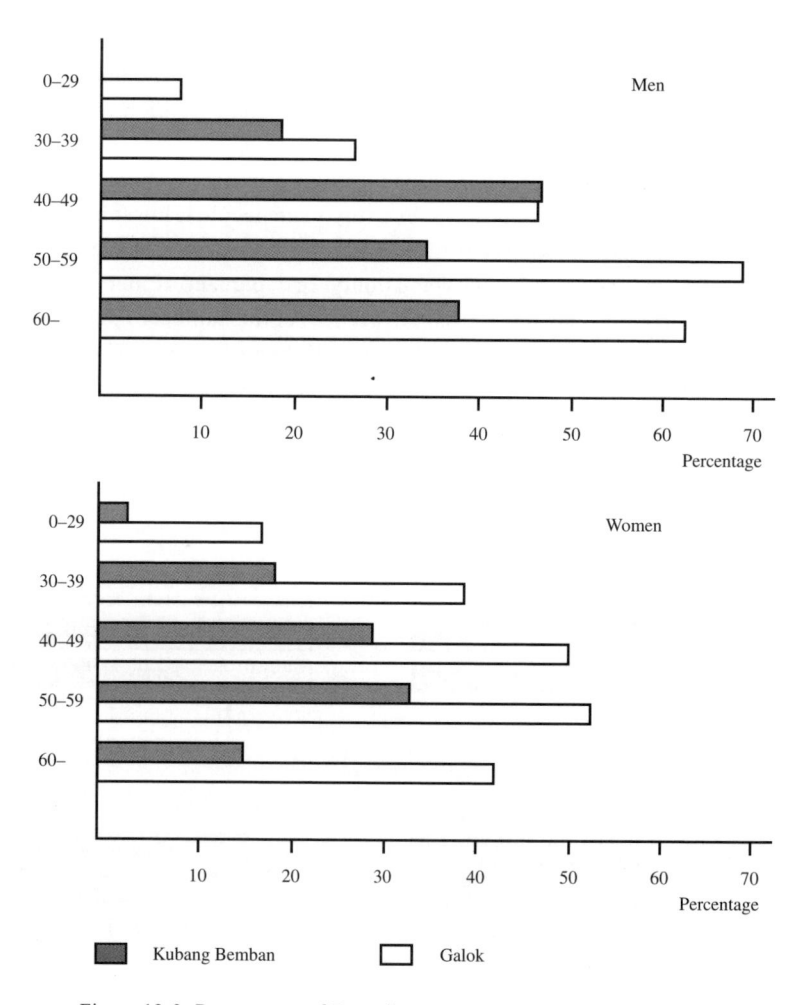

Figure 12-9. Percentages of Ever-divorced Persons among Ever-married

The duration of marriages ending in divorce is shown in Figure 12-10. In both villages, 80–90 percent of divorces took place within six or seven years after marriage. In Galok, many divorces took place shortly after marriage, with as many as 40–50 percent occurring within the first year, whereas very few divorces occurred shortly after marriage in Kubang Bemban.

In the case of male Galok residents, twice as many divorces were instigated by wives than by husbands (38 to 19), while in the case of female residents, wives instigated divorce 2.9 times more often than husbands (49 to 17). In Kubang Bemban, on the other hand, these figures were only 1.3 times (13 to 10) and 0.8 times (10 to 12), and the initiative of wives appeared to be much weaker. As data for Galok in particular is not entirely reliable, it is necessary to look at these data with some reservations; however, if this points to women in remoter villages being more powerful and independent, it is a very interesting phenomenon.

12.3. Education and Religion

Figure 12-11 presents the educational experience of residents in Kubang Bemban and Galok. The school education system was introduced in Kubang Bemban at a much earlier date than in Galok, and at the time of the 1971 survey, a few men over sixty and more than half of the male population in their fifties had received school education. In contrast, none of the male residents of Galok in the same age groups had been to school. School education for women was introduced considerably later in both villages, but women in Kubang Bemban had still received more schooling. There were a few female residents of Galok in their forties and fifties who had been to school, but they were originally from other areas. A similar trend can be seen in Figure 12-12, which presents the literacy rate for men and women in both villages. The fact that men over fifty in Galok had some degree of literacy even though they lacked school education reflects the role of *pondok* education in the village.

A more detailed look at the education of the 15–19-year-old age group is shown in Figure 12-13. The percentage receiving school education in this age group in both villages is fairly high, and little significant difference can be discerned. However, if we focus on the percentage of people who lack schooling and the percentage of those who continue on to secondary education, an obvious disparity can be observed in the state of education between the two villages.

The spread of school education reduced the educational role of the *pondok*. Both Kubang Bemban and Galok have a *pondok* nearby, but, as discussed previously, in 1971 elderly residents in the *pondok* in Galok had almost entirely

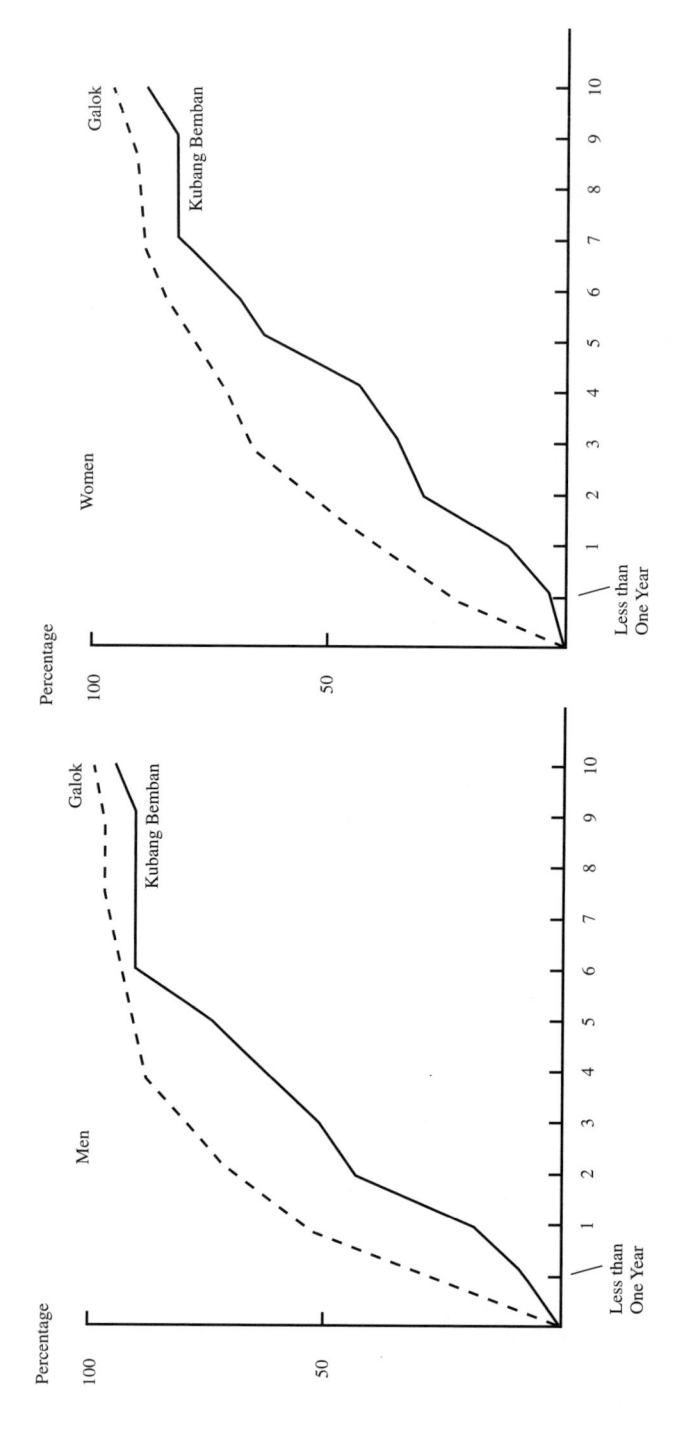

Figure 12-10. Duration of Marriage before Divorce (Aggregated Percentages)

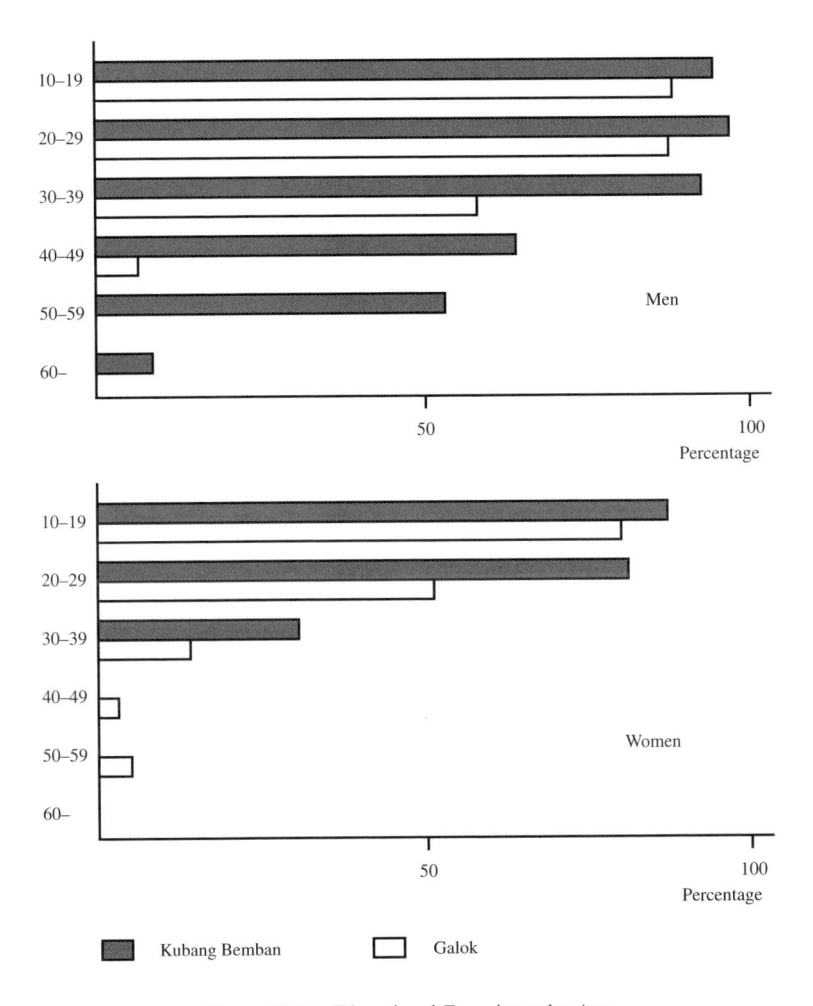

Figure 12-11. Educational Experience by Age

replaced young students, and it had taken on the role of an old peoples' home (11-6). Elderly residents were also increasingly replacing youth in the Kubang Bemban *pondok*, but as students commuting to the school in town used the *pondok* as a dormitory, outward change was less obvious than in Galok. Moreover, the guru in Kubang Bemban was well known and attracted a large audience, including youth, to his weekly religious sermon.

The combination of proximity to a town and a degree of economic surplus seems to have fostered religious activity. The mosque at Kubang Bemban was much more attractive than either of the two mosques in Galok, and it offered

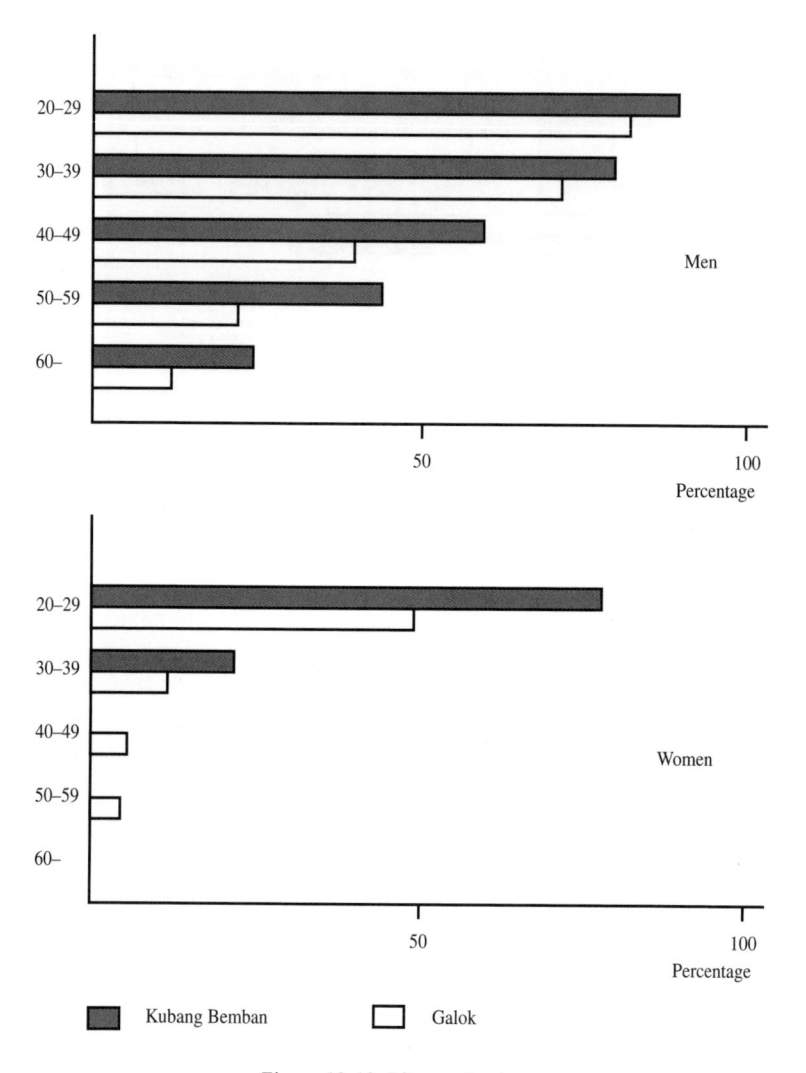

Figure 12-12. Literacy by Age

better meals during the month of fasting. A similar trend could be discerned in the number of people making pilgrimage to Mecca. Whereas a total of four people, one man and three women, from Galok had been on pilgrimage, representing only 1.3 percent of the population over twenty, a total of fourteen people from Kubang Bemban, nine men and five women, had been, representing 7.1 percent of the population over twenty. Moreover, of these, two had been on pilgrimage twice.

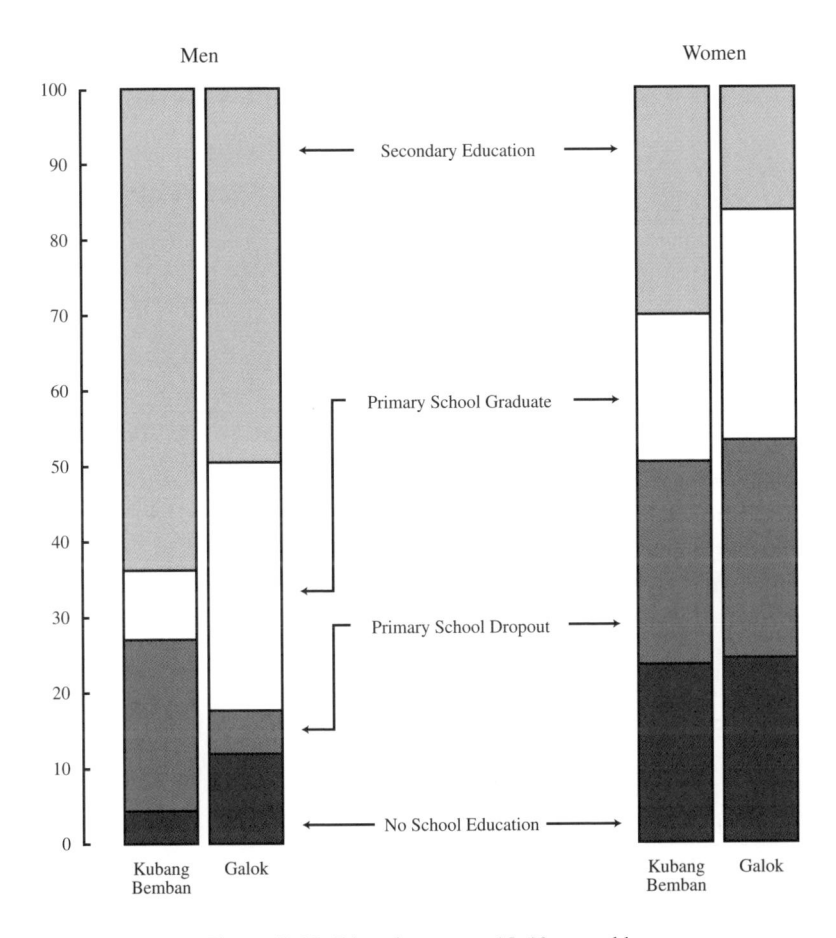

Figure 12-13. Education among 15–19-year-olds

12.4. The Concepts of "Town" and "Village" Among Malays

Villages located near towns undoubtedly assume many town-like characteristics. In this sense, when making a comparison of two "villages" they should perhaps be viewed as interrelated with or even as part of a continuous entity with nearby towns. In the multiethnic society of Malaysia, however, there are problems with thinking in terms of a continuum that extends from major urban centers to small villages. This was certainly the case in 1971. If we assume that the multiethnic society in Malaysian cities is moving from tradition towards a freer cosmopolitan world, then it is clear that trends among residents in the villages are not necessarily moving in the same direction. The same complexity is evident if we look at modernization. Although modernization is often assumed to be accompanied by increased secularization, in some cases, there were movements in the opposite direction, such as the increase in the number of Kubang Bemban villagers making pilgrimage. Secularization obviously can not be considered a requisite component of modernization.

In terms of the move away from agriculture-based income and the general rise in income, it may be possible to evaluate villages and cities in terms of a linear change. As their income increased, Malays strove to realize goals that had value for them. In cases where some of these aspirations are essentially traditional in nature, however, a linear configuration becomes more complicated. It is possible to hypothesize that tradition or aspirations to tradition represent the ideal Malay model, which would include placing importance on religion and strengthening traditions.

The structure of daily life in newly opened settlements was rough and simple. The villagers' aspirations revolved around the town where the Sultan lived and the prosperous villages nearby. The ideal model of Malay lifestyle was characterized by the upper classes of the more traditional, regional cities. While some of the material aspirations were realized through modernization of lifestyle, others were realized through the actualization of traditional ideals, such as the trend towards more elaborate marriage ceremonies, higher marriage payments, and increased pilgrimage revealed in the cross sectional comparison of Kubang Bemban and Galok, which can be seen as linear changes in terms of the actualization of traditional ideals.

In the 1991 Galok survey, we can see the same contrast that occurred between Kubang Bemban and Galok in 1971 occurring within the village of Galok. Improvements in transportation had some bearing on this change, reflecting the passage of time, and it must be noted that change is not always bound to a specific space or location. As has been pointed out, income from agriculture including rubber tapping and tobacco cultivation was replaced by an increase in income from wage labor in Galok. This was supported by migrant work in Singapore and other urban locations, with work in such distant places often forcing couples to live apart. Thus, despite the geographical distance, Galok has come to function as an essential component of the cities.

As for changes in family life, the potential for a move towards extended families was suggested from the comparison of Galok and Kubang Bemban in 1971, and the realization of this projection was confirmed by the survey conducted in Galok twenty years later. If we look just at the residents of single households, a tendency toward complex family composition is apparent in the towns. The view that nuclear families are an urban phenomenon cannot be said to be universal, and the idea that the trend towards nuclear families is universal should also be accepted with reservations. The findings also suggest that,

Plate 12-1. Ujung Galok mosque in 1971.

Plate 12-2. The same mosque in 1991.

particularly in poorer villages, the rural multihousehold compounds comprised of groups of small houses are no more than a temporary detour in an overall tendency toward the formation of extended family households accompanying the construction of larger houses.

One other major change in family life concerns marriage and divorce. In 1991, the age at which people married in Galok was much higher than the age in Kubang Bemban in 1971. The number of divorces had also markedly declined. This process of change occurred throughout Malaysia, diminishing the differences between Kubang Bemban and Galok so that the differences have become almost insignificant. Marriage payments exceeding RM1,000 became normal even in Galok. Increased economic prosperity has led to more elaborate marriage ceremonies in both villages, which is another manifestation of the same phenomenon.

The spread of education was the basis of the change in marriage and divorce described above. The higher age for marriage, and the reduction in divorce clearly corresponded to the spread of secondary education. Even in Galok there was a fairly large number of university graduates; a phenomenon not even guessed at in the 1971 comparison of the two villages. As a result of a government policy favoring Malays with government scholarships and student loans, even children from poor families could attend university. Children in rural areas were disadvantaged compared to city children in terms of opportunities for education, and the growing stiffness of competition is exacerbating this disparities, yet the effect of the government's preferential policy is still clearly evident.

It is important to note that the secularization of school education was accompanied by a marked increase in the religious activity of pilgrimage. The number of Galok villagers who had been to Mecca in 1991 surpassed those of Kubang Bemban in 1971.

The prospective changes indicated by the comparison of Kubang Bemban and Galok are now being realized. It is particularly interesting to see that both the secular and the sacred aspects have been reinforced. This phenomenon, which could not be mechanically predicted from the survey results, represents a new trend brought about by changes in society, including the spread of refrigerators, color televisions, telephones and cars which were hardly seen at all in Kubang Bemban in 1971, as well as changes in the education and marriage systems and their effects on society. Large urban centers may have provided the model for many material aspects of change, while the more traditional regional cities were models for other aspects, such as religious activities. The issue remains, however, as to whether these sorts of changes should be interpreted in terms of a single linear model or in terms of a double-track model.

13
The Study of Malay Villages and Related Subjects

13.1. Individuality and Universality

As mentioned at the beginning, this book in essence describes a community study. Assertions that can be made from findings in one village in a corner of the Malay peninsula over such an historically short period of time are, of course, limited. Nevertheless, the temptation arises to use this information as a basis for a discussion of Malay rural communities in general and to develop it into a theory of rural communities throughout Southeast Asia.

The problem with community studies is obviously the limited nature of the subject. The question is whether or not conclusions drawn from community studies can be considered representative of other areas. The complementary relationship between broad, shallow studies, and narrow, detailed studies has frequently been discussed. The most logical assumption is that the former serve to substantiate the latter, giving them a broader scope of application. In reality, however, it is impossible to establish positive evidence of correlation with a limited number of indicators. The degree to which a community study can be applied to a broader area depends upon which indicators are selected; some types of indicators will widen the scope of application while others will limit it.

The problem of applicability is related to the nature of comparison. The angle of perspective in a comparative study and the researcher's conclusions are determined by the researcher's approach, by whether he is seeking to identify similarities or differences. The choice to define common characteristics of Malay rural communities in Kelantan and Kedah or to contrast their differences is determined by the researcher's purpose in undertaking a comparison, and meaningful comparisons from community studies are largely dependent upon the researcher's choice of approach.

Another problem the researcher faces when attempting a comparison is deciding what and how to compare. When Japanese scholars conduct community studies, it is natural for them to compare the subject of their study with the society of Japan, the country in which they were born and raised. Although this type of comparison has meaning in itself, it cannot be considered sufficient if one is aiming to extract universal elements and apply them to a broader geographical area as described above. The researcher must include information concerning areas other than his native land when deciding whether a particular element is universal or not. In some cases, the researcher's view may be based on his own research or on shallower experience, or on the records of other scholars, and he will most likely need to collect data in a variety of forms.

One approach is to give information concerning other areas the same weight as data obtained in the community study; in other words, to regard one's own study as merely one among many. This approach takes the stance of scientific classification, placing great importance on objective data. To do this, the researcher must disregard the individuality of the specific study, dispassionately providing data. One drawback of this approach is that the wealth of specific data obtained during the community study is relegated to an extremely limited role, and the only part of the researcher's experience that will be conveyed is his world view, which was formulated during the study.

The significance of community studies has much in common with studies on the life history of individuals. In the latter, capturing the universality that exists within an individual case is the unspoken theme, not identifying individual peculiarities. In the case of community studies, the underlying theme is perhaps to capture an image of society. Although the society reflected in a community study is necessarily limited to a specific area, the study has sufficiently achieved its purpose if a subject of this scope can be even partially depicted. There are not many examples of community studies that have actually attempted to extend their scope in this way.

The researcher expands the scope of his study on the basis of his overall experience. In his work of contemplating the subject community and comparing it with other communities or areas he must rely upon his accumulated experience. Because his experience is that of an individual, it is not always objective, representing instead his subjective or world view. Area profiles extracted by using Human Relations Area Files (HRAF) will both support and conflict with the area profiles drawn up by individual researchers. The intuitive and subjective nature of the latter must be acknowledged. Careful examination is necessary to determine the difference between cases where understanding or comprehension is derived via individual experience and cases where it depends entirely on that which is objective or assumed to be objective.

13.2. Galok and the Image of the Southeast Asian Village

Setting discussions of abstract theory aside, let us consider what types of elements can be universally applied from specific examples when looking at Southeast Asia through the lens of a single community study. First let me propose a general model of farm villages in Southeast Asia using Galok as the basis. Like Galok, the majority of Southeast Asian farm villages were initially settled during the latter half of the 19th century, and bore, to a greater or lesser extent, the characteristics of pioneer settlements. Although the main occupation in most villages was paddy farming, the geographical location of many precluded the use of irrigation facilities, while the bilateral kinship structure precluded the formation of fixed kin groups despite the fact that daily activities were communal and centered around neighboring kin. The village itself also lacked group-like characteristics.

The above model of farm villages fits Galok but fails to reveal any of the specific details of daily life in that particular village. The tendency to engage in more than one occupation and in migrant work, flexible family ties characterized by comparatively easy divorce and remarriage and grandparents adopting their grandchildren, and the influence on daily life of Islam which has its own strength and versatility - such features as these are important in understanding daily life in this community yet they cannot be generalized as characteristics of all farm villages in Southeast Asia. Those elements of daily life that would be eliminated in the process of generalization are the very ones that vividly portray the lifestyle of Galok villagers. The portions present in the community study but lacking in the generalized picture are essential to real understanding.

From my experiences in other Southeast Asian farm villages, it is clear that each of them has some elements in common with Galok and others that are not. The generalization recorded above of the farm village of Southeast Asia likewise does not correspond to every farm village. In the following sections, I will discuss the differences and similarities that I have observed in Southeast Asian farm villages derived from my own experience.

13.3. Villages in the Malay Peninsula

In this section I will focus on several villages in the Malay peninsula. The first Malay village I visited was Padang Lalang, located in the Kedah plain.[1] Although I stayed only about seven months at the most in 1964 and 1965, this experience formed my first impressions of Southeast Asian villages. A ribbon settlement with indistinct boundaries, the houses were spread along a drainage canal constructed when people began settling in the territory. The village's northern edge was bounded by a small settlement of Chinese from Fuchien and Kuangtung provinces in China. Beyond this, Malay households regarded as belonging to the next village continued along the canal. Although few in number, the village included some households of Chinese from Chaozhou and Bengali Moslems married to Malays, showing the more liberal attitude of the village.

Paddy cultivation was rainfed and, without communal irrigation facilities, there was no need for communal work organizations. The water gate on the canal, primarily used for drainage, was operated by a worker from the Irrigation and Drainage Department. Farmers depended to a great extent upon hired labor for planting and harvesting, and in some cases, employed labor groups comprised of village residents. Such labor groups were usually organized by people whose property or social status gave them more social influence, but membership in the group was not fixed.

Money was a frequent topic of conversation. Although there was mutual trust between Chinese and Malay residents regarding the fulfillment of promises in business transactions, relationships between the two groups were restricted to the distribution of goods and money and limited contact based on an inherent distrust was maintained in social relationships. Individualism was the keynote in relationships among Malays, and land was rented even among parents and children, although if the child was poor, his parent rented land at a lower rate than for a stranger, and a child might care for his parents in their old age by paying a comparatively higher rent for use of their land.

If this lack of group solidarity is viewed as characteristic of communities that opened up new territory by settling in less advantageous agricultural areas dependent upon rainfed paddy cultivation, then it is a feature shared by Padang Lalang in Kedah and Galok in Kelantan. In Galok, which was situated on more undulating terrain part way up a river, the means of livelihood also included upland rice cultivation and rubber tapping. When the shortage of land in the village became more acute, migrant labor also became an important source of income, and the village entered a period where villagers seasonally traveled to work in other paddy-growing areas, including Kedah. In Padang Lalang and throughout Kedah state, on the other hand, paddy cultivation was the main production activity up until a certain point in time, and those who did not own land were able to make a living as farm laborers working other people's fields. With the Muda River Irrigation Project on the Kedah plain, double cropping was introduced, accompanied by the use of machinery and direct planting. In contrast, Galok villagers were becoming increasingly dependent on migrant work in Singapore and other cities, and the two villages appeared, at least superficially, to be diverging.

In the 1960s, notable differences between the two began to appear in the roles of men and women. Kedah was characterized by the division of labor according to gender and the segregation of the sexes, while in Kelantan women were actively involved in commercial activities and men and women were allowed to communicate freely. Divorce was common in both areas, but particularly noticeable in Kelantan. These cultural differences, which can be viewed as arising from a difference in receptivity towards Islamic teachings, colored the various practical aspects of daily life in both areas. Changes in attitudes towards marriage among Malaysian Muslims that accompanied revisions in the marriage laws in the 1980s markedly reduced divorce rates in both regions, resulting in more uniformity.

In comparison with the above two villages, slightly more differences can be found in Bukit Pegoh, another Malay farm village located in Melaka in the southern Malay peninsula.[2] This village was originally settled by Bugis from Sulawesi who moved into the Malay peninsula, and the village is located on an island of higher land and surrounded by rainfed paddy fields. The village was established relatively early, and therefore the pioneer nature of the settlement is weaker. Residual Bugis characteristics can be glimpsed in such factors as the higher number of first cousin marriages, but most indigenous characteristics have been lost and their identity as Malays has become firmly established. The fact that neighboring kin groups are not as common as in either Kedah or Kelantan may be due to the fixed nature of compound land and a lack of extra land for expansion. Migrant labor became an important source of livelihood in the village at an early date. Islamic education thrived, and, as divorce was frowned upon by Islam, the divorce rate began to noticeably decline sometime before that in Kedah and Kelantan. Despite the early loss of the village's characteristics of a pioneer colony and the changes brought about by the strengthening of religious beliefs, some aspects of social structure that corresponded to Galok were maintained, including flexibility of household composition and the adoption of grandchildren.

13.4. Villages in Continental Southeast Asia

Villages in the Chao Phraya delta of Thailand adjoining the Malay Peninsula also fall within the same category of pioneer settlements established in newly opened territory.[3] In this region, longitudinal and latitudinal canals were dug and excavated earth was used to create embankments along the sides. Houses were built along the tops of these and a variety of crops were planted on the land behind, with paddy gradually becoming the main crop. Paddy was well suited to the marshy delta land, and by taking advantage of natural flooding during the monsoon, it could be cultivated without any irrigation facilities. The organization of villages established in this type of area sometimes centered on the families of the original settlers, but they never dominated it. Rather villages spread along the canals remained loose entities without definite boundaries. As opposed to the Malay peninsula, Buddhism was the backbone of the villagers' spiritual life, and the Buddhist temple served as the nucleus of daily activity.

These characteristics were common not only to villages located along drainage canals but also to those along rivers. A little further up the delta, floating rice, which grows rapidly as flood levels rise, was cultivated, and villages were formed along the tops of the natural river banks. Although similar in appearance to the villages along manmade canals, it was clear when walking through the community that there was a greater distance between each clump of houses, and each appeared to be a well-defined group. These household groups were small, comprised of only a few houses, and in most cases the members of the different households were kin, centering on sisters and their husbands. Although they had the character of pioneer settlements, they also had more of an air of permanence.

In Thailand, land clearance was not limited to the delta. The same phenomenon was occurring simultaneously in the Northeast on the Khorat Plateau. Migration, denoted by the expression *ha na di* ("to seek good paddy land"), was an integral part of the value system governing people's behavior, and people sometimes moved long distances to obtain land. The village of Don Daeng[4], for example, was settled by people of Lao stock who moved along a tributary of the Mekong river in search of arable land, and made their livelihood by cultivating rainfed paddy. Don Daeng is a clustered settlement with clear boundaries. Within the village, it is common for married daughters to live close to their parents and for their households to share rice from a common granary. Although they cook and eat separately, the daughters' households are dependent upon the parents' land for production. Compared to villages that sprang up suddenly on the delta, this village seems to have more coherence.

Do such differences mean, however, that the lack of coherence in delta villages is due to their location on an alluvial flood plain? Let us shift our focus to the farm villages of the Mekong delta.[5] Many of these were settled around the same time as villages in the Chao Phraya delta. Here also, rainfed paddy cultivation was the main occupation. Inhabitants of this delta were mainly Vietnamese, but in some areas there were high percentages of Khmer. A marked number of villages were opened on the river's natural levees, but in comparison to villages in the Chao Phraya delta they appear to have more cohesion and tend to be of clustered settlement type.

In Vietnamese settlements along the Red River delta, which has a longer history of settlement by the Vietnamese, kinship structure was found to be based on patriarchal principles rather than the bilateral principle of Malay or Thai kinship. Villages are enclosed, and a shrine (*dinh*) forms the spiritual center of each. Villages in the Mekong delta are generally larger than those in the Red River delta, and their organization is looser. The Red River delta, relatively small for a delta, has a high population density and is intensively farmed. Even though pioneer settlements in the great expanse of the Mekong delta naturally exhibit some similarities to those in the Chao Phraya delta, they also share features in common with traditional Vietnamese farm villages. It is not, therefore, possible to claim that the location of a pioneer settlement in a particular natural environment will necessarily result in a loosely structured village with more flexible human relationships.

13.5. Villages in South Sumatra

As noted above, the settlement of new territory on alluvial plains or lowlands that preclude the use of irrigation facilities does not necessarily result in the formation of villages with weaker solidarity. This is shown by the farm villages on the Mekong delta cited above, and also by the villages in South Sumatra, Indonesia located along the lowlands of the Musi River and its tributaries. These rely on cultivation methods that do not require irrigation facilities, including paddy growing in the period of floodwater recession and upland rice cultivation.[6] Often villagers still remember the names of the settlement's founders, and village solidarity is stronger. In some cases, conflict with the indigenous inhabitants arose when the land was first settled, necessitating consolidation or maintenance of the group for self defense. Depending on the circumstances, the topographical location and surrounding conditions have no bearing on a village's solidarity; rather a community's group identity is strengthened or weakened in relation to the human environment rather than in relation to the natural environment. The type of villages with looser group identities and indistinct boundaries found in the Malay peninsula and Chao Phraya delta appear to have emerged in areas of relative peace and stability. In contrast, the village structure in Sumatra was characterized by the establishment of branch villages, a fact attributable to the need for self defense arising from the human environment. There was a marked group solidarity in villages that used the slash and burn method, despite the mobile nature of cultivation and the fact that boundaries within the jungle can only be vaguely defined. The longhouse style of communal dwelling found in places such as Borneo, for example, is not merely a large group of extended kin but rather the village itself.[7] This type of configuration might be expected to occur in areas with enemies, including headhunters.

13.6. Pioneer Settlements

The traditional village of Southeast Asia is dependent on paddy cultivation in irrigated fields. Such villages are often found in areas with small rivers that can be controlled without mechanical power, such as fan-terrace complexes and intermontane basins. The common ownership of irrigation facilities and the need for cooperative labor organizations for their maintenance strengthened group bonds among villagers and made group action and production activities essential. A meaningful comparison of the group solidarity in irrigated paddy-growing villages with that in villages in deltaic and lowland areas dependent on rainfed paddy cultivation can only be achieved by selecting villages among the latter that lack this feature. The lack of a cohesive group character is not universally found in non-irrigated agricultural areas but rather is restricted to a narrower range of criteria.

In addition to irrigation and other measures for production, or the necessity of self-defense, organization for administrative purposes must also be considered as a determinant of village boundaries. In Java, with its high density of villages, this more artificial type of framework is important. Village officials are appointed, lands are allocated to them in accordance with their office, and the boundaries are defined. Such villages, where the Javanese residents have a bilateral kinship structure, appear on the surface to have a solid framework, but internally they lack a strong sub-unit of organization larger than the family. In the mid 1970s, I visited Java with the late Koichi Mizuno to conduct a comparative study on paddy-growing villages, and I remember that he referred to Javanese villages as looking solid and firm yet if you shook them, they would quickly loose their shape like a rotten apple.[8]

When observing the relationship between the village and the sub-units that comprise its organizational structure, it is helpful to refer to the categories of clan ties and association-based ties defined by the late Japanese sociologist Tadashi Fukutake.[9] Clans in Japanese villages are made up of families that share a common ancestor and that recognize the relationship of main and branch households. These relationships are not between individuals but between households, and are maintained and perpetuated, forming a group that transcends generations. These in turn form the nucleus of the village's administrative organization. Neighboring kin groups and multihousehold compounds found in Southeast Asia are based on the parent-child relationship, and their structure is fluid and without strong generational continuity. Even if the parental generation in a multihousehold compound happens to have a leadership role in the village, the multihousehold compound does not act as a sub-unit of the village's organization. These facts reveal the weakness of the sub-unit forming the nucleus of the group and the lack of organizational structure in the village. Association-based ties should probably be understood in the same way.

It must be pointed out that in Japan strong group cohesion and solidarity were present at the outset when new settlements were established. Records concerning new villages settled on reclaimed swampland in the Niigata plain still exist. The land was naturally marshy and at the time of settlement, irrigation facilities were unnecessary, resembling farm villages on alluvial plains in Southeast Asia. Settlers of the new villages usually moved in from neighboring communities; however, village structure and characteristics basically followed the same pattern as the former villages, and they appear to have been organized as a group from the very beginning. The same is true for settlements in Hokkaido. At one period, groups of settlers were formed in Tohoku, Hokuriku and other areas and the members of each group migrated together, playing a major role in settling new villages. It is a characteristic feature of such pioneering efforts in Japan that even if houses were dispersed, a firm group structure bound them together.[10]

From the above we can see that village organization depends less upon topographical or environmental differences than upon cultural inclinations. However, there is a pitfall in developing the argument in this direction. When speaking of culture, one must consider how long it has existed. In Southeast Asia, there was an extended period of low population. Although the opening and settlement of new territory on the plains only began to dramatically increase in the late 19th century, it has a history of over 100 years. I believe that a century is a sufficient period of time for a culture to take shape with regards to the nature of its society, although the characteristics of a village were assuredly never fixed in the past and will continue to change in future.

It is also necessary to touch upon the subject of how long a new settlement maintains its pioneer character. I believe that the overall tendency for new pioneer settlements to be continually created is more important than the progress of land clearance within individual villages. In this sense, the fact that villagers consider it only natural for people to leave in search of new land before the population increases beyond the village's capacity is part of the culture of a pioneer society, and the fact that out-migration is given a positive rather than a negative value is one of its essential characteristics.

As has been stated before, not all farm villages in Southeast Asia are characterized as pioneer settlements. Although they are very prevalent, they do not represent every area, and in the long term, they are merely a temporary phenomenon. Nor does the nature of settling new territory dictate every aspect of the villagers' mode of behavior. Religion is another element that affects farm villages in Southeast Asia. Village life is, in reality, comprised of a combination of various elements, and in some aspects, religious influences are more obvious. When, for example, Masuo Kuchiba went to Don Daeng in Northeast Thailand to participate in a follow-up survey after spending some time surveying the Malay farm village of Padang Lalang in Kedah, he was struck more by the differences arising from Islam and Buddhism than by the common characteristics arising from both communities being pioneer settlements.[11]

13.7. Relationship to Southeast Asian Society

In closing I would like to consider the relationship between community studies on farm villages in Southeast Asia and understanding Southeast Asian society. Let me start by describing the composite nature of this society. Since the ancient past, Southeast Asia was characterized as a sparsely populated area connected to the outside world through trade in forest products. Large and small port cities functioned as a link between sites where forest products were extracted and their final destinations, and these drew outsiders of different ethnic origins who settled, forming a multi-ethnic population. Some Southeast Asian farm villages were established as bases to support this trade, but a dramatic increase subsequently occurred in paddy-growing pioneer settlements on the plains accompanying the process of colonization. Commercial centers with mixed ethnic populations were set up around such settlements, and as outsiders of different ethnic backgrounds began to settle in the latter, some aspects of their structure came to resemble that of the cities. This is somewhat removed from the image of closed and isolated farm villages and in that sense, understanding farm villages is not totally unrelated to an understanding of life in the cities.

It must be noted that even in the cities, segregated residence and cultural coexistence were prerequisite conditions to multi-ethnicity. In the last decade, however, this has changed rapidly with the marked progress of industrialization. In addition to the original foreign population that formerly comprised the main residents, Malay in-migrants from other areas have come to account for a significant portion of the urban population. Increased exchange between farm villagers and urban areas through former villagers living in the cities, commuters and migrant workers has brought urban lifestyles closer to the village. The number of people engaged in agriculture, which originally defined the nature of farm villages, has decreased, and there is a rising tendency to engage in several occupations. Electricity, running water, telephones, propane, cars, motorbikes, etc. have been introduced into the daily life of the village, and although there is still some discrepancy in income levels between farm villages and the city, the conveniences of daily life are almost identical. When I first began research in the Malay peninsula in the 1960s, villagers who had been educated and were employed in towns, and particularly those who had become civil servants, were aware that they could never adjust to living in the farm village environment again because it was too different from their lifestyle in town. Now, however, it is possible for people to return to the village to live when they retire. These types of changes are reducing the differences between villages and towns.

There does not appear to be any fundamental differences between families inhabiting farm villages versus those inhabiting towns in terms of organizational principles. The trend towards nuclear families in the cities likewise does not necessarily stand out in contrast with the farm villages whose basic family structure was already nuclear in appearance. Moreover, there is a tendency for in-migrating siblings and other kin to live together in the cities in order to help one another. There even appears to be a change towards the strengthening of family and kin solidarity occurring particularly in the cities. And with the active interchange between towns and villages described above, the principles distinguishing cities and farm villages are becoming less distinct. It will be very interesting if the principles of pioneer settlements that underlie these recent changes continue to be maintained.

The choice must be made as to whether to look at aspects of change or aspects of continuity in Southeast Asian society. This is equivalent to a synchronic choice between focussing on similarities or focussing on differences. We need to adopt a dynamic perspective that recognizes the temporary nature of the characteristics of a pioneer society yet at the same time sees them to some extent as a continuing undercurrent in present society.

Notes

1. Masuo Kuchiba subsequently continued the study of Padang Lalang. See Masuo Kuchiba, Yoshihiro Tsubouchi, Narifumi Maeda (1965).
2. A survey of Bukit Pegoh was conducted by Narifumi Maeda at the beginning of the 1970s. I accompanied him to this village when he first selected it, and visited him during his extended study. See Masuo Kuchiba, Yoshihiro Tsubouchi, Narifumi Maeda (1965).

3. I participated in a short-term study of three paddy-growing villages in the Chao Phraya delta and adjacent plateau in 1973. See Shinichi Ichimura (ed., 1975). Detailed records by staff of the Center for Southeast Asian Studies, Kyoto University on paddy-growing farm villages in Thailand also exist including those by Yoneo Ishii (ed., 1975) and Yoshikazu Takaya (1982).
4. There are many reports on Don Daeng including Koichi Mizuno (1981), Hayao Fukui (1988), and Masuo Kuchiba (ed., 1990). I visited this village three times with Hayao Fukui.
5. I accompanied Kazutake Kyuma and Narifumi Maeda on a survey of villages along the Mekong delta immediately prior to the fall of Saigon. We were able to visit many villages along the roads but none in more remote areas. See Yoshihiro Tsubouchi and Narifumi Maeda (1975b).
6 I worked with staff from the Center for Southeast Asian Studies, Kyoto University on a survey of South Sumatra from September 1978 to February 1979. At that time, I was primarily involved in interviewing residents along the Komering river, a tributary of the Musi, concerning the history of village formation. See Yoshihiro Tsubouchi (1979).
7. My experience with longhouse communities in Borneo was only short term. In 1976 I traveled with Hayao Fukui among others, visiting the upstream portion of the Baram river in Sarawak. Subsequently, I caught glimpses of longhouses in West Kalimantan and East Kalimantan in Indonesia in 1990, but the disintegration of the lifestyle of longhouse communities in this area was already pronounced, and the majority of residents lived in separate houses.
8. With Koichi Mizuno, I participated in a comparative study of three paddy-growing villages in Java conducted by staff of the Center for Southeast Asian Studies, Kyoto University, among others, in 1973. See Shinichi Ichimura (ed., 1975).
9. See Tadashi Fukutake (1949).
10. The study in Niigata was undertaken in 1974 with the objective of comparing these villages with farm villages in Southeast Asia. See Shinichi Ichimura (ed., 1975). Other studies on the Niigata plain were conducted several times before and after this period. As for Hokkaido, several short-term studies, including a survey of the formation of Shinto shrines during the development period, were undertaken with Saburo Takahashi and others, but the results were only used for a presentation at a meeting in Bangkok and were never compiled into a report.
11. See Masuo Kuchiba (ed., 1990).

14
Galok Thirty Years On:
The End of Ecological Adaptation

In July and August 2000, thirty years after my community study of 1970 and 1971 in the rural community of Galok, I carried out a follow-up survey of the same village on the east coast of the Malay Peninsula. I had also made follow-up surveys in 1977, 1984, 1991 and 1992, so this was not my first time back in 30 years. My 1970/71 survey was a comprehensive one, while in 1991 and in the present survey I focused on population and the family. In this chapter, I shall focus on the period since 1991, recording the changes that have occurred and discussing their significance. The "ecological adaptation" of my subtitle presupposes its role in explaining changes in population and family through its effect on occupations rather than a direct influence. The significance of ecological adaptation in present-day Malay rural communities has changed greatly and is perhaps in the process of being lost. In response to this, the characteristics of population and the family have also changed. Here I shall describe these changes and review the role that the ecological base has played in the lives of rural Malays, then offer my view of ecology-centered area studies.[1]

14.1. Changes in Occupations and Lifestyles

While some repetition may be involved, let me summarize the location of Galok and the changes in occupation seen there, describing additional features that I have come to consider worthy of note in the past decade. The survey village of Galok lies some 400 to 800 meters from the middle reach of the Kelantan River, along the road connecting Pasir Mas and Tanah Merah. The district capital of Pasir Mas is some 15 kilometers downstream, and beyond that, some 31 kilometers distant, is the state capital of Kota Bharu, on the lower reach. Fifteen kilometers upstream of Galok is Tanah Merah, seat of the district office of Jajahan Tanah Merah. Today, Galok is connected by road to these towns, but before the road between Pasir Mas and Tanah Merah was opened, reportedly in 1935, the Kelantan River was the principal means of transport.

Galok is thought to have been first settled in around 1890. The first settlements were formed at the northern and southern ends of Kebang Galok, a swamp, now drained and converted to paddy land, from which the village derives its name. The first settlers came from across the Kelantan River and established a livelihood based on upland rice and wet rice cultivated in rain-fed paddy fields. Settlers also came from Pahang state, but now only ten graves remain, their descendants having apparently moved on. At about the same time, a village of Fukkienese immigrants led by brothers said to have come from Kampung Kasar in Pasir Mas district was opened to the south of Galok on the Kelantan River. This settlement, now called Pasir Parit, has grown to encompass 156 households and is the largest agricultural settlement of overseas Chinese in the area. Padang Hangus, a Malay village neighboring Galok at a greater distance from the river, was settled later.

Development of this area entered a new phase with the introduction of rubber along the Kelantan River. Rubber was planted on a relatively large scale in plantations situated more than one kilometer from the river and on the upper reach, while around Galok it was planted on patches of high ground that were unsuitable for paddy cultivation. The main occupations in Galok thus became small-scale rubber tapping and paddy cultivation. Because the Kelantan River has high banks and no tributaries near Galok, it is impossible to stabilize agricultural production in the village by use of traditional technologies. In this sense, Galok can be characterized as a pioneer village established under limiting conditions for rice cultivation before rubber became the mainstay of development.

At the time of my 1970/71 survey, Galok's resources were already insufficient to accommodate and support the population that had grown up there. Tobacco cultivation, introduced around this time with the backing of the state government, was attracting back to the village, albeit temporarily, the young people who had left to plant rubber on the upper reaches of the Kelantan River. By 1991, tobacco cultivation was in decline, and migrant work in Kuala Lumpur and Singapore had become significant. Wage labor and permanent employment in Pasir Mas, Tanah Merah and other towns within commuting distance had also increased.

In 2000, Galok had 210 households. The most notable changes at this time were that migrant work had almost ceased, while permanent employment had increased further. In addition to the teachers of the past, villagers held various government jobs, such as nurse at the newly opened clinic, hospital assistant, and ambulance driver. The number of cars in Galok, as elsewhere, has grown in the past few years, and one household in three now owns a car, albeit second-hand. With the widening of the road between Pasir Mas and Tanah Merah and the increase in traffic, fourteen villagers now work as bus, shared-taxi, or long-distance lorry drivers.

By 1991, a lumber district had been established in Tanah Merah, where a collection of saw mills and plywood factories operated. One of the factories paid a daily wage of RM15 for men and RM13 for women, insufficient to support a family, providing no more than a supplement to the household budget. At this time, sixteen villagers, mostly men in their twenties, were employed as day laborers at a saw mill, but with the movement of young people of this age to Kuala Lumpur and elsewhere, the number of employees from Galok has declined. The owner of the cafeteria at the middle school in the neighboring village of Chekok lives in Galok, and he pays workers a daily wage of RM10. Similar work in and around Pasir Mas pays RM13. Clearly, subtle considerations determine the wage level, but it is also true that the wage system within the region differs from that in other parts of the country.

One notable development in the village has been the emergence of skilled workers. One of the villagers who worked in Singapore now meets local demand for the skills he acquired there in concrete-block construction and tile-laying. Twelve villagers are carpenters. With the recent rapid spread of the telephone, some villagers carry out wiring under subcontract. Within the village, the shops have grown in size and in the number of items they handle. Little coffee shops *(kedai kopi)* have also increased in number, and some of them now serve simple meals. Some villagers also peddle fish and vegetables by van.

In the midst of these changes, the number of people engaged in agriculture has declined. Seventy-one households grew rice in 1970/71, while only 36 did so in 1991. In recent years, however, the government has imposed strict controls on the import of Thai rice, and in 2000 the number of rice-growing households in Galok had risen to 42. Households tapping rubber, some of which also grew rice, numbered 94 in 1970/71, 53 in 1991, and only 38 in 2000. Tobacco cultivation, introduced in 1968 as a dry-season crop in paddy fields, attracted 124 households at its peak in 1970/71, and thereafter declined to 40 in 1991 and only 25 in 2000.

Rice continues to be cultivated in rain-fed fields, but tractors are now hired for plowing. Rice varieties recommended by the Department of Agriculture are widely used, being transplanted in the traditional way using family labor. Traditional harvesting operations have also been maintained, with reaping by sickle and threshing by beating sheaves against the rungs of a ladder set in a tub. The family still provides the main source of labor, although some households hire the large mechanical harvesters that come from Kedah. The harvested rice is still almost entirely for home consumption. Rubber production has changed greatly in recent years with a move towards the reduction of labor.

Plate 14-1. A furniture factory adjacent to Galok.

Plate 14-2. A peddler preparing for her rounds.

In the past, the collected latex was coagulated by adding acid, rolled, then dried naturally; but today it is left in bowls for several days, and the lumps of latex *(getah beku)* thus formed are loaded into sacks and sold to middlemen. This simplification of operations allows a larger area to be tapped, but in fact none of the villagers has expanded tapping to the limits of work capacity. Some villagers have shifted from tobacco to other field crops, including *kangkong* (a leafy vegetable), *timun* (a melon), *kacang* (cowpeas and other legumes), and *ubi keling* (a potato). One villager cultivates about two acres of tapioca *(ubi kayu)*.

These changes in agriculture involve elements of expansion, diversification, and intensification, but there has been absolutely no movement to seek new land for agricultural development outside the village. In the past, agricultural land within the village was also important, and the availability of land as a means of production influenced decisions on postmarital residence. This is no longer true. The pioneer spirit of peasants who sought through their own endeavors to build a livelihood around agriculture no longer exists. Land within the village, while supporting the livelihood of some residents and maintaining the village's agricultural landscape, is significant for many villagers only as residential land.

Plate 14-3. Vegetable cultivation.

The disappearance of the peasant lifestyle of a pioneering society is also apparent in housing styles. Cement-block houses standing on the ground were originally found mainly in the towns and suburbs. In the village, such houses mostly belonged to teachers, who had a stable income. Now there are a number of such houses belonging to people who were attracted to Galok by its relative convenience for transportation and low land prices, and who purchased land there with the help of distant relatives or acquaintances. Such houses are particularly noticeable along the road, although elsewhere in the village the rapid rise in lumber prices has also inevitably had an impact, with wood replaced by brick and finally by the cheaper concrete blocks. Of course, the period when wood exclusively was used was relatively short; before that walls were normally made of woven bamboo. The typical Malay-style stilted houses with raised floors under which water buffaloes and other animals were kept have all now disappeared, but stilted houses are still in the majority. These houses have been extended at ground level, starting with the rebuilding of the cooking area *(dapor)* in brick or concrete blocks. The bathing area, originally outdoors, has been incorporated into the house at ground level, as has the toilet, which was either completely lacking or housed in a temporary structure outdoors. The living space on the raised floor will also eventually be replaced at ground level in the course of expansion or rebuilding. The straw matting *(tikar)* woven of *mengkuang* or other natural fibers is being replaced by commercially available plastic matting, and drawing-room furniture is becoming a necessity in the ground-level houses. Television sets, electric fans and refrigerators are already standard. Houses are becoming larger and more permanent structures, and this itself is influencing the character of family and kin. The time has arrived to reconsider the composition and function of the multihousehold compound in the wider sense, comprising a group of small, simple houses, where a certain degree of separation of the constituent members and flexibility of composition were considered a matter of course.

14.2. Changes in Population

From the arrival of the first settlers until 1991, Galok's population grew steadily. In 1970/71, the population of 690 lived in 146 households.[2] By this time, 27 households owned neither paddy nor rubber land, and 44 households engaged in neither wet-rice cultivation nor rubber tapping. This situation was made possible by the introduction of tobacco cultivation, which provided a new, albeit small, source of income, and without which the village population would probably not have reached this level. Landholdings were already fragmented: the average holding of paddy land of households that owned such land was 1.2 acre (0.48 ha), and the corresponding figure for rubber land was 1.7 acre (0.69 ha). Some young couples left their children with grandparents and went to join the state-sponsored development of rubber plantations that was underway in Ulu Kelantan. With the introduction of tobacco cultivation, some of these people returned temporarily to the village for the dry-season cropping period. This may have been the last time that land pioneering still played a real part in daily life.

By 1991 the situation had changed. The village population had reached 1,064 people in 205 households,[3] agriculture was in decline, and migrant work in Singapore had become the new alternative source of income. In that foreign workers were not permitted to reside long-term in Singapore, the migrants were obliged to return to Galok, and in this sense the village was still their base. By 2000, the situation had changed again. With the industrialization of Malaysia, factories in Selangor, where Kuala Lumpur is located, and in Johor, the state adjoining Singapore, and restaurants and other service industries were providing job opportunities for young people. The number of households had grown slightly to 210, but the population, at 1,010, showed signs of decrease with the exodus of young people.

Figure 14-1 shows the age structure of the Galok population in 1970/71, 1991, and 2000.[4] In 1970/71, out-migration of 25–29-year-olds is evident in the narrowing of the pyramid for this age group. Their destinations were mainly the jungle development areas around Ulu Kelantan, although some were attracted to neighboring settlements with surplus land. The stagnation or slight decrease in the 0–4-year-old population is a result of the decrease in their parents' age group together with the influence of a family planning campaign that began at this time. This campaign, though reportedly not very effective among Malays, probably had some influence in Galok, since a number of villagers were included on the list of acceptors of the contraceptive pill at the health subcenter in Kangkong, some six kilometers from Galok.

In the 1991 pyramid, a narrowing is evident centering on 25–29-year-old males and extending to the older and younger age groups. In absolute terms, however, the population shows an increase relative to 1970/71 for all groups except men aged 20–24. The imbalance between males and females aged 0–4 years is due to a combination of errors in collecting and compiling data. Compared with 1991, the 2000 population structure is plainly gourd-shaped. The constriction has shifted from the 25–29-year-olds to the 20–24-year-olds, suggesting that, as the age of marriage has risen, many unmarried villagers have left the village. The predominance of males among out-migrants has declined, and females now apparently outnumber males among 20–24-year-olds. The 0–4-year-old population is markedly smaller than the

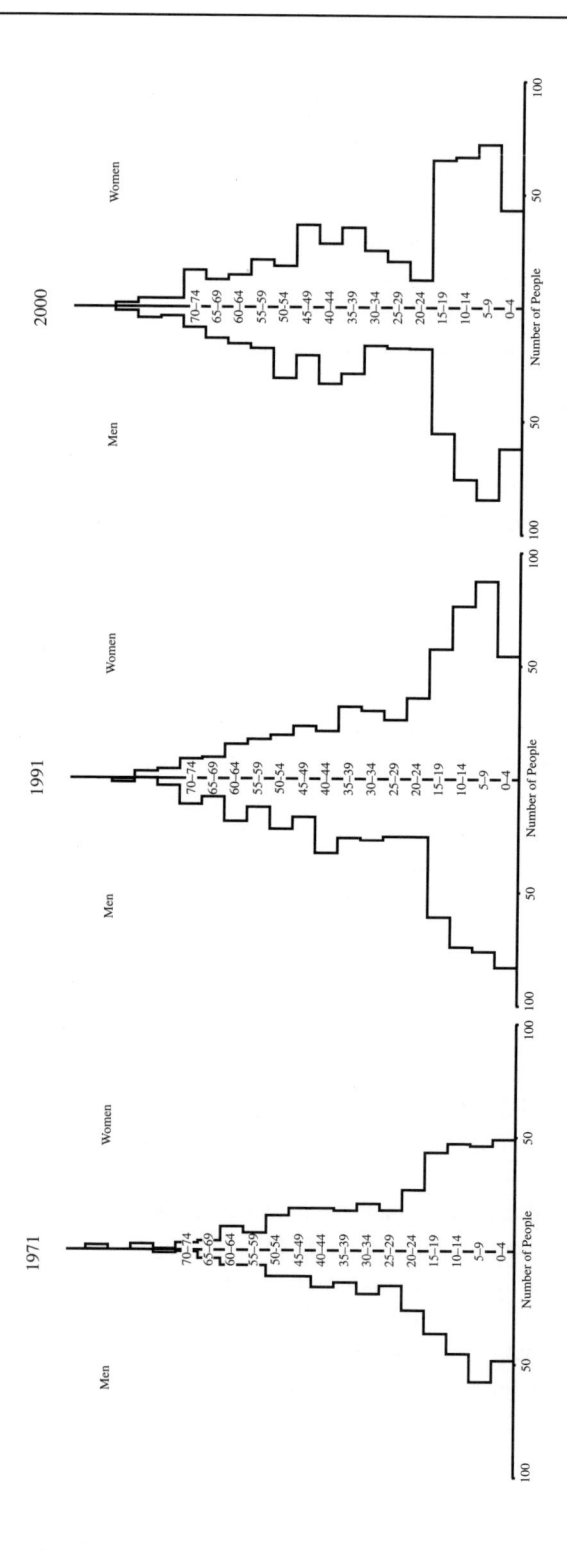

Figure 14-1. Population Pyramids for 1971, 1991 and 2000

5–9-year-old, reflecting the significant out-migration of their parents' age group.

In the 1991 survey, women were asked about their history of childbirth, and the age-specific fertility and total fertility rate (TFR) for the period 1972–1991 were calculated. In the present survey, this was repeated for the period 1991–2000. Table 14-1 shows the results. Fertility has clearly declined in the 15–19 and 20–24 age intervals, presumably because of the increase in the number of unmarried women of these ages resulting from the rising age of first marriage. In contrast, fertility in all age intervals from 25 years is virtually unchanged or even shows a slight increase. The TFR was calculated at 4.860 for 1972–1991 and 4.620 for 1991–2000. This slight decrease can be interpreted as a result not of a decline in fertility among married women but of an increase in the number of unmarried women. These observations of fertility show that the changes in the population structure of Galok are caused not by changes in the fertility of residents but by migration.

Table 14-2 shows the numbers and destinations of village residents in 1970/71 who had out-migrated by 1991, according to their age in the latter year. Table 14-3 shows similar figures for out-migration in the period 1991–2000. Since the former table covers a period of twenty years and the latter only nine years, comparisons in terms of age are difficult, but nevertheless several important changes can be noted. First is the increase in out-migration. Of the 1970/71 residents, 311 left the village in the following twenty-years; while of the 1991 residents, 382 had left nine years later. Second, the sex ratio of out-migrants became balanced: for the 1970/71 residents, 112 males left per 100 females; while for the 1991 residents the figure was 99. In particular,

Table 14-1
Age-specific Fertility and Total Fertility Rates

	Fertility	
Age	1972–1991	1991–2000
15–19	0.066	0.010
20–24	0.228	0.168
25–29	0.267	0.275
30–34	0.200	0.202
35–39	0.164	0.169
40–44	0.038	0.091
45–49	0.009	0.009
Total Fertility Rate	4.860	4.620

Table 14-2
Destinations for Out-migration from 1970/71 to 1991

Age in 1991	Kuala Lumpur*1		Other States		Ulu Kelantan		Tanah Merah		Kota Bharu		Pasir Mas*2		Other*3		Total	
	Men	Women	Men	Women	Men	Women	Men	Women	Men	Women	Men	Women	Men	Women	Men	Women
20–24	6	6	10	8	6	3	2	5	3	2	5	1	2	3	34	28
25–29	8	2	9	12	7	5	4	4	2	4	7	7	2	2	39	36
30–34	6	2	11	7	5	2	6	8	2	5	2	9	3	2	35	35
35–39	5	3	7	4	3	2	1	3	2	2	4	7		5	22	26
40–44			3		2	1	1	1			6	3		3	12	8
45–49			2					1		1	4	1			6	3
50–54					1	1	1		3		1				6	1
55–59					1	1	1							1	2	2
60–64						1			1	1	2				3	2
65–69							2	3							2	3
70–											1	3	1		2	3
Unknown							1								1	
Total	25	13	42	31	25	16	19	25	13	15	32	31	8	16	164	147

*1 including Petaling Jaya   *2 excluding Galok   *3 including unclear cases

among migrants to Kuala Lumpur and other destinations outside Kelantan State, the high figure of 152 males per 100 females of the 1970/71 residents dropped to 99 for the 1991 residents. Third is the change in destinations. Of the out-migrants in the earlier period, 35.7 percent went to Kuala Lumpur and other out-of-state destinations; while in the later period, the figure rose to 71.1 percent. Thus, the main flow of migration became directed to Kuala Lumpur and other distant urban areas. Of the earlier migrants, 13.2 percent had moved to Ulu Kelantan and other jungle areas within the state, while only 1.8 percent of the recent migrants did so. The fourth point is that the recent out-migrants tend to be younger. Because the results for the 1970/71 residents are aggregated over a long period, it is difficult to draw any firm conclusions; but at least it can be said that out-migration did not center on those in the 20–24 age group at the end of the period. For the 1991 residents, migrants clearly tended to be younger and to center on those aged 20–24 at the end of the period.

For the 1970/71 residents, their age at the time of migration is unclear, since data were collected twenty years later. However, the fact that the out-migrants included older villagers, some of whom must have been at least in their fifties, suggests that migration was a universal and commonplace activity, not one restricted to younger people who moved in search of work or as a result of marriage. The same is also true of the 1991 residents.

14.3. Changes in Household Composition

Household composition in Galok has in some aspects changed in concert with the changes in population structure discussed above. However, this is not the only factor involved. Another notable feature is that urban influences have eroded the principles that were created and maintained in relation to an agricultural pioneering society. Here I shall focus on the changes that have occurred in the family composition of households, based on the data presented in Tables 14-4, 14-5, and 14-6. (See also Figure 9-7 for the stages of the family career.)

The most salient change has been an increase in the number of unmarried children who have left the parental home. In 1971, there were only nine such cases. At this time it was normal for unmarried children to live with their parents and to leave the parental home only after marriage. By 1991, the number of households with absent unmarried children had risen slightly, but by 2000 the figure had leapt dramatically to 31.9 percent of the total households. This was due to the increase in age at first marriage and the out-migration of young people for education and employment. In 1971 it was not considered normal for unmarried children to live apart from their parents, but

Table 14-3
Destinations for Out-migration from 1991 to 2000

Age in 2000	Kuala Lumpur*1		Other States		Ulu Kelantan		Tanah Merah		Kota Bharu		Pasir Mas*2		Other*3		Total	
	Men	Women	Men	Women	Men	Women	Men	Women	Men	Women	Men	Women	Men	Women	Men	Women
0–4																
5–9			1	2			1		1	1	1			1	5	4
10–14			3	2	1		4	1	3	1	6	7		2	18	13
15–19	6	1	6	12	2		3	4	3		7	6	2	4	27	27
20–24	23	21	23	25	1		2	3	1	7	2	5		2	52	63
25–29	18	15	17	15	1		4	1	2	2	7	4	2	3	51	40
30–34	3	4	4	6	1			2	3	3		4			11	19
35–39	1	1	2	1			3		1		4	1		1	11	5
40–44	1	1		1			1			1	1	2	1	1	4	5
45–49			2					1			2		1		6	2
50–54				2			2		1			2			2	4
55–59		1									1	2			1	3
60–64														2		2
65–69						1										2
70–										1	2	3			2	3
Total	52	44	58	67	6	1	20	12	15	16	33	36	6	16	190	192

*1 including Petaling Jaya *2 excluding Galok *3 including unclear cases

Table 14-4
Family Composition of Households in 1971

Stage of Family Career	Total Number of Households	Households with Model Composition	Absent Members: Couple's Unmarried Child	Absent Members: One Spouse's Unmarried Child	Absent Members: One Spouse	Additional Members: One Spouse's Unmarried Child	Additional Members: Adopted Child	Additional Members: Parent	Additional Members: Divorced Daughter	Additional Members: Grandchild	Additional Members: Collateral Kin
I	3	2					1				
II	6	3	1				2				
III	59	41	7	10	2	6					1
IV											
V	30	12	1	1	4	4		1	5	12	
VI	18	5			10					7	
VII	14	6					3		1	5	1
VIII	16	8					1			7	
Total	146	77	9	11	16	10	7	1	6	31	2

Polygynous marriages are counted as two households because the husband is counted twice.
Source: Kuchiba, Tsubouchi, and Maeda (1976), p. 202.

Table 14-5
Family Composition of Households in 1991

Stage of Family Career	Total Number of Households	Households with Model Composition	Absent Members: Couple's Unmarried Child	Absent Members: One Spouse's Unmarried Child	Absent Members: One Spouse	Additional Members: One Spouse's Unmarried Child	Additional Members: Adopted Child	Additional Members: Parent	Additional Members: Divorced Daughter	Additional Members: Grandchild	Additional Members: Collateral Kin
I	3	1									2
II	1										1
III	103	64	13	1	13	3	2	1	11		7
IV	5	3	2								
V	51	26	4	1	12	1		3		9	
VI	10	1	2		2					7	1
VII	15	9			1				1	5	
VIII	17	11						1	2	4	
Total	205	116	21	2	28	4	1	15	3	26	11

by 2000 it had become quite natural. In 2000, households classified as having model composition had fallen to less than 50 percent of the total, reflecting clearly this change in the coresidence rule.

The number of unmarried children of one spouse (either husband or wife) counted as absent family members also decreased, from eleven cases in 1971, to

Table 14-6
Family Composition of Households in 2000

Stage of Family Career	Total Number of Households	Households with Model Composition	Absent Members: Couple's Unmarried Child	Absent Members: One Spouse's Unmarried Child	Absent Members: One Spouse	Additional Members: One Spouse's Unmarried Child	Additional Members: Adopted Child	Additional Members: Parent	Additional Members: Divorced Daughter	Additional Members: Grandchild	Additional Members: Collateral Kin
I	2	1					1	1			
II	2	2									
III	92	44	31	8		2		14			10
IV	2	1	1								
V	45	7	27	11		2	1		4		
VI	16	4	8	2					2		
VII	21	16						1	1	1	2
VIII	30	26						1			3
Total	210	101	67	21	4	3		17	1	11	10

two in 1991, and none in 2000. This is related to the decline in divorce, from an extremely common to a rare occurrence. In Kelantan, the number of divorces per 100 marriages fell from 52.2 in 1960 to 34.7 in 1970, 16.7 in 1980 and 4.6 in 1990/91. Underlying this decline has been a re-evaluation of marriage among Muslims in the whole of Malaysia and corresponding changes in legislation. The strict attitudes of 1990/91, however, have not since been maintained, and divorces per 100 marriages have fluctuated irregularly: 14.1 in 1997, 6.5 in 1998, and 15.5 in 1999. Whatever the case, there are now fewer children of an earlier marriage that has ended in divorce who live in a household other than that created by the parent's remarriage. Likewise, there are now fewer divorced daughters or grandchildren (the children of divorced daughters) living as additional members in parental or grandparental households.

The phenomenon of grandparents taking in their grandchildren was not solely associated with divorce. People who went to the jungle to clear land often left their children with grandparents because of the inconvenience of life and lack of educational facilities in remote areas. Old women who went to live in the *pondok* also often had a grandchild live with them. Cases of the former declined with the slow-down of jungle development, while cases of the latter declined because life in the *pondok* with a grandmother became incompatible with rapidly changing educational circumstances and living standards. In this way, although child numbers have been maintained and grandparents could still take in a grandchild, the circumstances surrounding this phenomenon have changed.

In both categories of parent and collateral kin as additional family members, the number of cases has increased. These changes do not, however, directly

Plate 14-4. A family with children.

indicate a change in household composition but should be seen in relation to change in the representative of the household arising from change in the means of livelihood. In earlier times when land was more significant, the ownership of paddy and rubber land by parents defined their role as the economic mainstay of the household. Once alternative sources of income became available, migrant workers of the children's generation naturally assumed a greater role, and their younger brothers and sisters came to be classified as coresident collateral kin. So, has there been a change in the proportion of households classified as so-called stem families? If we regard households with stem family composition as those in stages IV and VI of the family career together with those with a parent as an additional member, such households accounted for 13.0 percent of the total in 1971, 14.6 percent in 1991, and 16.7 percent in 2000. While slight, an increasing tendency can be observed. This is also related to the fact that, as pointed out in Chapter 9 herein, the increasing size of houses, and the provision of such facilities as electricity and mains water supply has decreased the number of aged parents, young couples and others living in temporary buildings near the core household.

14.4. Changes in Multihousehold Compounds

What are here called multihousehold compounds are groups of kin living in close proximity as a result of one or more children taking up residence on their parents' land.[5] In Malay rural communities, the cohesion of such groups through living and working together and sharing the fruits of labor is weak, and family relations within the group may diffuse via the coresidence of siblings to the coresidence of cousins. In 1971, 95 households lived in thirty-six multihousehold compounds in this wider sense, accounting for 65.5 percent of the villages total of 145 households (families of polygynous men residing in the same house were counted as 1 household). Table 14-7 shows the changes in the numbers of constituent households in these thirty-six compounds between 1971 and 1991, while Table 14-8 shows the corresponding changes between 1991 and 2000. In the earlier interval, seven ceased to be multi-household compounds through the loss of 1 of their 2 households, and by 2000 ten of the original thirty-six were reduced to 1 household. In all but one case, these had previously had 2 households. Conversely, in addition to the original thirty-six compounds, five new groups had been formed and were still in existence in 2000. At that time, 95 households occupied multihousehold compounds, and although this represents a relative decrease overall, it indicates that, continual changes in membership notwithstanding, the multihousehold compounds are being maintained.

The framework within which such groups have been formed in Galok is related to the process of clearance and subsequent partition of land. As long as people were dependent on a limited amount of agricultural land, expansion of the number of households was limited, and by 1971 a saturation point had been reached which affected the residence of kin in close proximity. Changes in occupation subsequently relaxed this limitation, but the increase in house size allowed parents and married children, who would formerly have lived separately, to live together in the same house, thereby changing the form of coresidence. Larger houses required more space and made it difficult to build several houses in the same

Table 14-7
Number of Households in 1991 in Multihousehold Compounds of 1971

Number of Households in 1971	Number of Households in 1991										Total
	1	2	3	4	5	6	7	8	9	10	
2	7	9	7	1							24
3		2	2			1					5
4		2	1	1	1						5
5											0
6						1				1	2
Total	7	13	10	2	1	2	0	0	0	1	36

Table 14-8
Changes in Number of Households from 1991 to 2000 in Multihousehold Compounds of 1971

Number of Households in 1991	Number of Households in 2000														Total
	1	2	3	4	5	6	7	8	9	10	11	12	13	14	
1	6	1													7
2	3	10	5												18
3	1	3	1		1										6
4					1										1
5					1										1
6					2										2
7															0
8															0
9															0
10														1	1
Total	10	14	6	0	5	0	0	0	0	0	0	0	0	1	36

compound. This encouraged the conversion of farm land to residential land and has led to the establishment of a "new village" (*kampung baru*) a little distance away from the original settlement, where twelve households now reside.

Changes in compound coresidence in Galok, particularly when siblings or cousins are involved, does not entail group formation. Such changes are merely the result of household formation. As we have seen, household formation is characterized by a notable decline in younger members, even though the number of households has not changed. Against the background of such a change in households, the residence of kin in close proximity is being maintained, while the presence of single old people and old couples living alone is becoming notable.

14.5. In Conclusion

Such have been the changes in Galok over the past thirty years. Changes in line with the out-worn framework of modernization appear, though belatedly, to have occurred here also and are evident in the pursuit of universal values as represented by Kuala Lumpur. The changes in occupation that have accompanied urbanization have undermined the basis of the mode of adaptation premised on the land pioneering that rural society in Malaysia, including Galok, had maintained since the mid-nineteenth century and that shaped the character of that society and found expression in the flexibility of family composition. The notion of flexible family and kin bonds has not been lost entirely, but it also true that occasions for its expression in visible form have decreased. The structure that permitted divorce is in the process of being lost due to strong central guidance, and the subtle relationships of dependence between parents and children living in the same compound are not formed because young people leave the village. Coresidence of grandparents and grandchildren is also less common than in the past, because of such factors as the decrease of out-migration for land pioneering, the spread of education and the difficulty for older people to deal with this, and the decline in divorce.

It may be superfluous to add that divorce among Malays was traditionally more common in rural than in urban areas. Life in pioneer villages, where educational opportunities were limited and opportunities for enjoyment few, early marriage was the rule, and when difficulties arose between husband and wife, whose cooperation was the basis of their livelihood, people quickly dissolved the marriage and sought a new chance. Divorce was common among the young, while as people grew older their marriage ties became more stable. The idea of limiting this inherent instability in traditional society, based on the urban or modern view that the nuclear family plays an exclusionary role, was applied to rural areas through the revision of legal procedures and resulted in a widespread decline in divorce. The fact that recent divorce figures for Kelantan have fluctuated irregularly is perhaps an indication that such measures were somewhat excessive.

The flexibility of bonds in Malay society and the Malay family are today perhaps more clearly observable in Galok's relations with urban areas than within the village itself. Examples include the mutual assistance exchanged between migrants to urban areas, the role of urban families as temporary recipients of rural migrants, the remittance of money to the villages, the frequent visits to and from relatives living in rural areas, and the return of pensioners to the villages. This trend remains linked to the mode of pioneering society based on agriculture, and in this sense a continuity can be recognized despite the change in the ecological basis. If such continuity is an intrinsic part of the Malay value system, then it will be the task of area studies to explore its new manifestations. If what is seen as continuity is no more than a large relic of the past, then pursuit of its characteristics in area studies will become meaningless. Even if continuity can be recognized, the question will still remain as to what extent it will find concrete expression in the family. The conditions that produced the frequent coresidence of grandparents and grandchildren and child adoption no longer remain in effect. The future subjects of observation and research will be the relics of spiritual or ideological aspects of the value system, and their renewal and reinforcement.

The direction of the modernization that has changed the system of livelihood in the village shows certain points in common with Japan, at least in the process of abandonment of agriculture. The next stage may be depopulation, of which the out-migration of young people is perhaps the harbinger. Alternatively, a circulation may be established between rural and urban areas, including the return of pensioners to their villages. Within Asia, will such changes be limited to Malaysia, or will they extend to Thailand and Indonesia, and eventually sweep across China, India and Bangladesh? Would such changes be for the best? If not, what is the logic for following a different path? What, beyond observation, should area studies aim to do? These are the questions we must ask ourselves.

Notes

1. On earlier surveys, see, for example, Kuchiba, Tsubouchi, and Maeda (1976).
2. Polygynous families living in the same house are counted as two households.
3. The figure of 211 households reported in the 1991 survey (see Table 9-5) was subsequently found to include duplication, which when subtracted yields a figure of 205.
4. The 1991 population figures were also subsequently found to include duplication, here corrected.
5. On multihousehold compounds in Northeast Thailand, see Mizuno (1981); and for a comparison of Northeast Thailand with Malaysia, see Kuchiba and Maeda (1980). It should be noted that the use of this term in the context of Kelantan involves considerable widening of the original definition.

Appendices

Gleanings from the Study of Kelantan

I have recorded surprisingly little information on how the field survey was conducted. The only printed record that remains is a report prepared just prior to the end of my field study in 1971 and published in the Field Report section in the Journal of *Tōnan Ajia Kenkyū* (*Southeast Asian Studies*). This was mainly an outline of study results with very little mention of the concrete procedures involved in implementation of the study. It is impossible at this date to recall every detail of the survey at that time, but if I do not attempt to record what I can still remember, it will be lost forever. Accordingly, I have included a brief account in the first appendix, written in 1995.

I have also reproduced the two field reports published in *Tōnan Ajia Kenkyū*. One was written in Alor Janggus, Kedah in 1965, and the other in Pasir Mas in 1971. The Alor Janggus report provides background and history to the Kelantan study. Alor Janggus remains imprinted in my memory, along with the names such as the *penghulu* of Padang Lalang, my landlord Tuan Haji and his nephew Harun, a junior high school student and one of my assistants, and my servants Sa'ad and Rokiah and their child Hamid, of all of whom have since passed away. The report from Pasir Mas reproduces my impressions exactly as they were at that time. Although there are many portions that overlap with the main text of this book, and despite the fact that some of the expressions and statements may be inappropriate, I venture to present the unrevised version here.

Appendix 1
One Year in Kelantan

I first visited Kelantan in 1965. Having completed a field study in Alor Janggus in Kedah, I traveled by propeller plane from Alor Star to Kota Bharu. Leaving the red earth of Kedah behind for the dazzling whiteness of Kelantan, I was particularly struck by the sight of women busily working in market. Although I still remained on the Malay peninsula, it seemed to be a different world. The hotel accommodations in Kota Bharu were slightly better than those in Alor Star in that my room came equipped with a place to bathe with water. At night, the roof was transformed into a kind of nightclub with bright lights and blaring music. Young Malay girls drank colored water and waited upon the customers, a scene unimaginable today when Islam exerts such a strong social influence.

Based on an agreement between the Center for Southeast Asian Studies, Kyoto University and the Faculty of Economics and Administration, University of Malaya, a comparative study of Malay paddy-growing villages was commenced in 1968. Villages in Kedah, Melaka and Kelantan were to be selected for field studies, and I returned to Kelantan once again for this purpose. I visited state government offices to gather information and at the same time, scouted villages in irrigated, coastal, and rainfed paddy areas. In the end, I selected Galok, a village in Mukim Jabo in the subdistrict (*daerah*) of Chetok in Pasir Mas district, because it was located in a rainfed paddy area where traditional cultivation methods were thought to be most preserved.

Galok is situated along a road that runs parallel to the Kelantan river at the midpoint between Pasir Mas and Tanah Merah, which are separated by a distance of thirty kilometers. Villagers engaged in both rainfed paddy cultivation and rubber tapping. The village was comprised of a total of 150 households and I felt that, with some effort, it would be possible to study every household. The lack of electricity and running water might be inconvenient for a prolonged study period, but I thought that I could either build or borrow a small house and asked the *penggawa* (head of the *daerah*) who was temporarily living in the village to arrange it. As I was scheduled to participate in a one-year training program on demography at Princeton University in the fall of 1968, the study period was to commence after that date.

In July 1970 I finally began the study. Originally, funds were to be provided by a grant from the Ford Foundation to Kyoto University, but this plan was abandoned due to student unrest at the university. Instead, thanks to the efforts of Professor Shinichi Ichimura, the Director of the Center for Southeast Asian Studies, Kyoto University at that time, support was obtained from the Kansai Economic Center and others. I was awarded US$450 per month for the study period, an unexpectedly large sum for a young assistant professor in view of Japan's economic situation in 1970.

I spent one-third of the study grant to procure a small vehicle known in Malaysia as a Toyota 1000. The purchase of a car greatly changed the initial study plan and also affected study methods. I had originally intended to live in the village and visit each household by bicycle, but a vehicle made it possible to live near Pasir Mas and commute daily to the study site. Although this meant fewer opportunities to have contact with the villagers in their daily lives, it had the advantage of permitting me to extend my observations to Pasir Mas district and Kelantan as a whole. In addition, it meant that I could use electricity at night, allowing me the luxury of an electric fan and also enabling me to organize my field data in the evenings.

Accommodation was arranged through Ramly Yaacob, a clerk in his midthirties, whom I happened to meet at the Pasir Mas district office. He lived in Kubang Bemban, a village suburb of Pasir Mas. Electricity supply lines had been installed along the road from Pasir Mas to about one-third of households in this settlement, and those connected to the power supply were considered part of Pasir Mas township. Ramly lived in one of three houses occupying a roadside compound, the other two of which were occupied by his wife's mother and adopted daughter, and by his wife's older sister and family. The house he introduced me to was a sort of two-storied duplex standing in the neighboring compound to his. Two-storied houses were very unusual in Pasir Mas at that time, and this one was actually a traditional house on high stilts, in which a ground floor had been made by enclosing the space under the stilts with a wall of concrete blocks set with windows. It lacked a proper entranceway or terrace, and instead a folding door opened directly into the front yard. The tenants renting the other half of the building were both teachers, the husband from Negeri Sembilan and the wife a native of Kelantan. The landlord lived in a separate house, a large structure with a raised floor located behind our rented quarters.

Rent for the unfurnished house was RM60 a month. (In 1970, RM1 = ¥120; RM3 = US$1.) The first floor had one large open concrete room, a kitchen, and an adjacent toilet-cum-bathing room, while the upper wooden portion of the house consisted of one room of about ten square meters and another of about seven square meters. I immediately set about purchasing the necessary furniture and appliances. The most expensive items were a refrigerator of about 90-liter capacity and electric fan, both considered luxury items at the time, and a propane gas burner, all of which I purchased at a Chinese store in town. I also bought a folding table and plywood chairs at the same store. I obtained a bed from a Malay cabinetmaker located along the Kelantan river. With the addition of pots, dishes, and cutlery, my preparations were complete. I subsequently rented accommodation in Pasir Mas on two other occasions for follow-up surveys, but as the period of time was very short, I chose much simpler lodgings. This first house represented the height of luxury during the study. Although I lived alone most of the time, my wife and 3-year-old daughter came to stay for a short period during the summer holidays and my daughter played in the backyard, chasing the free-ranging chicks and being chased by the hens. Here, at the junction of town and village, goats and water buffalo wandered freely into the front yard and in the landlord's backyard was a monkey tied to a tree.

Esah, the landlord's wife cooked for me. Fish and chicken were the main ingredients and these were grilled, deep-fried or stewed in curry with other ingredients. As I only needed enough for one, I stored the meals in the refrigerator and ate the same food for lunch and dinner. For breakfast, she bought me a type of rice mixed with fragrant leaves and other ingredients that was sold on the street. Abdul Rahman, my landlord, supplied a set of rattan chairs for the downstairs room and made a tin-roofed carport for my car.

Esah, proud to be a native of Kampung Laut, a village in downstream Kelantan with a long history, took me to a relative's wedding. Or rather, it transpired that I acted as chauffeur while she and many others piled into my car, far exceeding the legal number of passengers. That car carried many people during my stay. Although they try not to impose on each other, mutual dependence is a natural part of Malay lifestyle once people become more closely acquainted. Likewise, I not only depended upon them, but compensated by being depended on.

As a Japanese person was something of a novelty in this area, I had many visitors and I received many invitations to weddings and other events. Once I attended a district office picnic and crossed the choppy South China Sea to a small island where we cooked outside and slept on a mat gazing up at the starlit sky.

With the spread of school education, standard Malay was widely understood even in the rural areas of Kelantan. There were still many elderly people, however, who could only speak a local dialect, and it was necessary for me to find an assistant who could speak it fluently. I hired Wan Junoh, a youth just over twenty. He had been employed until recently gathering census information, but was presently out of work. His father was dead and he lived with his grandparents in Kubang Bemban. His mother was remarried to a policeman and was living in Chekok near the police substation.

The first month was spent in becoming accustomed to my new lifestyle and gathering general information. I then began the interview survey of Galok using a survey sheet that had been made for use in several areas as part of a comparative study on paddy-growing villages in Malaysia, and it was based on survey experiences in Kedah in 1964 and 1965. Because of its emphasis on paddy growing, however, there were no columns for rubber tapping or tobacco cultivation and no checklist for diverse sources of income. I therefore began inserting additional items where necessary, deciding to record everything that came up during the interviews. The survey was conducted at the slow pace of one household per day.

To each interview, I took gifts: ground coffee, condensed milk and a bag of sugar. These gifts were an inadequate expression of appreciation for their cooperation considering that one interview could take more than two hours. During the house-to-house survey I conducted in Kedah, I was usually served coffee or some similar refreshment at the homes I visited, but in Galok, this type of hospitality was very rare as most people had no thermoses to keep water hot and lighting a fire to heat water was very time-consuming. It seems that the gifts I brought were much appreciated. Twenty years later I met elderly women who remembered that I had brought them coffee.

The interviews took place on long benches attached to the verandas in front of the houses or in the front room immediately at the top of the ladder leading into the home. When I interviewed people in the latter, they would spread out a small mat that stood rolled up in a corner and politely invite me to sit down. I always tried to interview both the husband and the wife. Some of the houses were so small as to be more appropriately termed huts and there were times during sudden downpours when gusts of rain would spray through the gaps in the palm-thatched roofs or woven bamboo walls as we talked. My assistant, Wan Junoh, became very adept at questioning so that the interview was primarily carried out in the Kelantan dialect while I recorded the information in English on the survey sheet, occasionally asking additional questions or correcting any mistakes in my understanding.

We asked many questions concerning their private affairs such as property, inheritance, income, marriage and divorce, but as the villagers did not need to concern themselves with taxes and were not embarrassed by divorce, it was relatively easy to obtain answers. At the same time, however, they did not volunteer information of their own accord, only responding to questions, and we had to be careful not to omit any details in our inquiries. In the end, I visited each household at least three times to confirm data or obtain additional information. The fact that I was a foreigner worked in my favor as it was possible for me to ask questions that a fellow Malay might be reluctant to. At the time of the survey, I was consciously trying to move away from a qualitative anthropological approach and sought, as far as possible, quantitative data.

About halfway through the study I received the enlarged aerial photographs that I had ordered from the Survey Department in Kuala Lumpur. These, combined with a cadastral map traced onto semi-transparent paper, proved to be priceless, saving me the trouble of making a map of the village, and I was later to regret being too concerned about overspending to obtain aerial photographs of a larger area.

I wore short-sleeved shirts and sandals during the survey. The latter were convenient because whether we conducted the interview on the veranda or in the front room, I had to remove my shoes. A basin of water was placed at the foot of the ladder leading into the house with an empty can for washing one's feet before entering. Most people did not wear shoes then, and children ran naked through the house.

As the results of the survey are presented in detail in the main body of the book, I will not touch upon them here. The major changes that have occurred since that time are also recorded, but I would like to touch upon a few items of clothing, diet and dress that are not mentioned elsewhere. Excluding school and other uniforms, adults and children all wore sarongs. Even very small children could skillfully dress themselves. When I finished the survey, I traveled to Java in Indonesia, and was surprised to see so many people wearing slacks. It was very difficult for villagers to obtain fresh fish, and dried salted fish was a common side dish. Firewood was the main cooking fuel, and food was cooked over a hearth in the kitchen. As there were no toilets, people did their business in the bush, and partly for this reason, they harbored a large number of parasites. In stool tests taken by Dr. Hideo Takizawa as part of a support survey for health and environment, 79 percent of pupils at the elementary school near Galok tested positive for roundworm eggs, and 35 percent positive for hookworm. In general, people were poor, but I would not describe their lifestyle as tragic or destitute. Rather daily life was permeated with an undercurrent of cheerfulness, an attitude of living for the moment.

As the day of my departure approached near the end of my year-long study, I began to dispose of the equipment and furniture I had purchased. I did not have anything of real value, and decided to sell it all very cheaply. Although a Chinese man had been eyeing my car for some time, in the end I sold it to Ramly for a partial payment in cash and the remainder in installments. I used the cash to travel to Indonesia and to purchase books and documents. The remainder used as wages for Wan Junoh to conduct a survey in Kubang Bemban after I left. Wan Junoh wanted the refrigerator for his mother so that she could make ices to sell. In payment I was handed a wad of well-worn RM1 notes bound with a rubber band. Like many others in this region, she might have kept her hard-earned cash from making cakes in a bamboo tube above the ceiling. The propane gas burner I left as a gift for Esah, the landlord's wife, and although there were many people who wanted to buy my bed, I no longer remember what happened to it.

The house that I lived in during this first survey later burned down. Ramly's third daughter and her husband now live in Ramly's house, and his wife's elder sister, who used to live in the house in front, moved to another state with her son who became a customs officer. As for the landlord's household, all of his sons grew up and left home. Wan Junoh now works as a contractor. Married, he has five children and his eldest daughter works in a hotel in Kota Bharu. Ramly became the *penggawa* and since his retirement at fifty-five, he has lived on his pension. His lively younger daughter became a journalist and now lives in Kuala Lumpur with her husband, a native of Kelantan and a police inspector.

During the follow-up survey in 1991 and 1992, I lodged with Ramly in his house in Kampung Dangar where he had moved. His younger daughter lent me a car at a very low rate from among several Malaysian Proton Saga cars that she had bought to lease to car rental companies. As in Galok, the scope of people's lifestyles has broadened and kin members act as intermediaries between urban and rural areas.

APPENDICES

Appendix 2
From Pasir Mas (Field Report 1)

Project for a Comprehensive Survey of Malay Farm Villages

I have spent almost one year in Malaysia as part of a joint project by the Center for Southeast Asian Studies, Kyoto University and the Faculty of Economics and Administration, University of Malaya. Under this project, Masuo Kuchiba (Faculty of Letters, Ryukoku University), Narifumi Maeda (Center for Southeast Asian Studies) and myself have been assigned to socioeconomic field studies in Kedah in the northwest, in Melaka along the west coast, and in Kelantan along the east coast, with periodic visits from researchers specializing in irrigation, paddy cultivation, soil, and medicine who conduct surveys in each study area and advise the above three researchers.

Kuchiba's survey of Kedah ended in 1969 while Maeda's began only a few months ago. Although our study periods were staggered, we managed to get together this August for a meeting. Members of the natural science team are Keizaburo Kawaguchi, our team leader from the Faculty of Agriculture, Kyoto University, Yoshikazu Fujioka, irrigation expert from the Faculty of Agriculture, Kyoto University, Toshihiko Nishio, paddy cultivation expert from the Ministry of Agriculture, Forestry and Fisheries, Hisao Furukawa, soil scientist from the Faculty of Agriculture, Kyoto University and Hideo Takizawa, a doctor from the Faculty of Medicine, Kyoto University. Nishio's survey is to be carried out at a different time, while the other members, having traveled from Kelantan to Kedah and then to Melaka, are almost finished. I find myself very busy as I near the end of my stay.

Kelantan State

Before I leave Kelantan, let me describe the conditions where I have lived for the last year. I will present a proper report concerning the study results after my return to Japan, and I wish to make it clear that I am only jotting down my impressions here.

Kelantan is situated on the east Malay coast near the Thai border. At one time it paid tribute to the Kingdom of Thailand. The population is concentrated on the plains near the mouth of the Kelantan river where there is a broad belt of paddy land intermixed with rubber estates. Traveling upriver, the undulation becomes more marked and the number of rubber estates increases, finally disappearing into a vast expanse of jungle. The total population according to the 1970 census is 680,626, and unlike states along the west coast which have a high proportion of Chinese Malaysians, the population of Kelantan is characterized by a greater percentage of Malays. There are two flights a day from the state capital of Kota Bharu (population approximately 55,000) to Kuala Lumpur, although one of these is via Penang, and a mail train runs through the jungle three times a week. A paved road runs from Kota Bharu stretching about 400 miles along the coast through Kuantan and Kuala Trengganu.

Kelantan, which is controlled by the Islamic opposition party, Partai Islam, is isolated from the west coast and is known in Malaysia as a rather backward state where development projects lag behind those in other regions. Recently, however, many irrigation projects are being implemented such as the Kemubu Project, and the number of double-cropping regions which pump water from the Kelantan river has increased. The jungle is also being reclaimed through a state development project.

Pasir Mas

Kelantan is divided into eight administrative districts (*jajahan*). The district office for Pasir Mas district (total population of around 100,000) is in Pasir Mas, a small town of about 10,000 located on the west bank of the Kelantan river about ten miles from Kota Bharu. A long concrete bridge was constructed by the state government in 1964 to connect Kota Bharu with Pasir Mas and Tumpat on the opposite bank and it is a symbol of the state government's independence.

The center of Pasir Mas town is a market with small traders in farm produce, fish, meat, etc. surrounded by shops run by Chinese, Indians and Malays. Various government agencies such as the district office, post office, hospital and health center are located around this complex and there are also two cinemas. Malay women are actively involved in commercial activities at the market place, a phenomenon not found along the west coast. The majority are middle-aged women who pile their wares on trishaws early in the morning and head for the market from surrounding *kampung* (villages).

The Study Village Galok

The study village (Kampung Galok) is located about nine miles from Pasir Mas along the Kelantan river. A Malay village, it is a ribbon settlement with 150 households spread thinly for about a mile along the road and it is situated about a quarter to half a mile from the Kelantan river. Although there are some irrigation projects within the district including one in Lemal and another in Pasir Mas, Galok is upstream from these and remains totally dependent upon rainwater. As a study of double-cropping regions has already been undertaken by the government and other agencies, I chose a more traditional single-cropping area for the study. Undulation is more pronounced this far upstream, and inspection reveals differences in elevation between adjacent paddy fields. Compared to double-cropping regions, which are more economically stable, the poverty of the houses is noticeable. The village's name is reportedly derived from a swampy area named Kubang Galok that was formerly situated on the same site. Village history, however, is vague. Neighboring villages closer to the river such as Atas Beting and Jabo are said to have a history of almost one hundred years, while Padang Hangus which is located even farther from the river was only settled fifty-five years ago. It seems that the Galok area was settled about eighty years ago.

Land Ownership

Until the recent introduction of tobacco, the main occupations in the village were rain-fed paddy cultivation and rubber tapping, both of which were undertaken on a very small scale of only one or two acres. Land ownership was similarly very small in scale.

As in other parts of Malaysia, after the initial settlement of new territory, land was fragmented into increasingly smaller portions with each generation as property was divided in accordance with Islamic or customary inheritance laws. Unless excess population migrates to new settlement areas or is absorbed by the cities, the present rapid rate of population increase will make further fragmentation of land impossible in the near future. In Galok, customary law in which land is divided equally among sons and daughters is more common than Islamic law, although when there is only one son and several daughters, the son's portion may be somewhat larger.

Residential land, like agricultural land, is also subject to inheritance, but there are no rules determining which siblings leave and which remain. This depends instead upon incidental circumstances and postmarital residence can be fairly accurately predicted by the property owned by each spouse. Residence of parents and children or siblings in the same compound is thus opportunist and incidental in nature. The concept of individual ownership is very strong, and renting and selling of property among parents and children and among siblings is as frequent as that among kin and non-kin.

Sharecropping under the *pawah* system is very common. The landowner generally receives one half of the harvest and the tenant the rest, although this varies slightly depending upon the circumstances. Near Pasir Mas, for example, the landowner pays half of the cost of fertilizer application and pays the tenant in cash for harvesting, but each party transports his own share of the crop. In Galok, the sharecropper does not receive any compensation for such tasks.

The *pawah* system is also used in rubber tapping and livestock raising. In the former, part of the daily earnings is given to the owner, while in livestock raising, the offspring are shared. Although the *sewa* system, under which the tenant pays a fixed fee in cash or in kind, is very common on the west coast, in this area, it is only employed occasionally near the town.

Paddy Cultivation, Rubber Tapping and Other Occupations

As opposed to double-cropping regions where paddy has become a commercial crop, paddy is mainly grown for home consumption. Because cultivation is dependent upon rainfall, there may be almost no yield at all in drought years. Yield for this year was moderate, but the previous year it was very poor due to drought. Although *bahagia* and other new varieties are planted in double-cropping areas, only traditional varieties such as *intan belian* and *padi piah* are planted near Galok, and they are selected to suit the conditions of each paddy field.

Men plow the fields using water buffalo or oxen, women bundle the seedlings in the nurseries, and men and women together transplant them. In Kedah where the division of labor by sex is very clear, transplanting is done only by women, but in Galok men can often be seen doing this task. Women cut the grain at harvest time and men thresh it. Winnowing is predominantly women's work. Excluding the harvest, the above tasks are carried out entirely by the family unit, and organized labor groups are only occasionally employed at harvest time.

Paddy is stored in a granary called a *baloh*. For the majority of farm households, the yield is insufficient even for home consumption, and if there is some surplus one year, it is saved against shortages in the next year and only very rarely sold.

Rubber tapping was once a very profitable source of cash income. Unfortunately, however, the price of rubber has dropped drastically, and as the processing methods and quality of rubber produced in Galok are inferior compared to that produced on large plantations, profit per acre is only a little over RM1. Moreover, tapping is only possible for half the year because the trees cannot be tapped when it rains. Although men also engage in rubber tapping, the number of women is somewhat higher. Unlike on the large plantations, where work begins before sunrise, tapping in Galok starts at about seven in the morning and the sheets of rubber are finished before noon. The rubber, which is not even smoked, is very low grade, and it is either sold in bulk to a licensed store in a nearby village or in small batches to middlemen that visit the village almost every day.

In addition to paddy cultivation and rubber tapping, a few people (*penyadap*) are engaged in coconut-sugar (*manisan*) making which involves collecting sap from the flower stalks in bamboo pipes and boiling it down in an iron pot. Those with orchards or fruit trees in their compound obtain some income from selling *durian* and *duku*, but the fruit crop is extremely uncertain and at times trees may not bear any fruit at all.

Some villagers run coffee shops and stores that cater to the village. There are two coffee shops in Galok, both of which are run by divorced women, and many men congregate there, another phenomenon not seen in Kedah. The limited land area and unstable yields in the village make it difficult to secure a livelihood there, and consequently village men travel to Kedah to help with the harvest, taking advantage of the different harvest season on the west coast, or to Ulu Kelantan, Pahang or even Thailand to tap rubber under the *pawah* system.

Introduction of Tobacco Cultivation

The Malayan Tobacco Company (M.T.C.) established a station in Galok in 1968. When I first visited the village, a brick curing-shed had just been completed. The introduction of tobacco cultivation, which is concentrated around more than ten M.T.C. stations, has greatly changed villages that were dependent on single-cropping paddy cultivation in Kelantan, and Galok is no exception.

Leaf tobacco is grown in paddy fields during the dry season. Until last year each household was only allowed to cultivate 1,000 plants per season, but this year the restrictions have been eased. Villagers were also allowed to plant in both the first and third period of the three-part planting season instead of just in the first period. A tobacco station belonging to a rival tobacco company began operating in a limited area this year including a neighboring village, and the impact of tobacco cultivation on the lives of the villagers is steadily increasing.

Tobacco cultivation is strenuous labor, but the profit per unit area planted is comparatively high, and earnings of about RM250 can be expected from one-seventh of an acre of land planted with 1,000 plants. The village today might be more appropriately called a tobacco-growing village. In addition to cultivating tobacco, the daughters of almost every household are employed at the tobacco station during the four month season. The Galok station alone employs about 750 girls from villages in the area.

Youth who in the past would have been forced to migrate due to the shortage of land and seek their fortune elsewhere no longer need to leave the village thanks to the few months of tobacco work, and young couples who have moved to rubber tapping areas are returning during the tobacco season to grow tobacco, living temporarily with their parents. During the busiest part of the season, no one taps rubber, and small-scale rubber groves are frequently neglected. Some of those involved in making *manisan* (coconut-sugar), which is extremely hard labor, have switched to tobacco cultivation and the number of migrant workers to other parts has also decreased.

During the tobacco season, stalls selling cloth, meat, fish, etc. spring up along the road outside the M.T.C. station. Many of the stall owners come from town, but some youth from the village sell fish or sugar cane juice.

Cash income from tobacco cultivation also seems to have made it easier to continue on to secondary education. A secondary school was first opened four miles away in an abandoned elementary school building in Kankong in January 1965, and now almost all elementary school graduates enter secondary school. The closer proximity of the school is one factor facilitating the increase in secondary school attendance, but we cannot ignore the economic factor because a substantial sum of money is required for textbooks and transportation. The number of bicycles in the village used for commuting to school has also increased.

The *pondok*, a type of religious boarding school, on the other hand, is experiencing the opposite trend. Formerly many boys lived in small huts on *pondok* grounds and studied under *To'guru*, an elderly teacher, but with the spread of the school system, boys have almost disappeared from the *pondok*. There is one *pondok* near Galok, but the majority of residents are elderly women, and it appears more like a home for the elderly. Only four youth live there now.

Tobacco cultivation brought major changes to the village. However, it has not proved sufficient to ensure a stable and adequate livelihood. Tobacco cultivation is also dependent on rainfall, and last year's harvest was quite a disappointment to most of the village farmers. Moreover, most of those who have remained in the village to cultivate tobacco are unemployed for the rest of the year. It seems that it will not be so easy for Galok to rise above this trough in regional development.

The Survey

Life in the village is diverse, as can be seen even from the above glimpse at its economy, and it is also undergoing major change. The description in the previous section has, of necessity, been abbreviated, and a more detailed explanation and analysis must be postponed until after my return to Japan. The deeper aspects underlying the structure of Malay life, such as residence of family groups or parents and children in close proximity, the sale or rental of land after it has been divided for inheritance, life in the *pondok*, and pilgrimage are all closely interrelated with economic activities. Even if I were not already too pressed for time to write in more detail here, I am restricted by space limitations.

The majority of survey data was gathered through interviews with the villagers and each household was visited about three times. The villagers were generally simple people who responded without hesitation to questions concerning their private lives. At the same time, however, if the questions were not painstakingly detailed, only vague, general replies could be obtained, and it took much trial and error to identify what factors were important. A period of one year was the minimum required to obtain adequate survey results. People unintentionally forgot to tell us things or were mistaken in their information. Many of these errors we were able to correct by comparing information with that obtained from parents and children, siblings and kin or from the land register, yet most likely they are still somewhat less than perfect.

Language was another problem. The Kelantan dialect is quite different from standard Malay in both pronunciation and idioms. Quite honestly, I was almost entirely dependent upon my 23-year-old assistant Wan Junoh for much of the survey work. He understood my objectives very well and offered appropriate explanations where necessary.

The car, which I had purchased at considerable sacrifice, proved to be invaluable. For one thing, it allowed me to conserve my energy, a very important consideration in making a long-term field study both mentally and physically tolerable. Moreover, it also allowed me to make frequent visits to other areas, expanding the scope of the study. Even in the small state of Kelantan, there are many differences in lifestyle and simple generalizations are very dangerous.

Now, however, my period of stay is nearing an end. I must end this by expressing my deep gratitude to the people of Kelantan and my determination to return.

(September, 1971)

Appendix 3
From Alor Janggus (Field Report 2)

Return to the Village

I returned to Alor Janggus at noon on June 23 traveling from Bangkok via Kuala Lumpur. Sa'ad and his wife, who have been in our employ since last year, had been waiting expectantly from the previous day, and were very pleased to see me, complaining at my tardiness. They appeared to have thoroughly cleaned my quarters and there was not a speck of dust. They have taken very good care of our house. After describing with expansive gestures and much exaggeration everything that transpired in the month since the departure of Narifumi Maeda, an exchange student at University of Malaya who was looking after our house during his school break, they informed me that I was out of rice, kerosene, cooking oil, coffee, powdered milk, sugar, soap, etc. and I should go shopping immediately. Within a short space of time, I had spent a small fortune.

Alor Janggus

Alor Janggus, a small shopping center located in a paddy-growing area of Kedah in the northwest of the Malay peninsula, was selected as a site for a sociological and anthropological study by the late Dr. Joji Tanase, leader of the Malay study group, and Mitsukuni Yoshida, who came to peninsular Malaysia in June, one month before the main team, as part of the Malaysia and Indonesia project undertaken by the Center for Southeast Asian Studies. As this study area has already been introduced in letters from the field written by Dr. Tanase and published in *Tōnan Ajia Kenkyū* (*Southeast Asian Studies*) 2, no. 2, as well as in an interim report on the area's economic aspects by Kuchiba, Tsubouchi and Maeda presented under the title "Paddy-growing Villages in Northwest Malaya" in volume 3, no. 1 of the same journal, I will merely attempt to describe the material and human environment of the Malaya team in Alor Janggus.

Although Alor Janggus can be found on a map, determining its exact boundaries is rather complicated. The houses of Malays in this area are built along a canal and surrounded by palm trees. The villages (*kampong*) usually have a mosque at the center. Alor Janggus, however, is not the name of a single village, but rather merely refers to the geographical area centered on a collection of small shops run by Chinese at the meeting point of two villages, Padang Lalang and Kubang Siam. The seventy-odd Chinese shops and houses form a kind of foreign settlement within Malay society, yet it is too small to be called a town, and most of it falls within the administrative jurisdiction of Padang Lalang. Our study focuses on Malays residing in Padang Lalang (a little over 200 households), the Chinese shops and part of adjacent Kubang Siam.

Village Life

Our house, which is situated directly across from the elementary school at the entrance of Alor Janggus, is a Malay-style structure with a raised floor and four rooms of about ten square meters in size that we rent for RM30 per month (about ¥3,600 or US$10) from the landlord who lives behind the house. Unlike Malay houses in the village it is not surrounded by coconut palms, nor is it large with a long interior like Chinese homes. To make matters worse, it has a tin roof. It is the hottest house in the area, so much so that even our Malay servants escape on very hot days.

I say hot, but the indoor temperature usually hovers at about 32 degrees centigrade during the day. It is the monsoon season, however, and due to the high humidity, I am constantly perspiring, which is very unpleasant. The rain is violent and at times it makes the whole house shake. Last year the river flooded and the area around my house was like a swamp, making access to the outhouse fifty meters away rather difficult. There is less rainfall this year than last and weather conditions seem to be more favorable.

With the rains, people have begun planting, and every evening I see women returning in single file from planting the fields. About eighty percent of the work has been completed, which seems a little earlier than last year. Plowing the fields is men's work, but planting in this village is considered solely women's work. Seedlings are planted using a wooden-handled tool with a forked metal tip called a *kuku kambing* ("goat's hoof"), into which seedlings are inserted. One or two men assist groups of ten or so women by carrying seedlings but men claim that they would be ashamed to be seen planting by other men. While the women plant, the men stay out of sight.

Our Servants

As mentioned above, we employ a married couple as house servants and I will introduce them here in more detail as the Malays with whom we have the closet contact. The husband, Sa'ad, is 62 years old and his wife, Rokiah, is 46. Both are remarried, Sa'ad for the fifth time and Rokiah for the third, and their present marriage has lasted nine years. Sa'ad divorced three of his wives but is still married to one other, so he has two wives. According to Islamic law he is obliged to treat both wives equally, but Rokiah is young and has her own income, so he spends most of his time with her. Speaking of polygynous unions, the father of Halim, a secondary school student and our interpreter, has two wives, and he travels punctiliously back and forth between their two villages. In general, however, most men have only one wife. Rokiah divorced her first husband, whom she married when she was 12, and married Sa'ad after she was widowed by the death of her second husband. She has a 20-year-old son by her second marriage, but he does not get along very well with Sa'ad. It may seem that these two have been married many times but in fact it is not surprising to find people who have remarried eight or nine times.

Sa'ad's main job is to carry rainwater for cooking and showering from the tank at the elementary school. Rokiah's jobs are cooking, washing and shopping. As many men do the shopping in this area, I used to give Sa'ad money daily for the shopping when I first came. But he embezzled so outrageously that I began giving both the money for shopping and their wages to his wife. As this is a rare opportunity to make money, she also pockets some of the shopping allowance, but never as much as Sa'ad. The amount never exceeds RM1 a day (about ¥120) and accordingly, we have all turned a blind eye to it. I was surprised, however, to see that she had purchased a gold bracelet and necklace soon after we made her responsible for the budget. Together they must have cost about RM200 (¥24,000). As they can be sold for almost the same value or pawned, this represents the best means of saving for women in the area.

At the beginning of the month I pay them RM60 (about ¥7,200). For all but government officials in rural Malaysia, where wages are extremely low, an advance payment of RM60 a month plus board are excellent conditions. From this, Rokiah gives her husband an allowance. Last month (July), for example, she gave him RM10 and this month (August) RM5. Sa'ad enjoys mahjong, and he uses this money to bet, only to lose it immediately and be soundly scolded by his wife, a rare and unexpected scene in this Islamic society where men have such strong authority.

Although they have little hope of advancement in the world, Sa'ad is known for his witty remarks, and when he goes to a wedding or the Friday worship service (from which he sometimes plays truant) he wears good clothes and holds himself proudly erect. When he was young, he was nicknamed "Sa'ad Stockings" because he wore socks, which were very unusual in those days.

Rokiah has one major objective: to build a new house. She has been busy saving, and has already bought RM143 worth of lumber. The total construction cost will be RM300 (about ¥36,000), and they should be able to build a house smaller but sturdier than their present one. Rokiah's cooking is extremely simple, limited both by available ingredients and cooking methods. The main ingredients consist of three types of fish, chicken that is mostly bone and skin, bean sprouts, potatoes, chicken eggs and duck eggs, and she either fries these in oil or stews them as a curry. Lunch and dinner is exactly the same menu, and by the end of the week I have lost my appetite. Compared to last year, however, her cooking has improved considerably. Although a poor cook, she is an entertaining conversationalist and our kitchen is always full of neighborhood women, both young and old.

At night when the electricity comes on and the electric fan begins to whirl, Sa'ad and Rokiah close and lock all the windows against thieves that prowl the area. In August last year, the Alor Janggus police received a tip that a group of four robbers was on its way from another village, and, after waiting in ambush, they arrested them. This June a wealthy man in the next village was stabbed to death during a robbery. Our defense strategy has been to widely proclaim that we cannot exchange money unless we go to the bank.

Our Study

About twenty days after I arrived, Masuo Kuchiba came followed ten days later by Kiyoshige Maeda. Now that our house is fully occupied, Sa'ad and his wife, who were staying with me, return to their own home at night, coming to work every morning. Soon after Katsuji Fujimoto and Teruyo Umeda arrived in Alor Star and the Alor Janggus study team is at it full strength.

As Kuchiba already spent about six months here last year, he is well known and his name seems to have become a synonym for anyone who is Japanese. The postman calls out "Kuchiba" regardless of whether the letters are for him or for one of our other members, and when I or another Japanese walk down the street we are often addressed as "Kuchiba".

Kiyoshige Maeda, a lecturer from Tenri University who is fluent in Chinese, is conducting a survey of the Chinese residents of Alor Janggus. Since his arrival, our house has suddenly been inundated with Chinese guests. In addition to a young man named Moy from the goldsmith's shop who has been coming since last year, some of the regular callers include a man of around thirty who works at the rice mill and whom we have dubbed "Mourning Badge" because he wears a mourning ribbon on the shoulder of his shirt, and a sixth grade elementary school pupil who is the son of the laundry owner. As our contact with the Chinese has increased, we hear through the medium of Maeda much criticism of Malays. "Malays are lazy." "They just have to copy others, even borrowing money to buy a scooter." "Why do you employ a Malay when they're such bad cooks?" "Malay storekeepers don't know how to display their goods." "Malay gravestones are unseemly." "Malays don't cry even when their parents die." For a nation where ethnic groups with totally different languages, religions and ways of life must co-exist through close economic relationships, Malaysia has some difficult problems to surmount. Even the Chinese are not united, but suffer from conflict among themselves between those from Fuchien and Kuangtung, and between rich and poor.

Professor Fujimoto from Kansai University studies Islam, and as he can read Arabic, he is regarded with great respect by the Malays of Alor Janggus. He is rather stout, and has been nicknamed "Tuan Jatoh" (Fallen Master) because he fell through a thin spot in the floor last year. Sa'ad and Rokiah frequently mimic the cautious way he walked after the incident.

The number of people who find some excuse to walk by our house has noticeably increased since Ms. Umeda, a graduate student at Kansai University and the only woman in our group, began coming to our house. Malays and Chinese, men and women—everyone walks past to take a look. In Islamic society, it is very difficult for men to interview women. Even after all this time I have only just begun to have short conversations with the women who live in the neighborhood, so we are quite expectant of results with Umeda's arrival. In fact, soon after she came, she was able to observe a female circumcision rite, something we could never do, and she also received from the village midwife an abortive drug used by Malays. One glance revealed that it was alum.

Maeda visits the Chinese quarters daily, Umeda commutes by bus from Alor Star to visit Malay homes near our house, and Kuchiba and I get onto the bicycle we bought for RM120 (about ¥14,400) last year and cycle to houses in Padang Lalang, which stretches on and on for about two miles, proceeding steadily with our survey.

The road we are accustomed to take to Padang Lalang is a new road to Alor Star built very recently, and although last year it was just red dirt, this year it has been almost completely paved. The present bus route is circuitous, covering a distance of about nine miles whereas the new road is a much shorter five miles. These roads represent a significant change as prior to construction of the old road, people either walked through swampy ground or traveled several hours by river to reach Alor Star.

Although life has become more convenient, the population is rising due to in-migration and natural population increase. Seventy years ago this was a sparsely populated area, much of it covered by jungle, but now almost all of it has been transformed into paddy land and there is no room for further expansion. Due to Islamic and customary inheritance laws, land is becoming increasingly fragmented, and consequently, there are a considerable number of farm laborers who do not own any land. The same is true for the Chinese. As Alor Janggus has reached full capacity, many must commute to work in Alor Star.

Although we never heard any singing from the national Malay school across the street last year, this year they not only read the Koran on Fridays but we can also hear them singing, albeit slightly out of tune since they lack the accompaniment of an organ.

The number of people owning television sets in Alor Janggus has risen to three.

Malay farm villages are undergoing drastic change. Our house is made of Malaysian lumber, Swedish plywood, and Japanese tin sheeting, and the implements we use in our daily lives are from Malaysia, Japan, the United States, England, Germany, France, Holland, Australia, Hong Kong and China. It is not only material goods that are flowing into the village from the cities and foreign countries, but also new cultural and intellectual trends, all of which the villagers must deal with in some way. Our study is being conducted in the very midst of these changes.

In another twenty days, Fujimoto, Kiyoshige Maeda, Umeda and Kuchiba will leave. I myself will depart from Alor Janggus at the end of September, leaving only Narifumi Maeda from our Malay team, who is on his own in a Proto-Malay hamlet in Johor. At the moment, the villagers' main interest is the fate of our possessions when we leave, and Sa'ad and his wife are busy relaying requests to purchase beds, furniture, appliances, and our bicycle.

Our study is gradually coming to a close. I wonder how far we can analyze and reconstruct this society with the limited amount of data we have been able to collect. We can only do our best.

(From Alor Janggus August 8, 1965.)

Bibliography

Ackerman, Charles. 1963. "Affiliations: Structural determinants of differential divorce rates." *American Journal of Sociology* 69, no. 1.
Awang Had Salleh. 1977. "Institusi Pondok di Malaysia," in Zainal Kling (ed.), *Masyrakat Melayu: Antaratradisi dan Perubahan*. Utusan Publications & Distributors.
Azizah Kassim. 1984. "Women and divorce among urban Malays," in Hing Ai Yun *et al.* (eds.), *Women in Malaysia*. Petaling Jaya: Pelanduk Publications.
Burns, P. L. and C. D. Cowan (eds.). 1975. *Sir Frank Swettenham's Malayan Journals, 1874–1876*. Kuala Lumpur: Oxford University Press.
Biro Pusat Statistik, Indonesia. 1971. *Statistical Pocketbook 1970/1971*. Jakarta.
——— 1977. *Statistik Indonesia 1976*. Jakarta.
——— 1984. *Statistik Indonesia 1983*. Jakarta.
——— 1989. *Statistik Indonesia 1988*. Jakarta.
——— 1993. *Statistik Indonesia 1992*. Jakarta.
Castles, Lance. 1966. "Notes on an Islamic school at Gontor." *Indonesia*, no. 1.
Del Tufo, M. V. 1949. *Malaya: A Report on the 1947 Census of Population*. London: The Crown Agent for the Colonies.
Crawford, Hunter A. 1970. "The birth of the Duff Development Company in Kelantan, 1900–1912." *Malaysia in History* 13, no. 2.
Department of Statistics, Federation of Malaya. 1959. *1957 Population Census of the Federation of Malaya*. Report nos. 3–14. Kuala Lumpur.
Department of Statistics, Malaysia. 1992. *Mukim Preliminary Count Report (Population and Housing Census of Malaysia 1991)*. Kuala Lumpur.
Djamour, Judith. 1959. *Malay Kinship and Marriage in Singapore*. London: The Athlone Press, University of London.
——— 1966. *The Muslim Matrimonial Court in Singapore*. London: The Athlone Press, University of London.
Dodge, Nicholas N. 1980. "Population estimates for the Malay Peninsula in the nineteenth century, with special reference to the East Coast States." *Population Studies* 34, no. 3: 437-475.
Downs, Richard. 1967. "A Kelantanese village in Malaya," in Julian H. Steward (ed.), *Contemporary Change in Traditional Societies. Vol. 2. Asian Rural Societies*. Urbana: University of Illinois Press.

Fallers, Lloyd. 1957. "Some determinants of marriage stability in Busoga: A reformulation of Gluckman's hypothesis." *Africa* 27, no. 2.
Favre, P. 1848. "An account of the wild tribes inhabiting the Malayan Peninsula, Sumatra and a few neighbouring islands." *Journal of the Indian Archipelago and Eastern Asia* 2.
Firth, Raymond. 1966. *Malay Fishermen*, 2nd ed. London: Routledge and Kegan Paul.
Firth, Rosemary. 1966. *Housekeeping among Malay Peasants*, 2nd ed. London: London School of Economics.
Fraser, Thomas M., Jr. 1960. *Rusembilan: A Malay Fishing Village in Southern Thailand*. Ithaca: Cornell University Press.
Fujimoto, Katsuji. 1966. "Maraya ni okeru Isuramu kyōiku seido" (The Islamic Education System in Malaya). *Tōnan Ajia Kenkyū* (*Southeast Asian Studies*) 4, no. 2.
Fukui, Hayao. 1988. *Dondēn Mura: Tōhoku Tai no Nōgyōseitai* (Don Daeng: Agricultural Ecology of Northeast Thailand). Tokyo: Sōbunsha. Translated into English as *Food and Population in a Northeast Thai Village*, trans. Peter Hawkes. Honolulu: University of Hawaii Press, 1993.
Fukutake, Tadashi. 1949. *Nihon nōson no shakaiteki seikaku* (Social characteristics of Japanese rural communities). Tokyo: University of Tokyo Press.
Geertz, Clifford. 1960. *The Religion of Java*. Illinois: The Free Press of Glencoe.
Geertz, Hildred. 1961. *The Javanese Family*. New York: The Free Press of Glencoe.
Gluckman, Max. 1950. "Kinship and marriage among the Lozi of Northern Rhodesia and the Zulu of Natal," in Radcliff-Brown and D. Forde (eds.), *African Systems of Kinship and Marriage*. London: Oxford University Press.
Goode, William J. 1993. *World Changes in Divorce Patterns*. New Haven and London: Yale University Press.
Gordon, Shirle. n.d. "Marriage/divorce in the eleven States of Malaya and Singapore," *INTISARI* 2, no.2.
Government Printing Office, Singapore. 1967. *Singapore Year Book 1966*.
Graham, W. A. 1908. *Kelantan, A State of the Malay Peninsula*. Glasgow: James Maclehose and Sons.
Ichimura, Shinichi (ed.). 1975. *Ine to Nōmin: Nippon, Tai, Indoneshia ni okeru Hikaku Kenkyū* (Rice and Farmers: A Comparative Study of Japan, Thailand and Indonesia). Kyoto: Center for Southeast Asian Studies, Kyoto University.
Ishii, Yoneo (ed.). 1975. *Taikoku: Hitotsu no Inasaku Shakai*. Tokyo: Sobunsha.

Translated into English as *Thailand: A Rice-growing Society*, trans. Peter and Stephanie Hawkes. Honolulu: The University Press of Hawaii, 1978.

Jones, Gavin W. 1980. "Trends in marriage and divorce in Peninsular Malaysia." *Population Studies* 32, no. 2.

———— 1981. "Malay marriage and divorce in Peninsular Malaysia: Three Decades of Change." *Population and Development* 7, no. 2.

Khoo Kay Kim. 1980. "Nineteenth century Malay Peninsula III," in Zainal Abidin bin Abdul Wahid (ed.), *Glimpses of Malayan History*. Kuala Lumpur: Dewan Bahasa dan Pustaka.

Kitahara, Atushi. 1990. *Tai Nōson Shakairon* (Social theory of rural Thailand). Tokyo: Keisoshobo.

Kuchiba, Masuo. 1971. "Marē nōson no shakai kōzō: hitotsu no kadai" (Social structure in Malay rural society: one issue). *Buddhist Culture Research Center Bulletin*, 10.

———— 1972a. "Suitōsaku nōson Padanraran: sono shizenjōken to nikisakuka ni tuite" (Padang Lalang, a rice-growing village: Its natural environment and the introduction of double cropping). *Tōnan Ajia Kenkyū (Southeast Asian Studies)* 9, no. 4.

———— 1972b. "Kedā ni okeru Marē nōmin no minzoku shūkyō" (Folk religion of the Malay peasants in Kedah). *Minzokugaku Kenkyū (The Japanese Journal of Ethnology)* 37, no. 2.

———— 1990. "Taijin kankei no mekanizumu" (The mechanism of human relations), in Tsubouchi, Yoshihiro (ed.) *Tōnan Ajia no Shakai (Southeast Asian Society)*. Kobundo.

Kuchiba, Masuo (ed.). 1990. *Dondēn Mura no Dentō Kōzō to sono Hen'yō* (The traditional structure of Don Daeng and its transformation). Tokyo: Sobunsha.

Kuchiba, Masuo and Narifumi Maeda. 1980. "Yashikichi kyōjūshūdan to kazokuken" (Multihousehold compounds and the family circle). *Tōnan Ajia Kenkyū (Southeast Asian Studies)* 18, no. 2.

Kuchiba, Masuo and Yoshihiro Tsubouchi. 1966. "Maraya hokuseibu no inasaku nōson: kon'in, rikon, kazoku no tokushitsu ni tsuite" (Rice-growing villages of northwest Malaya: Characteristics of marriage, divorce and family), *Tōnan Ajia Kenkyū (Southeast Asian Studies)* 4, no. 1.

———— 1967. "Maraya hokuseibu no inasaku nōson: nōgyō rōdō ni tsuite" (Rice-growing villages of northwest Malaya: Farm labor). *Tōnan Ajia Kenkyū (Southeast Asian Studies)* 5, no. 1.

Kuchiba, Masuo, Yoshihiro Tsubouchi, and Narifumi Maeda. 1965. "Maraya hokuseibu no inasaku nōson: nōchi shōyū no reisaika ni tsuite" (Rice-growing villages of northwest Malaya: Fragmentation of landholdings). *Tōnan Ajia Kenkyū (Southeast Asian Studies)* 3, no. 1.

———— (eds.). 1976. *Marē Nōson no Kenkyū* (Studies of Malay villages). Tokyo: Sobunsha. Translated into English as *Three Malay Villages: A Sociology of Paddy Growers in West Malaysia,* trans. Peter and Stephanie Hawkes. Honolulu: The University Press of Hawaii, 1979.

Leach, E. R. 1957. "Aspects of bridewealth and marriage among the Kachin and Lakher." *Man* 57, no. 59.

Logan, J. R. 1847. "The Orang Binua of Johore." *Journal of the Indian Archipelago and Eastern Asia* 1.

Maeda, Kiyoshige. 1966. "Maraya hokuseibu ni okeru Chūgokujin shūraku no kōzō" (The structure of a Chinese community in northwest Malaya), parts 1 and 2. *Tōnan Ajia Kenkyū (Southeast Asian Studies)* 3, no. 5 and 4, no. 1.

Maeda, Narifumi. 1966. "Endaugawa ryūiki no Orang Hulu (Jakun) no kazoku oboegaki" (Notes on Orang Hulu (Jakun) Families in the Endau River Basin). *Tōnan Ajia Kenkyū (Southeast Asian Studies)* 3, no. 5.

———— 1967. "Maraya ni okeru Jakun no kazoku kōsei no tokushitsu" (Characteristics of Jakun family composition in Malaya). *Tōnan Ajia Kenkyū (Southeast Asian Studies)* 5, no. 3.

———— 1969. "Jakun (Oran Furu) no kekkon to rikon" (Marriage and divorce among the Orang Hulu (Jakun)). *Tōnan Ajia Kenkyū (Southeast Asian Studies)* 6, no. 4.

———— 1973. "Sōkeiteki sinzoku soshiki ni okeru itokokon no ichi kōsatsu" (A note of first-cousin marriage in a bilateral kinship system). *Tōnan Ajia Kenkyū (Southeast Asian Studies)* 10, no. 4.

———— 1974a. "Marējin no kazoku" (Malay families). *Tōnan Ajia Kenkyū (Southeast Asian Studies)* 12, no. 1.

———— 1974b. "The changing peasant world in a Melaka village: Islam and democracy in the Malay tradition. Ph.D. dissertation, University of Chicago.

Mizuno, Koichi. 1969. "Tōhoku Tai no shakai soshiki" (Social structure in Northeast Thailand). *Tōnan Ajia Kenkyū (Southeast Asian Studies)* 6, no. 4.

———— 1975. "Inasaku nōson no shakai soshikiī (Social structure of rice-growing villages), in Ishii, Yoneo (ed.), *Taikoku: Hitotsu no Inasaku Shakai* (Thailand: A rice-growing society). Tokyo: Sobunsha.

———— 1976. "Kazoku, shinzoku shūdan no kokusai hikaku: Taikoku to Nippon" (An International Comparison of Family and Kin Groups: Japan and Thailand). *Shakaigaku Hyōron (Sociology Review)* 26, no. 3.

———— 1981. *Tai nōson no shakai soshiki* (Social structure in a Thai village). Tokyo: Sobunsha.

Nishino, Setsuo. 1990. *Indoneshia no Isuramu Kyōiku* (Islamic Education in Indonesia). Keisoshobo.

Nugroho. 1967. *Indonesia, Facts and Figures*. Terbitan Pertjobaan.
Rauf, M. A. n.d. "Islamic education." *Intisari* 2, no. 2.
Raffles, Thomas Stamford. 1817. *The History of Jawa*. Two volumes. (Reprint ed., London: Oxford University Press, 1965).
Shaharil Talib. 1981. "Nineteenth century Kelantan: A tributary state." *Jurnal Anthropologi dan Sosiologi* 9.
——— 1983. "Voices from the Kelantan Desa, 1900–1949." *Modern Asian Studies* 17, no. 2.
——— 1995. *History of Kelantan, 1890–1940*. Monograph no. 21, The Malaysian Branch of the Royal Asiatic Society.
Siegel, James. 1969. *The Rope of God*. Berkeley and Los Angeles: University of California Press.
Skinner, C. 1966. "Abdullah's voyage to the east coast, seen through contemporary eyes." *Journal of the Malaysian Branch, Royal Asiatic Society* 39, part 1.
Sudjoko et al. 1974. *Profil Pesantren, Laporan Hasil Penelitian Pesantren Al-Falak & Delapan Pesantren Lain di Bogor*. LP3ES.
Surin Pitsuwan. 1985. *Islam and Malay Nationalism: A Case Study of the Malay-Muslims of Southern Thailand*. Bangkok: Thai Khadi Research Institute, Thammasat University.
Sugimoto, Katsuo. 1970. "Marēshia no nōgyō: Nikisaku no shinten to shomondai" (Agriculture in Malaysia: Progress and Problems in Double-Cropping). *Nettai Nōgyō Shūhō (Tropical Agriculture Report)*, no. 15.
Swift, Michael. 1963. "Men and women in Malay society," in Barbara E. Ward (ed.), *Women in New Asia*. UNESCO.
Takaya, Yoshikazu. 1982. *Nettai Deruta no Nōgyō Hatten: Menamu Deruta no Kenkyū*. (Agricultural Development of a Tropical Delta: A Study of the Menam Delta). Tokyo: Sobunsha. Translated into English as *Agricultural Development of a Tropical Delta: A Study of the Chao Phraya Delta*, trans. Peter Hawkes. Honolulu: The University Press of Hawaii, 1987.
Takizawa, Hideo. 1972. "Nishi Marēshia nōson no hoken to iryō" (Health and medical treatment in farm villages of West Malaysia). *Tōnan Ajia Kenkyū (Southeast Asian Studies)* 10, no. 1.
Tsubouchi, Yoshihiro. 1966. "Marējin no rikon: tōkeiteki bunseki no kokoromi" (Divorce among Malays: A statistical analysis. *Tōnan Ajia Kenkyū (Southeast Asian Studies)* 4, no. 3.
——— 1969. "Sōkeiteki shinzoku kōzō wo motsu Marēkei shominzoku no rikon ni tuite" (Divorce among Malay ethnic groups with bilateral kinship structure). *Tōnan Ajia Kenkyū (Southeast Asian Studies)* 6, no. 4.

―――― 1972a. "Kurantan no ichi nōson ni okeru tabako kōsaku no dōnyū to shakaikeizaiteki henka" (The introduction of tobacco cultivation and socioeconomic change in a farming village in Kelantan). *Tōnan Ajia Kenkyū (Southeast Asian Studies)* 9, no. 4 (1972).

―――― 1972b. "Higashi kaigan Marē nōmin ni okeru tochi to kyojū" (Land and residence among Malay peasants on the east coast). *Tōnan Ajia Kenkyū (Southeast Asian Studies)* 10, no. 1.

―――― 1972c. "Marēshia higashi kaigan no tensuiden chiiki ni okeru inasaku" (Rice cultivation in the region of rain-fed rice fields on the east coast of Malaysia). *Tōnan Ajia Kenkyū (Southeast Asian Studies)* 10, no. 2 (1972).

―――― 1972d. "Higashi kaigan Marē nōmin ni okeru kekkon to rikon" (Marriage and divorce among Malay peasants on the east coast). *Tōnan Ajia Kenkyū (Southeast Asian Studies)* 10, no. 3.

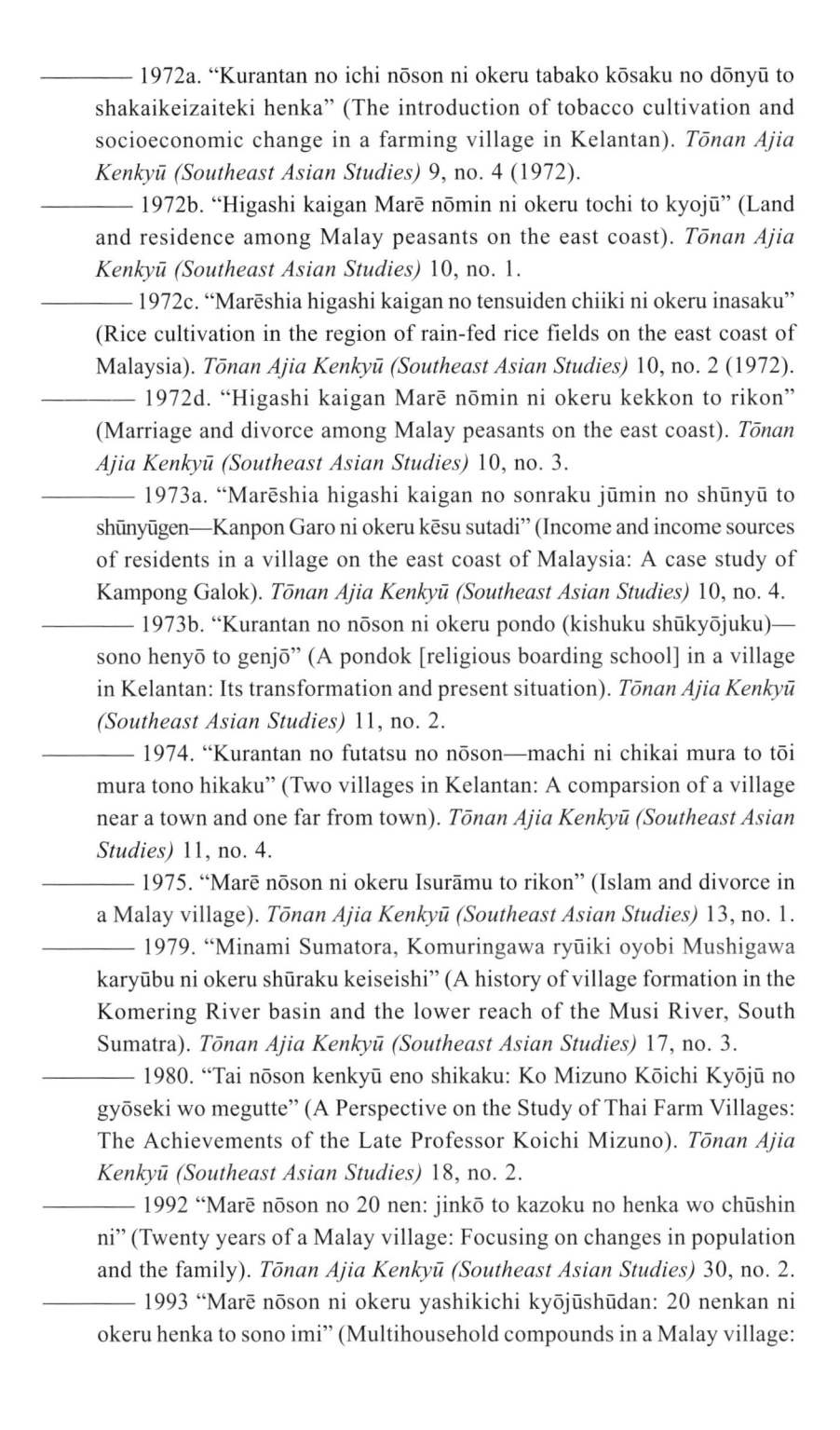

―――― 1973a. "Marēshia higashi kaigan no sonraku jūmin no shūnyū to shūnyūgen—Kanpon Garo ni okeru kēsu sutadi" (Income and income sources of residents in a village on the east coast of Malaysia: A case study of Kampong Galok). *Tōnan Ajia Kenkyū (Southeast Asian Studies)* 10, no. 4.

―――― 1973b. "Kurantan no nōson ni okeru pondo (kishuku shūkyōjuku)—sono henyō to genjō" (A pondok [religious boarding school] in a village in Kelantan: Its transformation and present situation). *Tōnan Ajia Kenkyū (Southeast Asian Studies)* 11, no. 2.

―――― 1974. "Kurantan no futatsu no nōson—machi ni chikai mura to tōi mura tono hikaku" (Two villages in Kelantan: A comparsion of a village near a town and one far from town). *Tōnan Ajia Kenkyū (Southeast Asian Studies)* 11, no. 4.

―――― 1975. "Marē nōson ni okeru Isurāmu to rikon" (Islam and divorce in a Malay village). *Tōnan Ajia Kenkyū (Southeast Asian Studies)* 13, no. 1.

―――― 1979. "Minami Sumatora, Komuringawa ryūiki oyobi Mushigawa karyūbu ni okeru shūraku keiseishi" (A history of village formation in the Komering River basin and the lower reach of the Musi River, South Sumatra). *Tōnan Ajia Kenkyū (Southeast Asian Studies)* 17, no. 3.

―――― 1980. "Tai nōson kenkyū eno shikaku: Ko Mizuno Kōichi Kyōjū no gyōseki wo megutte" (A Perspective on the Study of Thai Farm Villages: The Achievements of the Late Professor Koichi Mizuno). *Tōnan Ajia Kenkyū (Southeast Asian Studies)* 18, no. 2.

―――― 1992 "Marē nōson no 20 nen: jinkō to kazoku no henka wo chūshin ni" (Twenty years of a Malay village: Focusing on changes in population and the family). *Tōnan Ajia Kenkyū (Southeast Asian Studies)* 30, no. 2.

―――― 1993 "Marē nōson ni okeru yashikichi kyōjūshūdan: 20 nenkan ni okeru henka to sono imi" (Multihousehold compounds in a Malay village:

Changes in twenty years and their significance). *Tōnan Ajia Kenkyū (Southeast Asian Studies)* 31, no. 1.

――――― 2001 "Marē nōson no 30 nen—seitaitekiō no shūen wo haikei toshite" (Thirty years of a Malay village: With the end of ecological adaptation as a background), *Ajia-Afurika Chiiki Kenkyū (Asian and African Area Studies)* 1, no. 1.

Tsubouchi, Yoshihiro and Narifumi Maeda. 1975a. "Marējin kazoku niokeru kakusedai kankei" (Alternate Generation Relationships in Malay Families). *Tōnan Ajia Kenkyū (Southeast Asian Studies)* 12, no. 4.

――――― 1975b. "Chū seiken makki no Mekon deruta nōsonbu ni okeru rīdāshippu" (Leadership in rural communities in the Mekong delta at the end of the Thieu administration). *Tōnan Ajia Kenkyū (Southeast Asian Studies)* 13, no. 3.

――――― 1977. *Kakukazoku saikō: Marējin no kazokuken* (Reconsideration of the nuclear family: The Malay family circle). Kobundo.

Tsubouchi, Yoshihiro and Reiko Tsubouchi. 1970. *Rikon: Hikaku Shakaigakuteki Kenkyū* (Divorce: A comparative sociological study). Tokyo: Sobunsha.

Tweedie, M. W. F. 1953 "An early Chinese account of Kelantan." *Journal of the Malayan Branch, Royal Asiatic Society* 26, part 1.

Umeda, Teruyo. 1966. "Maraya no jōsei: Kedah shū ni okeru genchi chōsa" (Women of peninsular Malaysia: A field study in Kedah State). *Tōnan Ajia Kenkyū (Southeast Asian Studies)* 3, no. 5.

Winzeler, Robert. 1970. "Malay religion, society and politics in Kelantan." Ph.D. dissertation, University of Chicago.

Yano, Toru. 1970. "Minami Tai nōsonmin no songai kyojū keiken ni tsuite" (Extra-village residential experience of Southern Thai villagers). *Tōnan Ajia Kenkyū (Southeast Asian Studies)* 8, no. 2.

Yoshida, Mitsukuni. 1963. "Isurāmu no koyomi to nenjūgyōji oboegaki" (Notes on the Islamic calendar and annual events). *Tōnan Ajia Kenkyū (Southeast Asian Studies)* 1, no. 1.

Glossary

adat	customary law
alor	channel in river or a dry torrent-bed carrying occasional flows
anak sa-pupu (se-pupu)	child of first cousin
baewah	communal feast, known as *kenduri* in the western states
Bahagia	an improved variety of paddy
belanja	euphemism for gift
baloh	granary
bidan	midwife
bidan kampung	traditional midwife without formal training
bodoh	mentally handicapped
bomoh	traditional healer
budu	traditional fish sauce
Bulan Maulud	the month of Mohammed's birth
Bulan Puasa	the month of fasting
cabut semai (menyambut)	uprooting seedlings from the nursery
cedong	transplant
cerut	cut with a sickle
cok	hoe
daerah	sub-district, headed by *penggawa*
dapor (dapur)	cooking area
dua-pupu	second cousin
dusun dan macam macam	a category of land, fruits groves
fitrah	a kind of charitable donation under Islamic law
gala balek (gala lumat)	second plowing
gala beloh	first plowing
gantang	measure of volume, 1 *gantang* equals 1 British gallon or 4.546 liters.
gerap	harrow
getah	rubber
getah beku	coagulated latex
gila	mentally disordered
guru	religious teacher

guru kuran	Koran teacher
Hari Raya Puasa	the day of celebration of the end of the fast
hasil tanah	land tax
igu	yoke of plow
imam	religious official for the village mosque
Intan Belian	a traditional variety of paddy
Jabatan Ugama Islam	Department of Islam
jajahan	district
kacang	cowpeas and other legumes
kadhi	judge of the Islamic court
kampung (kampong)	hamlet or village
kampung baru	new hamlet
kankong (kankung)	a leafy vegetable
kati	a measure of weight, 1 *kati* equals about 600 grams
kedai kopi	coffee shop
keping	a counter for flat objects, including land
kerbau	water buffalo
kerja kampung	"village work," applied to various kinds of jobs
kubur	cemetery
kuku kambing	literally "goat's hoof," a transplanting tool
lembek	mattress
lembu	ox
madrasah	religious school building
Mahkamah Shaiah	religious court
Mahsuri	a high-yielding variety of paddy
masjid	mosque
mak sa-pupu (se-pupu)	parent's first cousin (female), see *pak sa-pupu (se-pupu)*
manisan	sweets, refers to coconut sugar
meminang	engagement gift
mengkuang	a kind of pandanus used for matting
mukim	the lowest administrative unit, headed by a *penghulu*
menabor	sow seed
nangar	plow shaft
nayer	part of a plow
nikah	marriage contract
padi	paddy
Padi Kedah	a traditional variety of paddy brought from Kedah
Padi Piah	a traditional variety of paddy, also known as Padi Ketip

padi semangat	ritual rice
padi tugalan	dry paddy sown with a dibble
pak sa-pupu (se-pupu)	parent's first cousin (male), see *mak sa-pupu (se-pupu)*
pasah	a divorce procedure, actually annulment
pawah	letting out land for half the crop in lieu of rent, or letting out livestock for a proportion of the young
pejabat tanah	land office
penggawa	head of a sub-district
penghulu	head of a *mukim*
penolok	part of a plow
penyadap	toddy-drawer
peratur	traditional wedding ceremony, literally "to sit side by side," known as *bersanding* in the western states.
petang	afternoon
Pok Dut	a traditional variety of paddy
pondan	male who behaves like a woman, a sort of sexual pervert
pondok	residential religious school, literally "a hut".
pot	a way of processing rubber scraps left in the containers
pulut semangat	cooked glutinous rice for ritual use
ringgit	Malaysian currency, abbreviated as RM; in 1970 the exchange rate was 1 ringgit = 120 yen, or 3 ringgit = 1 US dollar.
rojok (rujuk)	revocation of divorce
sadat	sickle
sambut menantu	to receive a daughter-in-law
sa-pupu (se-pupu)	first cousin
sarong (sarung)	skirt-like cloth worn by men and women
sekolah kebangsaan	national elementary school
sekolah menengah	junior high school
sekolah rakyat	communal elementary school
sembahyang hajat	prayers of supplication
sen	Malaysian currency; 1 ringgit = 100 sen
sewa	hire, rent
ta'alik	pronouncing of a divorce that comes into effect only when certain conditions are fulfilled.
talak	divorce, repudiation
tame	harvesting knife
tanah alor	paddy field on a channel

tanah dalam	deep-water land
tanah darat	upland field
tebus talak	literally to buy *talak*, a divorce procedure employed by women
teksi	taxi, *i.e.*, trishaw
telor semangat	boiled egg for ritual use
tepi sungai	river bank
tikar	mat
timun	a melon or a cucumber
tong	threshing tub
tugal	dibble
tulong (pinjam)	help without payment
tumpang	leasing land or a part of a house free of charge
tunggu kubor	watching the graveyard, offering prayers at the cemetery
ubi kayu	tapioca
ubi keling	a potato
upah	payment for service
wakaf	communal property

Index

adat 85, 128
adoption 28, 51, 71, 127, 130, 162, 165, 231, 257
age of marriage *see* marriage
Alor Janggus 258, 259, 272, 273, 275–277
Alor Pasir 9
Alor Setar 127
Arabic school 80, 185, 201
artisan 62, 207, 209
Atas Beting 9, 16, 99, 163, 164, 202, 267
Ayer Lanas 198

Bacho 4 *see also* Bachok
Bachok 201
Bahagia 15, 268
barber 62, 207, 209
Belimbing 198
betel nuts 6
bicycle 24, 36, 52, 59, 62, 65, 78, 80, 94, 212, 260, 270, 276, 277
bilateral kinship structure 153, 229, 234 *see also* neighboring kin group
birth rate 152, 154, 165
blanket 79, 80
British Adviser 9
budu 6, 51
buffalo 20, 28
Bukit Pegoh 127, 128, 131, 132, 134, 136, 137, 231, 237
bus 10, 11, 58, 241, 276

cake maker 64
Captain China 5

car 10, 240, 260, 261, 263, 264, 271
carpenter 5, 16, 17, 62, 94, 200, 241
Census of 1911 3
Census of 1947 2
Chabang Empat 197
Chao Phraya Delta 231–233, 238
charcoal maker 50, 64, 94
Chekok 21, 28, 36, 47, 51, 53, 54, 80, 98–100, 160, 194, 197, 198, 200–202, 241, 262
chemical fertilizer 28, 30, 39, 51, 211
Chenoh 202
Chetok 99, 100, 161, 164, 198, 259
Chinese 1–5, 11, 27, 36, 54, 58, 131, 210, 230, 240, 261, 263, 266, 273, 275–277
choice of residence 88
cinema 11, 266
clinic 11, 162, 240
coconut-sugar making 50, 71, 90
coffee shop *(kedai kopi)* 50, 51, 55, 59, 64, 160, 161, 200, 201, 241, 269
color television 226
communal feast *(baewah)* 97
communal labor organization 18
community endogamy 109, 115, 128, 136, 137
community study 1, 227–229, 239
compound. *see* neighboring kin group
contract work 45, 46, 49, 51, 54, 80, 164
copra 6, 9
cousin marriage. *see* marriage

customary law 85, 108, 128, 267 see also *adat*

death rate 86, 139, 144, 153, 154
dibble 14, 27
district office 10, 11, 87, 139, 239, 260, 261, 266
divorce 18, 71, 108–110, 112, 114–116, 119, 120, 122, 123, 127–132, 134, 136, 137, 139, 140, 154, 157, 158, 163, 190, 191, 197, 198, 201, 202, 216, 218, 219, 226, 229, 231, 252, 256, 262
  rate 108, 110, 112, 115, 122, 123, 125, 126, 131, 132, 137–140, 157, 165, 231
  condemnation of 130
  decline in 132, 134, 158, 252, 256
Don Daeng 167, 168, 232, 236, 238
double-cropping 15, 18, 21, 25, 56, 58, 127, 210, 230, 266–268
duck 19, 69, 70, 72, 275
duku 64, 65, 67, 269
durian 67, 269

education 55, 122, 125, 149, 161, 182–185, 203, 204, 206, 217, 219, 226, 231, 249, 252, 256, 261, 270
elder 33, 65, 72, 74, 94, 95, 119, 121, 122, 154, 157, 161, 181, 183, 185, 194–196, 198, 199, 201, 203, 204, 206, 219, 261, 262, 270
electric fan 80, 83, 201, 212, 244, 260, 261, 275
electricity 10, 80, 165, 188, 189, 197–202, 212, 254, 259, 260, 275

endogamy. *see* community endogamy
engagement gift *(meminang)* 102

family 15, 18, 23–25, 51, 67, 71, 75, 76, 78, 84–86, 92, 93, 102–105, 110, 112, 114, 115, 119–122, 125, 127, 129, 154, 157, 158, 162, 173, 175, 178, 183, 185, 190, 197, 199, 202, 206, 210, 211, 215, 216, 224, 226, 229, 234, 237, 239, 241, 244, 249, 251, 252, 254, 256, 257, 260, 268, 271
  cycle 120
  law 123
  planning 149, 245
  structure 120, 129, 237
  extended 92, 119, 166, 226
  stem 215, 216, 254
farm implements 16
Federation of Malaya 10
fertility 151, 152, 247
firewood maker 64
fish 5, 6, 11, 45, 51, 54, 138, 196, 241, 266, 270, 275
  dealer 51, 59
  fresh 80, 263
  salted dried 5, 6, 51, 263
fishing 5
fitrah 64, 77, 191
flight 10, 266
free of charge *(tumpang)* 21, 66, 75, 93, 94, 163, 164, 197
fruit grove *(dusun dan macam macam)* 84, 168
funeral feast 97

Galok 6–19, 21, 25, 27, 28, 30–33, 36, 38, 39, 41, 43– 47, 49–56, 58,

59, 62, 64–66, 68–72, 75, 76, 78, 80, 84–87, 92–95, 98–102, 105, 108–110, 115, 116, 119, 120, 122, 125, 127, 128, 130, 132, 134, 136, 137, 139, 140, 143, 145–149, 151–154, 156, 158, 160–166, 168, 169, 173, 176–181, 183, 185, 189, 191–195, 199, 200, 202, 203, 207–213, 215–217, 219, 221, 222, 224, 226, 229–231, 239–241, 244, 245, 247, 249, 254–256, 259, 262, 264, 267–270
gold 4, 6, 62, 103, 274, 275
granary *(baloh)* 24, 28, 127, 232, 268
Gua Musang 126, 148, 160, 162, 177
guru 97, 182, 183, 185, 186, 188–203, 205, 221, 270
gutta-percha 6

Hari Raya Puasa 97
harrow 20 *see also* paddy cultivation
harvesting *(cerut)* 16, 18, 23–25, 29, 30, 56, 57, 76, 211, 230, 241, 268
harvesting knife *(tame)* 23
high school. *see* shool
hire 18, 20–25, 27, 29, 30, 51, 54, 56, 58, 211, 230, 241, 261
hiring tractor 20
hoe *(cok)* 16–18, 83, 103, 104, 263
home 24, 25, 36, 55–59, 62, 64, 66, 67, 83, 93, 97, 99, 102–105, 120, 122, 154, 160–163, 177, 180, 183, 185, 189, 191, 192, 194, 196, 198–200, 202, 203, 212, 213, 216, 221, 249, 262, 264, 270, 273, 275, 276

home consumption 6, 13, 15, 16, 51, 58, 67, 69, 72, 76, 77, 97, 167, 210, 211, 241, 268
hospital 11, 201, 240, 266
house 4, 6, 10, 25, 36, 58, 59, 62, 66, 67, 72, 75, 79, 83, 88, 90, 92, 94, 95, 97, 98, 104, 105, 112, 116, 120, 155, 156, 160, 161, 164, 165, 168, 173, 176, 182, 183, 185, 186, 188–191, 197, 198, 200–203, 209, 213, 216, 226, 229, 232, 234, 235, 238, 244, 254, 257, 259–264, 267, 272, 273, 275–277
household 6, 12–23, 25, 27–31, 33, 36, 38, 41, 43–50, 52–54, 58, 65, 67, 69–72, 74–78, 80, 83–86, 88, 91–98, 100, 101, 119, 120, 122, 127–129, 143, 154–158, 162–171, 173, 174, 176–181, 188– 192, 194, 199–203, 207, 210–212, 215, 216, 224, 230, 232, 234, 240, 241, 244, 245, 249, 251–257, 259, 260, 262, 264, 267–271, 273
  composition 119, 120, 129, 143, 154, 156–158, 162, 165, 166, 203, 215, 216, 231, 249, 253
  independent 45, 71, 77, 91, 93, 96, 143, 147, 154, 168, 171, 173, 174, 180, 181
Hutan Mala 98, 99, 163, 164, 177, 196

imam 77, 98, 103, 104, 109, 123, 130, 131, 185, 200
income 28, 31, 33, 44–52, 54, 56, 58, 62, 64, 65, 67, 69–72, 74–78, 80, 84, 90, 128, 130, 161, 165, 179, 180, 191, 193–195,

198–200, 207, 209–213, 217,
  224, 230, 237, 244, 245, 253,
  262, 268–270, 274
Indonesia 139, 140, 233, 238, 257,
  263, 272
inheritance 12, 65, 72, 75, 84–100,
  112, 128, 129, 262, 267, 271, 277
Intan Belian 14, 15, 29
Intertillage 13 *see also* paddy
  cultivation
irrigation 7, 9, 12, 15, 55, 90, 96,
  127, 128, 210, 211, 229, 230,
  232–235, 265–267
Islam 2, 45, 102, 103, 108–110,
  127, 129–131, 137, 139, 140,
  191, 229, 231, 236, 259, 266,
  267, 274, 276, 277
 -ic court 85, 109, 110, 123, 130, 131
 -ic law 12, 64, 85, 86, 115, 116,
  128–130, 267, 274
 -ic modernization 140
 -ic Party 183
 -ization 2

Jabo 58, 98–100, 162, 164, 183,
  194, 196, 198, 200, 201, 259,
  267
Jabo Hilir 161, 197
Jakarta 140
Jalan Penggawa 10
Java 140, 234, 238, 263
Jeli 173, 196
Jintan 100, 164
Jogjakarta 140
Johor 160, 178, 200, 245, 277

kadhi 109, 122, 123
Kalimantan 238
kampung 64, 65, 98–100, 109, 255,
  266

Kampong China 5
Kampong Laut 4
Kampung Kuek 99, 100, 196
Kampung Tengah 99, 194
Kampung Tujoh 163
Kankong 185, 200, 270
Kedah 10, 18, 27–29, 56, 57, 127,
  129, 131, 132, 227, 229–231,
  236, 241, 258, 259, 262, 265,
  268, 269, 272
Kelantan 1–7, 9, 10, 12, 18, 19, 28,
  30, 32, 38, 45, 53, 54, 56–59,
  70, 77, 99, 102, 112, 119, 122,
  123, 125, 127, 129–132, 138,
  139, 147–149, 160, 163, 164,
  169, 176, 182, 183, 185, 192,
  199, 200, 203, 204, 210, 227,
  230, 231, 249, 252, 256–262,
  264–267, 269, 271
Kelantan River 2, 4, 6–10, 13, 76,
  239, 240
Kemubu 9, 266
Khorat Plateau 232
kin marriage *see* marriage
Koran teacher 64
Kota Bharu 4, 6, 10, 11, 19, 66,
  123, 163, 164, 173, 177, 191,
  202, 239, 259, 264, 266
Kuala Kerai 6, 126, 148, 204
Kuala Lumpur 10, 30, 108, 148,
  160, 162, 173–175, 177, 200,
  202, 240, 241, 245, 249, 256,
  263, 264, 266, 272
Kuala Trengganu 10, 266
Kuantan 10, 160, 161, 163, 266
Kubang Bemban 139, 207, 209–213,
  215–219, 221, 222, 224, 226,
  260, 262, 263
Kubang Kelian 98–100
Kuek 99, 100

INDEX 293

labor force 51, 74, 78
land 1, 4–7, 9, 11–15, 18, 20, 27–29,
    32, 33, 39, 43–45, 50, 54, 56,
    65, 66, 72, 74, 75, 83–96, 98,
    100, 101, 122, 125, 127, 128,
    163, 164, 166, 168, 179, 183,
    188, 191–193, 196–200, 209–
    211, 228, 230–235, 240,
    243–245, 252–256, 258, 260,
    261, 264, 266–271, 273, 277
  owner 33, 78, 88, 90, 210
  register 9, 84, 87, 98, 194, 271
  tax 84
  purchase 88, 100, 164
  subdivision of 12, 92
Lemal 9, 197, 267
literacy rate 219
lumber mill 11, 56, 162

Machang 201
madrasah 182, 185, 186, 188, 190
Mahsuri 15, 210
mail 10
mail train 10, 266
Malay Peninsula 1, 2, 3, 127, 139,
    140, 229, 231, 239
market 4, 11, 30, 45, 50, 58, 76,
    207, 259, 266
marriage 2, 95, 102–105, 107–110,
    112, 114–116, 119, 120, 122,
    123, 125, 126, 128–132, 134,
    136, 137, 139, 140, 143, 152,
    158, 165, 176, 183, 190, 191,
    197, 198, 201, 215–217, 219,
    226, 231, 249, 252, 256, 262, 274
  ceremony *(perator)* 62, 110, 224,
    226
  payment 102, 104, 105, 110, 115,
    128, 129, 217, 224
  age of 128, 136, 137, 245

cousin 108, 115, 128, 136, 137,
    231
  early 72, 102, 105, 256
  first 107, 115, 116, 119, 128, 156,
    178, 216, 217, 247
  kin 134, 136, 137
  prohibitions against inter 108
  sexual relations outside 102
mattress *(lembek)* 62, 79, 212
meat 11, 51, 59, 64, 67, 105, 266,
    270
Mecca 183, 196–201, 226
Mekong Delta 232, 233, 238
Melaka 2, 9, 127, 129–132, 137,
    139, 231, 259, 265
middleman 36, 50, 53, 64, 243,
    269
midwife *(bilan)* 64, 97, 162, 276
migrant 27, 50, 56–58, 65, 71, 80,
    95, 101, 125, 147, 148, 158,
    160, 161, 163, 164, 179, 207,
    224, 229, 230, 236, 240, 245,
    247, 249, 253, 256, 257, 270
milling 25, 27
modernization 125, 137, 140, 183,
    223, 224, 256, 257
monoculture 12
month of fasting *(bulan puasa)* 64,
    77, 97, 103, 222
mosque *(masjid)* 8, 84, 98, 99, 198,
    221, 273
motorcycle 10, 65, 78, 80, 212
motorized pump 83
mukim 2, 3, 58, 99
multi-ethnicity 236
multihousehold compound. *see*
    neighboring kin group

native healer 62
Negeri Sembilan 3, 10, 260

neighboring 9, 12, 15–18, 20, 25, 27, 28, 36, 47, 51, 53, 56, 64, 75, 91–93, 95–100, 104, 108, 109, 115, 139, 143, 160, 163, 164, 166–168, 193, 199, 211, 229, 235, 240, 241, 245, 260, 269, 275,276
neighboring (neighborhood) kin group 92, 95, 97, 166, 167, 168, 215, 231
compound 67, 75, 90–93, 95–97, 100, 101, 120–122, 167–169, 170, 171, 173–178, 180, 181, 190, 198, 203, 215, 231, 254–256, 260, 268, 269
multihousehold compound 167–171, 173, 175, 177–181, 215, 226, 234, 235, 244, 254, 257
nuclear family 90, 120, 122, 154, 166, 256
nuclearization 157
nursery 19–21

oil palm 12
oil palm plantation 9
out-migration 146–148, 152, 162, 165, 177, 181, 235, 245, 247, 249, 256, 257 *see also* migration
ox 10, 20, 21, 67, 199, 209, 268

Padang Hangus 9, 54, 98–100, 160, 163, 185, 194, 200, 240, 267
Padang Lalang 127, 128, 132, 134, 136, 137, 229, 230, 236, 237, 258, 273, 276
paddy
cultivation 12, 14, 18, 19, 30, 31, 33, 36, 38, 39, 49, 51, 67, 71, 77, 94, 127, 209–211, 229 230, 232, 234, 240, 259, 265, 267, 269

land owner 43, 44
varieties 14
padi semangat 28
padi tugalan 14, 27
Pahang 56, 58, 160, 163, 176, 191, 200, 240, 269
Paloh 185, 191
pasah 110, 112, 129
Pasir Mas 6, 8–11, 17, 18, 30, 41, 56–58, 62, 64, 76, 87, 97, 122, 123, 125, 160, 173, 183, 188, 202, 204, 207, 210, 239–241, 258–261, 265–268
Pasir Parit 100, 240
Pasir Puteh 4, 138, 178
Patani 5
Paya Mengkuang 17, 99
peddlers 18, 64, 65, 83
penggawa 28, 99, 259, 264
penghulu 58, 99, 258
Pengkalan Chupa 164
Perak 179
peratur (perator;beratur) 103–105, 115, 273
Perlis 10
pilgrimage 183, 196–199, 222, 224, 226, 271
pilgrimage to Mecca 192, 197, 199, 222
Pinang 163
pioneer settlement 6, 229, 231–233, 235–237
pioneering society 4, 244, 249, 257
plowing 20, 21, 28, 30, 39, 51, 241
plows 16, 17
police 4, 11, 108, 262, 264, 275
polygynous families 72
polygynous marriage 116, 119, 201
pondan 62, 108

pondok 66, 72, 80, 97, 98, 182–186, 188–206, 219, 221, 252, 270, 271
Pondok Sungai Durian 204
population 1–6, 10–12, 45, 51, 59, 86–101, 127, 143–147, 149, 152–154, 162, 164, 165, 169–171, 174, 179, 180, 206, 216–218, 222, 235, 236, 239, 240, 244, 245, 247, 249, 257, 266, 267, 276
  density 2, 4, 164, 233
  growth 1, 3, 147, 153
  movement 149
  of Kelantan 2–4, 12, 266
  pyramid 143–146
  female 153, 154, 169–171, 216
  male 2, 46, 152, 154, 169–171, 219
poultry 50, 59
poultry dealer 59, 90
propane gas 46, 261, 264
Pulai 4
push and pull 165

rain-fed rice cultivation 9
rainfall 7, 13, 15, 19, 39, 69, 75, 268, 270, 273
rajah 2, 4
Rantau Panjang 161
reclamation 4
Red River delta 233
refrigerator 80, 83, 226, 244, 261, 264
religious boarding school 182, 270 see also *pondok*
religious court *(mahakamah shariah)* 122 see also *kadhi*
religious judge 109, 110, 123 see also *kadhi*

remarriage 115, 116, 119, 139, 154, 157, 158, 217, 229, 252 *see also* marriage
renting 15, 29, 33, 38, 94, 95, 191, 201, 209, 260, 268
rites of passage 97
rojok (rujuk) 110, 123, 132
rubber 7, 9, 12, 27, 32, 33, 36, 38, 41, 49, 50, 51, 56, 58, 59, 64, 65, 69, 71, 83, 85, 87, 96, 100, 128, 168, 191, 192, 198, 200, 201, 240, 241, 245, 264, 266, 268–270
  cultivation 6
  land 9, 33, 50, 84–86, 88, 90, 95, 101, 180, 191, 196–198, 200, 201, 207, 210, 244, 245, 253
  tapping 32, 33, 36, 38, 44, 49, 50, 51, 56, 65, 69, 71, 77, 94, 95, 97, 125, 127, 178–200, 207, 209, 210, 224, 230, 240, 244, 259, 262, 267–270

Sabah 10, 163, 200
Salor 9, 25, 27, 57, 58
salt 5
Sarawak 10, 238
sarong 79, 263
school
  communal elementary *(skolah rakyat)* 184
  elementary *(skolah kebangsaan)* 44, 55, 66, 95, 182, 184, 200, 202, 263, 270, 273–275
  secondary ; high *(skolah menengah)* 11, 41, 80, 185, 270, 274
seamstress 62, 108
seasonal worker 41, 45, 55, 207, 230

secularization 224, 226
seed rice 19, 20, 27
seedling 6, 19–23, 30, 39, 47, 268, 273
Semarak 4
sewing machine 52, 62, 78, 83, 191, 212
sharecropping *(pawah)* 76, 95, 210
shop 11, 50, 59, 64, 69, 71, 90, 191, 192, 207, 241, 266, 273, 275
Siam 2, 9, 29, 273
sickle *(sadat)* 16, 18, 23, 28, 241
Singapore 5, 10, 30, 58, 122, 140, 240, 241, 245
soil 13, 27, 39, 54, 265
sparsely populated area 236, 276
stall 46, 51, 52, 59, 64, 66, 71, 80, 83, 97, 213, 260, 270
stem family. *see* family
sultan 2, 12, 149
Sumatra 1, 233, 238
Sungai Durian 174
Sungai Golok 196
Sungai Keladi 33, 197, 201
supplementary fertilizing 23

ta'alik 110
Tabar 4
talak 109, 110, 130, 132
tanah alor 14
tanah dalam 14
tanah darat 14
Tanah Merah 6, 10, 11, 56, 97, 125, 160, 162, 164, 173, 176, 178, 179, 185, 188, 191, 192, 195, 198, 200–202, 239, 240, 241, 259
teacher 44, 55, 56, 62, 65, 66, 72, 95, 97, 116, 131, 160, 163–165, 182, 183, 240, 244, 260, 270

tebus talak 110, 129
telephone 10, 80, 165, 226, 237, 241
television 80, 83, 198, 200, 201, 277
tenant 93, 95, 268
TFR(Total Fertility Rate) 151, 152, 247
Thai rice 30, 31, 241
Thailand 5, 30, 56, 76, 163, 164, 167, 176, 182, 200, 201, 231, 232, 236, 238, 257, 266, 269
thatched roof 185, 188, 262
threshing tub 16, 18, 24
tobacco 9, 28, 36, 38, 39, 41, 43–56, 58, 59, 62, 64–67, 69–71, 78, 80, 95, 112, 179, 191, 193, 194, 196, 197, 199, 200, 202, 243, 267, 269, 270
  cultivation 28, 36, 39, 41, 43–46, 48–52, 54, 56, 64, 65, 69, 70, 71, 74, 77, 80, 94, 178, 179, 193, 207, 212, 224, 240, 244, 245, 262, 269, 270
toilet 186, 189, 244, 260, 263
Tok Uban 200
transistor radio 52, 212
transplanting 15, 18, 19, 21, 22–25, 30, 39, 41, 241, 268
transport 49, 125
Trengganu 10, 160, 163, 173, 192
trishaw driver 62
trunk road 10
Tumpat 4, 10, 54, 123, 266

Ulu Kelantan 6, 33, 85, 116, 125, 126, 148, 160, 162, 163, 174, 176, 178, 204, 245, 249, 269
Unfederated Malay States 10
unhulled rice 6
upland rice 27 see also *padi tugalan*

uxorilocal residence 88, 89, 90, 128, 167, 171

van 65, 226, 241
vegetable farmer 64
village work *(kerja kampung)* 65
virilocal residence 88, 89, 128

Wachap Nau 4
wage earner 80
wakaf 186, 197, 198
washing machine 83
water buffalo *(kerbau)* 19, 20, 21, 67, 68, 104, 209, 244, 261, 268
water shortage 15
water supply 56, 97, 200–202, 254
wedding *(perator)* 23, 27, 62, 97, 103, 104, 191, 202, 261, 274
well 97, 186, 189, 197, 198, 200–202
wet-rice cultivation 244
woven bamboo wall 185, 188, 197, 262
wristwatch 80

yield 13, 15, 19, 27, 29, 30, 36, 47, 50, 69, 71, 75, 76, 168, 211, 257, 268, 269

zakat 191